"Insiders claim it should be titled *Daddy Dearest.*"

—*Chicago Sun-Times*

Bing Crosby was one of the most popular entertainers in showbusiness history. He appeared in nearly one hundred films. More than 500 million copies of his records have been sold. In fact, this enchanting and multi-talented performer, loved by countless millions, was one of the world's first true superstars . . . Hollywood's saint and America's idol.

But when the cameras weren't rolling, when the mikes were turned off and the curtains were down, Bing was irresponsible and lazy, cunning and cold. . . a man who double-crossed his way to the top, riding roughshod over friends and family alike. . . a man who left in his wake a heap of broken dreams and shattered lives. . . .

"We set out to write the story of a wonderfully witty, bright, talented and charismatic man, and found also the stuff that Shakespeare's plays are made of. And that was the last thing in the world that we expected to find. This man Bing Crosby was many things to many people, but he did some monstrously callous things to those who were nearest and who should have been dearest to him."

—*from Chapter Twenty-four*

Also by Robert F. Slatzer:

THE LIFE AND CURIOUS DEATH OF MARILYN MONROE

Bing Crosby

THE HOLLOW MAN

by

Donald Shepherd

and

Robert F. Slatzer

PINNACLE BOOKS   NEW YORK

BING CROSBY: THE HOLLOW MAN

A Pinnacle Books edition, published by arrangement with
St. Martin's Press.

First printing, March 1982

ISBN: 0-523-41729-2

Cover photo by Globe Photos, Inc.

Printed in the United States of America

PINNACLE BOOKS, INC.
1430 Broadway
New York, New York 10018

This book is respectfully dedicated
to the memory of

Dixie Lee,

a sweet and gentle woman who
revered truth but who would have
nevertheless given us hell for
revealing it;

Harry Lowe Crosby,

a lovable leprechaun who
cast no shadow
in his quiet light;

and Josephine Rinker,

whose flame burned but a moment
but whose warmth and light prevail.

Contents

Acknowledgments

It is usually axiomatic that the recounting of events and matters pertaining to a person's life benefits from the passage of time and from its perspective. But the axiom has not held true for the life of Bing Crosby, since it presupposes an accurate keeping of records, and the several written accounts of Bing's life have been anything but accurate.

We weren't far into our secondary research when we discovered that time has served to *obscure* the truth about Bing and to solidify a legend that Bing himself had helped to fashion—a legend that unwitting biographers used as a foundation to compile a considerable body of material that, taken as a whole, is a bewildering hodgepodge of conflicting "facts," apocryphal stories, half-truths, and even lies. And so, from the onset, we found it necessary to ponder even the most mundane of "facts" and to go into considerable detail in refuting previous biographers and documenting moments in Bing's life that may seem to the reader disproportionate in their relative importance to the amount of space given them. We have tried not to belabor such moments, but errors in fact told often enough are not easily laid to rest.

This is not to say that the several biographies of Bing were wholly without merit or value to us in our own effort; we have given credit to them where due, but for the most part each of the works has served to further litter an already obscure path. Consequently, we've concentrated more intently on gathering first-hand accounts and have had to focus on areas that we might not have had to explore so thoroughly. We are particularly indebted to those who aided us in doing so.

We approached this work knowing that Bing Crosby was an extraordinary and talented man but believing also that he was probably the least colorful of what are today called "superstars." But we found much more drama in Bing's life than we expected, and though we were frustrated by the mountain of printed misinformation pertaining to it, we were delighted to discover that although Bing's career spanned more than half a century, many of the players in the drama are still with us and are inordinately articulate, clear-minded, and perceptive in their recollections. Bing was a fascinating man, and so those with whom he came in contact had spent a good deal of time reflecting on his enigmatic nature and were as interested and eager as we to explore the enigma. We interviewed more than fifty people, and we have credited most of them in the text, but there are a few to whom we owe a special note of thanks.

Three of Dixie Lee Crosby's closest friends were especially helpful in "introducing" us to the real Dixie Lee, about whom very little has been written and too much has been rumored; they are Maybeth Carr Carpenter, Sylvia Picker McGraw, and Sue Carol Ladd. Kitty Lang Good, who is acknowledged by all as having been Dixie's dearest friend, chatted with us for several hours but is working on a book of her own and so declined—reluctantly—to grant us an interview. Kitty was center stage during much of the drama, so we hope that she finds an enthusiastic publisher for her work, which we look forward to reading.

In addition, we are indebted for first-hand account's of Bing's early life and career to Al Rinker, Loyce Whiteman Hubbard, and former Paul Whiteman sidemen Matty Malneck and Kurt Dieterle, all of whom were wonderfully patient with us despite our calling on them time and time again.

Several others who were helpful to us with their recollections of the Crosbys or of the entertainment business are Nancy Bacon, Teet Carl, Carroll Carroll, Dr. J. DeWitt Fox, Max Herman, Dr. George Hummer, Milt Lewis, Milo Marchetti, Bill Meiklejohn, Virginia Moberly, Glenhall Taylor, Rudy Vallée, Winstead "Doodles" Weaver, and Lawrence Zwisohn.

We are most grateful to Vernon Wesley Taylor for making available and allowing us to reprint the transcripts of his interviews with the late Kenny Allen and the late Burt McMurtrie, and for his account of a visit with Bing at Hillsborough. We must also acknowledge the late W. R. "Billy" Wilkerson, founder and publisher of *The Hollywood Reporter*. Mr. Wilkerson used his considerable influence and power for the betterment of the entertainment industry and was one of the few to criticize Bing publicly for what he considered an ungrateful act on Bing's part; his criticism, which is printed verbatim in the text, was instrumental in diverting us from the path that previous biographers had followed since the first Crosby biography was published in 1937. We're especially grateful to our friend Doug Warren, who brought Wilkerson's column to our attention and who took time to aid us in our research when he was himself under deadline pressure to complete a book of his own for our mutual publisher. That is, indeed, friendship.

Those who are not mentioned in this work but who gave us invaluable aid and support in our efforts are Al Stump, Moton B. Holt, Wilson S. Hong, Karla Cornejo, and Barbara Shepherd.

We also thank the employees of the Academy of Motion Picture Arts and Sciences; Joann Goldberg of the West Coast office of The Barbara Walters Specials; Ken Twiss, president of the Bing Crosby Historical Society of Tacoma, Washington; and Mark Sailor and Alan Siegal of Hollywood's Book City. All went out of their way to help us.

There are a few persons who granted us interviews but who requested anonymity; their requests have been honored and we thank them as a group for their participation.

There are also those whom we wanted to interview but couldn't. Kathryn Crosby closed her door and the door of the Crosby organization to us; we got her message through Sam Weiss, a former music publisher who had been associated with the Crosby organization and who was very close to Bing and Dixie. Mr. Weiss wanted to grant us an interview but was asked not to by Kathryn—through a Crosby-organization spokesman—because she was working on her own book. Her request of Sam Weiss seems to us an act of boundless temerity, for we know that her memoirs will have very little—if anything—to say about the first ·fifty-four years of Bing's life that she didn't share. Sam Weiss was keeping company with Bing and Dixie long before Kathryn was born, and he could have contributed much to our effort, but he honored Kathryn's request. A postscript: Kathryn's book is said to be complete and at her publishing house; we called Sam Weiss while writing these acknowledgments to· thank him for at least considering an interview, and learned that Kathryn had not asked him to contribute to her book.

No acknowledgment section worth its salt is complete without at least one cryptic entry, and so to the Reverend Monsignor J. Augustine O'Gorman of Santa Barbara, gentleman, scholar, and practitioner of what he preaches, our thanks. Monsignor O'Gorman had nothing at all to do with the content of this work, but much to do with half the team's effort.

Finally, we want to thank three men for doing what they do so well: Robert Miller, our editor, Tom Dunne, our executive editor, and Dominick Abel, our literary agent and friend. It was Dominick who first suggested the idea of this work and who brought us all together for its production.

Hollywood, California   D.S. and R.F.S.
January 1981

BING CROSBY:

The Hollow Man

Part One:

Summer and Winter, 1952

CHAPTER ONE

> We have only been married about
> six months, but we have
> already found out that we are
> not suited for each other.
>
> —DIXIE LEE CROSBY

Bing Crosby was in Europe for the location shooting of
Little Boy Lost when the gambling pool surfaced in the
fall of 1952. There were two illicit gambling pools
being circulated from the mail room of Paramount Pictures that year. One was the traditional World Series
pool, which went seven games before the Yankees took
the series from the Brooklyn Dodgers; the other was
macabre, even for the netherworld of Hollywood flesh
peddlers and users. It was called the Dixie Death Pool,
and it was doing brisk trade.

It was planned as a monthly pool. The October

1

board was divided into thirty-one days, with each day subdivided into A.M. and P.M., giving a total of sixty-two chances at five dollars a throw. The "lucky" bettor who would by chance get on the November board and draw the morning of 1 November 1952—the day Dixie Lee Crosby would die—would win $300, less the pool runner's commission, of course.

The Dixie Death Pool was circulated rather openly on the Paramount lot. It was probably kept from the Crosby-organization people and from people who worked closely with them, but even some of the hangers-on and Crosby partisans were on the board with apparently clear consciences.

Dixie's "villainy" was common knowledge to those who considered themselves familiar with intimate Hollywood goings-on; they saw her as a hopeless drunk who was given to savage verbal attacks on Bing—at the few social functions to which he took her—and who had caused him nothing but grief for more than twenty years, not the least of which was the grief brought upon him by the four sons that Dixie had borne him. Outsiders and the public believed—and still believe—that the Crosby marriage was an ideal one, made in heaven, and that Bing's loss of Dixie would be tragic. Insiders knew better. If Bing's marriage wasn't made in hell, they thought, it was certainly being dragged in that direction from purgatory. Bing was a devout Catholic for whom divorce was unspeakable, unthinkable. And in insiders' view, he could rise above his temporal purgatory only when he was free from the clutches of the drunken vixen who was dragging him down.

Nothing could have been further from the truth.

Those who thought themselves privy to Bing's private life didn't see it in the light of whole truth. They couldn't, for Bing and his organization—the keepers of the image and of the light, who were powerfully influential in Hollywood—kept drawing attention away from the real problem by focusing the light squarely upon Dixie.

The real problem was Bing himself.

2

It's a curious paradox that even the most hardened of film-colony cynics, whose eyes are instinctively drawn to the shadows, were distracted from them by the spotlight. They knew, of course, that there was a dark side to Mr. Crosby and that there were many women in his life, but that side seemed forgivable and was sheltered from light even by those who disliked him, not only because criticizing Bing Crosby in the forties and fifties was very nearly unAmerican—and very bad business, as well—but because it was believed that his dark side was an anomaly not of character but of circumstance.

Aside from Bing's brother, Larry, who handled public relations for the Crosby organization, and his brother Everett, who acted as Bing's personal manager, it appeared even to members of the Crosby organization and to other insiders that Bing was a martyr. It seemed obvious to them that he was cursed with an alcoholic wife and trapped by the tenets of his religion. Even those who were burned by the Crosbys and who left the organization with rancor—usually toward Everett or Larry—departed feeling no animosity for Bing. They pitied him; they suffered with and for him. Thus the Dixie Death Pool was accepted and entered into by people who might have been repulsed had they known the whole story.

Bing's few close friends certainly didn't know Dixie's side of the story. And while Dixie's few close friends were aware of her quiet desperation, of her frustration, loneliness, and tempestuous drinking bouts, of some of her separations from Bing and her numerous attempts at divorcing him, they were nonetheless perplexed. They were sympathetic toward Dixie and loved her dearly, but the relationship bewildered them; the effect it had on Dixie seemed disproportionate to the cause, which, as they saw it, was nothing more than Bing's inordinate absences from her.

Bing's career necessitated his being away from home occasionally, but even when he took time off from work and was "home," most of his time was spent—without Dixie—at the golf course or the track or hunting or fishing or at his ranch in Elko, Nevada, or just out with his cronies. To Dixie's friends, this was a lamentable situation, but it didn't represent a behavioral change on Bing's part; he had always been that way. Dixie shouldn't have expected him to change. Still, Dixie grew increasingly bitter and sullen. Few who were close to her realized that the absences about which she complained were merely symptomatic of a more profound problem: unrequited love. Bing Crosby was unwilling or unable to give of himself. Perhaps he was incapable of truly loving another person.

Dixie was basically a shy person, but she was outspoken and could be as bullheaded as Bing. She fought like a tigress when wounded, and Bing wounded her constantly, because he wouldn't change his ways, and couldn't without professional help. But Bing Crosby would never admit to needing professional help. So after putting up with Bing's errant behavior for years, Dixie began to drink. Her close friends were convinced that she drank out of spite. Bing hated for her to drink. Still, he triggered it by taking a trip and refusing to take her, or by going up to the ranch—which she grew to hate—and she'd drink to get even with him when he returned. Then he'd leave because she was drinking, and she'd drink because he was leaving again. To insiders, it appeared that Dixie was as much to blame as Bing for their bad marriage.

There's irony in that it was Bing, not Dixie, who had the drinking problem during their first years of marriage. And it was Dixie who gave him—indeed, insisted upon—the stability that was necessary for his success. Bing was never an alcoholic. He just liked to drink, and he drank too much, up to the time that he started gaining fame as a record, radio, and movie celebrity. Even in the relatively short time that he was in Hollywood prior to marrying Dixie, he had become notorious as an irresponsible playboy who blew every cent he earned on wine, women, and gambling. That he hadn't mended his ways upon marriage was evidenced when on March 5, 1931, the Los Angeles *Examiner* revealed that Dixie

4

Lee had separated from her husband and planned to file for divorce. The paper quoted her as saying,

We have only been married about six months, but we have already found out that we are not suited for each other. Our separation is an amicable one, and the only reason for it is that we just cannot get along. Bing is a fine boy as a friend, but married he and I just cannot be happy.

But Bing loved her in his fashion and couldn't tolerate the idea of divorce. His will prevailed. The reconciliation occurred ten days later in Mexico, where Dixie had fled to get away from him. They talked by phone; then Bing took a plane to Mexico (a daring feat in those days) and undoubtedly turned on his irresistible charm. Undoubtedly, too, he made promises he didn't keep, for variations of this scene were to recur for the next nineteen years. But toward the end, Bing's charm no longer worked, and he often enlisted the aid of other Crosby-clan members to help him change her mind. And Dixie always acquiesced.

Dixie was madly in love with Bing Crosby to her death. She adored him. There was never another man in her life. And yet, for the most part, the best that can be said of their relationship was that Dixie never wanted for material things. Bing was a good and generous provider, but aside from the four sons he gave her, he brought little pleasure to her life—and much pain. He was like a drug to her, a drug to which she was seductively, hypnotically drawn but from which she wanted also to be free. Bing wouldn't let her go.

For several years before her death, Dixie hadn't felt entirely well. No one knew how ill she was. In her last year, she was bedridden much of the time and should have been bedridden all of the time, but she was indomitable. She had an acute sense of duty as a wife and mother, and she hid her illness even from her sons. It wasn't Dixie's style to cloud the lives of her family or friends. Then in July of 1952, her doctor detected cancer and immediately arranged for exploratory surgery. It was discovered that the cancer had developed in her left ovary and that it had spread beyond control. Dixie was dying. The remainder of her life could be counted in months, if not weeks.

It was decided that the boys shouldn't be told. Although the eldest, Gary, who was nineteen, and the twins, Philip and Dennis, then eighteen, were mature enough to be told, it was probably decided that it would have taken more than an Academy Award—winning acting job on their parts to conceal the truth from their youngest brother, fourteen-year-old Lindsay. Come September, Lindsay would be the only one remaining home, for Gary was returning to Stanford, while Phil and Dennis would begin their freshman year at Washington State College. The shock of their mother's death would be traumatic enough for the boys when it happened, but expecting them to live with the specter of impending death was too much to ask.

Life would go on as usual. While Dixie was ostensibly recuperating from her surgery, the boys would join Bing at their Elko ranch to work. From there, they'd go on to Hayden Lake, Idaho, for their usual reward of recreation and rest from the hard work on the ranch, before returning home and then going on to school. Everything went off as planned. But then the life-as-usual routine that Bing planned for himself must have left even the believers of the "Dixie Demon" stories nonplussed.

In April, three months prior to Dixie's operation, Bing had signed with Paramount to do another picture, *Little Boy Lost,* which was scheduled to begin shooting in France the last week in September. Though Bing had the studio clout, good reason, and ample time between July and September to have the picture postponed or to have himself replaced as its star, he didn't. Instead, he returned from Hayden Lake, packed his bags and, leaving Dixie with round-the-clock nursing care, left for Europe. And while Dixie lay dying, Bing chose the slowest possible means of travel, spending at least two

6

more time-killing weeks en route than were necessary.

Rather than flying to France when it was time to begin shooting the film, Bing left early, booking passage on the French ocean liner *Liberté*. He landed at Plymouth, England, on September 18. He played golf in England, including a charity match at Temple course, and then performed in a charity show at the Stoll Theatre in London before taking a plane to France for location shooting on the film.

When the location shots were finished, Bing boarded another ship for his return home. From New York, he took a train to Los Angeles. Exactly a week from the day he arrived home, Dixie would be dead.

CHAPTER TWO

The car is as good a place
as any to die.

—DIXIE LEE CROSBY

During the two weeks that Bing was wending his way back from Europe, Dixie was undergoing daily blood transfusions to sustain strength and life. On the day of his return—without the knowledge of her physician, Dr. John H. Davis—Dixie got out of bed, put on her favorite lace dress, and was waiting at Union Station in Los Angeles when Bing's train arrived. According to Sylvia McGraw, Georgie, Dixie's companion-aide, was in anguish over Dixie's action, but Dixie told her, "The car is as good a place as any to die."

The following day, Sunday, October 26, 1952, she had a relapse. Two days later, she went into a coma from which she never regained consciousness. Gary, Philip, and Dennis were summoned home from college; Dixie's closest friend, Kitty Lang Good, arrived from Elko, Nevada; and the vigil began. It was short-lived.

On Thursday, it was announced that Dixie was still in a coma and was believed near death. The following day, the news was broken that she had been received into the Roman Catholic church. Monsignor Patrick Concannon, of the Church of the Good Shepherd in Beverly Hills, emphasized that Dixie had been baptized four days earlier, the day before she sank into a coma, and that "she had asked some time ago to be received into the church." By Friday, she had received the sacraments of the Catholic Church, including extreme unction—the last.

Dixie Lee Crosby was pronounced dead at 9:50 A.M. on Saturday, November 1, 1952. On Monday, November 3—the day before her forty-first birthday—she was buried in the Crosby family plot at Holy Cross Cemetery, next to the grave of Bing's father, Harry Lowe Crosby, who had died two years earlier.

The timing of Dixie's death created an embarrassing dilemma for Bing. He was supersensitive about his image and worried about public opinion. It had been announced that Dixie had had surgery in July and that she had died of cancer four months later. Even the most naive layperson could deduce that the surgeon must have discovered the cancer and that Bing must have known about it, must have known that she was dying while he was in Europe playing golf and making a movie.

Bing couldn't go to a golf course and putt this problem away, which was a technique he often used to "resolve" less weighty problems. Instead, he resorted to another technique that was characteristic of him throughout his life: he blamed someone else.

Just a few months after Dixie's death, Bing's autobiography, *Call Me Lucky,* was published; it was written by Bing and author Pete Martin, and was serialized in the *Saturday Evening Post,* as well. In it, Bing explains why he went to Europe as Dixie lay dying: ". . . her [Dixie's] doctors said, 'You'd better do it [go to Europe]. Every day you're here, she'll think you're staying because of her and it'll make her uncomfortable.' "

This wasn't the first appearance in print of Bing's incredible rationale. Two days before Dixie's death, Bing's brother Larry released to newsmen the same story, which was printed in the Hollywood *Citizen News* on October 30, 1952:

She . . . underwent a serious abdominal operation last July. Physicians at that time advised against Bing's plans to call off a film-location trip to France, saying it would be a bad psychological move.

The next paragraph of Larry's release named Dixie's physician as Dr. John Davis. Such "sage" advice from a competent medical practitioner or practitioners is difficult to accept on its face, let alone to contemplate.

Dixie's personal physician was, indeed, Dr. John H. Davis. It was Dr. Davis who discovered the cancer and who arranged for the exploratory surgery. It was Dr. Davis who attended her, making daily house calls at her Hombly Hills home during her last weeks, and it was he who signed her death certificate.

When we contacted Dr. Davis at his West Los Angeles office, we learned that he hadn't read *Call Me Lucky,* and he was surprised to hear that the rationale of Bing's trip had been attributed by implication—at least in part—to him. It had been twenty-eight years since Dixie's death, of course, and Dr. Davis didn't recall Bing's European trip, but he did recall that he was never consulted about a trip to Europe, and added, "I'd never give such advice. I'd personally consider it unethical to do so."

We showed Dr. Davis the passages in question. In an effort toward objectivity, Dr. Davis pointed out to us that Bing had referred to Dixie's "doctors," plural, and that the newspaper report, which had been released by Larry Crosby, had stated that "physicians," plural, had allegedly given Bing such advice. It was clear and understandable that Dr. Davis was reluctant to judge the alleged counsel of unnamed peers, but the fact remains that, in this case, Dixie had only one physician, her internist, Dr. Davis. There was the surgeon who performed the operation, Dr. Arnold Stevens, who has since died, and the surgeon who assisted him, Dr. William Ross, but even if they had been asked for advice, they would have deferred to Dixie's personal physician—which is the standard ethical practice.

The story as released to the newspapers and as related in Bing's autobiography was simply a lie. It was a rationalization for incongruous behavior. But, in fact, the behavior wasn't at all inconsistent with the true nature of Bing Crosby. Granted, no one in his right mind wants to stand witness to a loved one's wasting away from the ravages of cancer. But it must be done. To run away, leaving the loved one to die alone, seems incredibly callous. And to do so when all that your loved one ever wanted or demanded throughout her life was your attention, your *presence,* seems monstrously callous.

Such behavior is incomprehensible. It begs for explanation. If one can't find an acceptable rationale for it, then one looks for motivation, not for the purpose of passing moral judgment, but in order to throw light upon—if not solve—the mystery: how could the man we all knew and loved have done such a thing?

One begins, of course, with the assumption that Bing's actions regarding Dixie during those dark days were not characteristic of him. The assumption is that Bing fitted perfectly his fan-magazine and screen image, that privately he was what he appeared to be on screen: a warm, easygoing gentleman with a bent for self-effacement; a friendly man; a man who once won a Father of the Year award; an all-around guy who loved his family and fishing and ranching and hunting and golf and horses. Sure, writers had touched upon a fault or two, as had Bing himself in his autobiography. But such faults were either dismissed with a bit of humor or placed in contexts that made them seem momentary indiscretions rather than manifestations of character.

But the image is transparent under scrutiny. If one looks beyond his image to his actions, one gets quite a different and perplexing view of Bing Crosby. Even a cursory glance at his personal relationships with the people closest to him gives one pause and raises an uncomfortable subjective bias. And if one is to deal with the subject, one is led straight into a quagmire of psychological and philosophical considerations.

There was the first family: Dixie, and the boys,

whom Bing often told would be on their own at age twenty-one. But after Dixie died and Bing remarried, it appeared that "on their own" was Bing's euphemism for familial excommunication. The appearance may have been distorted, but one could hardly describe Bing's relationship with the boys as a close one.

The second family was heralded by Bing as his second chance. Presumably, things would be different this time, but there is little evidence that his second family fared any better than the first. Kathryn was more tolerant and flexible than Dixie and tried to be more of a buddy to Bing than Dixie had—not surprising, since she had the opportunity to learn from Dixie's "mistakes"—but her complaints after ten years of marriage could have been read straight from Dixie's script. And the second set of offspring was saddled with the same standards of exactitude and perfection as the first.

Bing's treatment of his brothers, too, indicated a good deal about him. Elder brothers Larry and Everett kowtowed to Bing and were for the most part kept in the fold, but elder brother Ted was more independent and bolted the Crosby organization after a brief encounter, ultimately returning to Spokane to stay. Kidbrother Bob was another independent one, and he had the temerity to light out on his own in show business. He was nearly cut off at the pass by brother Bing.

In 1931, Bob Crosby was the eighteen-year-old "baby" of the clan and was still at home in Spokane when he received a telegram from bandleader Anson Weeks offering him $100 a week to sing with the band at San Francisco's Palace Hotel. These were Depression years, and Bob was reportedly working the strawberry fields for 25¢ an hour. Taking a shot at singing was better than breaking his back in the fields for $10 a week, so Bob accepted the offer and headed for Los Angeles to get some pointers on being a band vocalist from brother Bing.

Bob had only a few days in Los Angeles before he was to assume his San Francisco job, but every time he asked Bing for advice, Bing changed the subject. On his last day in Los Angeles, Bob cornered Bing and forced the issue: "I've got this job," he said, "and I want some pointers about what I should do."

Bing patted him on the shoulder and said, "Just stay in tune, kid, and keep your nose clean." The discussion was closed.

Bob was infuriated by Bing's treatment of him, but for years he kept the Crosby ranks closed by saying: ". . . in effect, he was trying to tell me to stand on my own two feet. . . . He never let me feel that I had a crutch."

Indeed, Bing seldom offered crutches. But a good case will be made for the fact that he would never have reached superstardom had he not used a lot of them himself. In his autobiography, Bing suggested that part of his "luck" consisted in getting boosts from the right people at the right time. But the ones he named as having, in his words, "touched my life" were his attorney, his tax man, and three others who had nothing at all to do with his gaining stardom. Those who really helped him were, of necessity, mentioned in his book but were given little or no credit for their help in his rise to fame. And some, like brother Everett, were given credit for other people's work.

Bing left a trail of "crutches" behind him. All of them were used; some of them were used badly.

It's customary to speak of one's "personality"—singular—but in reality, we're all a complex network of many personalities, many selves. Most of Bing Crosby's several biographers have illuminated only his performing self and have either ignored the actions that seemed uncharacteristic to the self they were dealing with or buried them in contexts that precluded or defied explanation. Most, including Bing himself, placed "uncharacteristic" behavior in a humorous context, thereby precluding serious consideration of it and of its implications. A couple of his biographers did call attention to questionable actions but then backed off, seemingly as perplexed as their readers would be at the inexplicable "knobs" that protruded from an otherwise comfortable, smooth, and glossy surface image.

Professionally, Bing Crosby was an intelligent, witty, articulate, and enormously talented man. His performing self had profound sociological effects on America; it entertained us for more than fifty years, from the vaudeville stage to beams bounced from satellites in space. He appeared in nearly one hundred films. More than 500 million copies of his records have been sold. He was one of the most popular stars in the history of show business—perhaps the first true superstar, known the world over. But when the cameras weren't rolling, when the mikes were turned off, when the curtain was down and the stage dark, he was not his professional self.

Privately, Bing was many selves. Most of them were, or could be, charming; all of them were totally—and deceptively—self-centered and self-indulgent. His dominant self was a Hemingway protagonist personified: a man's man who was most comfortable in the company of men and who could drink neat (later in life, anyway), shoot straight, cast a fishing fly truly, and who, though a man of small passion, made the earth move beneath a bevy of beauties in his day—though, aside from his mother, there were only three women for whom he ever exhibited a semblance of genuine love, such as it was.

Bing didn't really understand women and apparently couldn't see them as other human beings who happened to be female. He was sometimes shy around them, uncomfortable. And if they were beautiful, he was often intimidated by them. When they became wives, however, he waxed medieval: the woman's place was in the home with *her* children; the husband was king of the castle, and he could come and go as the spirit moved him and without explanation; when he did return home, there should be a warm fire in the hearth, food on the table, an orderly house, "adult" children, and an uncomplaining wife who demanded nothing of him. Period.

14

He didn't understand children, either. Bing treated his children as extensions of his religious adult self; they should think and act accordingly. The fact that no child could come close to the "perfect" adult model that he would have them emulate simply wasn't acceptable to him. He would mold them in his image without regard for their individuality, and if they failed to respond, failed to be exactly like him in thought and deed, then they failed him. Period.

And Bing didn't understand himself, particularly in matters of ethics, of right conduct. He was raised with ethical standards that he knew to be right but driven by a natural inclination to go against them. This was most evident—with few exceptions—in his few close personal relationships. He was criticized often enough for being antisocial to make him aware that his feelings were somehow different from those around him, but there is little evidence that he had any remorse for such actions, unless, of course, they were made public. Bing worried inordinately about public opinion.

Crosby made an art of slipping through life sideways, of never confronting an adverse situation squarely and responsibly. Ironically, the trait worked to his advantage in public life, giving him a relaxed, happy-go-lucky image that we all admired and to which we all aspired: why can't we be like that? In private life, however, the trait was disastrous, for there it couldn't pass for what it appeared to be. It was what it was: irresponsibility.

To certain people, Crosby could be, and was, consistently warm, charming, very generous, and friendly: to people who were in the Social Register, people who were in impressive professions outside of show business, people in show business who didn't rival him, people who made no demands of him, and people who were useful to him. To these people, Bing Crosby and his screen image were synonymous; it's the only side they ever saw of him. To others, even upon first meeting, he could be rude, arrogant, cold, and even inimical. As one person who was once quite close to him but who wishes to remain anonymous said, "Bing was an enigma. He seemed, well, he was the kind of guy you just naturally wanted to befriend, but it was a mistake to try. I don't think Bing had any real friends—cronies, yes, but not real friends. He was cold. *Cold.* Maybe it was the power. I don't know. Power and influence and celebrity do strange things to people. I've seen him be icy to people for no reason at all. The man could piss ice water."

Bing Crosby always did exactly what Bing Crosby wanted to do. If someone helped him along the way during the times in his life when he genuinely needed help, no gratitude was shown. If someone was injured by his actions, the injury was not acknowledged and no apology was offered. If someone was left behind, he or she ceased to exist in Bing's mind. Bing never looked back, and it appeared that he just didn't give a damn. It was true of him when he was an international superstar, and it was true of him when he was just a kid named Harry Lillis Crosby back in Spokane, Washington.

Part Two:

Bing

CHAPTER THREE

> Bing? How that boy hated
> to exert himself.
>
> —WEBSTER GRADE SCHOOL TEACHERS

Al Rinker, who would play a major role in Bing Crosby's rise to success in the music business, first saw Bing at one of the two municipal swimming pools in Mission Park, on Spokane's east side. It was around the summer of 1916, as Al recalls, and Al was only about nine at the time, too young to be noticed by Bing's older crowd. But Al took notice of Bing because he stood out from the others. Al describes him as having been "kind of a character" around the park, "a towheaded, chubby little fellow who could dive well and swim excellently and who was very popular." Then, too, everyone called him Bing, and who could forget a name like that? He had a good sense of humor, a quick smile, and an even quicker tongue; he was the most articulate member of

17

his crowd, Al recalls, although he didn't appear to be its leader—if, indeed, it had one.

Al saw him at the park frequently after that first day, for Bing swam and played handball there often, but it would be another six years before the two of them would have their first fateful meeting.

Bing was thirteen when Al first saw him, but Al didn't know his age. In fact, in all their years together, the question of their age difference never arose. Al remembers only, upon reflection, that Bing seemed more mature and sophisticated than he. Perhaps owing to his relatively late start in show business, Bing was always deliberately vague about the year of his birth. And since he was born at home and since the filing of birth certificates in Tacoma at the turn of the century wasn't routine—at least for the Crosbys, for there are no birth certificates on file for Bing or for Everett and Ted, two of Bing's three elder brothers—his birth date isn't a matter of public record. Thus, all of Bing's previous biographers disputed the year of Bing's birth. And all of them were wrong.

Bing didn't help clarify the matter—quite the opposite. In *Call Me Lucky,* he said that he was born May 2, 1904, and added, "I've seen several dates listed for my birth in various publications, among them, 1901, 1903, and 1906. I'd like to take 1906, but 1904 is the one I was stuck with."

It's been the long-standing practice of movie companies, agents, personal managers, and other representatives to shave years from their stars' lives, and it would seem likely that if Bing was "stuck" with the year 1904, it was because that was the year chosen by his own organization. No doubt this assumption was made by those who erroneously claimed that he was actually born in 1901. The dispute over his birth date is understandable under the circumstances.

In the first biography ever written of Bing, published in Los Angeles in 1937 and written by his elder brothers Ted and Larry, the train trip that their mother, Kate, took with the children from Tacoma to Spokane in 1906 is described on page one. Bing's age is given as five. On page three, however, still aboard the train moments later, Bing's age is given as four. And toward the end of the biography, there's a 1929 scene in which they quote Bing as saying that he's twenty-five. Thus, according to the official family biographers, Bing was born in 1901, 1902, *and* 1904. All wrong, but the confusion didn't end there.

In 1975, London-based journalist Charles Thompson published an authorized biography with the same title as that used earlier by the family biographers: *Bing*. In the early seventies, he interviewed brother Larry Crosby for a BBC Radio anthology on Bing's life. Larry, who was Bing's public-relations director, told Thompson that Bing was born May 2, 1901, and added, "During his early days at Paramount, people thought that everybody had to be young and I let them think that Bing was born in 1904."

According to Bing's baptismal certificate, which came to light three days after Bing's death and which was furnished to us by Ken Twiss, president of the Bing Crosby Historical Society in Tacoma, Washington, Bing was born on May 3, 1903. And according to the present parish priest, Reverend Joseph Marquart, of St. Patrick's Church, where Bing was baptized, the baptismal dates are correct. Father Marquart added that it's not at all uncommon for people born around the turn of the century to be in doubt about or simply not know their actual birth date. Father Marquart says that the ages of twenty percent of the people over seventy for whom funerals are held in his parish are incorrect, because there are no birth certificates filed, and families simply forget when people were born.

However, a look at other Crosby-family baptismal records doesn't exactly inspire one to total confidence with respect to accuracy, despite Father Marquart's assurances. Brother Ted's baptismal certificate, for example, which was also recorded by St. Patrick's Church, lists Dad Crosby, Harry, as "Henry," and lists Mother Crosby's maiden name, which was Harrigan, as "Carrigan." Obviously, the record is in error, which raises the possibility—and in this case, the probability—that the day of Bing's birth was recorded in error as well, particularly since the church would have to rely on the parents as informants for the day of birth. And since Bing's parents always celebrated his birth on the second of May, one must conclude that the person who recorded the day of his birth on the baptismal record was in error.

The year 1903 is indisputable, though, because the baptism was recorded in a large ledger and was preceded and followed by other baptismal entries on the same page, all of which bear the year 1903.

Other than the baptismal certificate, the only other document that records Bing's true year of birth is a bound genealogy given by Bob Crosby to the Daughters of the Pioneers, who own Tumwater House, at Tumwater, Washington, the home built by Bing's grandfather, Nathaniel Crosby, in 1860. The genealogy lists Bing's birth as May 2, 1903.

It's possible, but unlikely, that Bing himself was somehow convinced that he was born in 1901. His elder brother, Larry, and his first wife, Dixie, certainly thought so. We interviewed Dr. George J. Hummer, who had been a close friend of Bing and Dixie's, and Dr. Hummer distinctly remembers attending with his wife a dinner party given by Dixie in May 1951 to celebrate Bing's *fiftieth* birthday. The date stands out in Dr. Hummer's mind because he and his wife were touring Europe with Dixie at the time, and the dinner was given in the south of France; Bing was back in Idaho, fishing at the time. It's questionable that Bing didn't know the true date of his birth by 1957, for that was the year he got a copy of his baptismal certificate in order to marry Kathryn. It seems unlikely that he wouldn't read it, but then, since his friend and aide Leo Lynn made the church arrangements, perhaps Bing didn't even see the certificate.

Finally, the year 1904 could be totally discounted even if there had been no baptismal certificate, for

Bing's sister Catherine was born on October 3, 1904, precluding Bing's having been born five months earlier. Catherine's birth certificate is a matter of public record in Tacoma. Thompson's biography lists Catherine's birth as 1905, but he was obviously given this information to cover for Bing's claim to 1904. Ironically, in all the confusion, Bing's grave was marked in error as well: 1904–1977.

He was born Harry Lillis Crosby on May 2, 1903, and was baptized on May 31, in a small Catholic church (which burned down the following year) on the southeast corner of North G Street and Starr, not far from his birthplace, a white, two-story house at 1112 North J Street, in Tacoma, Washington. He was the fourth child of Harry Lowe and Catherine Helen Crosby, née Harrigan, and his birth had been preceded by the births of his brothers Laurance Earl (Larry), January 3, 1895; Everett Nathaniel, April 5, 1896; and Henry Edward (Ted), July 30, 1900; and followed by the births of his sisters, Catherine Cordelia, October 3, 1904, and Mary Rose, May 3, 1906; and a brother, George Robert (Bob) Crosby, August 25, 1913. Bob was the only member of the Crosby family to be born in Spokane.

The maternal side of the Crosby family tree had Irish-Catholic roots. Bing's mother, Catherine Helen Harrigan, was the daughter of a carpenter, Dennis Harrigan, and Catherine Ahearn. Although Thompson's authorized biography states that Dennis and Catherine were born in Ireland, they were actually born in New Brunswick, Canada, and were married there before immigrating to Stillwater, Minnesota, where Catherine, known as Kate, was born on February 7, 1873. The Harrigans later migrated to Tacoma, Washington, where Kate met and married Harry Lowe Crosby.

The name Crosby is said to be of Danish origin, meaning "Town of the Cross." According to Larry, as related in Thompson's biography, *Bing,* the Crosby forebears are alleged to have been Vikings, Scandinavian pirates who settled in Ireland, Scotland, and England from the eighth through the tenth centuries. Thompson,

21

a free-lance journalist, says that Irish records show the establishment of an ancient House of Crosby, which was at Ardfert in County Kerry and which authorized a now-extinct title of earl of Glandore, and that in addition to there being a Bishop Crosby of Ardfert in 1601, there was also a knight, called Sir Pierce Crosby, who had a castle in what is today Ulster.

Inevitably, Larry also discovered a Crosby among the 102 founders who set sail aboard the *Mayflower,* a damsel who is said to have married Thomas Brewster, one of the Pilgrim Fathers. Larry traced a coat of arms, as well: a lion, above which are suspended two red hands. The coat of arms signifies a legendary bold deed by a seagoing Crosby ancestor. As the story goes, it was customary that the first person to touch newly discovered land could claim it. The Crosby ancestor sighted new land, but bad weather made landing impossible and, in an apparent fit of frustration, he cut off his hand and hurled it ashore, thus claiming it as his own.

Bing was proud enough of the family crest to risk his average-guy-next-door image by wearing it on his blazers while performing and by having the crest set in tile at the entrance to his second Palm Springs home, a place that he built in 1956, just prior to marrying his second wife, Kathryn.

The American roots of the Crosby branches are more substantial. Bing's paternal great-grandfather, Nathaniel (after whom a Liberty Ship was named in World War II), was a sea captain who left his home in Worcester, Massachusetts, and traded in the Far East before settling in Oregon, where he helped found Portland before moving north to help settle Olympia, Washington, where Bing's father, Harry Lowe Crosby, was born on November 28, 1870, and where, ten years earlier, Nathaniel built what is today known as Crosby House.

There's no record of whether Harry Lowe Crosby had finished his schooling, which included a year or so of college, before he met Kate Harrigan in Tacoma, Washington, or whether he quit school after meeting her. But quit he did, though not before getting enough education to become a bookkeeper. Kate was a pretty, level-headed Irish lass who shared Harry's love for music, and Harry went for her in a big way. Harry was a handsome catch for Kate, an educated man from a good family and with a good profession, and he was easygoing, gregarious, and charming. He sang her the latest songs, accompanying himself on mandolin and guitar, and he could even sing Chinese songs, which he had learned as a child from his family's servants. He was fun to be around, always carefree and debonair. The only obstacle was that Harry wasn't Catholic, and the devoutly religious Kate Harrigan would never submit to a "mixed marriage." So Harry converted to Catholicism, swept Kate off her feet, and they were married in the early 1890s.

By December 1902, the Crosbys already had three sons, and the fourth (Bing) was three months along when the local newspaper announced that Harry L. Crosby had purchased two lots on J Street, between North Eleventh and Twelfth streets, for $850, and planned to build a $2,500 residence there. The same page carried the news that Tacoma carpenters were about to get a 60¢ raise, to a steep $3.60 per day. The new house at 1112 North J Street was completed in time for Bing to be born there. Catherine was also born there the following year.

By the spring of 1906, things were going wrong for the Crosby family. Harry had been a bookkeeper for the county treasurer, but apparently owing to a change in political administration, he lost his job, and the prospects of finding another one didn't seem to be good. As did many other Coast dwellers at the time, he looked toward Spokane, two hundred miles to the east near the Idaho border, which was in a fertile wheat belt and which, as a railroad center, was becoming the logging and mining center of the area. Spokane was booming as Tacoma had. So the Crosbys sold their three-year-old house to Kate's sister, Anne, and brother-in-law, Edward J. Walsh.

23

The timing couldn't have been worse for an uprooted family of five children; their sixth, daughter Mary Rose, was due to be born the following month. Evidence indicates that the Crosbys rented a furnished house at 1214 South I Street as a temporary measure, for that's where Mary Rose was born on May 3, 1906. Kate was in no condition to make the long, hot train trip from Tacoma to Spokane, so Harry left the children with her and her sister, Anne, and went alone to Spokane looking for work. He found a job as bookkeeper for the Inland Brewery and began work. As the time neared when Kate had recuperated enough from childbirth to travel, Harry rented a house and had the furniture shipped to Spokane.

There is evidence that the financial problems of the Crosby family were more serious than simply the loss of Harry's job. Ted and Larry speak of a financial reverse and of their mother's attitude toward starting anew. In *Call Me Lucky,* Bing says that the family "arrived [in Spokane] on short funds, rented a house, and ran up a sizable grocery bill as well as a large tab for fuel and other household necessities." Bing also spoke cryptically of Spokane townspeople as being people who minded their own business and who didn't care who you were or what your reputation had been before you moved there. The statement makes one wonder whether the Crosbys had suffered something akin to the humiliation of bankruptcy—or worse—in Tacoma, and whether Kate's sister and brother-in-law had taken the house to save the Crosbys from foreclosure. This is pure speculation, but the sudden change from buying two lots and building an expensive home in 1902 to leaving town, renting, and buying necessities on credit four years later seems indicative of something more disastrous than being temporarily out of work. Then, too, the Crosbys (and the Harrigans) were deeply rooted in Tacoma and were well known; the stigma of financial failing or bankruptcy could be intolerable in a small-town, turn-of-the-century environment. As further indication that something went terribly amiss in Tacoma, there's an undercurrent of disrespect for Dad Crosby in Ted and Larry's biography that seems to stem from his being—in their and Kate's opinion—financially irresponsible. Whatever the problem was, the family never forgave Dad Crosby for it.

In July, Kate arrived in Spokane by train, the two-month-old Mary Rose in her arms and the other five Crosby children in tow. Harry met them at the depot with a rented horse-drawn carriage and took them through the business and manufacturing districts and then across the Spokane River to a pleasant residential area on the city's northeast side, to their yellow, two-story rented house on Sinto Avenue. It was a nice four-bedroom house with indoor plumbing and electricity, and it was particularly suitable for a large Catholic family. There were stores nearby and trolley lines to take them across the river to the business district. And within three blocks of the house was Webster, a grade school, and a Jesuit-run high school–college complex called Gonzaga, which was named for St. Aloysius Gonzaga, the patron saint of colleges, as was the adjoining church, St. Aloysius.

In September, Larry, Everett, and Ted were enrolled at Webster School. And with Harry again working and Kate at home with three-year-old Bing, two-year-old Catherine, and infant Mary Rose, the Crosby family settled into a comfortable if spartan routine. It was at the Sinto Avenue house, about four years later, that Bing was given his nickname.

Until about 1910, he was known only as Harry. But at about this time, when he was a second-grader at Webster, he became an avid reader of a humor feature called the "Bingville Bugle," which occupied an entire page of the Spokane *Spokesman Review*'s Sunday edition and which had the appearance of the front page of a newspaper published in a mythical place called Bingville. The "Bingville Bugle" page was filled with short, humorous, country-bumpkin stories about such mythical Bingville folks as Bale Hawkins, the widow Hinckley, Amzi Gookins, and the like, with a few humorous cartoon spots illustrating some of the stories. The following is taken from the October 10, 1910, "Bingville Bugle."

LOST

I went out and lost the stem outen my corncob pipe somers about the first of last week or the last of this week. I don't know where I lost it; if I did, I wouldn't ask you to find it for me. I'm awful put out because of this, being as I can't smoke an I haft to chew. Find it for me please.

HANK DEWBERRY,
Bingville

The "Bugle" 's logo was a horsefly, and flanking the mythical newspaper's title were the caricatures of two Bingville citizens. Young Harry Crosby had a next-door-neighbor chum named Valentine Hobart, who shared his enthusiasm for the feature. It was Valentine who noticed that the caricatures of the two Bingville folks had stocky, pear shapes and protruding ears exactly like those of his youthful friend, and Valentine began calling him Bingo from Bingville. Naturally, their peers echoed the alliteration, but soon they were calling him simply Bingo, and eventually the o was dropped and he was known to all thereafter as Bing.

The humor in the "Bingville Bugle" feature is reminiscent of country humorist Bob "Bazooka" Burns, who billed himself as The Arkansas Traveler and who Bing used on his "Kraft Music Hall" radio show (and in movies) for many years. The "Bingville Bugle" could well have been the publication of Burns's mythical Arkansas population, and foreshadowed Bing's fondness for Burns's brand of country humor.

That Dad Crosby hadn't mended his "spendthrift" ways was evident when he came home to the Sinto Avenue house one payday evening with two large packages containing a phonograph with a morning-glory-shape horn, which was the speaker, and several records featuring baritone Denis O'Sullivan, marches by Sousa and

26

other concert masters, and a light-opera group singing songs from *The Mikado*. Harry had made a special purchase that he thought might thaw the icy reception Kate would give him for wasting their hard-earned money on yet another needless item, one of the many he was forever bringing home. He included among his record selection the "Merry Widow Waltz," which was Kate's favorite song at the time. Even the level-headed Kate had to admit that having vocalists and bands that sounded as though they were right in the living room, playing at the family's command, was pleasant. Music was very important. But she took no stock at all in Harry's claim that a friend had given him the phonograph as payment for "some favors."

Dad Crosby was forever bringing music into the house. He went without a new suit he had been saving for in order to get a piano, too. And Kate saw to it that both girls took lessons, but none of the boys showed interest. When the children grew older, Sunday night became music night at the Crosby household. Dad Crosby would get out his mandolin and his four-string guitar, and the family would gather round to sing such favorites as "In the Good Old Summertime," "In the Shade of the Old Apple Tree," and Kate's all-time favorite, "When Irish Eyes Are Smiling." Kate had a rich contralto voice and had sung in the church choir in Tacoma before the children were born and she could no longer attend rehearsals. Dad Crosby had a good tenor voice for their songfests, and the children contributed harmonically as best they could—except for Everett, who even in his middle teens was exhibiting the gruff "whiskey" voice that characterized him throughout life. Everett was the only Crosby who couldn't carry a tune in a bucket, but that didn't discourage him. He made up in volume what he lacked in pitch.

Dad Crosby was always bringing home new records and the latest sheet music for the girls. While Ted and Larry seem to credit their mother's voice and influence as being most influential in the family's music interest, it was quite obviously Harry Lowe to whom homage should be paid for making music so important in the lives of all the Crosbys, especially Bing and Bob.

By the time Bing was approaching his teens, he was literally filled to overflowing with music. Barry Ulanov, who interviewed many of the Crosby neighbors and Bing's teachers for his book *The Incredible Crosby,* points out that everyone could tell when Bing was around, even before they saw him coming, for he was always singing, whistling, or humming. To them, he had an often pleasing but sometimes disconcerting penchant for breaking into song—anytime, anyplace. But even when Ulanov interviewed Spokane neighbors for his 1948 biography, none claimed to have seen any promise in Bing. Quite the contrary.

Even in grade school, Bing exhibited an indolence that, throughout his life, was as much a part of him, and as unlikely to change, as the color blindness of his blue eyes. He was even then what is called a quick study in show business; he had something akin to total recall. This was true for people's names and faces, which ingratiated him with the adults in his early years and with the relatively unknown technicians or bit-part actors he met during his professional life. But at Webster and at Gonzaga High School and at the college, his extraordinary ability was used to get ordinary grades with as little time and effort as he could get away with. As Ulanov says in *The Incredible Crosby:* "All of his grade school teachers remember Bing's laziness. 'Bing? How that boy hated to exert himself!' "

It's typical of him that he made music his life and made a fortune at it for more than fifty years, but he went to his grave never having learned to read a single note of it.

CHAPTER FOUR

The Crosby family was
a matriarchy, and Kate ran it
as though she had a direct hotline to God.

Of all the Crosby children, Bing was Kate Crosby's favorite, and she apparently made no effort to hide the fact. This is clearly stated by elder brothers Ted and Larry in their 1937 biography of Bing and is evidenced by anecdotes throughout their book. The reasons he was given special treatment by Kate seem obvious, though conjectural.

The Crosbys were a large and relatively poor family, in an era when sons were more valuable to the family than daughters. Sons could work when they were young and be of financial assistance, and when they eventually married, they'd be the breadwinners of their own families and therefore more able and traditionally inclined to look after their parents. And it appeared that Bing would be the last son born to Kate and Harry. His birth was followed by the births of his two sisters, Catherine and Mary Rose, and it was seven years after Mary Rose's birth—and a full ten years after Bing was born, by which time Kate and Harry were both in their forties and would least expect another child—that Bob was born.

For a decade, then, Bing was the baby boy of the family, and of the boys then born, he was the most like

Kate. He had his father's easygoing disposition but Kate's pragmatic emotional makeup. Finally, if it can be said that one can inherit the genetic material of an ancestor who had kissed the Blarney stone, Bing Crosby was so blessed. It was no accident that at school he excelled in elocution, and that despite his natural indolence, he ingratiated himself with his teachers, with adults in general, and with his mother in particular. Bing alone could sweet-talk Kate into almost anything. And sweet-talking Kate was the secret to preeminence in the Crosby household.

The structure of the Crosby family was that of an absolute matriarchy. Kate Crosby ran the family with an indomitable will and with the conviction of one who had a direct hotline to God. In familial matters, Kate's will would be done. The Church and the Crosby family were her life. She was devoutly religious, never missed mass, and often attended church several times a week. Things secular were never entrusted to chance or luck, for Kate made a practice of enlisting the aid of the Poor Clares—a community of nuns in Spokane—by petitioning them to offer special prayers for her family. In Bing's autobiography, he tells of mentioning to his mother the element of luck in his rise to stardom, to which Kate replied, "Your luck has been my prayers and the prayers I've asked the Poor Clare nuns to offer up for you."

Kate was the keeper of the family finances, the decision maker, the supervisor of religious education, and an inflexible disciplinarian. She spoke softly but wielded a heavy wooden hairbrush that even the fast-talking Bing couldn't avoid at times. When her children grew too old, and presumably too mature, for corporal punishment, she dealt with transgressors by assigning to them chores that they least liked and by giving them a "bludgeoning" stony silence and reprovingly cold glares that were tantamount to short-lasting, but nonetheless chilling, excommunication—a fate more unnerving than the ache of a throbbing bottom. This is not to say that Kate wasn't a loving mother, even a doting one. She was. But she was also the family sovereign and would remain so until her death in 1964, one month to the day from her ninety-first birthday. Her influence upon Bing, her favorite, was considerable even then.

Conversely, Harry Lowe Crosby quite obviously suffered the same fate as most fathers in matriarchal arrangements; he was acknowledged and cared for, but there is little evidence that he was accorded any significant measure of respect, at least by Kate and the first four Crosby sons. Though Ted and Larry weren't forthrightly critical of him in their book, they undermined his role in the family by constantly emphasizing mother Kate's problems, all of which, one is led to believe, were owing to Dad Crosby's inadequacy in providing for the children that he caused Kate to bring into the world.

Ted and Larry led one to believe that the bookkeeping father of the Crosbys was an impulsive spendthrift who had to be convinced by Kate that economy was necessary, had to be convinced that it was better for the family's health to economize on clothing rather than on food. And the boys point out that it was only through the miracles of Kate's sewing basket that the family appeared presentable to the outside world. Kate lamented that despite her prayers, Harry never got ahead in his job the way she thought he should have. He simply didn't make enough money, and the fact was often, and not too subtly, thrown up to him.

The Crosby family's counterpart to the Joneses was Kate's sister Anne and her husband, Edward Walsh, who had purchased the Crosbys' Tacoma house. Kate had come from a large family of five brothers and a sister, all of whom were left behind when the Crosbys pulled up stakes in Tacoma. Since Kate and her sister corresponded often, it was probably quite natural for Kate to measure her temporal success against that of her only sister. It was obvious that, in Kate's judgment, Anne had married well. And Kate was probably envious, if not a little jealous, of her—particularly since Anne now owned the home that Kate loved, in the city

Kate didn't want to leave, while Kate had to live in a rented place. The fact that the Crosbys had seven children while the Walshes were childless didn't deter Kate from comparing her financial circumstances with theirs, and it didn't deter her from keeping Harry pointedly abreast of Edward and Anne's success: unlike Harry, Edward was becoming a success in the hardware business; unlike Harry, Edward would soon become a partner in his firm; unlike Harry, Edward bought a new car so that he could take Anne on tours of Tacoma, while they had no car; unlike Harry, Edward was obviously making good money and didn't waste it.

Kate even used the Walshes to get Harry to have her mother's old piano shipped from Tacoma to Spokane. She pointed out to him that Anne missed the Crosby children since they moved, and that Anne had hinted that she'd like to adopt Catherine, if the Crosbys would consent, which would give them one less mouth to feed. Kate told Harry that she was probably being selfish, because the Walshes could give Catherine the things that she and Harry couldn't provide for her, like piano lessons. But she said she loved her six children—Bob had yet to be born—and really couldn't part with any of them.

Harry is said to have considered the problem for a moment and then to have decided to go without a new suit he had planned to buy and use the money to have the piano shipped from Tacoma instead. Kate patted his hand, saying, "I don't like to see you go without things, Harry." Dad Crosby puffed his pipe and replied that his college days were behind him and that he didn't have to be stylish anymore.

The family biographers even had Kate fantasizing what might have been had she entered the theater with her fine singing voice, rather than marrying the "carefree" Harry Crosby. But her fantasy is said to have ended with her saying, "Well, too late to change now."

By the time the family biography was published, the Crosbys had moved en masse from Spokane to Hollywood. Kate and Harry were living in a beautiful home in Hollywood's then-exclusive and fashionable suburb Toluca Lake, and Dad Crosby was in "semi-retirement" with the Crosby organization and gaining the nickname "Hollywood Harry" for his penchant of pridefully making the rounds with pocketfuls of clippings and notices about his famous sons, Bing and Bob. Bing wrote a typically self-effacing preface to the biography, saying that when his brothers asked permission of him to write it, he "blushingly consented," and attested to the truth of its contents.

The family biography was dedicated, "With Fond Recollections to Mother and to Bing." Dad Crosby's name was most conspicuous by its absence, and one wonders how he must have felt making the rounds after its publication.

If it occurred to Ted and Larry that any man with a wife and seven children to support would find the economic going tough, regardless of his occupation and regardless of whether times were good or bad, they didn't mention it. They even used the euphemism "manufacturing plant" for their father's first job in the brewery at a time when it was legal to make and sell liquor, but volunteered the information that brother Everett had been a bootlegger in Seattle and that, while visiting Everett, Bing had got himself thrown in jail and his brother in trouble with the law by stealing a meal from a Chinese restaurateur. It appears that their father's honest work in a brewery was shameful to them, but their own dishonesty was not.

Harry Lowe Crosby was known to raise a glass or two in celebration, even though Kate was against drinking. But there is no evidence that he drank more than the average working man. He worked regularly and was a family-loving homebody who labored uncomplainingly over dull ledgers at first in a brewery and then, during prohibition, a pickle factory. He was the sole breadwinner, keeping the family well fed and providing them with a warm family atmosphere. After a financial reversal, he had the courage to move his wife and children across the state to a strange new place for a fresh start. He saw to it that all his sons who wanted a college education got it. And in a ten-year span, he provided his large family with two new homes, houses that he had built especially for them. This is quite an accomplishment for a bookkeeper with seven children. But the family biographers leave the reader with the impression that Kate Crosby's sacrifices and shrewd economic planning did it all. One wonders how she could have accomplished it without the steady, hard work of Harry Lowe Crosby.

Dad Crosby didn't fare much better in Bing's hands, either. In *Call Me Lucky*, which was published three years after his dad's death and while his mother was still living, Bing gives his dad faint praise as the one from whom he inherited his ability to relax. He describes his father as a "casual" man who believed in "living in the present and in having a good time." He says that when his mother would fret about a financial problem, his dad would put his feet up, open the evening paper, and tell her not to worry because things would work out. Bing points out that things always did work out, too, but he attributes this to his "levelheaded" mother, who he says was the family's business manager and who stretched out dad's modest salary.

Bing, who became as devoutly religious as his mother, praised her for being the family disciplinarian, as well. His father, he said, could never get mad enough at the children to punish them; he'd leave the house when a disciplinary session was in order and wouldn't return until it was over. His mother, however, loved them as much as any mother could, Bing says, and that love included punishing them—because it was good for their souls—even though doing so hurt her.

Since this was Bing's only book (although he was working on another one at the time of his death), and since his father had died three years earlier, one might have expected him to dedicate the book to his father's memory. But he didn't; he didn't dedicate the book to anyone.

Aside from his mother, the most influential member

of the family in Bing's early childhood was one of Kate's brothers, George Harrigan, whom Bing admitted was his boyhood idol. According to Bing, Uncle George was a handsome man with black hair, freckles, blue eyes, a powerful Irish tenor voice, and "a colorful Irish personality." In *Call Me Lucky*, Bing described him as "a talented entertainer" who played in theatricals in Tacoma and Seattle and who was known statewide for his rendition of the song "Harrigan, That's Me." He was also, according to Bing, "a genius when it came to telling dialect stories." The only thing that kept Uncle George from going professional—and Bing was convinced that he could have been a success—was that, like Bing's father, he had a large family to support, and as a court reporter, he could never get enough money ahead to take a fling at show business.

Though Bing doesn't mention it, the family songfests, his mother's dream of going onstage, and the impressive performances of his Uncle George must have played at least a subconscious role in his ultimate attraction to show business. Certainly these influences dispelled any reservation Bing might ordinarily have had about performing in public, for even when he reached grade school, he would sing before anyone, anytime, anyplace without the slightest compunction, embarrassment, or self-consciousness—except for one time.

Kate arranged for him to take lessons from a singing professor for a short while. Under the professor's tutelage, Bing performed before a function, singing "One Fleeting Hour." The less-than-enthusiastic response he received cured him of singing in public until he began playing drums and singing with a band. That experience, and the professor's insistence that Bing practice scales and bring a degree of discipline to the study of voice, cured Bing of the professor, also.

Years later, when Al Rinker and Bing were performing as a duo prior to setting out for big-time show business, they got an engagement requiring Bing to do a few dance steps onstage with a trio. Bing, of course, didn't have the slightest aptitude as a dancer, and Al says admiringly, "I don't know how he did it, but he did it. Bing was really a gutsy guy onstage."

But as performers go, Bing was a late bloomer, and he'd be twenty-two before he seriously considered a career in show business. Meanwhile, he turned down an opportunity to take piano lessons, and he bolted from the singing lessons. And though he shared with his peers a common interest in the music of his day and often mimicked with a friend parts of the acts they had seen performed by vaudeville troops at the Auditorium Theater, Spokane's large opera house, he showed no interest at all in becoming a professional entertainer until he met Al Rinker.

In July 1913, the Crosbys finally left their rented Sinto Avenue house for a home they had built at 508 East Sharp Street. It was a fine two-story structure, with a formal dining room and a built-in buffet, two bathrooms, four bedrooms, and a second-story sleeping porch. As with the first house they had built on J Street in Tacoma—the one in which Bing had been born shortly after they had taken possession of it—this home, too, was "christened" with the birth of a baby boy who would one day gain fame as a performer. The following month, on August 25, the seventh and last Crosby child, Bob, was born. He was baptized George Robert on September 7, 1913, at St. Aloysius Church, and was named after Kate's favorite brother—and Bing's idol—George Robert Harrigan.

The move didn't necessitate uprooting the children, for their new home was just a few blocks from the Sinto Avenue house and even closer to Webster grade school—where ten-year-old Bing would be passing into the sixth grade, Catherine the fifth, and Mary Rose the third—and to the Gonzaga college and high-school complex just a block and a half away, where Everett was entering his junior year in the high-school division and Larry would begin his sophomore year at the college. Although all of the Crosby boys would follow brother Larry into Gonzaga College, Larry would be the only one of them to earn a degree.

By the time Bing entered Webster grade school, the faculty was well acquainted with the Crosby clan. Larry, small and bespectacled like his dad, had entered Webster in the seventh grade when the family had moved from Tacoma and had been a serious, model student who was happiest when absorbed in a book. Everett, large and muscular, entered in the fourth grade and dispelled whatever illusions the faculty might have had that the other Crosby boys would be well-behaved like Larry. Ev, as he was called, did well with his studies and was a good athlete, but he was short-tempered and given to punching his peers in the nose at the slightest provocation. Ted had entered Webster at the second-grade level, and if Ev's teachers were bracing themselves for another battling Crosby, they needn't have bothered, for Ted was the quietest of them all; he was a good, inquisitive student but not given to group endeavors and was happiest when left alone to his own thoughts.

So after studious Larry, pugnacious Ev, and introverted Ted came a short, stocky, blond-haired little fellow with protruding ears who, by the third grade, would be known to all as Bing. And his teachers soon learned that he was unlike any of his brothers. He was bright but exerted himself only enough to keep moving from grade to grade with his peers at Webster without tapping his potential. But he lagged considerably behind his peers in matters of deportment and had more than a nodding acquaintance with Webster's principal, C. J. Boyington, who at least once had to take the yardstick to Bing after numerous warnings and a note to Kate with respect to her son's apparent disregard for the gravity of the education process in general and the school's regulations in particular.

Bing also had more than a nodding acquaintance with the school's truant officers and with what Bing would have called the Spokane constabularies. On one occasion, he was playing hooky from school with a few of his friends when they chanced to see a local bakery's delivery wagon returning from its rounds still laden

with unsold pastries. The boys waited until the driver
went inside with his invoices, leaving the wagon unpro-
tected, and then raided it, taking a couple of pies apiece
and several bags of cinnamon buns. After eating their
fill, they were left with a surplus of cinnamon buns, so
they went down on Mission Boulevard and were glee-
fully pelting passing motorists with the pastries when
they had the misfortune of scoring a direct hit on an
otherwise unmarked vehicle occupied by several off-
duty policemen on their way home from work. The policemen locked the boys up in the juvenile-detention
ward and called their mothers. When Kate was notified,
she told them to keep Bing there overnight. "It'll do
him good," she said. And they did.

The experience cured Bing of stealing pastries, but
its doubtful that it put an end to his hooky playing; it
just wasn't natural for him not to take an occasional, if
unofficial, vacation from school in early summer to fish
or swim in McGolderick's Mill pond, or to smoke corn-
silk in Buck Williams's or MacGowan's barn, or, in
winter, to go bobsledding on Ligerwood Hill.

Most of the time, though, he stayed in school, and
most of the time he behaved himself. He wasn't a bad
student, just free-spirited and not easily motivated. He
loved sports and was quite good at them in grade
school. And when the class was called upon to sing, he
was outstanding. With all else, he simply endured, impatient to get into the high-school division at Gonzaga,
where he hoped to excel in football, baseball, basketball, and any other sport they offered.

Still, even at an early age, there was something
charming about him. His second biographer, Barry
Ulanov, visited Spokane in the late forties and found
two of Bing's former grade-school teachers, Nell and
Agnes Finnegan, who remembered Bing as Harry
Crosby and who weren't particularly impressed by him
at the time. They did recall a teacher named Margaret
Cox who had left Webster and returned for a visit; the
only student she was particularly anxious to see was
Harry Crosby. And when she saw him, all disheveled,

his shirttail hanging out, she was delighted that he hadn't changed a bit. The Misses Finnegan remembered Bing's singing and whistling. "We liked his singing as a youngster much better than we've liked it since," Agnes Finnegan said. Neither of the ladies cared for crooning.

Bing's boyhood on Spokane's northeast side was as close to idyllic as one could hope for. His family was relatively poor, because it was relatively large, but none of them ever wanted for necessities. They were close, with a solid religious base, and very secure. Bing also had the security of growing up in the same neighborhood from age three until he left Spokane at age twenty-two. He went through grade school, high school, and into college with the same friends. In his grade-school years, he was a member of the Boone Avenue gang, a neighborhood social group that operated out of MacGowan's barn, which they called the Sinto Avenue Club and from which were organized sandlot football and baseball teams, and boxing teams, which challenged other neighborhood groups.

Boxing was very big in Bing's middle-childhood years. His uncle George Harrigan had been an adept amateur boxer and taught Bing something of the art. Bing remained interested in boxing throughout his life and invested money in several prizefighters, just as he invested in several other sports. Unlike his brother Ev, Bing was easygoing and not at all pugnacious; his only street fight that can be documented was one in which he defended his kid sister's honor.

Mary Rose was decidedly plump, and a young man at Webster made the mistake of illustrating the fact by drawing a fat stick figure on the blackboard and putting her name beneath it. Bing challenged the offender to an after-school fight, which was the talk of the school and which drew a large crowd. Bing dispatched the chalk artist with a bloody nose and assorted bruises. Later that evening, the boy's father called Dad Crosby to complain of Bing's barbaric behavior and was assured that Mr. Crosby would take the steps necessary to set

39

his son back on the right path. Then, according to Ted and Larry, Dad Crosby took Bing into the basement, where, rather than punishing him, he drew up a chair and eagerly asked for a blow-by-blow account of the battle. Kate didn't believe in fisticuffs, but she, too, looked upon her son's battle of honor with silent pride.

The family biographers and Bing himself added to the image of him as a young Irish scrapper by relating an incident that was supposed to have taken place several years later, when Bing was singing and playing drums with The Musicaladers. They were appearing at a roadhouse about ten miles out of Spokane when a young tough made a remark about how, in his opinion, only sissies sang songs. One account has Bing jumping from the stage—midsong—and decking the heckler on the dance floor. Another has Bing inviting the heckler outside, where he dealt with him swiftly. But, according to Al Rinker, no such fight ever took place. There are, in fact, several stories in the family biography and in *Call Me Lucky* that simply weren't true and were apparently added to the books to make them more entertaining.

Bing was a proud young Irishman with athletic ability, but he wasn't physical and he was very slow to anger. There was only one incident in his life in which he was angered sufficiently to lose control and react physically. It was a minor incident involving a schoolboy crush—his first—on a girl named Gladys Lemmon. Gladys was transferred to Webster from another school district; she was a pretty, golden-haired lass, and Bing couldn't keep his eyes from her long enough to avoid tripping over his own feet in her presence. He began carrying her books home from school and then taking her bobsledding on Ligerwood Hill and generally spending a lot of time with her. They became quite an item in the Crosby home, for it was the first time that Bing had shown an interest in anything besides sports.

One evening Bing was late for dinner and had no sooner sat down at the table when Larry jokingly asked, "Where've you been? Out squeezing that Lemmon again?" According to Ted and Larry, Bing exploded and threw a slice of buttered bread at Larry. But by the time Bing related the same incident in his own book sixteen years later, the object he had thrown took on a considerably larger form. Bing reported that he hit Larry with an entire leg of lamb.

Bing continued seeing Gladys Lemmon until he was invited to her birthday party. It was his first dress-up party, requiring a suit and a stiff collar. And he apparently decided that no girl was worth all the torture he suffered, for the day after the party, he made excuses about having to practice for football, and he was never seen in her company again.

If anything at all can be said with incontrovertibility about the enigmatic Bing Crosby, it is this: boy and man, professionally and privately, the three greatest influences in his life were religion, sports, and music. And the experience that gave profundity to his religious bent—which had been instilled by his mother—was his entry to the high-school section of Gonzaga in September 1916.

Gonzaga was an all-male, Roman Catholic educational complex operated by the Jesuit order and consisting of a college, a four-year high school, dormitories for out-of-state students, and St. Aloysius Church. The complex was located on Boone Avenue, just a block and a half from the Crosby home.

While Bing had slipped through Webster effortlessly, the curriculum at Gonzaga's high school was a considerable challenge to him. He was required to take four years of Latin and two of Greek, two years of mathematics and of history, a year of chemistry or physics, and four years of English, stressing not only grammar and syntax but elocution, in addition to the usual courses in English and American literature. All he needed was the motivation to shift out of his intellectual lethargy, and one of the Gonzaga priests, Father Kennelly, gave him that.

Father Kennelly, whom the boys called Big Jim behind his back, was a 280-pound dynamo who, among other duties, was the prefect of discipline at the high school. He carried a considerable number of keys on a long key chain, which he kept coiled beneath his cassock and which he could flick, according to Bing, "with the accuracy and speed of a professional fly-caster." He'd stand outside his office during change of classes, and if any of the students broke the mandatory hallway silence or committed any other infraction, they'd feel the bite of Big Jim's keys. Naturally, it became great sport to provoke him and then to move one's anatomy out of key-chain range.

Father Kennelly was also a sports enthusiast who often tucked his cassock under his belt and joined the boys in yard baseball or football games. Bing had been at Gonzaga only a few days when he informed Father Kennelly of his athletic aspirations, and that's when Big Jim gave him the sobering news that to participate in organized sports, one had to have good grades. Thus Bing found the motivation to study.

Gonzaga divided its competitive sports program by age. There were two groups: the Junior Yard Association, for boys sixteen and under, and the Gonzaga Athletic Club, for the older boys. Bing played center for the JYA team and made the Athletic Club's baseball team, in addition to other intramural sports. Basketball was out for him; he just wasn't fast enough on his feet. But he was an excellent swimmer. As one of his classmates pointed out, Bing didn't move fast on land, and in almost all sports other than swimming, his enthusiasm was far greater than his ability. It's interesting to note that he didn't take up golf until he quit school at twenty-one, and he eventually got good enough to turn pro if he had wanted to.

Bing had won a number of first- and second-place medals at swimming in a Mission Park swimming competition just a few weeks before entering Gonzaga. He was proud enough of this athletic achievement to have told his second wife, Kathryn, about the medals when he was courting her, forty years after he won them. But if it hadn't been for Kate's outsmarting him, he would

42

never have won the medals. Kate had heard about the swimming competition from Larry or Ev, and had asked Bing if he was going to enter. Bing was cool to the idea but changed his mind fast when Kate said she'd let him out of his chores for the day if he agreed to sign up. Bing figured he'd pull a fast one on the family and agreed. His plan was that while his brothers did his chores—Kate assigned them to Larry, Ev, and Ted—he'd hop a trolley and pick up some extra spending money by caddying at the Downriver Golf Course.

On the day of the meet, Kate sent Bing off to the park to practice for a couple of hours, and when he returned, she had his favorite meal—pork chops—waiting for him. He really thought he was in heaven when, after lunch, Kate suggested that he rest for a couple of hours until the meet. So he lay on the living-room sofa, king for a day, while his brothers went about grumbling and doing his chores. He even made Catherine stop practicing her piano lessons because "the racket" was disturbing him.

When it came time to leave, Bing got his bathing suit and said good-bye to Kate, ready to bolt for the golf course. But to his surprise, she got her hat and announced that she was going with him. He tried to talk her out of it, to no avail, and was forced to enter the meet. He took first place in most of the events and placed in all of the others, winning six or seven medals.

Between his studies and his part-time jobs and his sports, Bing somehow found time for other activities. He joined the band and was given a snare drum to beat on, and he did so with far more enthusiasm than technique. The fact that he never really applied himself to learning proper technique early on is probably owing to his motivation for taking it up in the first place: it was his "ticket" to all the varsity football games. Had he known that it would also be his ticket into show business, he might have taken it more seriously—maybe.

He also got involved in school politics, but only because sports were involved. Six members of Bing's class of 1920 formed an organization called the Dirty Six, one of whom eventually became president of the senior class and all of whom were influential in student activities simply because they were organized and the other students weren't. Bing didn't care about their activities until they formed the Derby Club in their sophomore year, which was formed to patrol all the varsity athletic events and which meant that members of the club not only got to see all the athletic events, but got to see them close up.

To Bing, this was power worth fighting for, so he formed a Loyal Opposition of at least twelve students, and since the news of the day was concerned with a revolution that was taking place in Russia—which would end in November of Bing's sophomore year—and since the opponents of the royalists were known as the Bolsheviks, what better name for his Loyal Opposition group? They dubbed themselves the Bolsheviks.

Whether the Bolsheviks managed to horn in on the athletic events isn't known. But elocution and debate were big at Gonzaga, and the Dirty Six and the Bolsheviks clashed in many debates. The Bolsheviks usually won because Bing was their leader, and he was an outstanding elocutionist. But for the most part, the two groups' chief endeavor seemed to be that of pointing fingers at one another. If one of the Bolsheviks got involved or was suspected of being involved in some mischief, he inevitably blamed the Dirty Sixers, and vice versa.

It's interesting to note that biographer Barry Ulanov reports accurately on Bing's formation of the Bolsheviks—indeed, he named them himself—in his book *The Incredible Crosby*, which was published in 1948. But five years later, when Bing's autobiography was published in the wake of McCarthyism, Bing claimed to have been a member of the Dirty Six. Considering the insane paranoia that still gripped Hollywood even then, one can hardly blame him. All that was needed was for someone to come across the information that Bing had once led a group of Bolsheviks at some strange-sounding "college" in the north, and who knows what could have happened? People got burned in Hollywood for less than that. It's obvious, though, that Bing's 1918 sophomoric group couldn't have had the faintest notion of what the Bolsheviks were or what they were up to.

Despite the discipline necessary to the running of a campus filled with boys and men, and despite the influence of Jesuit priests like the key-swinging Father Kennelly, Bing's deportment didn't improve visibly. Offenders at Gonzaga didn't get off with simply the swat of a yardstick or a note to their mothers; they were sent to the penance room, which the students referred to as the Jug. In the Jug, one was given a piece by Ovid or Virgil to memorize in Latin. And one had to recite it or write it from memory to get out. The more grievous the offense—or the more frequent the offender—the longer the piece assigned. If the offense was considered very serious, one had to memorize the piece backward.

Bing spent a lot of time in the Jug, and he could probably quote Ovid and Virgil in his sleep—and backward, too. Sometimes he was in the Jug for scholastic reasons, but more often than not, it was because of deportment. There seemed no defiance in his offenses, simply a lack of concern about them. Time was a problem. It meant nothing to him, and he was almost always the last one to class and often late. He didn't break rules indiscriminately or even deliberately, but he simply ignored them if they interfered with something that he wanted to do. This was true of all things secular, but religion was quite another matter.

Kate Crosby had always wanted one of her sons to be a priest. This is emphasized in the family biography and is mentioned in Bing's book as well. Since Bing was Kate's favorite, and since for a period of ten years, she thought him to be the last Crosby son, there is good reason to believe that her religious training of Bing was more intense than that of Larry, Ev, and Ted. It's a matter of conjecture, of course, but what is not a matter of conjecture is that Bing was the most religious of the boys. Kate had instilled in him an unshakable, visceral belief, and Gonzaga not only nurtured his belief but gave it intellectual substance.

Along with the secular educational program, boys at Gonzaga were given a four-year course in religion, from the fundamentals to a thorough philosophical exploration and interpretation of Catholicism and of the most learned Christian apologetics. And in addition to such instruction, the fathers at Gonzaga celebrated mass at St. Aloysius Church, and their students attended mass there, as well. Of the several hundred students at Gonzaga, only about eight were chosen as altar boys, and Bing was one of them.

Each altar boy served seven straight days every three weeks, and the service required that he be there at six-thirty every morning. According to Ulanov, who interviewed several of the priests who were at Gonzaga when Bing was in school, there is no evidence of his ever being late or derelict in his duties as altar boy. So in ecclestiac matters, Bing was most attentive and responsible, but in the secular world, he gave free rein to his irresponsibility, a curious paradox that one sees interwoven throughout his life. He compartmentalized his religion and seemed unable, or unwilling, to generalize its philosophy and apply it to worldly matters. He adhered to the moral imperatives of Catholicism as strictly as any mortal could, but used them in an almost Procrustean manner to make judgments of others, including family members. He judged and did not forgive. And it seems apparent that he sicced his unmerciful judgment on himself, as well.

By the time Bing reached his sophomore year in high school, there were a number of changes at home. Larry and Ev were in the army, Bob started school at Webster, and Catherine and Mary Rose had gone on to North Central High School. When the war ended, Larry, who had graduated from college, came back and began teaching at Gonzaga's high-school section, while Ev, who had quit college, went up to Seattle, where he bootlegged liquor for a while. In the early twenties, Ev moved to Los Angeles, where he became a truck sales-man for the White Truck Company.

Bing graduated from the high-school section in June of 1920 and entered the college in the following September. He wasn't required to choose a major until his junior year, so his first two years were spent completing his general education requirements. He wasn't as active in sports as he had been in high school; he made the college baseball team but was too small and light for football, so he became an assistant cheerleader, which enabled him to see all the games.

He also joined the college band, where he gained access to a bass drum and where he met six other musicians who, along with him, formed a dance combo called The Juicy Seven. They weren't very good. They used stock arrangements—music pieces arranged by a professional for large bands and printed commercially in quantity—which were not only terribly dated but also called for instrumentation the small band didn't have. But they got jobs playing for high-school dances at Gonzaga and an occasional off-campus dance or party. The off-campus jobs were often difficult to make, because most of The Juicy Seven were out-of-state students who lived in the dormitory and were subject to restrictions and to curfew. Also, they had to use the school instruments and had to sneak them off the grounds whenever they got off-campus jobs.

Sneaking a clarinet or cornet out of the basement band room and off campus was easy compared to sneaking an entire set of drums noiselessly away. In those days, the set was usually comprised of four pieces: a cymbal and three drums, including a huge bass drum. Then there was the problem of returning them to the basement without waking the entire campus after the job was over. The drums were such a problem that Bing finally invested in a set of his own.

In his junior year, which began in September 1922, Bing decided to become a lawyer. He was a good orator, he was fascinated with criminal law—he could see himself arguing dramatically before the bench—and he was of the opinion that all lawyers made good money. He soon learned otherwise.

To enhance his studies and to earn pocket money as well, Bing got a part-time job working in the law offices of Colonel Charles S. Albert, who was a legal counsel for the Great Northern Railway. Bing's job was recording the garnishments brought against railroad employees and occasionally typing out briefs for the colonel and his assistant. It was pretty mundane stuff, and the only excitement Bing got out of it was when he'd find the name of an old high-school or neighborhood friend and would warn the friend to draw on his pay before the judgment was served.

By this time—late 1922 and early 1923—The Juicy Seven combo wasn't very active, so Bing settled into a routine of morning classes at Gonzaga and humdrum work at Colonel Albert's offices in the afternoon. His only diversion was listening to records at a friend's house or taking in a vaudeville show whenever one came through Spokane. Most of his time was spent hanging around Benny Stubeck's Cigar Store with the gang and trying to scrape up enough money among them to buy liquor. But one afternoon a young man named Al Rinker called Bing, and that telephone call was to change Bing's life.

Part Three:

Crosby and Rinker

CHAPTER FIVE

> Listen, if you ever talk
> to *me* like that, I'll give
> you a punch in the nose!
>
> —BING CROSBY TO AL RINKER

Alton Rinker was born December 20, 1907, on a farm near Tekoa, Washington, about sixty miles southeast of Spokane, the son of Charles and Josephine Rinker, née Lee. He had two brothers, Miles and Charles, and a sister, Mildred, who gained fame as Mildred Bailey, the first non-black female singer to be accepted in jazz and the first female big-band vocalist.

Al's father, Charles, was a former railroad man turned farmer, and his mother, Josephine, was one-quarter Coeur d'Alene Indian, and inherited more than 640 acres of wheat land from the Coeur d'Alene Tribe in nearby Idaho. Josephine, who was known as Josie, was Catholic, and studied under the tutelage of nuns at a convent called St. Joseph's Academy, in Tekoa, where

49

she learned to read music and to play piano. She was an excellent pianist, and could play classical and ragtime with equal facility. No one knows how she learned to play ragtime or even where she heard it in a "frontier" farming community of eight hundred people in those preradio days.

There was always a piano in the Rinker household, even on the farm, and when Mildred and Al exhibited not only an interest in it but also an astonishing aptitude for it and an inborn sense of rhythm and harmonics, Josie taught them to play. Mildred, who was six years older than Al, also studied for a while with the nuns at St. Joseph's Academy.

In 1912, the Rinkers left the farm and moved to Spokane, where, a few years later, Josie died of tuberculosis. She was only thirty-six when she succumbed to the "white man's" disease for which the Coeur d'Alenes had little resistance; Josie's brothers, Miles and Charles, after whom her first two sons were named, had both died of tuberculosis before her. A few years after Josie's death, Al's father married a woman who Al says could have been the model for mean fairy-tale stepmothers; to complete the tableau, she even had a spoiled daughter, whom she favored over the Rinker children.

Miles, Charles, and Al endured the mean stepmother, but Mildred, who wasn't easily trod upon, battled with her and with the stepdaughter before finally bolting from the household to live with her aunt Ida in Seattle in 1918, where she got a job in a Woolworth store demonstrating sheet music by singing and playing piano. It was in Seattle that Mildred met and married a young man named Bailey. The marriage was of short duration, but when Mildred divorced Bailey and left Seattle for Los Angeles to try her luck at singing, she kept her married name because she thought it more professional-sounding than her maiden name.

The Rinker boys were too young to leave home, so they used music to drown the discord created by the two nightmarish fairy-tale interlopers. Al continued developing his piano playing, and Miles took up the alto sax. Their playing intrigued two neighborhood boys, Clare and Bob Pritchard, who talked their parents into buying them musical instruments—a banjo for Clare and a C-melody sax for Bob. The Pritchard boys soon learned to play well enough to join Al and Miles, and in the few months before Al called Bing Crosby, he had begun to pull the group into a semblance of organization; the group began calling itself The Musicaladers (which they pronounced Musical-*aiders*).

Al could read a little music but not well, and none of the others could read a note. "The only reason I was the leader," Al says, "is because I was the only one who knew what notes each of them should be playing."

But that really wasn't the only reason, for as Bing discovered, and as he relates in his book, ". . . Al was a genius at listening to phonograph records, absorbing their arrangements, and committing them to memory by ear." And it was this uncanny ability that made Al's budding Musicaladers different from the other neighborhood bands and that gave them cohesion and potential.

Al made a practice of going down to the Bailey Music Company—a local record store that provided listening rooms and demonstration records—where he'd listen to the latest songs played by such groups as The Memphis Five, The Mound City Blues Blowers, and McKinney's Cotton Pickers. Then he'd run home, work the arrangements out on piano, and sound the chords and notes out for each member of the band. After a few weeks' practice at Al's house or at the Pritchards', who also had a piano, the boys worked up six or seven tunes for their repertoire.

It was at this point that they added a fifth member to the band, a would-be drummer named Ted Healey. Ted had a new set of drums, and at first The Musicaladers thought that was recommendation enough—like the kid who owns the only football on the block; whether he's liked or can play well is irrelevant. But it was soon discovered that Ted Healey had no musical talent at all;

he couldn't keep a beat. Dismissing the only guy they knew who owned a set of drums wasn't an easy decision, but it was finally agreed that, though a nice guy, Ted was dragging the whole band down and had to go. As Al told us, "We politely got rid of him. He didn't like it, but he left—under duress."

The Musicaladers were desperate and at a low ebb when Al learned that a fellow named Bing Crosby owned a set of drums. Al remembered seeing Bing at Mission Park, so he called him on the telephone and explained the band's plight, asking if Bing would be interested in coming over to his house and sitting in with the band.

"Yeah," Bing said. "I'll come over and try out."

Bing had given up on The Juicy Seven and had been forced to confine his drumming and singing to party gatherings, so he no doubt looked forward to the meeting at Al's that afternoon, hoping for the best. But the group was made up of high-school students, all of whom were younger than he, and it's doubtful that his expectations were very high.

When he arrived, Al introduced him to the others, and Bing set up his drums; they were an inexpensive set but flashy enough, with an oriental sunset painted on the bass. Bing had also brought along a small megaphone, which the others paid little attention to. They didn't know he could sing, too.

The band began playing, and Bing was surprised to find himself leading the percussion not to conservative, stock arrangements of old songs but to the latest hits, like "Margie," "Hindustan," and "Angel Eyes." And they were played with the harmonies, phrasings, and voicings of the hot, avant-garde bands that Bing had heard and enjoyed on records. The band was pleasantly surprised with Bing, too.

"We went over a couple of tunes," Al told us, "and we knew right away that this guy had a beat. Not only that, but he picked up his megaphone, and he could *sing!* So this was *great,* a real surprise to us."

The band had a few more practice sessions, and

while Al remained the leader, Bing put him on notice at the second or third session. "I was kind of bossy then," Al says, "kind of drunk with power, showing the guys their notes. But I remember he [Bing] bawled me out once for the way I talked to the guys. He said, 'Listen, if you ever talk to *me* like that, I'll give you a punch in the nose!' I was the younger guy, so I straightened out. I was careful how I handled him from then on."

The band added more tunes, with Bing singing all the vocals, and they started playing for high-school dances with their five-piece group for whatever they could earn—usually about one to three dollars apiece. Shortly thereafter, they rounded out the band's sound by adding a cornet, played by another North Central High student named Jimmy Heaton, who would eventually go on to play first trumpet with Hollywood orchestras at such studios as Goldwyn and Twentieth Century-Fox.

Bing and Al hit it off well and soon became inseparable. They worked nights, and when Bing finally dropped out of Gonzaga they had lots of spare time during the day to indulge in a sport that had attracted both of them but which neither of them had ever tried: golf. They each bought themselves an old, used set of mismatched clubs and some used "repaint" balls and began frequenting the Downriver Golf Course to teach themselves the game. In the following years, they would haunt golf courses all over the country, and both would become excellent golfers. When they weren't on the golf course, they were hovering around the Bailey Music Company listening rooms like vultures, with Al plucking out the latest and best of songs and arrangements, and Bing picking at the styles and vocal tricks of the vocalists.

It wasn't long before The Musicaladers became quite a novelty in Spokane, particularly with the younger generation, who didn't care much for the "old-fashioned" music of their elders that was slavishly being played from stock arrangements by the other bands in town. The Musicaladers weren't exactly accomplished musicians, but as Bing pointed out, ". . . our technique was

53

modern and advanced. The other musicians could read notes, but they couldn't play stuff the way we played it."

The boys' biggest thrill came when they were offered a week's engagement at the Casino Theater. "The reason they put us on," Al says, "is because it was kind of a novelty to have neighborhood boys with a band. You didn't find six-piece bands like that in Spokane. And it was a lot of fun. We even had all the professional musicians from the Davenport Hotel—the top hotel in Spokane—coming down to hear us. So we were *all* kind of puffed up a little bit; we thought that was great—and I guess it was, at the time, considering that we were just kids."

After the Casino engagement, the band was offered better-paying jobs. Besides the high-school dances and the parties, they were booked into the Pekin, a Chinese restaurant on Riverside Avenue that was a favorite Friday- and Saturday-night hangout for high-school kids. This was followed by a summer-long, three-nights-a-week engagement at Lareida's Dance Pavillion in Dishman, about ten miles east of Spokane.

By September of 1925, after about eighteen months, Bing and Al watched helplessly as the band dissolved around them. Al's brother, Miles, left for Champagne, Illinois, where he attended the University of Illinois; the Pritchard brothers left for Washington State College, at Pullman, Washington; and Jimmy Heaton headed for Los Angeles, where his cousins had a band at the time. Al and Bing were left with nothing but their ambition and the band car, a 1916 topless Model-T Ford that had seen better days, and which The Musicaladers had purchased for $30.

Bing and Al continued hanging around together, playing golf and going to parties, where they began forming a singing duo. They didn't do so intentionally; it was just a natural extension of their mutual musical interest and association. They began at first by just entertaining friends. "We'd just fool around at parties," Al says. "I'd play for Bing; he'd sing, and I started harmonizing with him, just naturally, and it sounded—I don't know how it sounded—but it was kind of natural for us."

At about this time, a man named Roy Bommer was looking for a quartet to put on a stage show between pictures at the Clemmer Theater, which was a fine theater, several cuts above the Casino, where the band had appeared. Someone told Bing and Al about Bommer's intention, so they got hold of three other singers, including a boy soprano, rehearsed a few numbers, and auditioned for Bommer. Al went along to accompany the quartet.

Bommer liked what he heard and hired the quartet, along with Al as accompanist. It was decided that they'd do numbers in keeping with whatever picture was playing—something like a musical thematic prologue to the bill. Al worked in the orchestra pit, which at the Clemmer was visible to the audience, and the quartet worked onstage. "They did this thing about Norway," Al says, "something about far away in Norway. They did it for about a week, and it didn't seem to go over very well. So Roy Bommer decided to get rid of the three who had been singing with Bing, but he must have seen something in Bing. I don't know what it was—maybe his personality, or something—so he kept Bing and let the other three people go—which was a very smart move on his part, incidentally. So Bing said, 'Well, what do you want me to do?' And Roy said, 'Don't worry about it. Just come onstage and sing.'"

As Al told us, this was a big thing for Bing. He'd never done anything onstage except a couple of school plays, and he had never performed alone. Bing said to Al, "Oh, lord, what'll we do?" The two of them worked up a few songs for him to sing solo. "Bing was outgoing," Al says. "He could talk and he could move, and he was very witty. So he came out for the first show and did a song called 'Red Hot Henry Brown.' He sang, then did a couple of dance steps, then sang a couple more songs, including 'Save Your Sorrow 'Til Tomorrow,' and did them well—he sang great even then, and sang them right out, no megaphone or anything. He had a lot of nerve for a young guy."

Bing sang solo for a few shows, but he didn't like doing so. Finally he went to Bommer and said, "Look, I don't feel good out there. It's very strange out there by myself. I'd like to do some songs with Al Rinker; the two of us have got some songs we've done at parties." And Bommer said, "Oh, what the hell, go ahead and do it. I don't care."

Bing joined Al in the pit, where the piano was, and they did the tunes they had worked up at parties, including "Five Foot Two" and "Paddlin' Madeline Home." And, as Al says, "The audience loved us. So we stayed there about five weeks, making about thirty dollars a week each, and this was big money for us. That's how we began singing together professionally."

By this time, Bing had given up the idea of studying law, particularly when he learned that he was making more money on the side with music than Colonel Albert was paying his assistant attorney for full-time work. He discussed with his mother the idea of giving up law, and as he says in his book, Kate resigned herself to the fact that Bing wouldn't be happy unless he "took a whirl at show business." But when Bommer went back to showing motion pictures without a stage show, the boys were suddenly out of work. It was October 1925.

Bing and Al discussed their problem at length. They had worked up an act that quite obviously went over well with audiences, but there was no place in Spokane for them to perform. Finally, it was Al who came up with what he thought was a wild idea. "Listen," he said, "why don't we drive down to Los Angeles and see my sister, Mildred? I know she's singing in speakeasies down there."

Bing didn't give the idea a moment's thought. "Sure," he said, "why not?"

The boys went home separately to tell their parents what they had decided to do. Al's father had no objection. Neither did Dad Crosby, who thought it was a good idea. But though Bing was now twenty-two, Kate was concerned, if resigned to the idea. She took solace in the fact that Everett was in Los Angeles selling White Trucks; he could look after Bing. Then, too, as Bing intimates, Kate probably thought that their trip would be nothing but a short vacation and that the boys would soon be back in Spokane, broke.

Al had saved about sixty dollars, and Bing, though he was not much of a saver, had fifty dollars. With gas selling at ten cents a gallon, they figured they had more than enough money to make the trip. The evening of October 14, Al took the band car to the neighborhood service station to get it ready for the long trip, something akin to a tuneup, an oil change, and some minor repair work, all of which cost a total of three or four dollars.

One of the previous band members had painted "Eight million miles, and still enthusiastic" on the canvas that stretched over the spare tire attached to the back of the Model-T. Neither Bing nor Al knew whether the old flivver was enthusiastic enough to make a journey of more than a thousand miles down the Pacific Coast, but they were young and adventurous, and neither gave it more than a moment's consideration.

CHAPTER SIX

Crosby and Rinker . . . stole
the show from those billed as stars.

—SAN DIEGO NEWSPAPER REVIEW

It was about nine o'clock on the morning of October 15, 1925, when Al drove over to get Bing. Owing to the excitement of their impending trip, Al hadn't slept well the night before, but the prospect of their adventure kept the adrenaline flowing, and he wasn't tired. He knocked on the door, and Kate answered, inviting him inside.

"He's still asleep," Kate said. "You can go up and wake him."

Bing was usually an early riser, so Al was surprised that he was still in bed. He went upstairs and knocked on Bing's bedroom door, but Bing was sleeping soundly, and Al finally had to go in and shake him awake before going back downstairs and waiting for him with foot-jingling restlessness. After a few minutes, Al went back outside to give the old car a last-minute checkup and to expend some of his nervous energy; he was anxious to get on the road. After a while, Bing came downstairs with his suitcase, and Al helped him load his drums and golf clubs in the backseat of the Model-T.

Kate and Harry followed the boys out to the car.

Harry smiled and wished them luck. And as Al cranked the car to a start, Kate kissed Bing on the cheek, then rattled off a list of motherly instructions: write regularly, eat properly, keep away from alcoholic spirits, dress warmly, say hello to Everett for us, get your rest, and the like. Bing climbed into the car with Al, assuring his mother that he would do all of the *do*s and that he wouldn't do any of the *don't*s, and the boys waved as they drove off.

Since they had to pass Al's house on the way out of town, Al had left his suitcase at home, and they stopped by to pick it up and to bid Al's parents good-bye. Charles Rinker had since divorced the woman who had caused so much dissension in the family and had married a Swedish woman named Elsa Honit, who had studied at the Stockholm Academy of Music and who had since taught Al a good deal about classical music. Elsa, a kind and loving woman, was the antithesis of Al's first stepmother, and there was a bond of genuine affection between them.

The Rinkers were more worried than the Crosbys about the boys' adventure. Though Bing was twenty-two and had been away from home before while working during the summers, Al was only seventeen and had been no farther than sixty miles from home. Still, it was a man's world in 1925, and it wasn't uncommon for "men" of fifteen and under to strike out on their own in those days. And Al was mature beyond his seventeen years. The Rinkers embraced Al and wished the boys luck as Al coaxed the old flivver away from the house and toward the main road leading from Spokane to Seattle, two hundred miles away.

Though the trip west to Seattle was the first leg of their journey before heading south, it wasn't the easiest. They had to cross over the Cascade Mountains in an open car with no top. The scenery was magnificent, but some of it was lost or ignored in the early-winter mountain snow flurries they drove through. Fortunately, they were young and warm-blooded and flushed with the spirit of adventure. And on the positive side, their trek through the snowy Cascades was one of the few times during the journey that they didn't have to worry about the radiator boiling over.

Actually, they paid little attention to the snow and to the possibility that the old car might wheeze its last dying gasp at any moment—particularly since it would be subjected to the extremes of the icy Cascades and the hot high-desert areas of southern California. The boys were too intent upon establishing the routine that would occupy them throughout their entire thousand-mile journey: they sang. They sang because they were young and suddenly on their own—free from parental restraint, free to drink moonshine if they wanted to or to stay up all night if they wanted to or to chase women if they wanted to—and free to take an unfettered fling at show business. But mostly they sang because they loved to. They sang all the way to California, and they had plenty of time to do so, for the old flivver's top speed was thirty miles an hour.

It was on the first leg of their trip that they also devised a "unique" plan to secure shelter at minimal cost during their journey. There were no motels in the entire United States at the time (the very first would open in December of that year at San Luis Obispo, California), so they had to stay in hotels, which invariably had desk clerks. But since their funds were limited, they devised a plan where one of them would enter the hotel and pay for a single, and the other would sneak in later and spend the night, thus avoiding the price of double occupancy. "We'd get in fast, and out fast in the morning," Al recalls. "And it worked all the way to Los Angeles." What they didn't realize at the time was that they were practicing a well-worn money-saving tradition that show folk had established generations before and that was known in show-business parlance as going two-fers—two for the price of one.

They arrived in Seattle at about nine that night and put their two-fer plan into operation at one of the less-expensive hotels. The following morning Bing telephoned an old buddy named Doug Dykeman, who had been a football star at Gonzaga. When Dykeman learned that Bing and Al had worked up an act and were striking out for a show-business career, he insisted on introducing them to a friend of his named Vic Meyers, who had a small band in Seattle and who would one day become the state's lieutenant governor. Meyers, in turn, introduced the boys to a friend of his named Jackie Souders, whose orchestra was appearing in the main ballroom of the fashionable Butler Hotel. Meyers also persuaded Souders to put the boys on that evening as an added attraction at the Butler, which he did. The boys weren't paid for the performance, but they were anxious to try their act out before a new and perhaps more sophisticated audience.

The ballroom at the Butler was beautiful and ornate, with a grand piano and an audience that included a large number of college youths, and the boys were well received. Al and Bing would soon learn that while they had great appeal to everyone, they were even more enthusiastically received by members of the younger generation, who were caught up in what Easterners were calling hot jazz. And since Crosby and Rinker had culled the best from the wide range of music being recorded in New Orleans, Chicago, and New York and had fashioned and presented it in a style uniquely their own, they were destined to become show-stoppers in the West. There was nothing quite like them, even in the East.

"We went over very well in Seattle," Al told us, "and that made us feel great. We had gone over well at the Clemmer, but now we were learning how to put a song over."

The response to the boys was so enthusiastic that Souders offered them a job with the orchestra if they'd stay on in Seattle. "We had our hearts set on going to Los Angeles," Al said. "I wanted to see Mildred, and I guess Bing wanted to see Everett, so we thanked him but told him we had to be on our way."

They gassed up the car and finally headed south, singing and two-fering and fixing flats all the way.

Among the places they stopped overnight was California's state capital, Sacramento, where they were drawn to an enormous movie palace, the largest they had ever seen, which was featuring a stage show produced by Fanchon and Marco, vaudeville impresarios who produced shows in dozens of theaters along the West Coast from their offices in Los Angeles.

After checking into a hotel, Bing and Al went to see the stage show and were very impressed. "It was big," Al said. "We'd never seen such a big show and such a large theater. There was a full orchestra, dancers, girls. It impressed us." Neither of the boys could imagine at the time that within three months, they would return to that same theater but would be onstage, not in the audience.

They left Sacramento the following morning and drove toward Bakersfield, totally amazed and excited by the climate, the farms and cotton fields stretching to the horizon. Cotton, and in early winter; they hadn't even imagined such sights and such weather. They stopped for gas in Bakersfield in preparation for the Ridge Route, a seventeen-mile stretch of road that climbed several thousand feet over the Tehachapi Mountains, which separated the high desert from the Los Angeles basin.

Al and Bing got out of the car to stretch their legs as the service-station attendant hand-pumped gasoline into the large, graduated, cylindrical glass bowl at the top of the pump. And as the attendant placed the nozzle of the hose into the gas tank to feed the gas by gravity from the glass bowl, he took a long and critical look at the Model-T. "I don't think you fellas are going to make it with this jalopy you've got here," he said.

The boys looked at each other, then surveyed the steep grade ahead. "We'll make it," Al said.

"Sure, we'll figure something out," Bing added.

There wasn't much conviction behind their words, but there was a great deal of optimism and determination. They were just a little over eighty miles from their destination, and they had no intention of being bluffed by a little hill or a pessimistic gas-station attendant. When the car was gassed up, Al revved the engine and took a running, thirty-mile-an-hour start at the grade. An hour later, with the radiator shooting steam overhead, they reached Wheeler Ridge, from which they could see stretched below them much of the more than six hundred square miles of Los Angeles County. The rest of their trip was, literally, downhill.

In *Call Me Lucky,* Bing says that the Model-T blew up at Wheeler Ridge and that he and Al hitched a ride into Los Angeles on a vegetable truck. Except for Bing's 1948 biographer, Barry Ulanov, writers have repeated the story and enlarged upon it. But according to Al Rinker, the story simply isn't true. The Model-T not only made it to Los Angeles but was also used by the boys to get around town for a while. As for Bing's version, Al says, "I think he was just trying to add a little drama to his book."

The San Fernando Valley was another wonder to them, with its date palms and citrus groves and crops growing along the old Ventura Road. They took the Cahuenga Pass south through the low range of Santa Monica Mountains that separate the valley from Hollywood, then they turned east on Sunset Boulevard to Coronado, past the temple of Sister Aimee Semple McPherson, asking directions along the way.

No one had told Mildred that the boys were coming to Los Angeles, and when she answered the door, she was astonished to find Al and Bing standing there. She was a pretty, round-faced brunette whose dark Indian complexion led many to mistake her for black and who even then was beginning to put on the weight that was to plague her for life. She was also very sentimental, and she burst into tears at the sight of Al. "Oh, my God!" she said, throwing her arms around him. "I don't believe it!"

Al introduced Bing to Mildred, and she had them bring their baggage into the house. Bing's drums were finally carried to the basement, where they remained. He hadn't touched them since the Musicaladers broke up, and he never played them again. No one knows what became of them. Bing did utilize one of the small cymbals, though, which he played in their act.

Mildred Bailey had married a man named Benny Stafford, whom Bing and Al liked very much. Benny, a quiet, gentle man, was a bootlegger. Their home on Coronado was in the fashionable Silver Lake district, and what caught the boys' eye first was the expensive grand piano in the living room. After the boys put their luggage in the spare bedroom, Mildred fixed them a meal, and they talked. When she learned why Bing and Al had come to Los Angeles, she turned over the guest bedroom to them for as long as they wanted it.

After they ate, Al asked Mildred to sing for Bing. She did a couple of songs, then asked to hear them. "We couldn't wait to get to the piano," Al told us. "We practically tripped over each other. We sang a couple of things, and Mildred clapped her hands in surprise and said, 'Hey, you guys are *good!* I didn't know you could sing like that. You're really good. You could do something with this. You could be onstage.' "

That evening Mildred and Benny invited the boys to the speakeasy where she was singing at the time. The boys didn't need to be coaxed; they'd never seen the inside of a real speakeasy. "Swell!" they said. Benny drove them over, and since they were with Mildred, the boys had no trouble getting past the guard at the door, who was always looking out for strangers who might be local or federal officers. The place was called The Swede's, and it was located in the Hollywood Hills, above Hollywood Boulevard. It was a classy place that catered to the Hollywood elite who could afford the high tariff for bathtub gin and "stuff right off the boat."

Mildred was accompanied only by a piano player, and she sang that evening either standing beside the piano or strolling among the tables. The boys were amused by the way she handled the patrons. She didn't tolerate them if they drank too much and got loud or interrupted her. She'd say, "Listen, do you want me to sing or not?" And they'd quiet right down. She was a fine singer. She had a small voice, with perfect intonation and pitch. Her interpretation of lyrics on ballads was spellbinding, and she was superb at up-tempo tunes, where her knowledge of harmonics was utilized to sing variations on the melodic theme that were years ahead of her time.

The boys enjoyed themselves immensely. Benny Stafford bought the drinks all evening, and as Al recalls with some amusement, "I had a couple of drinks. I wasn't used to drinking much, but Bing kept drinking and Benny kept buying, and Bing got loaded. He didn't do anything wrong, but he got very high and was feeling good. That wasn't the first time we had drunk anything, of course. We used to hang around Stubeck's Cigar Store, and we'd get this moonshine that even the lumberjacks wouldn't drink. We'd drink anything. But that was kid stuff; we all did it. Bing drank pretty good then, too. Later, he had a reputation for being a pretty good drinker, and under certain conditions he did drink a lot, but he wasn't a *good* drinker. He never held his liquor very well. I've been to many parties with him, and he drank, but when he got to a certain point, he'd just lie right down wherever he was—on the floor, or the sofa, or wherever—and that was it. He drank a lot, but he couldn't hold it. For a while, he had the reputation of being an alcoholic, but I don't believe it. He was a periodic drinker."

Benny and Al helped a very sleepy and happy Bing out of the speakeasy that night.

Bing and Al whiled away a couple of weeks in Los Angeles, playing golf, visiting Everett, and joining Mildred at The Swede's in the evening. Meanwhile, from the first day she heard them sing, Mildred used her show-business contacts in an effort to find the boys work. Finally she arranged an audition for them. Bing's book states that Mildred took the boys to Mike Lyman's Tent Café, where they performed, but Al Rinker says that she didn't. "It's not true," Al told us. "I don't know why Bing put that in the book. Mike had a popular place, but we never performed there. Mildred arranged an audition with Rube Wolf, a producer for the Fanchon and Marco Time—the same ones who produced the show Bing and I saw in Sacramento. The audition was held at the Boulevard Theater, which was on the southeast side of town, near the University of Southern California."

Mildred drove the boys over to the audition and sat out front to watch them perform. "We were nervous," Al recalls, "because we knew that this might be a chance for us to get into *real* show business. So we went into the theater, and Rube Wolf was there and Fanchon and Marco were there. We got onstage—Bing with his cymbal and me at the piano—and we were really nervous. But we sang about two or three songs, and I'll be damned if they didn't hire us."

They were to be a part of a new traveling show called *The Syncopation Idea,* and they were put into the show with sixteen dancing girls—an all-English group called the Tiller Girls, who specialized in high-kicking, precision chorus-line dancing similar to that of New York City's famed Rockettes. The boys were contracted at $75 a week each, which made them very happy. And the prospect of working with sixteen beautiful English girls put perpetual smiles on their faces. Al remembers saying to Bing, "This is a rather nice way to break into show business." Bing seconded the thought.

The Syncopation Idea was a variety show with jugglers, comedians, dancing girls, and the like, and it played throughout California for thirteen weeks, starting out in small cities like Glendale, Long Beach, and Pomona, and working north to San Francisco and Sacramento, where the tour ended. Rather than traveling by train with the rest of the troupe, Al and Bing had junked the Model-T and bought a used Dodge roadster from Al's father, who had moved to Los Angeles to be near Al and Mildred and had opened a Dodge agency in Pasadena. So the boys traveled the circuit by car, but they didn't travel alone; they had taken up with two pretty Tiller Girls, who kept them company for the entire thirteen weeks.

We asked Al Rinker if the Tiller dancer was Bing's first serious romance, and he said that he wouldn't describe it as a romance in the true sense of the word. "Bing went with a blond girl," he said, "and she was a good dancer. But as with all of the girls we went with when we were in show business together, Bing's relationships were casual, very casual. It was different with me and the girls I went with; nothing serious, but not casual, either. I liked them, and there was a nice relationship between us, but with Bing, there was no depth to his relationships at all. He might see one of them a few days after a relationship and simply nod, or wave and say, 'Hi, nice seeing you again,' as though he had had only a nodding acquaintance with them."

The thirteen-week Fanchon and Marco tour ended in Sacramento, at the theater they had visited on their way to Los Angeles, and the boys drove back to Los Angeles, where they took an apartment. With the tour behind them, they were now considered professionals. *The Syncopation Idea* show had given them an opportunity to polish their act, and they had been well received. By tour's end, they were doing encores.

They were back in Los Angeles only a few days when they learned that an impresario named Will Morrissey was putting together a musical show to be billed as *Will Morrissey's Music Hall Revue*. Morrissey and Arthur Freed, who later became a movie producer, had combined their talents; Freed wrote music for the show and arrangd financing for its production, and Morrissey produced the show and performed in it. The team set up the production in the Majestic Theater in downtown Los Angeles, but moved to the Orange Grove in an apparent attempt to give the revue a classier-sounding home.

Bing and Al auditioned for them and were hired at $150 a week for the act. They were billed as "Two Boys and a Piano."

The revue's opening at the Orange Grove was successful, and the fact that Bing and Al had polished their act and had learned the business quickly was evident

67

when they began stopping the show, with audiences calling for encores. Morrissey liked the boys and their act, and in addition to the revue, he booked them for a huge entertainment at the Olympic Auditorium in Los Angeles, a one-night-only affair, where the boys took the stage with such notables as Eddie Cantor, Irvin S. Cobb, Fanny Brice, Ruth Roland, Bebe Daniels, Eddie Peabody, George Jessel, Jackie Coogan, Pola Negri, and Charlie Chaplin—along with a host of others and seven masters of ceremonies.

Morrissey also took the boys with him to Hollywood parties. The most notable was one thrown for the cast of *Charlot's Revue,* an English entertainment starring Beatrice Lillie, Jack Buchanan, and Gertrude Lawrence, which opened Hollywood's first legitimate theater, El Capitan, on May 3, 1926. The party was held at a lavish home in the Hollywood Hills. "Actually," Al said, "Will took us along strictly to entertain, but it was a fine opportunity for us to meet those great English stars."

Al and Bing performed several numbers, and Al accompanied Bea Lillie and Gertrude Lawrence, who did songs from their revue. And according to Al, one of the evening's highlights was when Bing soloed, doing a song by Tommy Lyman called "Montmartre Rose," which Al and Bing had lifted from a record Mildred had of the song. "It was a beautiful song," Al said, "and I suggested that Bing sing it for them. He did, and the people loved it. He sang it great; it was a lovely song. After we had performed, Bea Lillie, Gertrude Lawrence, and Buchanan all came over and told us how much they had enjoyed us, which was a big thing for us—my God, just two *kids!*"

The boys were going over extremely well in the Morrissey Revue, too. Sylvia Picker, who in three years would become very close to Bing Crosby and Dixie Lee, saw the Morrissey Revue so many times that she memorized some of the songs and can still remember many of the comedy bits. Sylvia was in a boarding school in Hollywood, and went with her boarding-school friend Consuelo Bell to see the revue.

"Crosby and Rinker came on with their 'Two Boys and a Piano' act and stopped the show," Sylvia said. "They were wonderful, and so handsome that I fell in love with Bing Crosby, and Consuelo fell in love with Al Rinker. Well, we were so mad about them that we went to every Wednesday and Saturday matinee for as long as the show played in Los Angeles, which I believe was six or eight weeks. We kept going just to see Crosby and Rinker. But we weren't content with just seeing them onstage; we went backstage to see them after each performance.

"The thing was, Consuelo was the daughter of Monta Bell, the great MGM director who directed Greta Garbo's first American film. And I had been in San Diego theater since I was quite small, and had also partici-pated in the international grande ball at the Hotel Del Coronado—I was a toe dancer then, and lousy, but I had a lot of nerve for a youngster, so the newspaper used to do a photo feature on me for this society ball, and they dubbed me San Diego's Fairest Rosebud.

"So Consuelo and I—we were just thirteen at the time—thought we were really show-biz sophisticates. After every matinee, we'd go backstage to 'charm' Crosby and Rinker. Consuelo would name-drop, telling them that she had put in a good word for them with her famous father, and I'd remind them that I was really quite well known as San Diego's Fairest Rosebud.

"We had a terrible crush on them, and what we were really angling for was this: next door to the theater was an ice-cream parlor called The Pig 'n' Whistle, and we figured that if we impressed them with our show-biz backgrounds and sophistication, they might take us next door and buy us an ice-cream soda.

"How Crosby and Rinker kept from laughing in our faces or throwing us out on our pseudo-sophisticated you-know-whats, I'll never know. But they remained cordial to us matinee after matinee, week after week.

Needless to say, we never did get those ice-cream sodas, though."

After the Los Angeles run, the Morrissey Revue went to San Diego's Spreckels Theater for a short engagement, where the boys were taken out of the pit and given a special platform that extended out into the audience. A San Diego newspaper review bannered: "Crosby & Rinker Walk Away with Show at Spreckels Theater." The following is the review verbatim:

"If they like that, give 'em some more. There's a few things about our show they don't like."

So Will Morrissey instructed Crosby and Rinker, two young men whom the audience at Morrissey's revue at the Spreckels Theater last night wanted to take home and use for permanent amusement.

STEAL THE SHOW

Crosby and Rinker, who, by the way, sang all of the "red hot mama" songs that have been written in months, did "give 'em some more," stealing the show from those billed as stars.

The "few things" which was really only one thing the audience didn't like will be mentioned lower down, but not as low down as they really were.

In the meantime, however, a few of the 20 or 30 acts that should fill the theater for the rest of the week by the time first-nighters have recovered from their hysterics long enough to tell their friends, will be mentioned.

BLUES SINGER SCORES

Next to Crosby and Rinker, Lee Kent, a red-headed mama herself, who sang all the songs that the two men had left out, scored the biggest individual success.

Then there were Eddie Borden and Midgie Miller, the principals, a pair of delightful damphools who kidded Aimee McPherson; Smedley Butler; San Diegans; and others—indiscriminately.

H. Pierre White, late leading man of Rose Marie, and Lucy Day in several song numbers apiece, and Jack Eddy and "Delores," a dance team that could headline any vaudeville show, were the rest of the best, except for Morrissey himself.

And Morrissey is a great laugh-getter himself, but was responsible, we suppose, for one chorus girl who gave a startlingly realistic imitation of Joyce Hawley without the bath tub. There wasn't much excuse for this last, this reviewer thinks, but he may have misinterpreted the gasps of the audience.—B.A.A.

After San Diego, the revue played the Capital Theater in San Francisco for six weeks, then moved to the Lobero Theater in Santa Barbara, where the show closed. This time, however, Bing and Al weren't stranded.

Before the revue left Los Angeles, Jack Partington, of Paramount Publix, saw the "Two Boys and a Piano" act at the Orange Grove and called them. Bing was out playing golf at the time, but Al was in their apartment and took the call. Partington introduced himself and asked Al to drop by his office that afternoon.

Al went to Partington's office and, after discussing the boys' availability, Partington offered to sign them at $300 a week for the act. Paramount Publix owned a string of theaters at the time, but wanted to book Al and Bing for their two main West Coast theaters, the Granada in San Francisco and the Metropolitan in Los Angeles. The plan was for the boys to alternate back and forth. If they signed, Partington told Al, they'd be joining a vaudeville troupe of name entertainers, led by the M.C. Eddy Peabody, the comic banjo player.

Al went back to the apartment that evening and told Bing about Partington's offer. It didn't take much discussion between them. Al and Bing were getting good notices, but the Morrissey Revue couldn't last much longer—though it did last eight more weeks. So the day after Al's meeting with Partington, the boys went down to the Paramount Publix office and signed with him. Their contract would go into effect as soon as the Morrissey show closed or when the Morrissey contract ran out, whichever was first. And when the revue closed in Santa Barbara, they were free to join the new show—at double their earnings with Morrissey.

Paramount Publix would eventually play an important role in establishing Bing Crosby as an international star, for it was the forerunner of Paramount Pictures. But at this time—the summer of 1926—Paramount Publix was concerned primarily with its string of movie houses and with distributing motion pictures and booking stage shows to perform with them; in those days, one saw a movie and a stage show for the price of one admission.

Al and Bing joined the troupe in Los Angeles at the Metropolitan (which is called the Paramount today). They were booked as Crosby and Rinker and, with the rest of the troupe, they played four shows a day—five on weekends. The boys joined the "big time" with confidence in themselves, but with a degree of trepidation regarding the theaters they were to play. The Granada and Metropolitan were huge, with a seating capacity of 2,500; they knew they'd have no problem projecting enough to be heard in the back rows and balconies with their up-tempo and novelty tunes, but two small voices without amplified sound doing ballads like "In a Little Spanish Town" in those cavernous interiors was another question entirely. But as Al recalls with a good deal of wonderment, the audiences grew so absolutely still whenever they sang their ballads that the silence was eerie.

The audiences were far from silent at the end of each number, however. The applause was thunderous. "We just weren't two guys starting out anymore," Al recalls. "We knew something had happened since our days at the Clemmer Theater, and now at the Metropolitan, we were coming up." They were coming up fast, too. Very often they stopped the show—that is, after they had done their usual three or four numbers, had taken their bows, and had gone backstage, the audiences wouldn't let Eddy Peabody announce the next act. Instead, they kept applauding and cheering until he brought the boys back out for an encore or two—sometimes more.

The word that best describes audience reaction to Al and Bing at this stage of their careers is *delight*. Their zest and energy and enthusiasm were contagious. Their musical ability knew no bounds, and they continually nudged at—and often broke through—the very limits of contemporary music of the day, with a good measure of jazz worked into the fabric of their presentation. Young people loved them because they were the vocal avant-garde in popular music, and they would become widely imitated. Adults found them inordinately entertaining because they offered their wares without pretensions, with a dash of humor, and always with exquisite and marvelously subtle musical taste.

The boys even employed the lowly kazoo in their musical numbers for fill and to voice jazz phrases with remarkable effect, for both Al and Bing had impeccable intonation, and kazoos in their hands were extensions of their voices and unique style.

They were innately musical; the subtleties of music and intricate rhythm were gut level in them. In Bing's later years, one remembers the bubbly *b*s and rippling, rhythmic cadence of his conversational voice, reminiscent of the vibrant tones of a soft, laid-back string bass. Al Rinker's conversational tone even today has a muted-brassy intonation and a decidedly rim-shot, jazzy cadence.

As a duo, their voices complemented one another, and with Al's arrangements, they'd break from the melody line, exploring the subtleties of minor chords or the augmented and diminished facets of major chords before modulating ingeniously back on track, the throbbing, relentlessly hypnotic rhythm driving them along. And their audiences followed them, Pied Piper-like, joyous and astonished at the new avenues of musical exploration. Technically, the audience didn't know what the boys were doing, but they liked it. And the

73

boys were probably not technically analytical about what they were doing, either; it was gut level, and it worked.

They sang beautifully arranged renditions of ballads in which Bing's beautiful mellow baritone, with its delicately burred metallic trailing edge, fit snugly against Al's harmony, which was vibrantly brassy, with a soft trailing edge that resulted in perfect counterpoise to Bing and often seemed to take on the tonality of one voice. And after mellowing an audience with a warm and inventively presented ballad, the boys would explode with a comedic rendition of a tune like "Get Out and Get Under" or "Paddlin' Madeline Home" or "Baby Face." With the latter, for example, they'd play on the lyric in what was even then considered the corny manner of the old barber shop quartets: "Ba-a-a-aby, baby-baby / ba-a-a-aby, baby-baby / ba-a-a-aby, baby-baby," modulating to higher and higher keys with each phrase. Then they'd break into the exaggerated histrionics of very bad tap dancers before returning to the lyric—all done with gentle, humorous satire that was delightful, not at all biting, and very, very inventive.

An analysis of their performance reveals the fact that Al Rinker was never given the credit due him by Bing's biographers or by Bing himself. There was no shortage in the twenties of duos who could sing and play piano—and with pleasing voices, too. Every small city in the country could turn out a dozen of them to form the lines outside vaudeville producers' audition halls—fresh kids with good voices, pleasing personalities, and talent. But for any such duo to crack vaudeville—which was just as hard to break into as television or motion pictures is today—to steal shows from seasoned, professional headliners, and then to rocket straight to the top as a featured act with the most famous popular orchestra in the world at the time—all in less than a year—is the stuff of Hollywood movies. It couldn't happen in the real world. But it did. The explanation of their incredible feat boils down to one rock-hard fact: the act rested and rose on Al Rinker's arrangements; without

them, as good as their voices and show-business instincts were, they would have been just another singing
duo and piano act with pleasing voices. Mr. Crosby notwithstanding, it wasn't luck. And while today, Al
Rinker refuses to follow us to such a conclusion, the
facts make it incontrovertible.

Such was the boys' act, then, when they began stopping shows at the Metropolitan for Paramount Publix.
After the first four weeks, the troupe moved to the
Granada in San Francisco, where Bing and Al continued to stop the shows. Before their four-week stint was
up at the Granada, they were given the most coveted
position on the program: the next-to-closing act. They
had also begun drawing heavily from the University of
California at Berkeley, across the bay, where by word
of mouth, it had become known that the two young performers were not only in the vanguard of new and contemporary music, but also were unique in their style
and delivery. They were an unqualified hit with everyone who saw them and the craze of the college set.

By this time, Eddy Peabody was in a snit. He was
not only the emcee but also the star of the show—at
least that was the way he was billed. But for him time
and again to see those two wet-behind-the-ears huckle-
berries from Spokane hypnotizing audiences that were
quite willing to let Peabody and other headliners leave
the stage without encores was a little too much for his
ego to withstand. At each performance, he did his best
to kill Crosby and Rinker's encores: he'd try to tell
jokes so that the audience would quiet down to hear
what he had to say; he'd wait in the wings to delay the
show; or he'd go onstage and try to wait the audience
out, hoping they'd grow weary of applauding and cheering, so that in the momentary lull, he could introduce
the next act on the bill. But more often than not, the
audience outlasted him and wouldn't be denied, and
Peabody, exasperated, would finally have to wave the
boys back while he retreated to the wings, mumbling to
himself.

When it was time to return to the Metropolitan for

another four weeks, Al decided that they shouldn't be slaves to train and taxi schedules in their trips back and forth between Los Angeles and San Francisco. "Before we left San Francisco," Al said, "I decided to buy a sporty Mercer roadster, which was something like the Stutz Bearcat in style, so that Bing and I could drive back to Los Angeles. I'll never forget our first trip down the Pacific Coast Highway. We had the top down and were sailing down the road when we saw a chauffeur-driven limousine ahead, also with its top down. We drove past to see who was in the car, and recognized the occupants as John Barrymore and his wife, Dolores Costello. It was quite a thrill for us to see them."

While they were playing their second engagement at the Metropolitan, the boys had an opportunity to see another celebrity. They learned that Paul Whiteman was coming to town for an engagement at Sid Grauman's Million Dollar Theater in downtown Los Angeles. Bing and Al hadn't overlooked Paul Whiteman's recordings when they were haunting the Bailey Music Company in Spokane. Whiteman had yet to hire many of the great jazz musicians who later worked with him and was pretty conventional and staid at the time, but the boys had admired his recordings of "Whispering," "Japanese Sandman," "Three O'clock in the Morning," and others.

It was on February 12, 1924—at a time when the Musicaladers were playing high-school dances and parties—that Paul Whiteman made musical history by having George Gershwin appear as guest pianist to play his new composition, "Rhapsody in Blue," which established Gershwin as a serious composer and helped elevate Whiteman as an internationally popular orchestra leader. So when Bing and Al learned that he and his orchestra would be arriving by train at Union Station, they couldn't pass up the opportunity of seeing the famous group. They went down to the station and waited for the train to arrive.

Seeing Whiteman's sidemen was thrill enough, but

the big man himself more than fulfilled their expectations—all three hundred pounds of him. Though a man of considerable bulk, Whiteman was a natty dresser, a flamboyant personality, and very charismatic. And his orchestra was in keeping with his size—thirty pieces, including twelve strings. "It meant a lot to us at the time to actually see in the flesh the guys we had listened to so often on record," Al said.

Less than a week after they had visited Union Station, the phone rang in their apartment, and Bing answered it.

"I'd like to speak to Bing Crosby or Al Rinker," the caller said.

"This is Bing Crosby."

"Mr. Crosby, this is Jimmy Gillespie, Paul Whiteman's manager. I'm calling you for Mr. Whiteman. Could you come down to the Million Dollar Theater tomorrow, about mid-morning, to meet with Mr. Whiteman?"

"C'mon," Bing said, "what's the joke?"

"It's no joke."

Bing was halfway convinced that he was being victimized by a prankster. "What the hell does he want with us?" he said.

"He wants to talk with you fellows."

"Sure," Bing said, still unconvinced. "We'll meet with him."

"Good. Just ask for me when you get here."

Bing hung up and told Al about the "screwy" call. Both of them wanted to believe that they had just heard from the manager of the great Paul Whiteman, but show people were always pulling such "ribs" on one another. It seemed just too coincidental to be offered a chance to meet Whiteman when, only a few days before, they had lounged around the train station just to get a glimpse of him.

The boys simply couldn't believe it, but they wanted to believe it too much, and they decided to get an objective opinion; they called Mildred, asking who she thought could be playing such a trick on them. She told

77

them that she didn't think it was a joke. "Go on down there tomorrow," she said. "What have you got to lose?"

Though it might prove a little embarrassing, they decided that Mildred was right; they had little to lose. The following morning they went down to the Million Dollar Theater. When Jimmy Gillespie met them at the stage door, they knew it wasn't a rib, but they still couldn't think of a reason Whiteman would summon them.

Gillespie ushered them back to Whiteman's private dressing room. The big man, with waxed mustache and dressed in a silk lounging robe, was just finishing brunch, and Gillespie introduced the boys to him. Just shaking hands with him was enough to keep Al and Bing's feet off the ground for a week. Though Whiteman traveled first-class wherever he went, he was not, as Bing reported of their first meeting, sipping champagne and eating caviar. As Rinker recalls, Whiteman was having a regular lunch, which included beer, not champagne. Whiteman was fond of beer.

There were no preliminaries and no audition. It's known that Gillespie had seen Crosby and Rinker at the Metropolitan, but to this day, Al Rinker doesn't know whether Whiteman had seen their act. Thompson, in his biography *Bing,* says that Whiteman sent viola player Matty Malneck and pianist Ray Turner to see the act and quotes Malneck as telling Whiteman that the boys had an infectious style, "like hearing a great jazz player for the first time." And while biographers Thompson and Ulanov were both victims of misinformation given to them by their sources, Thompson's story rings true, for Whiteman wouldn't have called for them purely on his manager's recommendation.

Whiteman, as always, got directly to the point. "I'd like you boys to join my outfit," he said.

He didn't even ask if they wanted to join; it would have been a foolish question. Bing and Al stood blinking at him, momentarily stunned. Prior to this, Al Rinker doesn't recall their ever envisioning that Whiteman might want them in his organization; Whiteman already had a trio and a male vocalist. They hadn't had time to think before they were led into Whiteman's dressing room.

"I'll start you at $150 a week each," Whiteman continued, "and you can make extra money from recordings and from a couple of Broadway plays we're going to be in; we're signed to do a show called *Lucky* and one called *Whoopee*."

The reality of the scene was almost too much for the boys to grasp. "Whiteman just *talking* to us like that was enough," Al recalls. "We were glassy-eyed. We couldn't believe it. But I remember coming to my senses long enough to remind Bing in front of Whiteman that we were still under contract to Paramount Publix until around the end of October, and we had to finish that one out."

"I'll tell you what we'll do," Whiteman said. "We're going to be in Chicago December fifteenth, playing three theaters there, the Tivoli, the Chicago Theater, and the Uptown. You can join us there."

The boys were ecstatic. When the contracts were ready, Bing signed his, and Al, who was then only eighteen, had his dad sign for him. Eleven months from the day they had driven their old Musicalader Model-T out of Spokane, they had signed a contract with Paul Whiteman. They left the Million Dollar Theater that day reeling from the heady experience and feeling like a million dollars themselves.

Before they finished their contract with Paramount Publix, and perhaps owing to the news that they had signed with Paul Whiteman, Don Clark, a former Whiteman sideman whose orchestra was appearing in the grand ballroom of the Biltmore Hotel in Los Angeles, approached them to cut a record with his orchestra. It was to be the first recording Bing Crosby and Al Rinker ever made.

Biographers have reported that the recording was made in an old converted warehouse, but in fact it was recorded in the grand ballroom of the Biltmore, which is still in use today. On the afternoon of October 18, 1926, Bing and Al, the Don Clark orchestra, and a few engineers and recording technicians gathered in the ballroom, rehearsed, and cut a recording of the song "I've Got the Girl," with music and lyrics by Walter Donaldson, who did both music and lyrics for many great standards, including "Carolina in the Morning" and "My Blue Heaven." The flip side of "I've Got the Girl" was a Don Clark orchestra instrumental titled "Idolizing"; Bing and Al did vocal recordings of two songs that day, but the second, "Don't Somebody Need Somebody?" was never released. The boys' first record didn't sell well—for good reason—and was all but forgotten for nearly fifty-four years.

On April 15, 1980, the Bing Crosby Historical Society of Tacoma, Washington, issued a limited-edition 7-inch souvenir LP that includes among its selections "I've Got the Girl." Curiously, the society's cut of the record is more esthetically valuable than the original, for as the two Crosby fans—Bill Osborn of Seattle, Washington, and Vernon Wesley Taylor of Portland, Oregon—who contributed cuts for the album note, the record company (Columbia) that issued the original apparently thought that the master cut of the record was slow, so in an attempt to make it sound jazzier, they speeded it up when they cut the duplicates for release. The result was terrible. And as Al and Bing have both remarked during interviews—long after their embarrassment had given way to humor—they sounded to themselves like a pair of chipmunks chattering in the background. Indeed, the speed of the original cut is so fast that it's impossible to discern all of the lyrics.

For the limited-edition recording issued by the Bing Crosby Historical Society, the speed of "I've Got the Girl" was modified to more closely approach the tempo at which the song was performed. After listening to it, Al Rinker agreed that the society's cut of the song is, indeed, the tempo at which they originally sang. It's a great up-tempo tune, and the boys' jazzy rendition of it makes the listener firmly convinced that the record would have been a hit if the engineers hadn't modified the speed. Technically, its only flaw is a sound imbalance; Al's harmony overpowers Bing's melody line. But considering the recording conditions, it's excellent. Not only is it the first record that either Bing or Al ever made, but it's the only record of what Bing and Al sounded like at the time Paul Whiteman put them under contract. And though the boys were restrained by the band's arrangement, the listener gets a delectable but all too brief taste of Al Rinker's vocal arranging and a hint of why the great jazz artist Matty Malneck was so enthusiastic about Crosby and Rinker.

When their contract with Jack Partington was fulfilled, the boys decided to spend a week or so in Spokane before leaving for Chicago. Al sold his newly acquired Mercer roadster, and the boys bid good-bye to Mildred, Everett, and Al's parents before boarding a train for home. It would be quite a homecoming for them.

Spokane folks had kept abreast of Bing and Al's rise in show business. The Spokane *Spokesman Review* had run "local boys make good" stories at each progressive stage in their astonishingly fast climb from the neighborhood theater to the ranks of big-time "eastern" show business. And the hometown people weren't going to let their new celebrities' triumphant return pass unnoticed. Bing had written his parents with the good news and their plans to come home before going East, and Ted Crosby had acted in the boys' behalf by arranging a one-week engagement for them at Spokane's Liberty Theater; they would play there from Monday, November 21, through Sunday, November 27, which would not only give the Spokane populace an opportunity to see what it was those people in the East were so all-fired excited about, but would also give the boys an opportunity to break in a few new numbers in preparation for joining Whiteman. They were paid $175 each for the week.

Their return to Spokane couldn't have been more timely. They'd be home for the Thanksgiving holidays, which meant that even their college friends, including Bob and Clare Pritchard, would be there to see them. Al Rinker recalls their return fondly: "Here these two guys from Spokane—who had left in an old, beat-up Ford—were coming back to the Liberty Theater, en route to joining Paul Whiteman. You can imagine how we felt—you know, big shots now. Everybody came to see us, all the guys that we knew, and it was marvelous.

"My father and his wife were living in Los Angeles at the time, so we stayed at Bing's place with his folks. Of course I knew them very well. Bing and I spent a lot of time at each other's houses before we left Spokane, so I was at ease with them. They had a big house—kind of an empty house, sparsely furnished. Bing's dad was working in a pickle factory at the time—I think it's still standing—and he didn't want for anything, but they lived frugally.

"Bing's mother, Catherine, was a very strong Catholic. Mine was too, but Bing's mother was a strong Irishwoman—small, but she ran that household. She wasn't at all equivocal: 'We're going to do this and we're going to do that. We're going to church. Be there!' A strong woman, very tough. She was a matriarch in every sense of the word.

"But the old man? He was something else. I always liked the old man; he was always smiling and friendly. I asked Bing what his dad liked to drink, and Bing used to tell me about him, acting out the dialogue:

'You wanna try a little wine?' Bing would ask him.

'Well, don't mind if I do.'

'Or I've got some whiskey here. How about a little whiskey?'

'Sure, I'll try some of that, too.'

"I liked the old man. I *really* liked him."

The boys had no sooner carried their bags into the Crosby household when their friends began arriving, congratulating them and eager to hear of the stars they had seen and performed on the same bill with. It was a fine reunion with family and friends, and their appearance at the Liberty was heralded by the following ad in the Spokane *Spokesman Review*:

ADDED

PAUL WHITEMAN'S SENSATIONAL
ATTRACTION OF 1926

BING

CROSBY

AND

AL

RINKER

TWO LOCAL BOYS THAT HAVE MORE THAN MADE GOOD.
THEY ARE HOME FOR A VISIT AND WILL APPEAR FIVE
DAYS ONLY AT THE LIBERTY BEFORE GOING EAST.

POSITIVELY CLOSING THEIR ENGAGEMENT SUNDAY,
NOVEMBER 27TH

The theater was packed for every show, and many in attendance were repeat ticket buyers, particularly friends and acquaintances and teachers who weren't satisfied with seeing just one performance. Except for Everett, who was in Los Angeles, and perhaps Larry, who, it's thought, had given up teaching at Gonzaga by then and was living in Seattle, the whole Crosby clan had front-row seats. Naturally, after fifty years, Al Rinker doesn't remember specifically how the Crosbys reacted to seeing the boys' new professional performance, but one can imagine their pride. The newspaper gave them rave reviews, of course. They could probably have gotten onstage and made faces at the audience to great reviews, but this was their homecoming, and they gave it their all. As Al sums up the engagement: "*Now* we knew what we were doing."

The only incident that marred their return occurred

when one of Bing's friends sneaked backstage while the boys were performing and stole money from his billfold. Bing reported in his book that all of his and Al's money was taken, but, in fact, only the amount he was carrying at the time—$60—was taken. But Bing was very upset that a friend would do such a thing to him, and he never forgot the incident.

After finishing their engagement at the Liberty, the boys boarded the Great Northern for Chicago. All of their friends and Bing's family were at the station to see them off. They waved from the train until it had pulled from sight, then settled back for the trip. They were leaving Spokane again, but this time they were traveling in style, and they weren't facing the unknown. They had two thousand miles of track and the prospect of big-time show business ahead of them. The whole country—and the Windy City and Broadway—lay before them, too, and their festive mood didn't wane for the entire trip, not with contracts in their pockets signed by Paul Whiteman.

Part Four:

The Rhythm Boys

CHAPTER SEVEN

> I'd say to Bing, "Are you ready?
> Okay, one, two, three, *boom!*"
> And we'd pull the curtain right on cue.
>
> **—AL RINKER**

Bing and Al were met at Chicago's Dearborn Station by four other Spokane boys, all graduates of North Central High School, who had formed a singing group called The Foursome and who were appearing in Chicago in the hit musical *Girl Crazy*. Among the chorus girls in the show was a redhead named Ginger Rogers who, of course, went on to bigger things, but The Foursome, though they were very good, never rose above the status of supporting acts, and eventually disbanded. Ironically, another North Central High graduate and Spokane pal of Bing and Al, organist Don Isham, was appearing in a small theater on Chicago's outskirts at this time, but his friends didn't know it. Isham would later work the same large theaters that Bing and Al worked with Whiteman in Chicago.

The six Spokanites repaired to a nearby restaurant and had a rousing reunion—they would go out on the town together several times before their shows left Chicago—but it was apparent that The Foursome were just as baffled by the big city's size as were Bing and Al, for rather than directing the boys to a hotel near the Tivoli, they let them settle in at the Eastgate Hotel, which, they learned the next day, was miles from the Tivoli Theater.

After breakfast the following morning, the two boarded another train, but unlike the one that had brought them from Spokane, this one was suspended above the ground, and their fascination and amusement alleviated some of the embarrassment they felt at having chosen a hotel so far from the theater they'd be working. They had a wonderful tour of the city as the elevated wended its way to Chicago's south side.

The boys arrived at the Tivoli long before anyone else, and they sat alone in the dimly lit backstage area until members of the orchestra began arriving. They had met Whiteman, but they had yet to meet his sidemen, and as those famous musicians began arriving—Matty Malneck, Henry Busse, the trombone-playing vocalist Jack Fulton, and others—Bing and Al pointed out to one another the few they recognized. Finally Whiteman himself strolled in and saw them sitting alone, wide-eyed and in awe of what was going on about them. "Hey!" he said. "You two sprouts made it on time!"

"Whiteman was a very interesting man," Al recalled, "and when he came in and called us *sprouts*, it kind of put us at ease, made us feel part of things and comfortable. He had a good sense of humor, really sharp and quick—he was a character, Whiteman—a wonderful guy. A real personality, too. No matter who was in the room when he walked in, Whiteman got the attention."

Whiteman introduced Bing and Al to the band members. "These two boys, Bing Crosby and Al Rinker, are going to join us," he told them. Then he said to the boys, "I want you to do the show today. I'll put you on and introduce you, but don't be nervous; you watch the first show so that you can see what we're doing."

The contract at the Tivoli called for four shows a day, so Al and Bing knew that after watching the first show, they had three chances to put themselves over that day. They were apprehensive, because they were entirely out of their element. Chicago wasn't the West Coast; it was, in fact, one of the chief entertainment centers in the Midwest and the music mecca of the North. Chicago's theatergoers were sophisticated; they had seen the best and heard the best, and they expected nothing less. The opening in Chicago was, as Al recalls, the acid test for Crosby and Rinker.

Bing and Al sat with the audience and were spellbound by the first show. It wasn't until the orchestra's closing number, "Rhapsody in Blue," that they suddenly became conscious that the butterflies in their stomachs were multiplying and that what Bing would later call flop sweat was forming on their palms. They went backstage after the performance, and Whiteman was very reassuring and calm. He told them again not to be nervous, but his words fell on ears that could hear only the pounding of their own hearts. His advice was like telling two condemned men to relax on their way to the gallows.

It no doubt seemed to Bing and Al that the second show began only a couple of thundering heartbeats after the first had ended. In one wing was a small upright piano on wheels that could be rolled downstage near the audience. The boys had to do the rolling. So not only did they have to remember once they got on-stage what it was they were going to sing—and if they could remember some of the lyrics, that would be helpful, too—but they had to push a piano out there, as well. During one performance in Chicago, the piano tipped over as they were attempting to wheel it offstage, and as the audience roared with laughter, it took Al, Bing, and Whiteman to get it back on its wheels so that the show could continue. Fortunately, this didn't happen the first day.

When it came time for the boys to go on, Whiteman strolled center stage and said casually: "I want to introduce two young fellas who are joining my band—this is the first time they've been with us. I picked them up in an ice-cream parlor in a little town called Walla Walla, Washington. I thought they were too good for Walla Walla and that's why I brought them here. I want you to meet them: *Crosby and Rinker!*"

Bing and Al went on, and by the first four bars of their first number, the jitters left them; they finished it to good applause. After their second—concluding—number, the audience exploded with applause and cheers for an encore. "Well," Al said, "that was it. We were with Whiteman! We were equally pleased that we went over well with the band, too; they were *professional* critics. One of the songs we did that day was the ballad 'In a Little Spanish Town.' We didn't know it at the time, but their vocalist, Jack Fulton, had been singing that number with the full Whiteman orchestra behind him. But after Whiteman heard us sing it—which the audience loved—he turned to Fulton and said, 'Jack, from now on the boys will do that number.' That was quite a compliment. Whiteman never did tell us what to sing. He'd just ask us what numbers we intended to do so that he'd know."

During their three-theater run in Chicago, the boys were invited to cut a second record—their first with Whiteman. It was recorded on December 22, 1926, at the Concert Hall on Michigan Avenue. Bing and Al sang "Wistful and Blue," and Matty Malneck, who would soon play a key role in the boys' career, was the featured violinist. They also sampled Chicago nightlife, often accompanied by other members of the Whiteman group. They were particularly impressed by a young trumpeter named Louis Armstrong, who had come up from the South with King Oliver's band and was appearing at the Sunset Café. Whiteman also took them to numerous places and parties, introducing them to important people. He did this in every city they played. "Whiteman seemed to be quite proud of us," Al recalled. "We were young and eager, and I think it was because we were fresh and very enthusiastic that he took more than a casual interest in us."

After Chicago, the band took a zigzag route on their way to New York, playing numerous cities, including Indianapolis, Cleveland, and Detroit, where Crosby and Rinker were as well received as they had been in Chicago. But the date they were looking forward to most was their New York City debut at the Paramount Theatre on Times Square. They were real professionals now, and as with all professional entertainers, they wanted to open in the Big Apple with something so new and fresh that it would be the talk of the town.

The Whiteman group opened at the Paramount in January 1927. The boys could hardly contain themselves in the wings while Whiteman introduced them. And when he finally said, "I'd like you to meet them: *Crosby and Rinker!*" they took the stage with authority. And they bombed. They finished their act to a smattering of very restrained and polite applause, and even *that* wasn't accorded them by all members of the audience. The boys thought—and hoped—that it was just that particular audience; crowds have personalities, too, and occasionally one will run up against an audience that simply won't respond to anything. But it wasn't just that particular audience. They bombed during the next show, and the next, and the next day, and the next. They were crushed. They were totally bewildered. From the day they had driven out of Spokane in their Model-T, they had never experienced failure—quite the opposite. No one could figure out how they could be such a smash everywhere but at the Paramount. Whiteman was puzzled; his sidemen were puzzled; and the boys were in despair.

The situation got so bad that Bob Weitman, the Paramount's manager (who later became head of MGM and then Columbia Pictures in Hollywood), finally insisted that Whiteman take them out of the show. He did, and the boys cooled their heels in bewilderment for the rest of the Paramount run. It was a tough reality to face: they had been fired from the New York Paramount, and their cancellation wouldn't go unnoticed by critics, theater managers, and show-business folks, who had a grapevine on which news traveled fast and far. And they knew it.

While Whiteman and his orchestra had been away, his newest business venture was being readied—The Paul Whiteman Club, a huge second-story restaurant-nightclub that occupied the site of a former ballroom and spanned an entire block on Broadway between Forty-seventh and Forty-eighth streets. The opening was scheduled to coincide with Whiteman's return to New York, and he was sure that Crosby and Rinker would be well received in his own new club. "Don't worry about it, fellas," Whiteman remarked about their failure at the Paramount.

Much to Bing and Al's relief, the Paramount engagement finally ended. Whiteman opened his club on February 18, 1927. *Billboard* magazine reviewed its opening:

WHITEMAN'S OWN CLUB HAS
GRAND OPENING

New York, February 19—Paul Whiteman opened at his own restaurant, 48th Street and Broadway, last night, and played to a packed house, numbering approximately 900 friends, admirers, and prohibition agents, at $10 per head. The old Cinderella Ballroom has been renovated at a big expense and is beautifully decorated in black and gold. . . .

The rest of the review was favorable and listed about fifty prominent people in show business who attended the opening; many of them gave unscheduled performances for the gala. *Billboard* concluded by noting that twice as many tickets could have been sold had there been room, and predicted that Whiteman would clean up on his new enterprise.

Crosby and Rinker weren't mentioned among the

performers, for they had performed during intermission and were all but ignored. They had bombed again, and to such an extent that for most of the run at Whiteman's club, they worked as stagehands, raising and lowering the curtain for the show.

"We had our timing down pretty well," Al recalled. "I'd say to Bing, 'Are you ready? Okay. One, two, three, boom!' and we'd pull the curtain, right on cue. At least we were doing something *right* for a change. But I thought, my God! From success to *this*? To pulling curtains? We were both *very down*; you can imagine."

Many people have speculated about why Crosby and Rinker bombed so badly in New York City, and some, including a couple of Bing's biographers, have suggested that the Paramount was so large that they couldn't be heard. But this seems unlikely. And Al Rinker doesn't believe it at all. The Paramount was no larger than most of the theaters the boys had played; in fact, it was a new theater, and its acoustics may have been even better than some. It was true that they couldn't be heard at the Whiteman club, but this was because Whiteman put them on during intermissions when people were moving around, talking, and eating dinner. And they were put on during intermissions because New Yorkers simply didn't like them.

It was a mystery that Al Rinker addressed fifty-three years later. "I finally figured out in my own way," he told us, "why it was these two young guys had gone over so well in all the other theaters, and then when they got to the New York Paramount, they bombed. People didn't seem to understand what we were doing! We'd go: bop-bop-de-do-do/de-doodle-eeaaaa [snapping his fingers while singing scat] and stuff like that. And they didn't know what the hell we were doing! And now that I think about it, I don't blame them. The New York audience was mostly Jewish— provincial in its own way—staid; you know what I mean. They were used to great entertainers of a certain tradition like Jolson, Cantor, and Sophie Tucker, who were *belting* out songs. [Imitating Jolson here] Mammmeee! Mammmeee! They'd *really* let you have it! But we were *intimate*. That wasn't what they expected, and they didn't like it."

Rinker's analysis is logical. New York theatergoers of the day were, musically speaking, traditionalists; they were used to songs emotionally and stirringly delivered. Crosby and Rinker's delivery was controlled, and their arrangements were subtly esoteric, with jazz voicings that fell on New York ears like the babbling of foreign tongues. It was no accident that jazz took northern roots not in New York but Chicago. Café audiences were attuned to jazz, but the theatergoers wanted their popular music straight, like a shot of whiskey that would hit them fast, with gut-level impact. And if you tried to water it down with bubbly stuff, then you could peddle your wares elsewhere.

So, in effect, New Yorkers were quite willing to send the babbling Whiteman boys on their way—nowhere. What good were they to Whiteman if they couldn't make it in New York? What good were they if he had to pick and choose where they could and could not be presented? They could always go back to regional vaudeville, of course, but the top would be off limits to them, and what was the use?

Regardless of the reason they had bombed, they knew they were in deep trouble. And while they were expecting and waiting for the worst, Whiteman's featured violinist, Matty Malneck, came to the rescue.

Malneck had a friend named Harry Barris, who was under contract to Whiteman but was in danger of being let go because Whiteman couldn't find a spot for him in the organization. Barris was a budding composer and a good singer and piano player, but Whiteman was up to his ears in piano players—he always used two pianos in his orchestra—and to make matters worse, Barris couldn't read music.

Barris and Malneck's friendship went back a number of years to Denver, Colorado, where they were both in a pickup band that played social functions and high-school dances much as the Musicaladers had done. Among the members of the Denver band were Barris on piano, Malneck on violin, Glenn Miller on trombone, and Ted Mack (of "Original Amateur Hour" fame) on sax. So this friendship, together with Barris's plight—he was the father of a baby girl, so he had a family to support—gave Malneck more than a little incentive to help him.

About the time that Barris was worrying aloud to Matty that he was going to lose his job with Whiteman and had no immediate prospect for another one, Bing and Al deposited a very large egg onstage at the Paramount, then duplicated that effort in Whiteman's club. So Bing and Al and Harry Barris were all facing the distinct possibility of getting the bum's rush out the stage door and into the alleys of New York City. And it seemed to Malneck that all three were talented, and that if he could get them together as a trio, they might work well enough to salvage their careers and perhaps reestablish themselves with Paul Whiteman.

Malneck approached Harry Barris with the idea, and Harry was willing to give it a try—he was willing to give anything a try, for he didn't want to go back out on the vaudeville circuit now that he had a family. Then Malneck went to Bing and Al and explained his idea. "I want you guys to get together," he said.

"Well," Al recalled, "we had nothing to lose. We were desperate."

Matty took Barris over to the Belvedere Hotel, where Bing and Al were staying, and the four of them got together around the piano in the ballroom of the hotel. "Matty introduced us to Harry Barris," Al said. "We talked, then Barris played a couple of his songs. One of them was 'Mississippi Mud,' which he had composed—James Cavanaugh had done the lyrics—and we liked it. We talked some more, fooled around at the piano a bit, then we said, 'Let's learn it.' So we started harmonizing and arranging it, all four of us chipping in ideas, and when we finished, it sounded great to Bing and me because we had another voice there. And Barris could *really* swing, you know. So we learned 'Mississippi Mud' and another number, 'Ain't She Sweet.' We thought that was great, too, because it was another song for us, and we were anything but intimate in our delivery."

The boys hit it off well, and Malneck was impressed. "I want Whiteman to hear this," he said. And he herded the new trio over to Whiteman's club, where they did the two numbers, using two pianos—Barris and Rinker playing, Bing working with a hand-held cymbal, and all three singing. Whiteman was delighted and decided immediately to put them on at the club. The boys worked up three-part harmony arrangements of numbers that Bing and Al had been doing, added a few new songs, and made their debut. They were enthusiastically received, and they were very relieved.

All three were happy to be back in the fold, this time as a trio now billed as Paul Whiteman's Rhythm Boys. Had it not been for Matty Malneck's matchmaking and the talent of Harry Barris, it might well have been the end of the line for Crosby and Rinker.

Harry Barris was born in New York City on November 24, 1905, but his family moved to Denver, Colorado, when he was in his early teens. Denver was Paul Whiteman's hometown, and Harry studied music at East Denver High School under Whiteman's father, Wilberforce Whiteman. After working in the aforementioned pickup band, Barris formed his own five-piece jazz band and toured the western states, including an appearance in Seattle. In the four years from the time he left Denver until he joined Crosby and Rinker, Barris toured the Far East and the Philippines, worked briefly with the *Gus Edward's School Days* touring group and the Paul Asch orchestra in Chicago, and then toured the Paramount Publix vaudeville circuit before marrying and fathering a daughter, Hazel, known today as Zelle Lippencott.

By the time Matty Malneck took Barris to see Bing and Al, Harry was delivering a song as though he had a built-in bullhorn in his throat and at least three hands.

He pounded the piano unmercifully (and well), banged the piano lid in time with the rhythm, and belted out a song with such power that it could be heard not only in the back row, but out in the lobby and halfway down the street. Like Crosby and Rinker, Barris was rhythm personified. And he didn't just sing a song, he sold it, and he had some good songs to sell, including those of his own composition.

Al and Bing liked Harry Barris. He was a meticulously natty dresser—the exact opposite of Bing—and had a cocky and confident manner that earned him the affectionate sobriquet "Mr. Show Business" from Bing and Al. He was a wiry little guy—an inch or two shorter than Bing's five-nine—with a big talent and boundless energy. He looked, and was, intense, with sharp features, slicked-back hair parted in the middle, and piercing dark eyes that could stare right through you. But his intensity was tempered with a quick smile and an excellent sense of humor. He was sure of his talent, and rightly so, but beneath his brashness he was very sensitive and not a little insecure, which may well have contributed to his major shortcoming: he drank too much. Unlike Bing, who was a periodic drinker, Harry had gotten into the habit—or need—of drinking a little bit all the time. Unfortunately for his health, he could hold his liquor too well, and it was to interfere with and shorten what otherwise could have been a brilliant and productive career.

It wasn't long before Paul Whiteman's Rhythm Boys became one of the hottest trios ever to perform. And with Bing now back in Whiteman's good graces—at least temporarily—he made his first record as a solo artist; the tune was "Muddy Water," and it was recorded with the Whiteman orchestra at Leiderkranz Hall in Manhattan, where Whiteman always recorded for Victor when he was in New York; the recording date of Bing's first solo effort was March 7, 1927.

Two weeks later, on March 22, Whiteman opened at the New Amsterdam Theater in the musical *Lucky*, which was created by Jerome Kern, Otto Harbach, Bert

Kalmar, and Harry Ruby and which starred Mary Eaton, Skeets Gallagher, Ivy Sanyer, Ruby Keeler, and others. The Whiteman orchestra made a brief, late-evening appearance in the show each night, and The Rhythm Boys did a number called "Sam, the Accordion Man." During their run in *Lucky*, The Rhythm Boys made their first record with Whiteman: "Side by Side," which was recorded on April 29, 1927, also on the Victor label.

Despite the outstanding talent associated with *Lucky*, it didn't draw well and closed after seventy-one performances. After it closed, The Rhythm Boys left the Whiteman orchestra for at least a year. Other biographers have reported that Whiteman toured Europe in late 1927 and that he didn't take The Rhythm Boys with him because they had been so busy chasing golf balls and girls that they had neglected their act and hadn't added one new number to it. The only truth to this report is that, except for Harry Barris, who was married at the time, the boys did indeed devote a lot of their energy to chasing golf balls and girls (in that order), but they certainly didn't neglect their act, and Whiteman didn't go on another European tour.

The rise of Paul Whiteman's Rhythm Boys was nearly as phenomenal as the rise of Crosby and Rinker. We say *nearly* because The Rhythm Boys were not only show-business veterans but had the Paul Whiteman orchestra as a showcase, advantages that Crosby and Rinker didn't have when they started in the business. The Rhythm Boys organized in February of 1927, and by June they had their own recording contract with Victor, independent of the Whiteman orchestra. Shortly thereafter, they were headlining in vaudeville. They were still very new as a group and very enthusiastic, so there is no question of their slacking off, as biographers have stated. They didn't.

Paul Whiteman did schedule a concert tour in the fall of 1927, but it was a tour of the United States, not Europe. And instead of taking the boys with him, Whiteman booked them on the vaudeville circuit for forty-five weeks. Why he didn't take The Rhythm Boys on tour is a question that may never be answered to anyone's satisfaction. Matty Malneck doesn't recall, but he thinks the action strange because Whiteman was quite possessive of his troupe, and it wasn't like him to book any of them elsewhere, particularly since Whiteman used such specialty acts even in concert. Al Rinker's recollection is that they didn't accompany Whiteman because he didn't think The Rhythm Boys' act suitable for concerts. Biographers Ulanov and Thompson, both of whom had the cooperation of the Crosby organization in the writing of their books, say that the boys were sent on the vaudeville tour in disgrace. To say that the information furnished by the Crosby organization, including Bing and Larry, was unreliable is gross understatement. But there may be a grain of truth in their report.

Paul Whiteman developed quite a fondness for Bing and was very impressed with his talent. Conversely, he could get incensed at Bing's indifference to his responsibilities. Numerous people who were around Crosby in those early days—including a couple of musicians who were with Whiteman—have told us that Crosby caused Whiteman a lot of grief. He frequently missed engagements, and on at least three occasions, Whiteman sent someone out looking for him and found him literally in the gutter, passed-out drunk in front of some speakeasy or other watering hole. On one occasion in Philadelphia, they found him in the gutter during winter, lying in the snow and ice. That's the way booze affected Bing, but he wouldn't stop drinking.

It's possible that Whiteman may have banished The Rhythm Boys to vaudeville owing to Crosby's penchant for doing what he damn well pleased and without the knowledge of Harry Barris or Al Rinker. It should be noted that Barris and Rinker weren't exactly goody-two-shoes when it came to what Crosby called the flowing bowl, but liquor didn't affect them the way it affected Bing. Most show-business people drank quite a bit, but most, like Rinker, don't get hooked on the stuff.

On one occasion, though, all three of them got in trouble with Whiteman. They met a young man at a party who owned a sailboat, and they all decided to leave the party and go sailing on Long Island Sound. Bing, Al, and Harry all took their Ziegfeld-Follies-girl dates, and somehow during their adventure Bing fell into the ocean. It was fortunate that he was a good swimmer, for by the time the sailboat was turned around, Bing was just a drunken speck on the horizon. They finally managed to pick him up, however, and everyone, including Bing, thought it was very funny. They were having such a good time, that after they went back to Manhattan and Bing changed out of his wet clothes, they continued the party through the night, forgetting completely their evening performance. It didn't seem quite so funny to them the next day when Whiteman summoned them. That was the one time that they came very close to getting fired.

On June 20, 1927, The Rhythm Boys had their first recording session independent of Whiteman, during which they made two records: "Mississippi Mud" / "I Left My Sugar Standing in the Rain" and "Sweet Li'l"/ "Ain't She Sweet." It was a few weeks after this session that Whiteman had them booked on a vaudeville tour as Paul Whiteman's Rhythm Boys. He supplied them with a huge blow-up portrait of himself—to be displayed onstage—and a record of his voice introducing them, which was played for the audience just before they went onstage.

"Whiteman placed us on the Keith-Albee-Orpheum vaudeville circuit," Al told us. "That was a top circuit in those days, and we were headliners. We got our act together and opened in Yonkers."

Rinker doesn't recall the month that they began touring, but they did two shows a day, and *Billboard* magazine reviewed their August 9 appearance at Keith's 81st Street Theater in New York City:

Harry Barris, Bing Crosby, and Al Rinker, billed as *Paul Whiteman's Rhythm Boys,* have personality, good voices, and a way of putting their song numbers over effectively. Enough comedy is introduced to keep things moving rapidly while they are on the stage.

They have the art of rhythm perfected to a stellar degree, and add a brilliant touch to the song numbers constituting their repertoire. An act worthy of big-time booking, and a distinctive asset to any bill.

It's obvious that the boys hadn't let the act deteriorate. In fact, they were commanding an astonishing $1,000 a week for the act and had improved it considerably since they had joined as a trio six months earlier.

"In addition to our singing," Al recalled, "we did a spoof on tap dancing, as Bing and I had done as a duo, and a comic 'mind-reading' act. By this time, people knew us from our records on Victor, and we were well received, playing almost the whole circuit over the next forty-five weeks."

The circuit incorporated the East and the northeast section of the Midwest. The tour was tantamount to a holiday for them; they toured Pennsylvania, Illinois, Michigan, Minnesota, Wisconsin, and Ohio during the football season, and took in as many games as they could. And since they played just two twelve- to fifteen-minute shows a day and made, along with the money for their recordings, more than three hundred dollars a week each, they had a good time. As celebrities, they got invitations to play golf at the best private country clubs in every city they played. And as their fame spread, there was no shortage of twenties-style groupies, either. It was in Chicago that Bing finally met a girl that he didn't treat casually. He does not mention the affair in his autobiography—and for good reason—but his brothers did in their biography of him, indirectly.

In the family biography, Ted and Larry change the names of people and places for what they call obvious reasons. Events that took place in one city are said to have occurred in another. So they seem to have changed one true and embarrassing affair into two apocryphal stories in which Bing emerges as a man who thrust aside wealth owing to his show-business dedication and who was a quasi-innocent victim of circumstance, cleverly sidestepping implication in a murder and a police shoot-out.

One story relates Bing's involvement with a beautiful Akron, Ohio, socialite named Jane Rankin, to whom, the brothers intimate, Bing responded with more than casual interest. "They went the rounds together—football, golf, and close harmony." But, as the story goes, when Bing learned that Jane was the daughter of a millionaire—out of his class—and when she suggested that he could stay in Akron with her father's firm, Bing responded that he could never give up the "show game," and he extricated himself from the situation as graciously as possible.

In the second story, which is told by the brothers and by Bing himself, he struck up a friendship and went speakeasy-hopping with a couple of interesting characters who turned out to be gangsters. Bing is said to have been given knockout drops in one of the too-many glasses of bathtub gin he hoisted on the occasion, and to have regained consciousness two days later in a hotel room in which several armed gangsters were holed up. Among the gangsters was one of his speakeasy-hopping friends; the other one had been eliminated, gangster-style. When Bing regained consciousness, we are told, he realized that he had missed several Rhythm Boys engagements, and while he was in the hotel bathroom freshening up, the police broke into the hotel room and had a shoot-out with the gangsters. The story ends with Bing ingeniously talking his way out of the hotel by complimenting the officers on their splendid work.

This second story was repeated to Charles Thompson, who wrote the authorized biography, *Bing*. And either Bing or Larry Crosby told Thompson that Bing's surviving gangster acquaintance was the infamous Machine-gun Jack McGurn, who is alleged later to have been involved in Chicago's St. Valentine's Day

Massacre. Thompson's biography was published in this country only a year before Bing died; it's astonishing that even in the mid-seventies, Bing continued to mislead serious biographers with dozens of such stories.

Neither of the stories checks out. Bing may well have encountered McGurn, for the gangster was an avid golfer, and he may well have been chased by dozens of socialites, for women were inordinately attracted to him, but Al Rinker was with Bing all the while, and has no knowledge of either story. He would have known about the Akron socialite, for the books intimate that all the boys knew her and that Harry was the one who told Bing that the girl was the daughter of a millionaire. And as to the gangster incident, even if Bing hadn't told them about it—which was highly unlikely—Al and Harry would certainly have noticed his absence for two days and four performances. Both stories seem to be based on an incident that did cause Bing to miss performances, did involve a girl, and did take place in Chicago.

While the boys were still on the vaudeville circuit, they were booked into Chicago at the same time that the road company of the Broadway musical *Good News* was playing there. The star of the road company was a pretty brunette actress-comedienne named Peggy Bernier, whom Bing had met a year earlier when he and Al were playing the Granada in San Francisco on the Paramount Publix circuit. Bing renewed his friendship with Peggy in Chicago and started dating her. They became a very serious item around the Windy City, but the relationship was apparently more serious to Bing than to Peggy. For once, Bing seems to have gotten a taste of his own indifference; he was accustomed to having women trip all over themselves for him. But with Peggy Bernier, Bing did the falling and tripping, and Peggy refused to take *him* seriously.

According to Sylvia Picker McGraw, who was under contract at Fox when Dixie Lee was there and who knew Dixie, Bing, and Peggy Bernier, Peggy later married another singer, and Bing took the news of her marriage very badly. Sylvia also told us that when she first saw Bing's second wife, Kathryn, she knew immediately what had attracted Bing to her: she was the image of Bing's lost love, Peggy Bernier. "Kathryn might have been a little prettier than Peggy was," Sylvia told us, "but she certainly looked like her."

Ironically, Peggy's understudy for *Good News* was a young singer-actress named Dixie Carrol, whose name was later changed to Dixie Lee when she was put under contract by the Fox Film Company. And though Bing used to pick up Peggy at the theater for their dates, he neither saw nor met Dixie until he went to Hollywood two years later.

Bing's memory of Peggy Bernier, his relationship with her, and the event that took place following their last date seem to form the basis for the apocryphal stories conjured up by Bing and his brothers to add mystery, excitement, and romance to their books. What really happened wasn't exciting or romantic, but it did contain an element of mystery. Al Rinker laughed while recalling the incident, but neither he nor Harry thought it funny at the time.

"We had just finished our date at the Orpheum Theater in Chicago," Al told us, "and our next stop was at Rockford, Illinois. So Barris and I took the train that night to Rockford after the show. Instead of joining us, Bing went out that night with a girl he had met in San Francisco named Peggy Bernier, a very good actress. She and Bing had a little romance going. In fact, she was the only girl other than Dixie that I ever saw Bing pay any real attention to.

"Bing told us he'd stay behind and catch the early-morning train to Rockford. Barris and I checked into the hotel, and the next morning we went down to the theater to rehearse the show's orchestra. Our first show was scheduled for two o'clock in the afternoon, but Bing was nowhere around. We couldn't figure out what had happened to him. When it got close to two o'clock and Bing still hadn't shown, Barris and I talked it over and decided we could cover for Bing by working as a duo. The manager was understanding, and when we told him that we could go on as a duo, he told us to go ahead and do what we wanted. But we were still worried about Bing.

"We ad-libbed while playing the two pianos and singing. The audience didn't seem to mind, so we got by *that* performance. But when it came time for the next one, Bing was *still* missing. Now we were really worried. We had no way of calling him or locating him. We finally told the manager that we'd have to do a duo again and that we were extremely worried. Time for the night show came, and no sign of Bing. So Barris and I did the second show and got by. When it was over, I called our hotel, and lo and behold, Bing answered.

"What had happened is that he and Peggy had gone out on the town the night before, and Bing really got loaded. He was drunk when Peggy put him on the train, and he slept all the way to Rockford—about 90 miles west of Chicago. When he got off the tarin, he was still falling-down drunk and the cops picked him up and threw him in jail. He was in jail all day—*loaded!* We didn't know where to get in touch with him, and they wouldn't let him make any calls. Here we were, knocking ourselves out doing the shows, and he was in jail. Barris and I were furious. We were really mad, so we said, 'Let's fix him up!'

"There was a guy in the show named Tim Ryan, a sharp Irish comic, really sharp, and, of course, we played on a different bill at each theater, so Bing had never seen Ryan. We said to Ryan, 'We want you to come over to our hotel with us and pretend to be the theater manager and really tell our partner off.' And Ryan said, 'Sure, I don't mind, as long as I'm not hurting anybody. If it's just a gag, I'll do it.'

"We walked into the hotel room with Ryan trailing behind us, and there sat Bing on the edge of the bed, head in hands, *totally* hung over. Barris and I both told Bing, 'We brought the manager over; he wants to talk to you.' And Bing groans, 'Oh, boy. . . .'

"Ryan really waded into Bing. He said, 'What kind

of a trouper are you, letting these guys down? Do you know that they can cancel the act for this? They can write to the head office. This is a breach of contract! You could ruin the whole thing for these two!' And Bing just moaned, holding his head. Ryan kept it up for about five minutes, and the real manager could never have done as well. And Ryan was right, of course. If word had gotten back to the head office, we'd have been in trouble.

"Finally, Barris and I called Ryan off and told Bing that it had been a rib. And as it turned out, the real manager never did report Bing. We were all fortunate that he didn't."

Much has been written about the boys' hijinks on their vaudeville tour. It's been said that they got into trouble with theater managers and with the New York office because they turned their act into a comedy routine with little music, and that Bing's gambling caused them to work without their wardrobe on one occasion, and that the boys missed play dates by getting their schedule mixed up, and so on. But the Keith-Albee-Orpheum circuit wouldn't have put up with such behavior even once, let alone numerous times. The fact is, such anecdotes were invented by Bing, Ted, and Larry to enliven their books and were repeated by other biographers because they had been presented as factual. Boys will be boys at play, of course, but professionally, other than the Rockford, Illinois, incident, everything ran smoothly. They headlined throughout, missed no engagements, played to good reviews, and had more than a dozen recording sessions during the tour.

The forty-five-week tour ended during the summer of 1928, and though the exact chronology is lost, the Whiteman office seems to have continued booking The Rhythm Boys in and around New York for the next few months, with only an occasional date with the orchestra. One notable gig they played with Whiteman about this time was the Midnight Frolics Room, an exclusive club run by Flo Ziegfeld, which was located on the top floor of the New Amsterdam Theater. The room didn't open until eleven at night and played mostly to the after-theater crowd. Matty Malneck conducted the Whiteman orchestra during most of the engagement, for Whiteman was away on business, perhaps regarding their upcoming Universal film. The featured vocalist was Ruth Etting, and a young French entertainer named Maurice Chevalier made his American debut, holding New Yorkers spellbound, during the Whiteman orchestra and Rhythm Boys' engagement there.

The composition of the orchestra the boys returned to was quite different from the one they had left when they went on tour. Whiteman had long before assumed the title The King of Jazz, and even though music critics today question the title, they can hardly dispute the fact that the musical organization Whiteman was building in late '28 and early '29 was capable of playing some of the best symphonic jazz of its day. Any argument becomes one of semantics when it's considered that Whiteman added Bix Beiderbecke to the trumpet section; Frankie Trumbauer, Jimmy Dorsey, and Izzy Friedman to the reed section; and Bill Rank and Tommy Dorsey to the trombone section in 1928. And in early 1929, Whiteman added two of the best strings in jazz, with violinist Joe Venuti and the equally incomparable guitarist Eddie Lang, two South Philadelphia buddies who later became very close friends of Bing Crosby.

Other changes had been made, as well. Whiteman jumped from the Victor label to Columbia, and The Rhythm Boys followed suit. He had also signed to do a radio program for Old Gold cigarettes. Pops had been one of the last big-name holdouts to sign with the new medium, for it was still generally feared that being on radio would hurt record sales and personal appearances. Besides, Whiteman didn't relish the burden of putting together a radio show on a weekly basis, which often called for six A.M. rehearsals on broadcast day. But then the Old Gold company made him an offer that

105

he couldn't refuse: a budget that would allow him to go on the air first-class, which was the only way Pops did anything.

The concept of commercial broadcasting was totally new; and that the networks themselves were yet to realize its full potential was made clear to Whiteman when he walked into the NBC Radio headquarters with a package deal that would make today's network executives drool: Whiteman offered NBC his popular orchestra, The Rhythm Boys, and a very fat-budgeted Old Gold cigarette account. To Pops' total astonishment, NBC turned him down because, as they explained to him, "We already have a cigarette account." So Pops took his package to CBS.

"The Old Gold–Paul Whiteman Hour" began broadcasting from the CBS studios in New York City every Tuesday night at nine o'clock to an estimated fourteen million radio sets, including one in Spokane that Dad Crosby brought home when it became known to the family that Bing was going to be on the radio. And when Whiteman signed to do a motion picture to be titled *King of Jazz* and to be written especially for him and his orchestra, Old Gold agreed to participate in a very expensive radio tie-in. Rather than going straight out to the West Coast, an entire train would be leased for the trip, an all-compartment special of eight coaches, including three baggage cars (one contained Paul's auto), a dining car, and a club car. The entire train was painted gold, with huge letters proclaiming it the Old Gold–Paul Whiteman Special. The coast-to-coast trip would take twelve days, with stops at sixteen cities, including Philadelphia, Pittsburgh, Detroit, Chicago, Indianapolis, St. Louis, Omaha, Kansas City, Denver, Salt Lake City, and Los Angeles. Free concerts were scheduled at each stop (the stops were only for an hour or two), and Whiteman's weekly radio show would be broadcast from local theaters and auditoriums in some of the cities.

As the trip west was being planned, the Whiteman orchestra and The Rhythm Boys played in their second

Broadway musical: on December 4, 1928, *Whoopee* opened at the New Amsterdam Theater, starring Ruth Etting and Eddie Cantor. Besides its regular pit orchestra, the musical was apparently designed to feature a number of popular orchestras onstage, for the Whiteman orchestra replaced George Olsen's orchestra in the show and was, in turn, replaced by another when Whiteman left for the Coast. Most Broadway-play references don't even mention Whiteman's participation in the show.

Regardless of Whiteman's reason for sending The Rhythm Boys on the vaudeville circuit, he put them back in the band in late 1928, featured them on his radio show, and scheduled them for the trip west. On December 11, 1928, The Rhythm Boys recorded the hit song for *Whoopee,* "Makin' Whoopee," on the Columbia label.

Bing made his first record for Columbia as a solo artist on Thursday, March 14, 1929, when he recorded "My Kinda Love" and "Till We Meet," accompanied by piano, violin, and guitar only. Then, in May, The Rhythm Boys joined the Whiteman orchestra on the Old Gold–Paul Whiteman Special, along with representatives of Universal Pictures, Columbia Records, the Old Gold company, Whiteman's valet, and members of the press. Burt McMurtrie, who later retired in Tacoma, was also aboard the train. McMurtrie, who worked for CBS through the Lennen and Mitchell Agency, had conceived the special-train idea (he later wrote and produced Bing's Woodbury Soap radio show, and became fairly close to Bing). In all, there were about fifty people aboard; it was strictly a stag affair, and very informal and festive. Abel Green of *Variety* called it ". . . a night club, all stagg, on wheels, excepting that the club is going at all hours, day and night, in the club car and all over. No rough stuff, and everybody well behaved. . . ."

"So we headed for the West Coast," Al recalled. "We stopped at numerous major cities along the way and did our radio broadcasts—even from the Indianap-

107

olis Speedway. We all had compartments and traveled in style. I shared a compartment with Matty Malneck, for we had become good friends; we had a lot of fun on that trip to Los Angeles."

Bing shared Al's enthusiasm for the trip. In a letter he wrote to Kate from Chicago, he said that he was ". . . having a truly marvelous time of it." He also said that the trip was worth the trio's going back with Whiteman, intimating that he, and perhaps Harry and Al, felt somewhat restricted by being attached to the orchestra, and foreshadowing The Rhythm Boys' eventual break with Whiteman. One also senses from his letter, written toward the end of May 1929, that Bing was beginning to think not in terms of the trio but in terms of his own career as a single. He wrote: ". . . my name is being prominently featured in the newspapers and in the broadcasts, and considerable invaluable publicity thus redounds to me."

The family biographers say that before leaving New York for the trip, Bing was approached by a well-known agent who made him an attractive offer to stay in New York, under the agent's personal management. It's said that the agent offered to pay Bing's expenses until he got work for Bing in radio and possibly musical comedy. Bing is said to have been tempted but to have turned the agent down because he had a good thing going with The Rhythm Boys and doubted his ability as a single, and because the agent's offer was just too speculative.

The story may be true—at least in part. If we think of Bing as the superstar he eventually became, with his obvious talent, we wouldn't doubt the story at all. But in 1929, Bing Crosby was just a member of a fairly well known trio. And that's all. He certainly didn't have a voice for the musical-comedy stage, and the few solo records he had made to date weren't hits by any means. It would be a couple of years before the radio networks would begin looking for someone to rival Rudy Vallée, who in January 1929 had just begun to broadcast on radio from the Heigh Ho Club on East Fifty-third

108

Street with his Connecticut Yankees band. But the family-biography story does indicate that Bing was not including Al Rinker and Harry Barris in his future plans. Al and Harry knew that the trio wouldn't go on forever, but they had no idea that their pal would sacrifice their careers to further his own. But that's what Bing would eventually do, and ruthlessly.

CHAPTER EIGHT

> Kurt, this is Bing. I'm in the
> Lincoln Heights jail, and
> it's freezing down here.
>
> —BING, PHONING KURT DIETERLE

On June 6, 1929, the Paul Whiteman–Old Gold Special steamed into Los Angeles's Union Station. It had been nearly three years since Bing and Al had left the West Coast to join Whiteman, and they were happy to be back in California. Bing's brother Everett, who had married in his absence, was at Union Station with his new wife, Naomie, when the train arrived.

The Whiteman aggregation debarked reluctantly; it had been a wonderful trip—almost a vacation, considering their means of travel and despite their hectic twelve-day schedule—three thousand miles of partying and jam sessions with the likes of Eddie Lang and Joe Venuti. But had Whiteman's sidemen known in what mysterious ways Hollywood studios often worked, they wouldn't have been quite so sorry to see the trip end. Had Pops Whiteman known, however, he would have ordered the train East as fast as its engine could pull it.

Actually, their arrival in Los Angeles was a formality, officially ending the Old Gold Special's run. They went to San Francisco the following day for a week's engagement at the Paramount Theatre, then returned to

Los Angeles on the fourteenth for a two-week engagement at the Los Angeles Paramount before reporting to Universal Studio on the twenty-eighth.

Carl Laemmle, the majordomo of Universal Pictures, rolled out the red carpet for Whiteman's orchestra; their arrival was announced with great fanfare, ceremonies, and get-acquainted parties in a special rehearsal and recreation building that had been constructed especially for the band's private use. It was modeled after a rustic hunting lodge—a huge one—and contained a large rehearsal-recreation hall, complete with piano, pool table, and comfortable furniture, as well as showers and locker facilities. The lodge was purposely built in an isolated area at the end of a trail on the back lot, near *The Hunchback of Notre Dame* and *The Phantom of the Opera* standing sets. The late *Variety* editor Abel Green noted that the lodge was "removed from any supervisory interference . . . made to order for some of the cut-ups." And he added, "This was Hollywood. The lot was loaded with girls, girls, girls as part of the filmusical avalanche."

Laemmle, a German immigrant who founded and ran Universal, had coasted along with his silent films, thinking that the talkies were a fad that would quickly pass. But then the Warner Brothers had dropped their surprise blockbuster, *The Jazz Singer*, which had attracted unprecedented numbers of moviegoers and had rocked the industry. Laemmle was one of the moguls who scrambled for the cover of sound stages. By late 1929, according to *Billboard* magazine, there were fifty musicals scheduled for production by Hollywood studios: "100% all-talking, all-singing, all dancing." Laemmle may have been a slow starter, but he wouldn't be outdistanced in the stretch. *King of Jazz* would be not only all-talking, all-singing, and all-dancing, but all-color as well. The famous Technicolor process bore little resemblance to the quality of today's incomparable product, but it was color, and it drew audiences. It was with the idea of making his competitors pale by comparison that Laemmle contracted the entire Whiteman orchestra

111

for his musical extravaganza and budgeted his spectacular entry at a staggering (for 1929) $2 million.

There was only one little problem. Universal had yet to fashion a script for *King of Jazz*. Months had elapsed since Whiteman had contracted to do the film, and he was stunned by the revelation. To Whiteman, it was tantamount to his contracting for a concert, assembling his orchestra onstage poised and ready to play, then offhandedly informing the theater manager that everything was ready except that they hadn't gotten around to working up a book of arrangements to play. Fortunately, Whiteman had had the foresight to contract with Universal on a weekly, rather than a flat-fee, basis. The movie company was picking up the tab for the band's payroll, which amounted to more than nine thousand dollars a week, not including what Pops himself was making for the film. The Universal people assured him, though, that the script was being readied; it would be only a matter of days. Meanwhile, the preliminaries could be tackled while the script was being finished.

The first few days were spent doing tests with the band: lighting tests, film tests, and sound tests. The sound tests were the most unnerving to Whiteman and his sidemen, who were required to play through their entire book several times for reasons that were beyond their comprehension. Sound men were kings of the talkies in Hollywood at the time, and they justified their presence—more of them than were actually needed—and reinforced their images as wizards of the mystical "new" science by scowling and stringing wire and moving mikes and throwing switches and turning knobs and conversing in bafflegab in an apparently deliberate effort to mystify "scientifically ignorant" outsiders.

Whiteman wasn't impressed. It seemed to him that most of their circuslike antics and their nonsensical mumbo-jumbo were needless. Sound wasn't new to him; he was a veteran of countless recording sessions at a time when recording studios were yet to be built. He recorded in theaters, concert halls, churches—almost anyplace that had four walls and decent acoustics. So when the movie sound men would ask him to run through a number for the umpteenth time, Pops would grumble, "What in hell do these people think they're doing?"

It wasn't until Whiteman's manager, Jimmy Gillespie, pointed out to him that, as with bureaucrats, it was only by buzzing around, poking at things, throwing switches, turning knobs, and talking gobbledygook in an "expert" manner could the small army of sound technicians maintain their power on the lot that Whiteman finally understood and grudgingly submitted to their indignities.

When the band members were finally released from the clutches of lighting, color, and sound experts, they scattered in all directions to pursue their separate interests. They wouldn't be needed again until the script was completed, and Whiteman had yet to see a page of it. In the interim, a Ford dealer had approached the group and offered them spiffy little Model-As at fleet rate and on time payments, complete with spare-tire covers bearing Whiteman's famous caricature. Bing and most of the musicians bought them—Bing chose a convertible—and once they were on wheels, they rolled. *Variety's* Abel Green intimated that the more than thirty Whiteman personnel had a penchant for craziness and mischief, and added, "Worse, the city-slicker musicians soon learned they needed cars to get anywhere, and Pops had his hands full with bail money on that score alone, with the merrymaking musikers [sic] tearing up Ventura and Sunset boulevards."

The lodge that had been built for the band went largely unused. And after a week or so of waiting for the script, most of the sidemen even stopped reporting to the studio at all. According to Matty Malneck, some of the guys didn't even bother to pick up their weekly paychecks at the studio—they sent for them.

Since it had originally been estimated that *King of Jazz* would be four months in the making, Bing and two violinists, Mischa Russel and Kurt Dieterle, rented a house on Fairfax in Hollywood and hired a cook—they

113

had had enough of hotels. It was a large house (which still stands today), and it became the unofficial party-time headquarters for the Whiteman band members during their long stay.

As the days passed into weeks, Bing, Al, Kurt Dieterle, pianist Roy Bargy, and another musician or two joined the Lakeside Golf Club near Hollywood and spent most of their days there. As Kurt Dieterle told us, "We played so much golf every day that we retained full-time caddies. We'd play eighteen holes in the morning, break for lunch, then play another eighteen in the afternoon. Bing and Al were very good golfers, and there was a lot of betting going on between them." (Bing worked from an eight to a four handicap that summer; Al was a three-handicap player. Eventually Bing became champion of Lakeside.)

When he wasn't playing golf, Bing made the rounds of the movie studios. In *Call Me Lucky*, he describes being talked into going out to William Fox Studios by Raymond Keane and of being turned down by a casting director without benefit of a screen test because of his protruding ears. But according to Glenhall Taylor, a retired West Coast radio executive and author of an authorized but unpublished biography of Paul Whiteman that is still tied up in the Whiteman estate, Pops told him that Crosby had made the rounds of almost every studio in Hollywood except Universal. He also told Taylor that the studios spent, collectively, more than seventy thousand dollars in screen tests on Bing, and none offered a contract. Which, Whiteman intimated, shows how visionary the Hollywood experts can be.

The exact chronology of The Rhythm Boys' activities at this time is difficult to establish, for reasons that will become obvious. But there is some evidence that it was during this summer of 1929 that they played the Montmartre Café. Regardless of whether they played there in late '29 or early '30, however, it was an important appearance for them. It was their first engagement on the West Coast since their return and helped develop a following among the influential members of Holly-

114

wood's film colony that would later work to their advantage.

The Montmartre Café was an exclusive dining and dancing spot established by Eddie Brandstatter on the second floor of the C. E. Toberman Building at 6757 Hollywood Boulevard in downtown Hollywood. (The building still stands today, and the floor occupied by the café was most recently the West Coast branch of Lee Strasberg's Actors Studio.) It was a modest-sized, dance-hall-like room, far from opulent, with its white-cloth-covered tables and black-lacquered kitchen chairs and small dance floor. But for a while, it was the place to be seen in Hollywood—at $10 per person cover charge. Author Bruce Torrence, in his book *Hollywood: The First 100 Years,* says that the café was frequented by so many movie-colony favorites, with the fans gathered in such numbers on the sidewalk in front of it, on the stairs leading up to it, and in its foyer, that the café's illustrious patrons complained to the owner that they had great difficulty getting into the place.

Though The Rhythm Boys appeared at the Montmartre for only a few weeks, they became the "discovery" of the movie colony and the talk of the town, and their popularity was no doubt an important factor in their decision to talk their way out of the Whiteman contract and to stay on the West Coast after *King of Jazz* was completed.

While the rest of Whiteman's group was basking under the sun at golf courses, beaches, and swimming pools or seeking shade at the local watering holes, a committee of writers at Universal was still kicking around ideas for a Whiteman script. Most of the ideas were bad. It's alleged that they finally came up with a script or scenario of a love story in which Pops would be required to play a romantic lead. Whiteman is said to have nipped that bizarre bud quickly: he wasn't subject to Hollywood fever. He had no illusions about his acting ability, and he certainly couldn't be deluded into thinking that his three-hundred-pound frame could cut a matinee-idol figure on the huge silver screen.

To complicate matters, Universal was also having director problems. They had imported a director from Germany named Paul Fejos and had assigned him to the film. Then they decided that Fejos's European approach to filmmaking was too arty for *King of Jazz*, and they finally replaced him with John Murray Anderson. So while Universal continued to fiddle with the project, Whiteman burned.

Whiteman was concerned with his forced layoff, paid or not. He was a man who enjoyed performing and who liked being on the move, and for seven weeks, he and his orchestra had absolutely nothing to do except gather each Tuesday for their weekly "Old Gold–Paul Whiteman Hour," which was broadcast from the KHJ Radio studio in Los Angeles. He had some of the best musicians in the world in his orchestra, but Paul was of the opinion that one engagement a week wasn't enough to keep them from getting rusty as a unit—particularly when, it seemed to Pops, some of them were of the opinion that the rust was alcohol soluble. He knew also that the Whiteman name couldn't be kept alive with the nonradio-listening public while his orchestra was in semi-retirement beneath the palms and sunny skies of southern California.

Despite reassurances by studio brass, Universal was no nearer to coming up with a script than they had been when Whiteman first arrived. So Whiteman arranged for an engagement at the Pavilion Royale on Merrick Road in Long Island, an open-end engagement that would last until Universal got their act together and called him back for some serious filmmaking.

The Rhythm Boys returned East with the orchestra, which stopped at Detroit for a week's engagement at a Pontiac car convention before going on to the Pavilion Royale. They had been at the Long Island club for six weeks when Universal finally crafted a script that met with Whiteman's approval, and the band returned to the Coast to begin filming on November first—almost six months from the time they had first reported on the lot.

Knowing that they would eventually return to the Coast, the band members had kept their Fords in storage. But not knowing when they would return, Bing, Mischa Russel, and Kurt Dieterle had given up the large house on Fairfax, and Bing and Kurt rented an apartment upon their return. One evening Bing didn't return to the apartment from the studio, and at about two A.M., the phone rang and Kurt answered it.

"Kurt, this is Bing. I'm in the Lincoln Heights jail, and it's freezing down here."

"Jail? What happened?"

"I got in an accident. Listen, there's no heat, and they don't have blankets down here for me. Bring me a couple of blankets, will you?"

Kurt got out of bed and drove down to the jail with Bing's blankets. What had happened was that a party had been given at the lodge on the Universal lot to celebrate the end of the first week's shooting on the film. Bing had participated in the entertainment and merrymaking and had dipped too often into the "flowing bowl." He had escorted a young woman to the party, and when the time came to drive her home to the Hollywood Roosevelt Hotel where she was staying, Bing was in no condition to drive. Actually, according to Al Rinker, Bing wasn't a very good or attentive driver even when he was sober, and on this night, it's doubtful that Bing could even pronounce sobriety let alone effect it. In fact, he was so intoxicated that he had forgotten all about his date, and it wasn't until he suggested to Joe Venuti that they go elsewhere in search of entertainment that Joe reminded him about the girl and the fact that she didn't have a ride home.

Bing and the girl got into his convertible, and though it was a chilly November night, he left the top down and sped over the Cahuenga Pass toward Hollywood Boulevard. He made the few miles without incident, but when he reached the intersection of Hollywood and Orange Drive, where the Roosevelt is located, and as he was making a left-hand turn across traffic, his car apparently collided with an oncoming car, and the girl

117

was thrown over the windshield and onto the pavement. We say that this *apparently* happened, because there is no longer a record of the accident on file, and we have to rely in part on Bing's account of it.

According to Bing, the accident was a miraculous one that defied the laws of physics. He claimed in his book that his car was struck from *behind* at the intersection and that the girl was thrown *forward* onto the street, which, of course, is quite impossible. Bing also claimed that the driver of the other car was drunk and that he himself had had only a few drinks. But according to the account of the accident published earlier in the family biography, Bing and Joe Venuti had been ordered by a patrolman to move on when he had discovered them sitting drunkenly beside the road in front of Universal. And this happened only minutes before Bing got into his car to drive the girl home.

Fortunately, the girl wasn't seriously injured, though she was bloody and unconscious. Bing carried her into the hotel lobby and got someone to attend to her wounds before returning to the scene of the accident, where he was promptly arrested for driving under the influence and hauled down to the Lincoln Heights jail for the night.

Whiteman had Bing bailed out the next morning, and he was back on the set at Universal. He reported to court a week later for his hearing, ready to pay the fine for his misdemeanor. But he had spent the morning playing golf, as usual, and showed up in court still dressed in his golfing knickers, loud socks, and even louder sweater. When his case was called, the judge, who Bing says was a hardnosed guy from another district who wasn't as tolerant about drinking as were the local judges, studied his report for a moment, then said, "It says here, HBD [had been drinking]. Is this true, Mr. Crosby?"

"I had a couple of drinks," Bing said.

"Are you familiar with prohibition? The Volsted Act?"

118

"Sure," Bing said. "But nobody pays much attention to it."

"Well, Mr. Crosby, I'm going to give you thirty days to pay attention to it."

"How much is the fine?" Bing asked.

"No bail," the judge said. "Thirty days."

Bing spent more than a week in the Los Angeles County jail before Universal could use its influence to get him transferred to the Hollywood division, from which he was allowed out every day to work on the film, and locked up again at night. His daily release made it possible to do The Rhythm Boys' segments of the film, but Whiteman either couldn't or wouldn't hold up the filming of a feature solo, "Song of the Dawn," which had been promised to Bing but which was shot with John Boles while Bing was locked up in the county jail. Bing was bitterly disappointed about losing the solo.

During the filming at Universal, Whiteman became the first orchestra leader to hire a female band vocalist. Al Rinker had mentioned his sister Mildred to several members of the band, and they wanted to meet her, especially since Al told them that Mildred made the best home brew on the West Coast. So Al set up a party at Mildred's house.

"She had a big house up in the Hollywood Hills by then," Al told us, "and I arranged for all the guys to come up, even Whiteman. They soon learned that I hadn't exaggerated about Mildred's home brew. They all said, 'Wow. This stuff is great!' Mildred put out a buffet, and we began eating and drinking and having a good time. Hoagy Carmichael was there, too; he played some of his songs on Mildred's Steinway, and so did Roy Bargy (Whiteman's first pianist). Soon, all the activity centered around the piano in the living room.

"Finally, Bing asked me to get Mildred to sing. I guess he had asked her a few times, and she had refused. I knew she was playing hard to get, so I asked her and she agreed. I accompanied her on piano, and after her first song, she got tremendous applause from the guys. Nobody had heard her sing before—they didn't even know she was a singer. For an encore, she did 'Sleepy Time Gal,' which got even more applause and even brought Whiteman away from the food in the kitchen. He came into the living room and asked Bing who the girl was that was singing so great. 'That's Millie,' Bing told him.

"Whiteman looked at me, grinning, and said, 'Don't tell me there's *one* in the family who can sing!' Then he edged his way through the guys and gave Mildred a kiss, asking her to sing some more. She did a few more tunes, and when she finished, Whiteman said, 'I want you to be on my Old Gold show next week.'

"And that's how it started. The next week she appeared on the show as a soloist. I remember the first song she sang: 'Moanin' Low.' And that was the start of her career."

Mildred Bailey was put on salary at $75 a week. Within a year, Whiteman was paying her $1,250 a week. When she had finally asked for that amount, Whiteman had joked, "I'll tell you what. You give *me* $1,250 a week, and I'll give *you* the band!" But Pops paid her that amount and didn't resent doing so. Whiteman's father had always told him, in effect, "If you make a lot of money, it's because your musicians are doing a good job, and they should share proportionately." Whiteman practiced what his father preached. No one who ever fronted an orchestra paid his men better than Paul Whiteman. He was a very fair and honest man. Many people in the limelight are in the position to plug a song to fame, and all too often they'll insist on being given "songwriting" credit, along with the true authors, as a price for plugging the song. Whiteman considered this practice odious and dishonest, and he never did it. But Bing Crosby did.

Whiteman was amply rewarded by Mildred Bailey for his generosity. According to Matty Malneck, Mildred almost single-handedly saved the Whiteman orchestra from going under financially. After 1930, there was so much competition that bookings were down, and Whiteman was faced with the probability of having to cut the size of his orchestra and of having to let Mildred Bailey go. But when they were at the Edgewater Beach Hotel in Chicago, Mildred came across a number called "Ol' Rockin' Chair's Got Me," and sang it one evening on their weekly radio program (the song earned her the sobriquet "The Rockin' Chair Lady" and became her theme song). The response from listeners was phenomenal. Immediately after the show went off the air that evening, Western Union was bombarded with so many laudatory telegrams for Mildred that the company didn't have enough messenger boys to handle them all, so they installed a telegraph receiver backstage at the Edgewater. The publicity put Whiteman back on top, and Pops, who had given Mildred her break, was repaid in kind.

King of Jazz was finished in March of 1930, but it's possible that the Whiteman orchestra had finished its part in the film earlier. From Universal, Whiteman was scheduled for a tour starting in San Diego, then on to Portland, Oregon, and Seattle, Washington, before going on up to Canada and east. The Rhythm Boys accompanied the orchestra to San Diego, Portland, and Seattle, but at Seattle, they left Whiteman for good.

The boys had never really been enthusiastic about going back with Whiteman after they finished their vaudeville tour. They had had more freedom as an individual act; they weren't subject to the discipline that Whiteman insisted upon; they didn't have to sit through hours of performance holding dummy instruments on the bandstand; they had had star billing, rather than being an appendage of a famous orchestra; and finally, they wanted to stay on the West Coast, where they felt assured of starring as a trio and of getting movie work as well.

Thus Harry, Al, and Bing were all for breaking with Whiteman, and Bing, who had other plans as well and who stood to gain most from the break, was the spokesman for the group. According to Bing, as related in his book, the final break was precipitated by, of all things, a bottle of Scotch. Bing alleges that the band's bootlegger tried to collect money from him in Seattle for a bottle of Scotch that he never received. When Bing refused to pay, the bootlegger went to Whiteman, who paid for the Scotch and deducted the money from Bing's salary.

Bing says that he confronted Whiteman over the deduction and that an argument ensued that finally led to Whiteman's telling Bing that he was more trouble than he was worth and that he and Al and Harry could leave the band if they wanted to. That, according to Bing, is when and how The Rhythm Boys severed their alliance with Whiteman and struck out on their own.

It's a curious story, and the more curious because there isn't an ounce of truth to it.

Al Rinker doesn't know why Bing came up with such an account. According to Al, Whiteman had told them in Los Angeles that they could leave the band after the Seattle date. And Whiteman's side of the story bears Al out. Whiteman had the boys under a five-year contract and could have held them to the contract for another two years had he wished to. Years later, he told Glenhall Taylor that he had resisted their leaving at first, but had finally decided to let them go because they wanted to stay in California and because there seemed to him little advantage to keeping three disgruntled employees under contract. Then, too, it's known that Whiteman tried to get them a contract with Universal before he left Los Angeles, knowing that they were leaving the band with no engagements lined up.

In the family biography, Bing contradicted his own story in a letter written to his mother before they left Universal. He wrote to her that although Whiteman was reluctant to let the trio go, all had reached a "moderately satisfactory" understanding. He then described the trip they would take up the coast to Seattle, where they would leave the Whiteman organization and return to Los Angeles. So it was obvious that their break with Whiteman had been discussed and agreed upon before they left Universal. The "Scotch" story conjured up by

Bing fifteen years after the family biography was written seems to have no purpose, except that the break was a major transition in Bing's career and has its parallel in the equally spurious story Bing concocted later as a rationale for breaking his contract with the Cocoanut Grove, which was also a major transition in his career. Then, too, if the "Scotch" story were to be believed, it would appear that Bing wanted his readers to think that Paul Whiteman had fired The Rhythm Boys.

Rinker recalls that although Whiteman would have preferred that the trio stay with the band, he understood their desire to go out on their own, and the parting was amicable. Years later, Whiteman's recollection was the same as Rinker's; it was a mutually agreed upon split, without rancor.

It's possible that there was secret rancor, though, and that it was on Bing's part only. The family biography mentioned Bing's disappointment at not getting the "Song of the Dawn" solo in *King of Jazz* and emphasized how bitterly disappointed Kate was at the news. Bing told Ev that they (Whiteman and Universal) could have held the spot for him had they wanted him to do it. And more than forty years later, Bing was still talking to interviewers about "Song of the Dawn" and speculating about what might have happened to his career had he sung it. His remark to Everett makes one wonder whether Bing thought Whiteman had given the song to John Boles out of spite, to punish him for all the problems he had caused Whiteman in the past. And given that *King of Jazz* was more a loosely knit revue than a plotted story, perhaps Whiteman did; Bing certainly deserved it.

Back in Los Angeles, the trio contracted with a booking agent named Leonard Goldstein, who later became a prominent motion-picture producer. Goldstein had caught their act at the Montmartre and liked them. But despite the trio's popularity with the Hollywood set, there were no immediate openings for them, and they were out of work until they chanced to meet an executive with an oil company that sponsored a local radio variety show emceed by Walter O'Keefe. They were booked on the show for thirteen weeks.

Meanwhile, Goldstein contacted Abe Frank, who managed the Ambassador Hotel and its nightclub, the famous Cocoanut Grove. Frank liked The Rhythm Boys and thought that they could outdraw the Biltmore Trio, which was appearing at the Biltmore Hotel in downtown Los Angeles, the Ambassador's chief rival for the affection of the nightclub set. And though Frank couldn't pay the kind of money The Rhythm Boys expected, the Grove's prestige more than made up for the difference in pay, and they jumped at the offer Abe made them. There certainly was nothing to lose.

CHAPTER NINE

Most of us (singers) were not only
afraid to do it (sing in Bing's new style),
we hoped the whole idea of it would go away.

—KENNY ALLEN

When Bing went into the Cocoanut Grove with Al
Rinker and Harry Barris in the late spring or early
summer of 1930, he was a very frustrated man. He was
now twenty-seven, in a town where sixteen- and
seventeen-year-olds were under contract and on their
way to stardom. He had been in show business for five
years but was still relatively unknown, and he had been
rejected by nearly every studio in Hollywood. Bing
wanted to strike out on his own but seemed no closer to
making a name for himself than he was when he and Al
first joined Whiteman in 1926. In the interim, he had
blown a chance to solo in a $2 million picture, and his
solo-record efforts with Whiteman were undistinguished
and critically ignored. It was at this point that Bing
Crosby began to change—or, rather, that a facet of his
personality that had lain dormant began to emerge. It
was a subtle evolution, and an insidious one. When the
change was finally manifest in actions, it was abrupt
and callous. Al Rinker was bewildered by it; Harry
Barris was at first stunned and then nearly devastated
by it.

When Bing's career was launched in 1925, he had more or less hoisted anchor without enthusiasm and had drifted along without purpose. At first, Al Rinker did the rowing, then when Harry Barris came aboard, he, too, pulled his weight. This is not to say that Bing contributed nothing to their progress; he did, and he was indispensable. But he joined in only after Al—and then Harry—initiated the motion. And even then, he spent most of his time resting on his oars, just going along for the ride, for the good times. But when their vaudeville tour ended in 1929 and Whiteman took them back in tow, Bing seems to have suddenly taken an interest in his whereabouts and his destination. He had tasted the good life and found it to his liking. At a time when one could live very well on $50 a week, when a good hotel room could be had for $3 a week, a complete breakfast for 25¢, and a filet mignon at the finest of restaurants for $1, the young man from Spokane had been making $150 a week with Whiteman, then $300 a week (working only two hours a day) on the vaudeville circuit, and then $400 a week while working at the Montmartre and filming *King of Jazz*. Yet, when The Rhythm Boys separated from Whiteman in Seattle, Bing was flat broke; it had been easy come, easy go. His financial embarrassment was so acute that he wouldn't make the short trip from Seattle to Spokane to see his family, whom he hadn't seen for nearly three years.

Brother Larry was working in Seattle for a public-relations firm when The Rhythm Boys came to town for their last appearance with Paul Whiteman. And it was to Larry that Bing confided he didn't want to go home and face what he called the local scoffers broke and with his career in limbo. He used the term local scoffers, but he obviously meant his mother. Kate's opinion was the only one he valued—and feared. In effect, he realized that he had pulled what the family biographers would have called a Dad Crosby; he had let the good times roll and had blown all his money—a small fortune to Kate during those years—without a

126

moment's thought about the future. Even Larry was astonished that Bing hadn't saved a cent.

Bing knew that had Kate learned the truth about him, she would have held as little esteem for him as she did for his father—perhaps less, for Bing had earned more than his father could dream of earning and had blown far better opportunities. So rather than face the indomitable Kate, Bing hightailed it back to Los Angeles. The implication is clear: he couldn't go home again until he was successful, and success to Kate Crosby meant money and astute money management, not fame.

When The Rhythm Boys found that the City of Angels wasn't exactly awaiting them with open arms, and when they were out of work for a short time before their agent finally got them a contract at the Grove for no more money than Bing and Al's starting salary had been with Whiteman in 1926, Bing must have felt the sting of it even more than Al and Harry. And the money that individual performers were making in show business must have seemed even more enticing. He had seen people in the business with less talent and ability than he making astounding sums of money. There was no question that he was in the right business, but he was obviously going in the wrong direction. It was as though he had stumbled across what he knew to be a rich, unclaimed gold mine but couldn't find its entrance. Or, having discovered the means of entry—going it as a single—found himself frozen at the threshold, afraid to enter it alone.

Even before he arrived with Whiteman to do the Universal film, Bing's letters to Kate indicated a lack of satisfaction with the progress of his career and a new awareness of the need to get his own name before the public. Kate, of course, was ecstatic that he was at last serious enough about something to really apply himself for a change. But to Bing, this newfound seriousness was distasteful and presented a dilemma. Despite an awakened desire to succeed, he lacked the initiative to try it on his own. He was afraid of failure, and his philosophy seemed to be: nothing ventured, nothing lost.

127

Bing would have broken from the trio in a minute had conditions been right. But his conditions were almost impossible to meet. He had the talent and desire, but someone else would have to furnish the initiative and persistence, for these qualities were alien to his nature. He required someone to chart a well-defined course for him and to accompany him every step of the way, prodding, pushing, sometimes dragging him despite himself. Someone had to share the blame or criticism with him, had to take the fall with him if he didn't succeed. Bing wouldn't accept responsibility for his own failures.

A number of people had counseled him to strike out on his own. But they didn't meet his requirements. The New York agent offered him no guarantees, so Bing turned him down. Brother Larry thought he should try, but Larry offered no plan. And when he returned to Los Angeles, his brother Everett was constantly trying to instill him with initiative—Kate was behind Everett's constant prodding—but Bing told him to mind his own business—selling trucks. Everett, though, was the executive arm of Kate's influence and was in many ways as indomitable as his mother. He would persist.

If Bing had been left to his own devices early on, he would have ended his career in the nearest speakeasy and would have probably drifted back to Spokane and Stubeck's Cigar Store. Bing gave ample evidence to support such conjecture from the very beginning, when Al Rinker had to roust him from bed to get him out of Spokane and into show business. Later, it was owing only to Bing's ingratiating personality and obvious talent that people like Whiteman put up with his irresponsible ways, dispatching emissaries to search speakeasies and gutters for him when he failed to show up for engagements. Bing Crosby was a most unlikely candidate for fame.

Most of Bing's fans have assumed that, owing to his lack of ambition, he didn't seek fame; that because of his incomparable talent, he didn't have to *goniff* his way to the top and didn't step on anybody on the way, as other stars are known to have done. These were reasonable assumptions considering Bing's attitude toward fame; he hated it, and even if he hadn't hated it, he truly felt that he wasn't worthy of it. Time and time again, he told his fans, through interviews, in effect: "Oh, I'm just an average guy with a passable voice and a facility with words who got lucky." And this seemed the truth, though we chuckled admiringly when he described one of the best and most famous singing voices in the world as "passable." He was certainly one of the most unassuming performers ever to gain stardom. He remained relatively untarnished by fame, and we admired him for that. He didn't step on people for ego satisfaction, and we admired him for that, too. He was one of the most uncolorful celebrities who ever lived; so unlike other stars and superstars that he was fascinating. Hundreds of what's-a-nice-guy-like-this-doing-at-the-top stories were written about him for decades. "Luck," Bing told us. But one doesn't rise to the land of towering egos on luck and talent alone. It takes tremendous dedication and drive to reach the top and to stay there. And that kind of drive necessitates something akin to obsession.

Most performers are obsessed with fame, driven by it. They want to be known to everyone and to be admired and noticed and loved by everyone. They live to perform, for the recognition and applause. If they're very good at what they do, their audiences respond with admiration or love, even adulation. For most performers who reach the top, the power to command the apparent, if fickle, "love" of the masses is so seductive that it corrupts them, causing them to become locked into their performing selves, in constant need of nourishment in the form of attention, praise, adoration—forms of applause—even in their private lives. It was toward such people that a satirist once attributed the lines: "But we've talked enough about me. Now let's talk about *you*. What do *you* think of me?" This, of course, was the antithesis of Bing Crosby.

Bing was different. Perhaps due in part to his mother's influence and to his father's "negative" influence, Bing lusted for fortune, not fame. Ironically, he was gifted with a magnificent voice and extraordinary musical talent and so found himself in a profession in which fortune is a by-product of fame. And for a man who valued his privacy and personal freedom above all else, and who couldn't even deal with a simple compliment—let alone the adulation that inevitably accompanies fame—celebrity was a terribly restrictive yoke.

This is not to say that Bing went into the Cocoanut Grove with his eye fixed firmly on his goal, an ingenious plan to reach it, and uncharacteristic determination. Nothing could be further from the truth. He saw the Grove engagement as the only game in town and not a very good one at that, since it bound him more firmly to the trio for relatively low remuneration. But he did enter the Grove with a little less indifference toward his future, and though he continued to backslide occasionally, it was due to his recordings of Harry Barris compositions and to his great popularity at the Grove that the odds of his making it as a soloist turned slowly in his favor.

The Cocoanut Grove was a huge room in the Ambassador Hotel on Wilshire Boulevard, which took its name from the dozens of full-size imitation palm trees that had once been used on the sets of Rudolph Valentino's *The Sheik* and had been purchased from Paramount to lend the room a semitropical, oasislike motif. The room could accommodate several hundred dining and dancing patrons, and from its beginning in 1921, it was frequented by socialites, influential studio brass, and Hollywood's most glittering stars. It remained popular for decades, a chic room famous for its Saturday-afternoon Tea Dances, its Sunday-evening radio interviews with its celebrity patrons, and its fine orchestras and specialty acts.

The hotel and Grove room were run by Abe Frank, an elderly gentleman who hired and managed all the Ambassador Hotel's employees and who booked talent for the Grove. The Cocoanut Grove was Abe Frank's passion, and under his expert management and constant attention, it flourished. Abe was a hard taskmaster, but he was also kind and gentle, with an eye and appreciation for talent. He presided over the Grove from his table near the bandstand, which he occupied every night and from which he enjoyed the entertainment as much as his patrons did.

Abe was a show-business visionary, too. When radio was just developing, he converted a small upstairs room to a radio studio, complete with a control booth and numerous microphones, which he could control separately; thus, the quality of his musical radio programs, which were broadcast nightly from ten to twelve, was better than those originating from some of the local radio stations. His two-hour shows were broadcast along a small Pacific Coast network that reached as far north as Seattle and, depending upon weather conditions, drifted as far east as Denver. The Grove's radio shows made the club famous for hundreds of miles and offered performers like Bing Crosby an astonishingly large audience on the Pacific Coast.

The club offered a diversified entertainment program. In the early twenties, there were musical spectaculars complete with chorus lines, but the shows grew more sedate by the thirties. Abe Frank was a man of fine musical tastes, and he hired only the best. When The Rhythm Boys began at the Grove, two full orchestras—Gus Arnheim and Carlos Molina—and a trio called The Three Cheers were providing continuous entertainment. Arnheim's was the main orchestra, and Molina's orchestra, which specialized in Latin rhythms, played during Arnheim's breaks and when members of the Arnheim group were playing for the nightly radio broadcasts upstairs. One of Arnheim's violinists was a young man named Russ Columbo, who would shortly begin his solo singing career in New York, rivaling Bing Crosby.

It was inevitable that a man as well organized and attentive to his club as Abe Frank would clash with the irresponsible Mr. Crosby, and clash they did—

spectacularly. But not at first. Frank kept up with show-business goings-on, and in those days before Bing became so popular with the public and so powerful within the industry that no one whispered a discouraging word about him, he had been dubbed "Binge" Crosby, and Frank knew it. Frank also knew of Bing's jail sentence of a few month's earlier, as did everyone else in town. But he liked The Rhythm Boys and no doubt reckoned that since they had just split with Whiteman and were on their own for the first time, they would probably be on their best behavior. And he was right. The pronoun *they* was always used; Al and Harry were guilty by association. Most people assumed that whatever mischief Bing got into must have involved the other two members of the trio as well. But Abe Frank eventually learned otherwise.

For the first few months at the Grove, Bing was a model of professional decorum; he needed Abe Frank more than Abe needed him, and so he toed the mark. It wasn't until Bing began soloing with Gus Arnheim, drawing large and enthusiastic fans of his own, and making moderately successful records with Arnheim on the Victor label, that Bing felt he had enough leverage to bend the provisions of his contract by putting his own personal desires above his obligations to the Grove and to Al and Harry.

While Bing was on his good behavior, The Rhythm Boys became the hottest act in town. Fans they had cultivated at the Montmartre followed them there. Grove regulars quickly became fans. And when the socialite college students from the nearby privately owned University of Southern California discovered them, word on campus quickly spread, and the Grove's maitre d', Jimmy Manos, was kept hopping as never before, particularly on Friday and Saturday nights.

Winstead "Doodles" Weaver was one of the USC students at the time for whom going to the Grove was an absolute Friday- and Saturday-night necessity. Weaver, who later gained fame as a singer-musician with the Spike Jones orchestra, fondly recalled those

132

weekend evenings at the Cocoanut Grove. "The Rhythm Boys were popular with the college crowd," he told us. "We'd go there purposely on weeknights just to listen to that trio. They were the sensation of our time, singing our kind of songs—Barris banging away on the piano, doing those funny bits, and singing along with Al Rinker and Bing. They were wonderful."

Besides hitting his stride as a fine entertainer, Harry Barris also hit his stride as a composer while at the Grove. Earlier, he had written several songs, but only one, "Mississippi Mud," had become a hit. During his short tenure at the Cocoanut Grove, however, Harry wrote several hits, including "At Your Command," and two that became standards: "I Surrender, Dear" and "Wrap Your Troubles in Dreams." Unfortunately, this creative period was the high point of his music-writing career, and except for "Little Dutch Mill," which he wrote later, he never again equaled his production at the Grove.

The one who benefited most from Barris's extraordinarily productive period was Bing Crosby. When Barris wrote his first song at the Grove, "It Must Be True" (with Gordon Clifford), he rehearsed it with Bing, and after Jimmy Grier arranged it for Arnheim's orchestra, Bing was allowed to sing it solo. The same is true for "At Your Command" and "I Surrender, Dear." All of these songs were recorded, bringing Bing a good deal more attention than he had received from his recordings with Whiteman. And "I Surrender, Dear" would be instrumental in Bing's rise to stardom.

The audience response to Bing's solos at the Grove was astonishing, even to Bing. "When Bing did one of his solos," Doodles Weaver told us, "everything stopped. People would stop dancing and would just gather around the bandstand, swaying with the music and listening. He brought the house down with that slick delivery of his. I remember after he'd sing one or two solos, we'd all start cheering and applauding, and he'd come back for encore after encore. Sometimes he'd sing several more songs than he obviously had planned.

133

That's one of the things that made him the focus of attention at the Grove and brought him a measure of fame on the West Coast—that weekend college bunch who flocked there like sheep just to hear him sing. He was marvelous."

What particularly impressed the Grove patrons was Bing's innovative singing style, one quite different from that which he had used on his occasional solos with Paul Whiteman. The style seems to have evolved during this period, perhaps inspired by his new resolve and concentration on making it as a soloist. Prior to this time, Bing was delivering songs in a smoother manner not unlike the lyrical style used by Irish tenors of the day, concentrating on producing "pretty" pear-shaped tones and adhering to the melody, which resulted in his sounding much like the voicing of a technically correct but uninspired alto saxophone solo. But at the Grove, Bing seems to have brought all of his musical experience to bear on his delivery, and the result was the first stage of a totally new style of singing, different from that of any singer before him and much copied by all who followed.

The late Kenny Allen, who was a vocalist with The Three Cheers Trio when The Rhythm Boys were at the Grove, was interviewed shortly before his death by Vernon Wesley Taylor, a Portland, Oregon, business executive and Crosby fan who has published many articles on Bing and who was kind enough to supply us with a transcript of his interview with Allen and to allow us to quote from it. We were particularly interested in Allen's comments, because he was not only a fine singer himself and a student of pop singing but also an eyewitness to Bing's development as a soloist. The following are excerpts from the interview:

> Taylor: Was Bing really terrifically popular at the Grove?
> Allen: I was going to say: just as soon as he did his first solo. But he sort of dominated that trio he was in. And I suppose that's why they had him begin his soloing. In a place like that, you see,

with crowds stopping their dancing and crowding around the apron so they could listen, it didn't take long for the powers that be to figure out what was going on.

Taylor: A great many theories have been advanced as to just what made Bing so popular; I've even read that it was the resonance that the microphone gave to his voice.

Allen: You hear all kinds of theories.

Taylor: As a singer yourself, who worked in those days at the very same place, what is your theory?

Allen: Oh, I've never had one single thing convince me.

Taylor: You don't care to commit yourself? Was it his style? His range? His phrasing?

Allen: Well, it had to be all of those things—and more. He used no gimmicks. . . . He didn't use schtick like wrestling with the mike or lounging against the piano or some such thing. He didn't actually *do* very much except sing. Still, he had several pretty good things going for him, and they all seemed to work well together; they made sense. I've never been able to get over how he delivered his lyrics with such a strong intonation—gave him finesse.

Mr. Taylor pressed Kenny Allen about his observations and got an interesting professional singer's insight into Bing's hypnotic style, and then also got a humorous retort that exemplifies how difficult it is to analyze and then express in words the properties of any art form.

Allen: I'll be honest with you, Vern. I've given a lot of thought to the phenomenon of the popular singer. After all, I tried to be one myself. Well, Bing, besides that intonation of his, had a very nice sense of swing; that's hard to manage even once in a while. Most of us were not only afraid to do it, we hoped the whole idea of it would go away. But Crosby did it all the time—fast songs, slow songs, silly songs, sad songs. It didn't seem to matter with him. He didn't look like he gave a

> damn, and yet he still managed to make you think
> he did. Does that make sense?
> *Taylor:* I think so.
> *Allen:* Okay, then explain it to *me!*

The style that Bing was developing was less tonic, more relaxed and laid-back, allowing space and time for rhythmic patterns—the "sense of swing" that Kenny Allen spoke of. Bing would perfect it over the next few years, incorporating the tonality and phrasing of, as we commented earlier, a soft, laid-back string bass. Eventually, he would abandon the high-baritone key that was popular at the time and which nudged at the tenor range, giving his voice a very thin quality in the top notes. His natural range was much lower than the range he tried during his early years. The lower range was not only more natural but more comfortable for him and suitable to the style he was developing.

As with any art form that is executed perfectly, Bing's style seemed effortless, easy, just as Fred Astaire's dancing seemed easy. But pros like Kenny Allen knew better, and that's why they wished that it hadn't been developed.

After *King of Jazz* was premiered at the Roxy Theatre in New York in June 1930, The Rhythm Boys were offered more film work, though on a far more modest scale. Pathé studios, which was doing a series of "two-reeler" musical shorts, hired them to star in two of them. The first, titled *Ripstitch the Tailor*, directed by Raymond McCarey, was never released. The second, titled *Two Plus Fours*, was released in 1930. Next came *Check and Double Check*, an RKO release starring the popular radio comedy team Amos and Andy (Freeman Gosden and Charles Correll). The Rhythm Boys appeared with Duke Ellington's orchestra singing Harry Ruby's "Three Little Words," which they also recorded with Ellington on August 26, 1930, on the Victor label. The female lead in the picture was Sue Carol, whom Bing didn't meet during the filming but who was soon to become a very close friend.

136

The Rhythm Boys also had at least one musical sequence in a Paramount film titled *Confessions of a Coed,* released in 1931. Bing is generally credited with singing—unbilled and off camera—"Just One More Chance" in the film, but Al Rinker remembers that all three of them worked in the picture. Whether Al and Harry sang backup to Bing or whether The Rhythm Boys did numbers that were eventually cut from the film isn't known. Rinker never saw the finished film.

Bing appeared in another film that was also shot in 1930 and released in '31. It was the United Artists feature-length film *Reaching for the Moon,* starring Douglas Fairbanks and featuring Bebe Daniels. It's notable because it's the first film in which he appeared without Al and Harry, the first in which he sang a solo, and the first in which he had speaking lines—two words: "Hi, gang." It also resulted in his first review as a motion-picture player. *Variety* gave the film a lukewarm review and devoted much space lamenting the fact that most of Irving Berlin's songs had been cut from it, but the picture evidently left the unnamed reviewer wanting more of Crosby. The following is excerpted from the January 7, 1931, issue:

> None of the Berlin songs is left other than a chorus of hot numbers apparently named "Lower Than Lowdown." [Bing had done a chorus of "When Folks Up North Do the Mean Low Down."] Tune [sic] suddenly breaks into the running in the ship's bar when Bing Crosby, of the Whiteman Rhythm Boys [sic], gives it a strong start for just a chorus which, in turn, is ably picked up by Miss Daniels, also for merely a chorus. . . .

Aside from the few films mentioned, during the first few months at the Grove, Bing and Al spent most of their days playing golf together at the Lakeside Golf Club. Bing was dating an actress named Ruth Taylor at the time—she played the blonde in the original version of *Gentlemen Prefer Blondes*—and Al and his girl friend double-dated with Bing and Ruth frequently. Harry Barris didn't socialize with Bing and Al much; he

137

had gone through a troubled period with his marriage, which ended in divorce, and then had thrown himself into his composing, which he spent his time doing almost every waking hour that he wasn't performing.

It was at the height of their popularity at the Grove, perhaps three or four months into their engagement there, that the trio began falling apart. There were several contributing factors to the dissolution, but chief among them was Bing's gradual emergence as a soloist and his running battle with the Grove's manager, Abe Frank.

Frank was delighted with The Rhythm Boys; they were drawing large crowds and they were very popular on Frank's nightly radio programs. He was delighted, too, when Bing began soloing and developed a personal following that was keeping the Grove's cash register ringing. What didn't please him was that once Bing had gained a personal following and felt that Frank now needed him, he lapsed into his old ways. He began not showing up for work.

Both Bing and the family biographers say in their books that The Rhythm Boys frequently let their play time interfere with their work at the Grove. According to both books, the boys frequently got carried away with reveling at Agua Caliente (a legalized gambling complex with casino and racetrack across the Mexican border from San Diego) or at Palm Springs, the playground of the movie colony. But in fact it was Bing, and not Al and Harry, who frequently missed engagements. Bing had begun hitting the bottle more, and because of his intolerance for alcohol, it quite literally put him out of commission for two or three days at a time. Usually he couldn't work while drinking, but on at least one occasion, he tried.

Dr. J. DeWitt Fox, now a prominent neurosurgeon in Los Angeles, recalls attending a function at the Beverly Wilshire Hotel at which Gus Arnheim's orchestra appeared. (Arnheim frequently played such special engagements, particularly on Monday nights, when the Grove was dark.) Gus had brought along Bing as the band's soloist. Dr. Fox says that when it came time for Bing to do his first number, he stood pale and unsteady at the mike while the orchestra played the introduction to his song. Then, as Bing opened his mouth to sing, he vomited—on his suit front, his shoes, and on several members of his socialite audience, who had gathered close to the bandstand to hear him sing.

Bing's errant ways can't be blamed solely upon his drinking problem, however. There were many times that he missed engagements simply because what he wanted to do at the time was more important to him than showing up for work. But regardless of the causes, his absences were disruptive. Unlike the vaudeville days, when Al and Harry could cover for Bing because the audiences were paying not only to see The Rhythm Boys (and didn't know whether it was a duo or a trio), but the rest of the bill as well, the Cocoanut Grove patrons were coming to see The Rhythm Boys perform and to hear Bing Crosby solo. And when Bing didn't show, Al and Harry had to sit the evening out, while Abe Frank absorbed complaints from irate and disappointed patrons and tried to make excuses for Bing.

Frank was as charmed by Bing as everyone else who worked with him. Bing could be so witty, such a good storyteller and listener, so friendly and so pleasant to be with, that one was drawn to him and eager to be among the first to forgive him—even to defend him—for his occasional excesses. This was true of most of his acquaintances throughout his lifetime—and even today. But there's a limit to such loyalty in those who had to depend on Bing for one reason or another. And Abe Frank had his limits. The first few times that Bing missed work, Frank gave him a fatherly lecture and let him off. But when it became exasperatingly evident that his lectures were falling on indifferent ears, Frank took measures that got Bing's undivided attention.

After one Sunday-night show, Bing went down to Agua Caliente and spent the better part of the next twenty-four hours at the crap table. By Tuesday morning, his bankroll was nearly depleted, but rather than taking his losses philosophically and heading back to Los Angeles—a three- or four-hour trip in those days—he tried to win his losses back. He lost every penny. According to his autobiography, he didn't even have funds to get back to Los Angeles, and by the time he found a ride back, he had missed the Tuesday night show at the Grove.

When Bing showed up Wednesday night, Abe Frank didn't take him aside for his standard lecture. On payday, Bing found out why. Frank had docked him a day's pay. Bing was mad as hell, and to Abe Frank's astonishment, he protested Abe's action, as though Abe were deliberately and unjustly persecuting an innocent victim of circumstance. That was the beginning of a running and fiery battle between Bing and Abe, for Abe continued to dock Bing for days missed. For a while, Bing missed work less frequently. It was obvious that the way to his conscience was through his pocketbook.

Bing began concentrating on his solo work several months into their Grove engagement, and it cut into The Rhythm Boys' trio time. The fans didn't seem to mind, for they loved Bing's singing. Harry Barris, now pushing himself hard and successfully at composing, didn't mind either. He could put less energy into performing and rehearsing and more into creating, so he was content. The Rhythm Boys continued to perform, of course, with Harry playing accompaniment on the fast tunes and Al accompanying the ballads, but with less show time and performing, the enthusiasm began waning, and the boys eventually stopped rehearsing the trio altogether. The new numbers that were developed were being sung by Bing.

"Bing got popular singing those solos," Al Rinker told us, "and this is where he started to get his break—not as a member of the trio, though the people liked us, too, but as a soloist. And Barris was very instrumental in Bing's success because of the things he wrote for him, like 'I Surrender, Dear' and 'It Must Be True.'

There had never been a better pop singer than the young Bing Crosby. He was just great."

Upon reflection about the trio, Rinker told us, "We all lost enthusiasm and interest in it. The loss of enthusiasm was really gradual, subtle, and contagious. I had less and less to do at the Grove, but I had my own interests apart from work, and I really didn't give it much thought at the time. We all knew, without putting it into words, that a group like that doesn't go on forever. But I didn't anticipate that it would end quite so soon or so abruptly."

Al and Bing and Harry may not have been worrying about the trio, but Everett Crosby was. Unknown to Al and Harry—and perhaps to Bing—Everett was making the rounds of radio stations in an effort to find additional work for them. Glenhall Taylor told us of an encounter with Everett.

"When The Rhythm Boys were working at the Grove," he told us, "I was manager of KTM (radio). Everett came into our studios one day and introduced himself. He said, 'I'm not an agent. I'm in the truck business. But my brother's Bing Crosby, and they're singing down at the Grove. I'd like for them to get on radio. I'd like to sell you on the idea of a half-hour program once a week.'

"I told him that we were a small, independent radio station without much of a budget and that I didn't think we could afford The Rhythm Boys. But Everett said that we could have them for a half-hour, once a week, for just seventy-five dollars for the act. I recall his saying that we could have them cheap because, he said, 'They haven't learned a new song since "So the Bluebirds and the Blackbirds Got Together." They're singing the same old stuff over and over at the Grove. They haven't learned a new tune since they've been there, and I figured that if they were on the radio, they'd learn some new numbers.'

"I told Everett that I'd have to talk to my boss about it, which I did the next day. And my boss said, 'Oh,

141

hell, that's just another drunken trio!' I tried to reason with him. I said, 'I know this Crosby is so damn good that he'll be making shorts some day, and maybe we can sell his contract for five or ten thousand dollars.' But my boss wouldn't buy the deal at all."

While Ev was casting around for something that would act as a stabilizing influence on Bing, Bing was quietly contemplating an action that would, indeed, give him some of the stability he needed. He had met a young actress named Dixie Lee, and he had fallen for her even harder than he had for Peggy Bernier. For the first time in Bing Crosby's life, he was seriously considering marriage.

Part Five:

Dixie Lee

CHAPTER TEN

Dixie Lee . . . has an infectious smile (and)
two feet that answer to no conscience. . . .

—THE *Ohio State Journal*

When sound came to the motion-picture business in the
late twenties, Hollywood studio executives looked East
and began soliciting the services not only of actors and
actresses with what they thought were trained voices,
but of musical talent as well. So it was that the William
Fox Film Corporation hired De Sylva, Brown, and
Henderson, a team who had written dozens of popular
songs like "Birth of the Blues" and "The Best Things
In Life Are Free," and who were also producing smash
Broadway musicals like *Good News*. When the team
was summoned to Hollywood in 1929, they brought
with them a number of young, talented people whom
they had under contract when Fox hired them. They
were the hottest team on Broadway at the time, and

they wanted to insure their success by bringing along people that they knew they could work with.

One of the young singers who was under a road-company contract and who came West as part of the team's package deal with Fox was Dixie Carrol, the understudy of Bing's old Chicago flame, Peggy Bernier—the same Peggy who had "poured" Bing into a train bound for Rockford, Illinois, nearly two years earlier.

Dixie was just seventeen when she arrived in Hollywood with her parents in the spring of 1929 and settled into a small house in a bungalow-court on Crescent Heights Boulevard, just south of Sunset. She was an enormously talented girl. She could dance, had a fine voice and singing style, natural acting ability, and a finely honed sense of comic timing. She was beautiful, too: five-foot-three, with platinum-blond hair (bleached—she was a brunette), large fawnlike brown eyes, a delightful and lovely pixielike smile, and a stunning figure. And her cerebral qualities were as impressive as her physical ones: she was intelligent, with a delicious sense of humor and a lightning-fast wit. All who saw her perform or heard her voice have said that had she been inclined to stay in show business, Dixie could have been a very great star.

Privately, Dixie wasn't an easy person to get acquainted with. She was painfully shy and terribly nearsighted; she couldn't distinguish one face from another at a distance of six feet. And in those days when contact lenses were unheard of and, as Dorothy Parker had remarked, men didn't make passes at girls who wore glasses—especially in Hollywood—Dixie could see beyond arm's length in public only when she had occasion to wear her prescription sunglasses.

Another reason that Dixie wasn't easy to know was her candor. She was one of the most honest persons ever to sign a Hollywood contract. It was best not to ask Dixie's opinion of *anything* unless one was prepared for an honest answer. Dixie's answers were delivered straight from the shoulder; she said exactly what she thought. She hated phonies, phoniness, and hypocrisy;

this, together with her penchant for telling the truth, made her circle of close friends in Tinsel Town extremely small. She got along very well with men and preferred their company to women. Her women friends probably numbered fewer than a dozen, and every one of them was, like her, unpretentious and candid. Once one gained friendship with Dixie, however, one had a friend for life; come hell or high water, come fame or infamy, her generosity toward friends was incomparable and her friendship unshakable. Dixie never turned her back on a friend.

Even at the age of seventeen, Dixie drank. In those days before tranquilizers, and owing to her painful shyness, Dixie built courage for auditions, for performing, for meeting studio brass, and for public appearances by drinking. Not much, but often. She built such a tolerance for alcohol that by the mid-1930s, she could drink two-fisted drinking men under the table while she gave the appearance of being stone-cold sober.

During her first year in Hollywood, Dixie got away with drinking at home in the presence of her parents by surreptitiously pouring "medicinal" drugstore gin into her Coca-Cola and drinking the mix from the bottle. It was a habit formed to alleviate the horrors of her chosen profession. Almost all performers who have contact with reality and who care about the acceptance of their work suffer stage fright to some degree prior to and often during the first few minutes of their performance. But at some point, the stage fright mercifully vanishes; if it didn't, the experience would be so excruciating as to be unbearable. Dixie once told her friend Dr. George Hummer that she was terrified every moment that she performed; her stage fright never left her. She was drawn to performing, and very gifted, but the terror of it never ceased; thus, it was no great sacrifice when she eventually gave up her career.

Dixie had chosen the stage name Dixie Carrol when she had begun singing in Chicago. But when she reported to the studio in 1929, the first thing Fox did was change her name again. They already had a star on the lot named Sue Carol, with whom Dixie would soon begin a lifelong friendship, and it was studio custom to avoid the confusion of conflicting names. Her first name, Dixie, they thought was fine, but the last name had to go. When it was discovered that she was originally from the South, they decided on a totally Southern name: Dixie Lee, after Robert E. Lee, the great Civil War general. And on April 10, 1929, *Variety* printed her photograph along with the following announcement:

DIXIE LEE

Now under contract to Fox Studios. When playing the Zelma O'Neal part in *Good News,* the *Ohio State Journal* said: "Dixie Lee, a pert pepper-pot, goaled them. She has an infectious smile, two feet that answer to no conscience, and an over-abundance of youthful energy."

Dixie Lee was born Wilma Winifred Wyatt on November 4, 1911, in Harriman, Tennessee. She was one of three daughters born to Evan E. and Nora Wyatt, née Scarborough. Although Dixie told her friend Mrs. Maybeth (Carr) Carpenter that she had two older sisters who had died, no one knows why or where they died. Evan and Nora Wyatt were natives of Tennessee, but when Dixie was quite young, they moved to New Orleans, where she was raised and where, very much influenced by the City of Music—and especially Dixieland Jazz, which continued to be her favorite music (and Bing's)—she studied voice and dancing before moving with her family to Chicago.

It was in Chicago that Dixie entered and won a singing contest sponsored by The College Inn, an elegant nightclub in the Sherman Hotel. The contest was held to find the girl who sang most like Ruth Etting, the popular singing star of the day. The prize was a two-week engagement at The College Inn, and it was during her appearance there that she came to the attention of the *Good News* producers, who signed her as an understudy to Peggy Bernier and who finally brought her to

Hollywood, along with numerous other hopefuls who were under contract to the music writing–production team.

About the time that the Old Gold–Paul Whiteman Special was en route to the Coast, Dixie Lee was beginning to rehearse for the *Fox Movietone Follies of 1929,* which would be her first film. Because of her shyness, she had become acquainted with only one person on the Fox Hills lot—Mable Cooper, who worked at Fox for the songwriters as an accompanist and who was Jackie Cooper's mother (Jackie was just beginning his extraordinary career at the time). Dixie was apparently on her way to see Mable at the music bungalow one morning, and she arrived just in time to help another fair young damsel who was very much in distress at the moment Dixie first saw her. Her name was Sylvia Picker, the same young woman who had had a crush on Bing Crosby when he was appearing in *Will Morrissey's Music Hall Revue* at the Orange Grove Theater.

Sylvia, known today as Sylvia Picker McGraw, had been brought to Hollywood from the San Diego repertory theater group. "I was under a provisional contract to Fox," Sylvia told us, "and they were going to try to make something out of me—I was a comedienne and couldn't sing a note, but they were going to make me sing. So I had spent weeks rehearsing one of De Sylva, Brown, and Henderson's songs, 'Button Up Your Overcoat.' And believe me, not only can I not carry a tune, but my range is from B-flat to B, which if you know anything about music, is just half a note—no range at all.

"So now comes the day when the powers that be are going to hear me. I'm in the music bungalow—a little tiny room—and Mable's at the piano. Seated right in front of me are not only De Sylva, Brown, and Henderson, who wrote the song, but the two Fox studio heads, Winnie Sheehan and Sol Wurtzel. I was at the ripe old age of sixteen and a half, and I was scared—just scared to death.

"Mable played the vamp for me; I opened my

147

mouth, and not a sound came out. Mable looked at me and started the vamp again, and again my voice wouldn't respond. Meanwhile, the moguls are sitting there, staring at me and growing impatient, with expressions on their faces like, 'What the hell is *this?*' Mable started the song for the third time, and this time the song is belted out in *terrific* voice—but it wasn't *mine.* I turned around, startled, and there in the doorway stood Dixie—I had no idea who she was—and she's singing *my* song!

"I was *furious!* I thought, what is she *doing?* And then suddenly I lost my fright—thinking, she can't do this to me!—and I sang the song. When I finished, Mable introduced me to Dixie. I was mad at first, but then I realized that she was a very shy girl and that she obviously hadn't been trying to embarrass me. 'I knew exactly what you were going through,' she said to me. 'It's happened to me many times—where I'd freeze. I knew that if I'd start the song, you'd get into it.'

"Well, I was very grateful."

Sylvia took an immediate liking to Dixie, and as they talked that morning she learned that Dixie was new in Hollywood and didn't know anyone but Mable. Sylvia was a charter member of the Thalians, a society of actors and actresses from all the studios who had a rented beach house at Playa del Rey, so she said, "Why don't you come down to the Thalians' beach house with me this afternoon, and I'll introduce you to all the kids." She did, and they remained close friends until Dixie's death.

A month or so after Dixie came to Sylvia's aid, the studio began shooting *The Fox Movietone Follies of 1929,* where Dixie met and formed a lifelong friendship with one of the film's stars, Sue Carol, known today as Sue Carol Ladd. She was a star at Fox when Dixie signed as a contract player. Sue eventually gave up acting and became an agent, discovering among others a young radio actor named Alan Ladd, whose career she guided and whom she later married; they remained married until Alan's death, and Sue never remarried.

"I first met Dixie in *The Fox Movietone Follies*," Sue told us, "and I liked her immediately. She sang—had a wonderful voice—and we were in several pictures together. In one of them—*The Big Party*—we had sort of equal parts, although I guess mine was the larger part, at first. But I was lying on a bed during the shooting of one scene, and an electrician threw an oil can to another electrician who was up on the rafters. It came over the top of our set and landed on the bridge of my nose. And in about two minutes, my nose was twice its normal size. The studio executives whisked me away somewhere and had me sign all kinds of papers absolving Fox studios of any damage in the accident. I couldn't work for four to six weeks; they tried to shoot around me, but it finally worked to Dixie's advantage because she did most of my part."

Ironically—and characteristically—the Fox Film Corporation, whom Sue let off the hook for damages, didn't even have the decency to protect her reputation as one of its stars by informing the trade papers of the accident's consequence. A review of *The Big Party* in *Variety* leaves the reader with the impression that Fox may have been downgrading Sue Carol as an actress. The reviewer wrote: "Despite Sue Carol carrying top billing, it's Dixie Lee who is the real feature and who runs away with the picture. . . ." The reviewer extolled the "beauty" of Dixie's "blonde presence" and her abilities, then noted: "Sue Carol is entirely subordinated."

"I was happy it was Dixie," Sue says, "because we were good friends by then, and she needed the break at the time."

By the time Dixie had finished her first film, Sylvia Picker had found a larger house for the Wyatts, across from her place on Kilkea, near Beverly Boulevard. Dixie was kept busy at the studio; by the end of 1929, in addition to the films already named, she appeared in four others: *Happy Days, Cheer Up and Smile, Let's Go Places,* and *Why Leave Home?* Her social life was equally active. Sylvia had put her up for membership in

149

the Thalians, and young men had begun drawing around her like moths to a flame—nothing serious, but Dixie had more offers for dates than she could accept. She was much sought after by young actors like Johnny Darrow and Rex Bell (who later married Clara Bow). And one in particular, Raymond Keane (the Universal contract player who had taken Bing to Fox studios), was particularly partial to her; in fact, head-over-heels partial. But, to young Keane's chagrin, he was a party to getting Dixie and Bing together, with results that he hadn't anticipated.

Matty Malneck remembers the first meeting. Keane had taken Dixie to the Cocoanut Grove, and Matty, who had met Keane at Universal, was sitting at their table when Bing Crosby walked in. It was the winter of 1929, and The Rhythm Boys were still working in Whiteman's picture, *King of Jazz*; they hadn't yet begun working at the Cocoanut Grove. Bing stopped by the table to greet Matty and Keane, and Raymond introduced him to Dixie. It was a casual first meeting, and neither Bing nor Dixie showed inordinate attention to one another. Dixie was a fan of The Rhythm Boys and of Bing in particular; she collected all their records, so she was obviously impressed with meeting Bing, but that's all. Bing seems to have put the meeting out of his mind until he saw Dixie again a few months later.

Raymond Keane was a party to the second meeting, too. By the spring of 1930, The Rhythm Boys had finished their parts in *King of Jazz* and were booked into the Cocoanut Grove. Since Sylvia Picker and Dixie Lee went everywhere together, Raymond Keane was trying to talk them both into attending a party he was giving at his apartment in the La Leyenda, which still stands today at 1737 N. Whitney Avenue in Hollywood. Sylvia said that she'd go if Dixie went, and vice versa. Finally, when Dixie seemed cool to the idea, Keane played his trump card: The Rhythm Boys, he told her, would be coming to the party after their late show at the Grove. It worked. Dixie was suddenly interested in Raymond's party, and she called Sylvia.

"Raymond said The Rhythm Boys are going to be there," she said.

"Maybe," Sylvia said, "but I think Raymond is just saying that to get you to the party."

"Well," Dixie said, "let's go."

Dixie didn't have a car then, but Sylvia did, and they drove over to the La Leyenda in her car. "By the time The Rhythm Boys arrived, it was pretty late," Sylvia recalled. "When Bing walked in, someone was playing the piano and Dixie was singing. Bing headed straight for the piano; he was fascinated with Divie's voice because she was great, just great. And when she finished singing, he began talking to her. They had a lot in common, of course, both having known Peggy Bernier and having been in Chicago at the same time."

Bing's astonishing memory for names and faces didn't fail him the night of the party. When he was introduced to Sylvia, he looked at her curiously for a moment, then said, "You look very familiar to me."

"My mind flashed back to the time when Consuelo Bell and I had schoolgirl crushes on Al Rinker and Bing, when they were appearing in *Will Morrissey's Music Hall Revue*," Sylvia recalls. "Now I was seventeen but still not mature enough to admit that I had been one of the two little gadflies who had buzzed around them after every matinee, dropping names and trying to impress them with our sophistication. I evaded his remark somehow and breathed a sigh of relief. But every once in a while he would look at me, puzzled. Or he'd say, 'I know you from somewhere,' and I'd make some inane reply. Before long, though, it came to him, and he said, 'San Diego's fairest rosebud!' And I must have blushed the color of a rosebud when he found me out. He got a big kick out of it, and he never let me live it down, either. For years, he kept reminding me of it.

"As the evening wore on, Bing and Dixie kept talking and talking, and finally I was getting tired, and kind of sleepy, too, so I said, 'C'mon, Dixie, I think we ought to go.' And Dixie said, 'Oh. . . .' more than hesitantly; obviously, she didn't want to leave."

151

"Oh," Bing said, "do you *have* to go?"

"Well, that's my ride home," Dixie said.

"I'll take you home," Bing said.

"Well," Sylvia continued, laughing, "I was *so* mad, and so *hurt*. Nobody said to me, 'You stay, too.' No, nothing like that. They practically said, 'Good-bye—here's your hat; what's your hurry?—good-bye.' So I drove home alone, and that was the beginning of Bing and Dixie."

Sylvia saw Dixie the next morning, and she was still thrilled at having "dated" Bing Crosby. "Truthfully, there wasn't a girl in town who wasn't nuts about Bing Crosby," Sylvia told us. "He was darling. I asked Dixie if she thought he would ask her out again, and she said, 'He already has.' "

It was soon evident to Sylvia that she had lost a chum, for Dixie went out with Bing almost every night from then on. "I missed the good times we had together," she said, "and I was more than a little jealous, too, to tell the truth. As I said, there wasn't a girl in town who wasn't nuts about Bing Crosby, and I was no exception. And when an old high-school friend of Dixie's, Betty Zimmerman, came to town and started double-dating with Bing and Dixie, I was cut out completely for a while, and I was hurt about that, too. Of course I never let on to Dixie how I felt."

Bing and Dixie's dating became the talk of the town—and the talk wasn't good. One got the impression that Dixie had fallen into the clutches of another Attila the Hun. "The minute Dixie started going with Bing, everyone was screaming at her," Sue Carol Ladd told us. "Because Bing had apparently been a pretty heavy drinker when he was with Whiteman."

Sylvia Picker McGraw concurred. "Even the studio brass tried to talk her out of dating Bing," she said. "I think Buddy De Sylva and Sol Wurtzel talked to her about it. Her family was against it, too. I think Dixie used to sneak out at night to see Bing. But I don't think the criticism of Bing was that valid; it was based mostly on the reputation he got from his first trip out here with

Whiteman—when he had that accident and was thrown in jail. That was big news at the time. He was supposed to be such a big boozer. Everything he did from then on was attributed to his drinking."

To illustrate her point, Sylvia recalled a time when she and Bing and Dixie were at the Thalians' beach house, and Bing invited her to join them at the Cotton Club in Culver City that evening. Louis Armstrong was in town—one of Bing's favorite people—and there was to be a jam session after the club closed.

"You have to work," Sylvia said.

"Oh, to hell with that," Bing said. "I'm not gonna miss *Armstrong*."

Bing even called Sylvia's parents—they liked Bing very much—and asked their permission, telling them not to worry because they'd be getting home late. Then they all went to the Cotton Club, and Bing missed a night at the Grove. "The next day," Sylvia said, "there was publicity and talk about how Bing had gotten drunk and missed another night at the Grove. He wasn't drunk. He went to the Cotton Club that evening, and we all had a wonderful time. Some of the crazy things that Bing did—like not showing up at the Grove, or whatever—he didn't do because he was drunk. He was a very independent soul. A real free spirit."

There is, of course, substance to Sylvia's point of view. If one has a reputation for drinking, then just pausing before a pub is enough to set tongues wagging. And with a fellow like Bing Crosby, who did the unexpected more often than not, his often-puzzling behavior was, to others, quite easily attributed to alcohol. Undoubtedly, Bing was on his best behavior during his courtship of Dixie Lee, and that's the side of him that Sylvia saw. But he was still using a big dipper in the flowing bowl.

Perhaps because of the furor raised by their dating, Bing and Dixie didn't confide in their close friends about their future plans. Matty Malneck was in his apartment at La Leyenda—which he was sharing with Bing—when Dixie telephoned Bing one day. Bing talked with her for a few minutes and, when he hung up, he turned to Matty and said, "I'm going to marry that girl." Coming from the secretive Bing Crosby, the revelation wasn't a burst of candor; it was a multimegaton explosion. So Matty Malneck was probably the only one who knew that there were wedding bells in Bing and Dixie's future. But he was far away—on the road again with Whiteman—when the event occurred.

On Monday morning, September 29, 1930, Sylvia got a phone call. It was from Bing.

"What are you doing this afternoon?" he asked.

"Nothing. I may go to the Thalian beach house."

"Well, I've got something better for you to do. How about coming to the Blessed Sacrament Church. . . ."

It was both a wedding announcement and an invitation—Crosby style.

The wedding ceremony was held in the vestry of the Church of the Blessed Sacrament on Sunset Boulevard. It was informal, with about a dozen people in attendance, and was held in the vestry because Dixie vehemently refused to convert to Catholicism and even put up a battle with Bing over the need for her promise to raise their children as Catholics. (It should be noted, however, that Dixie was a woman of her word. Though her closest friends say that she never herself attended Catholic church with Bing or the boys, she saw to it that her sons adhered to the faith; she never let them miss a Sunday mass.)

Among the guests at the wedding were Sylvia Picker; Johnny Truyens (of the wealthy Pasadena Truyens), who was an actor and a friend of Bing's; Harry Barris; Gordon Clifford (the lyricist); Burt McMurtrie (who would soon produce one of Bing's radio shows); and a few of the Thalians. Sue Carol was on a publicity tour of the East and so couldn't be present. Al Rinker wasn't present, either; he wasn't invited.

Before we found and interviewed Rinker, we were puzzled that he hadn't been among the guests at Bing's wedding. He had been instrumental, we knew, in getting Crosby and Rinker on the road to show business;

they had been inseparable for seven years; they had lived with one another in small hotel rooms and apartments during the lean years; they had played golf together almost daily since they had both learned the game together in Spokane; and by all accounts of the people who knew them both, they had never even had a difference of opinion, let alone a falling-out. Never. When we finally had an opportunity to ask Rinker why he hadn't been invited to the wedding, he said he didn't know the answer. He knew only that Bing could be very enigmatic.

Later, we came across facts that explained—to our satisfaction, at least—not only why Al wasn't invited to the wedding, but also why The Rhythm Boys had eventually disbanded in such a mysterious fashion. The latter will be addressed in the following chapters, but to answer the question posed here, we'll have to borrow a verb form coined by Joseph Heller in his novel *Catch-22*; Bing didn't invite Al Rinker to the wedding because he had "disappeared him." By the dawn of Bing's wedding day, he had used on Al Rinker the strange mental trick that we alluded to earlier in the book: Al Rinker had ceased to exist in the mind of Bing Crosby. It was as simple and as complex as that.

The Hollywood Reporter noted Bing and Dixie's marriage with a small blurb published September 30, 1930:

HONEYMOON LANE

Dixie Lee, Fox contract player, was married to "Bing" Crosby, member of the Gus Arnheim orchestra, yesterday at the Church of the Blessed Sacrament in Hollywood.

Miss Lee used the name of Wilma Wyatt at the marriage license bureau, which also accounts for the church not being filled to capacity for the ceremonies.

The real reason that the church wasn't filled to capacity was that the invitations were extended by phone and no one knew of the wedding until the morning that it was to take place—including Dixie's parents. Everett Crosby was best man (all the other Crosbys were still in Spokane and Seattle), and Dixie's Chicago friend, Betty Zimmerman, was the bridesmaid. Much has been written about how the newspapers reported the marriage; Bing and numerous biographers have claimed that newspaper accounts named Dixie as a Fox star and either called Bing an obscure crooner or misspelled his name. This misinformation was played for irony, of course. But in fact Dixie was not a star—though she was being groomed as one—and Bing wasn't unknown; he was better known outside Hollywood than Dixie, and in Hollywood, for that matter. Los Angeles is a movie town, so the newspapers did report the marriage under Dixie's name (Bing wasn't a movie actor then), and they did feature her photo and not Bing's, but one of them identified Bing as a "member of Gus Arnheim's orchestra and one of the original Rhythm Boys," and another called him a "well-known singer, appearing with Gus Arnheim's orchestra."

The reception following the ceremony was given at Ev's new house in Nichols Canyon, where another dozen or so people joined the wedding celebration, including Maybeth Carpenter and her brothers, who had received a call from Bing asking them to come over to Ev's because he had an announcement to make. Maybeth told us that she thought Bing was going to announce his engagement to Dixie, so she was very surprised to find it a fait accompli.

Aside from the attention given the bride and groom, the hottest topic was Everett's new place. Many wondered how Everett, a truck salesman, could so suddenly afford to move from a small apartment on Franklin Avenue to a spacious home in an exclusive section of the Hollywood Hills during the second year of the Great Depression, when companies were going bankrupt and selling their trucks, not buying them. There was also speculation as to what kind of cargo went along with the trucks that Ev was supposedly selling—a not-so-subtle reference to his bootlegging background.

Bing and Dixie spent their first few nights together at Everett's, which is another indication that their marriage had been a spur-of-the-moment decision; the Crosbys hadn't found—perhaps hadn't even looked for—a place of their own. It's generally thought that they were broke, but this is highly unlikely. They were both working, and both continued to work. Their combined weekly pay is estimated at more than three hundred dollars.

As it turned out, Bing and Dixie didn't need to go apartment or house hunting. Sue Carol gave them an incomparable wedding present: while she was in the East, she turned over her house—at 4961 Cromwell Avenue in the exclusive Los Feliz section—and her servants to them for several months. It was a very pleasant and luxurious way to begin a marriage. Even so, their marriage was nearly on the rocks before the honeymoon glow had faded. It was quite evident that even though Bing quite obviously adored Dixie, he didn't love her in the sense of a man and woman becoming as one. Bing wouldn't even *share* himself, let alone *give* himself to anyone. Not even Dixie. He loved her in his own fashion, but it was a passionless love on his part. Passion has an overpowering and compelling effect, and Dixie had no such effect on Bing—nor did anyone else, ever. Francois de La Rochefoucauld said it best: "Absence diminishes little passions and increases great ones, as wind extinguishes candles and fans a fire."

Bing's was the candle; Dixie's was the fire.

CHAPTER ELEVEN

. . . the crooner is telling the world that
he is sick of paying 20 percent to the man
who made most of his success possible.

—*The Hollywood Reporter*

There was no time for a honeymoon. Dixie had to be
back at work on the Fox lot the following day, Tuesday, September 30, and Bing was back at the Grove
that evening. It's ironic that when Bing finally had the
kind of reason for missing a Tuesday-night show that
Abe Frank might have excused, Bing showed up for
work. But now things were different; Bing had a wife to
support, and it was a matter of personal pride, too.
There were all those scoffers to prove wrong, the ones
who had warned Dixie that if she married Bing Crosby,
she'd have a drunken playboy on her hands whom she
might have to support for the rest of her life. And Bing
didn't want to be known around town as Mr. Dixie Lee.

For the first few months of their marriage, Bing re-
doubled his efforts at the Grove as a soloist and made
the rounds of clubs, where he often sang a number or
two with the bands just for the exposure. He did this
occasionally at the Hollywood Roosevelt Hotel, where
influential people like Mack Sennett had "permanent"

tables and where, on Monday nights, when the Grove was dark, the elite of the film colony used to dine and dance in the Blossom Room.

On the home front, life went well at first for the newlyweds. They had a fine place (Sue Carol's) to come home to, and they enjoyed late candle-lit suppers together. Early in their marriage, there was no call for Bing to sacrifice any part of his lifestyle. Quite the opposite. With Dixie coralled, he didn't have to chase after fillies any longer. And when Dixie was working on a picture, he was free to chase golf balls all day long, which he did. But when Dixie was between pictures and could spend more time at home, Bing continued to chase golf balls, leaving her at home by herself. It didn't take long for the new bride to figure out the running order: it was Bing first, golf second, and his new bride a distant third. That was bad enough, but when she began running sixth, behind his buddies, booze, and gambling, Dixie pulled hard on Bing's reins for the first time and found that they weren't attached. Even if they had been, though, it would have been like trying to rein a mule.

Bing's firm resolve to prove the local scoffers wrong had withered with the realization that the burden of proof lay squarely on him and that it was easier to shrug the burden off than to carry it off. The first blush of the honeymoon glow had no sooner begun to fade when Bing's cronies began gathering at the Grove once more. Author Leo Walker, in his book *The Wonderful Era of the Great Dance Bands,* relates a Crosby anecdote that Gus Arnheim's arranger, Jimmy Grier, was fond of telling. According to Grier, there was always a large company of Crosby cronies holed up in his dressing room at the Grove, waiting for Bing to get off work. They usually had a hot card game going as they waited and had the radio tuned in on the upstairs radio show, listening to Bing. Grier said that one night Bing must have been losing in the card game before he was called upstairs for the radio show, for as he finished his last number on the show, he announced along the entire Pacific Coast network: "Deal me in, boys, I'll be right down."

Sometimes their card game would be resumed elsewhere when the Grove locked up for the night. Or sometimes Bing would lead his entourage to the Cotton Club, if there was something going after hours there. Or sometimes they'd reassemble at Marchetti's, a plush restaurant owned by Milo Marchetti on the southwest corner of Fifth and Western, near the Grove. Marchetti's was a favorite hangout of studio executives by day, where probably more movie business was conducted than at the studios. At night, it became a gathering place for musicians, as well, for it was the first fine restaurant in Los Angeles to remain open twenty-four hours a day. Very often, Bing would return home to his bride at dawn, which displeased Dixie because she was on early-morning call at the studio. But often Bing would get drunk and not come home at all, which more than displeased her.

It became apparent to Dixie that Bing was taking his marriage vows very casually. It was bad enough to have the golf links separating her from her new husband, but when a pack of drinking, gambling cronies began running interference for him as well, Dixie stopped competing for Bing's attention, packed her bags, and left him for parts unknown.

On March 5, 1931, the Los Angeles *Examiner* reported that Bing and Dixie had separated after just three months of marriage. The following is the news item verbatim:

When Bing Crosby, singer with Gus Arnheim's orchestra, croons into the microphone, feminine hearts skip a beat, but not so his wife Dixie Lee.

She admitted to *The Examiner* last night that they were separated and that she would soon file a divorce suit against him, charging mental cruelty.

"We have only been married about six months," [sic] she said, "but we have already found out that we are not suited for each other. Our separation is an amicable one, and the only reason for it is that we

160

just cannot get along. Bing is a fine boy as a friend, but married, he and I just cannot be happy."

Miss Lee, Fox contract featured player, is 19. She came to Hollywood from New York about two years ago. Miss Lee is credited with being the originator of the dance, varsity drag, and her off-stage name is Wilma Wyatt.

As indicated earlier, Dixie was an intelligent woman and an honest one. She chose her words carefully for the newspaper release, and when she referred to Bing, who was two months away from his twenty-eighth birthday, as a fine *boy,* she had, as usual, thrust straight to the heart of the truth. No doubt her three months with Bing had seemed like the six that she indicated, and no doubt she often remembered her prophetic words: ". . . married, he and I just cannot be happy."

Dixie had turned the tables on Bing by fleeing to his favorite reveling spot, Agua Caliente, and when Bing learned she was there eleven days after she had left him, he flew there to effect a reconciliation. Just as Abe Frank had learned that the way to Bing's conscience was through his pocketbook, Dixie learned that the way to his attention was through the threat of divorce— particularly a public threat; he was as repelled by it as Count Dracula was by the sign of the cross.

The cause of their separation had been more than a lovers' quarrel over something that could later be laughed about or perhaps even eventually forgotten. It was a fundamental problem that time wouldn't heal; it would become worse with time, because Bing was naturally inclined to make it worse and because whatever feelings he had for Dixie early on could only diminish. But what could Dixie do? All of her intelligence and perception were lost to emotion. She was nineteen, and very much in love. She obviously had delusions about Bing's ability to make good his promise that he would change if she'd come back to him. Under the circumstances, she couldn't see—or didn't want to believe— that he was incorrigible. She had his career to think

161

about, which divorce, in those days, could damage. She had his religion to think about.

In all fairness, Bing did worship Dixie at this early stage of their relationship. But the evening of March 15, 1931, was Dixie's moment. Characteristically, she focused her concern on him, rather than on her own welfare; uncharacteristically, she let her emotions override her reason and made a decision that she regretted time and time again for the rest of her life: she went back to him.

At about the time Bing and Dixie were reestablishing their marital relationship, Bing came to the attention of one of Hollywood's best-known producers of two-reel comedies, Mack Sennett. According to a history of the Lakeside Gold Club, written for the club's fiftieth anniversary by its historian, Norman Blackburn, and published privately, Bing claims to have met Sennett at Lakeside and that it was because of this chance meeting that Sennett dropped by The Cocoanut Grove to hear Bing sing. He was impressed with what he heard and saw and invited Bing to stop by his office to discuss the possibility of their doing a film.

Sennett had worked for D. W. Griffith and was one of the foremost pioneers of screen humor. By the midtwenties, he had earned the title "King of Comedy" for introducing moviegoers to the likes of Charlie Chaplin, Harry Langdon, Charlie Chase, Roscoe "Fatty" Arbuckle, Chester Conklin, The Keystone Kops, and countless pie-throwers. He was also credited with discovering such luminaries as Carole Lombard, Gloria Swanson, Wallace Beery, and dozens of others. But by the time Bing met him, Sennett had fallen on hard times, and his empire had shrunk from his own huge studio complex to that of a small, independent company that rented office space and sound stages at Educational Studios on Santa Monica Boulevard. Though his empire had withered, Sennett's talent had not, and he was again doing quite well with slightly more sophisticated two-reeler talkies than he had produced with his own studio.

Bing dropped by Sennett's office, and the producer

162

made him an astonishing offer: he proposed a musical-comedy short that would star Bing, who would play himself, Bing Crosby, in the film. It was a most uncommon offer, considering that Bing was a relatively unknown singer and had yet to prove that he could even act. Bing would no doubt have been satisfied just to have a film executive of Sennett's stature do something besides stare at his ears, let alone make such a proposal. But Sennett did more than that. He had a contract made out; Bing would get $750 to do the film, which would take from two to five days at most, and an option for three or four more films if the first one made money. Bing signed.

At the time of the meeting, Bing's Victor recording (with Gus Arnheim's orchestra) of the Harry Barris–Gordon Clifford song "I Surrender, Dear" was doing quite well. And somehow it was decided that the song would not only be used in the film, but also as the film's title—without securing the right to do so from the song's publisher, Richard J. Powers, Ltd., of Los Angeles. So when *I Surrender, Dear* was released, the publisher immediately sued for copyright infringement, and Sennett settled with them out of court. It was a curious incident. Mack Sennett wasn't new to the picture business, and he was certainly no innocent regarding copyright law. He wasn't in the business of taking absurd risks, either; the two-reeler could have bombed, for all he knew, and he would still have had to pay damages to the song publisher. It's possible that Sennett was under the impression that he had clearance or a right to use the song and its title, for when the sheet music had been published earlier, it bore a photograph of Bing, along with the words "Suggested and Introduced by Bing Crosby of the Three Rhythm Boys." Bing had maintained that he had suggested the theme of "I Surrender, Dear" to its composer, Harry Barris, and thus had claim to it.

In addition to "I Surrender, Dear," which Bing sang at the opening and the closing of the two-reeler, he sang two other songs: a fine Johnny Green–Edward Heyman song called "Out of Nowhere," which was Bing's first recording for Brunswick, done on March 30, 1931, the month that he made the Sennett film, and "At Your Command," another Harry Barris tune, written with Harry Tobias and for which Bing is also given writing credit.

When Mark Sennett saw the rushes (the unedited, rough footage) of *I Surrender, Dear,* he was elated; he had been in the business long enough to recognize a money-maker when he saw it. Whether he communicated his enthusiasm to Bing at the time isn't known, but judging from Bing's action at the Grove, it's probable. Bing began playing out his role at the Grove like a poker player holding a royal flush. He began pressing Abe Frank with demands that Abe surely thought unreasonable from a guy who was disrupting his nightly presentations and rankling his patrons by showing up for work only when he felt like it—or, rather, only when he didn't have something better to do. Bing's manner and his actions and irresponsible bent made it clear to all who were connected with the Grove that a falling out with Abe was inevitable.

Frank wouldn't fire him, of course, for by March of 1931, Bing had established himself as a soloist and a local favorite. But Frank had no intention of being caught off guard in the event that Bing disappeared completely. Bing was under contract to him, and it's doubtful that Abe really expected Bing to just walk off into the sunset, but Bing was very unpredictable and was drinking very heavily at that stage of his career. So for insurance, Frank cast around for another soloist and found one in Loyce Whiteman, who became America's second female band vocalist and was very nearly the first—Paul Whiteman (no relation to Loyce) had hired Mildred Bailey only a few months before Abe Frank hired Loyce.

Loyce, today known as Loyce Whiteman Hubbard, was born in Dallas, Texas, and raised in Glendale, California, where she attended public school (she was a freshman at Glendale High School when John Wayne was a senior there). Like Dixie Lee, Loyce got her start in a singing contest (sponsored by *Radio Entertainment Magazine*), which led to a job as a vocalist for radio station KTM in Los Angeles—the same station that later refused to hire Bing—where she was known as a blues singer and where she became so popular that she was wooed away by radio station KFWB in 1930, the top station in Los Angeles at the time. It was while she was at KFWB that Abe Frank contacted her to audition for the Cocoanut Grove. Although Loyce didn't know it at the time, it was Frank's hope that Loyce's popularity would rival that of Crosby's at the Grove, thus taking some of the wind from Bing's sails.

The Rhythm Boys weren't present at the audition, but Loyce would soon meet them and would marry Harry Barris within the year. The full Arnheim orchestra accompanied Loyce for the audition. Frank asked her to sing two Barris tunes, "Wrap Your Troubles In Dreams" and "I Surrender, Dear." After she sang them, Frank was ready to sign her immediately, but she was a slight woman with a build like one of today's high-fashion models, and that worried Abe Frank. "Do you think you're strong enough to do these late-night jobs?" he asked her. "You're such a skinny little thing." When Loyce assured him that she was stronger than she looked, they got down to talking business.

"I didn't even know how much to ask for," Loyce told us. "I was making $50 a week at KFWB, and that was a fortune to me, but Arthur Freed (the producer who had backed the Morrissey show and whom Loyce had consulted when Abe had asked her to audition) told me to ask for $150. I told him that I couldn't, that I didn't have nerve enough to ask for so much, but he convinced me that I should, so I did. And Abe hired me at $150 a week."

Loyce opened at the Grove on Easter Sunday night, April 5, 1931, and The Rhythm Boys were there. Her audition stage fright was nothing compared to her opening-night jitters. Until that time, for the most part, she had been an unseen radio vocalist, and now she had to sing before an audience of hundreds. Bing was beside her just before it came time for her to go on, and she nervously commented to him that she didn't know what to do with her hands.

"Bing did a sweet thing that night," Loyce said. "He said, 'Don't worry about it. I'll hold your hand,' and he accompanied me to the mike, held my hand, and sang half a chorus with me to get me started. I'll never forget that. But that was our only close companionship; after that, he hardly ever spoke to me. He didn't speak to anyone, particularly. He went his own way. That's the way he was."

Bing had already, in effect, withdrawn his friendship from Al Rinker. "There was no well-defined break," Al told us, "no point at which it was evident that our close friendship had ended. As friends, we just started drifting apart. He had his friends and, of course, I had mine. He had gotten very popular as a soloist and was on his way up."

What the others didn't know, of course, was that Bing was playing a waiting game and couldn't care less about the Grove or the people associated with it. A small announcement in *The Hollywood Reporter* on June 16, 1931, signaled that the time for Bing to put his plan into operation was growing near:

BING CROSBY CLICK
MAY LEAD TO MORE SENNETTS

Mack Sennett's enthusiasm over Bing Crosby's initial two-reeler comedy, tentatively titled *I Surrender, Dear,* has caused the producer to plan a series of three or four shorts in which the actor-singer will star. . . .

So Bing had a new title: actor-singer. But his big break came when the film was reviewed. The following is a review from the June 25, 1931, issue of *The Hollywood Reporter:*

NEW SENNETT SHORTS
CLICK IN BIG STYLE

A winner! The tremendous popularity of Bing Crosby would have been sufficient to insure the success of his first short for Sennett, but in addition to his unquestioned "draw," *I Surrender, Dear* is packed full of laughs, love interest and everything it takes in the way of entertainment values. Exhibs can depend on it to bring in the crowds and keep them satisfied if the rest of the program is weak.

Bing gets ample opportunity to croon his well-known song from which the picture takes its name, as he plays himself in the picture. He meets a girl and falls in love with her; the rest of the picture is devoted to his efforts to know her better and win her from her jealous fiancé.

The gags are clever and well put over. Direction and photography excellent.

The entire cast does fine work. Arthur Stone, as Bing's pal, is especially good.

Though the review smacks of public-relations influence with respect to its references to Bing's "tremendous popularity" and "unquestioned 'draw'" (such reviews are presumed to be written for exhibitors and other industry people nationwide, not just locally, and Bing was neither tremendously popular nor an unquestioned draw outside Los Angeles at the time), it was otherwise right on target. Bing is excellent in the film, and *I Surrender, Dear* holds up well and is genuinely funny and entertaining even by today's standards. The film is particularly noteworthy with respect to Bing's career for three reasons:

First, the film could have been titled *The Road to I Surrender, Dear,* for it's the prototype of all the *Road* pictures that Bing and Bob Hope were to initiate at Paramount nine years later. The character that Arthur Stone played against Bing's flippant, happy-go-lucky casual characterization would be considerably broadened by Hope, of course, and Hope would bring his unique talent to bear on it, but one can't view the film today without realizing immediately that it was the sire of all those to follow.

Second, the character that Bing fashioned for *I Surrender, Dear* is the one he continued to play for the rest of his life; it's the screen image that moviegoers identified with him and that most of us mistook for the real Bing Crosby. Though he was billed as himself, he was, in fact, playing a character part, but Bing was shrewd enough to "trademark" a winning formula when he saw one—particularly when reviewers and moviegoers instantly identified with and accepted the character on screen. To some extent, the screen image was a self-parody of the drunken Bing Crosby. Bing was a much nicer, wittier, funnier, and more charming man when he was drinking than when he was sober. Alcohol lessened his severe emotional restraint to a degree. Somehow he managed to portray a semblance of that part of his character on screen, and it was a brilliant characterization and proof to anyone who knew the real Bing Crosby that, despite what some critics said of his acting, he was one of the best character actors ever to step before a movie or television camera. This point can't be brought home more tellingly than by a viewing of his early, "serious" films, such as the 1935 release *Mississippi*, which is frequently rerun on television. It was Bing's first "costume" picture, and he had not yet learned to transpose his screen character to the more restrictively plotted format; then, too, the Paramount writers had yet to realize the necessity of tailoring their scripts to Bing's image. *Mississippi* has its moments, as with Bing's scenes with W. C. Fields (which, obviously, require no emotional depth), but overall, his performance is wooden, and one can see traces of the real Bing Crosby, very much out of his element and uncomfortable.

Finally, his experience with Mack Sennett and *I Surrender, Dear* convinced him that he could, indeed, make it as a single, and this conviction, together with the knowledge of promising career developments in the East on his behalf, put him in position to carry off a villainous scenario.

We stated earlier that Bing wouldn't strike out on his

own without help and that his conditions for attempting it seemed impossible to meet. But Bing finally found the man who could help him. His name was Roger Marchetti, a name that won't be found in the family biography or in Bing's autobiography or in the several biographies of Bing Crosby because, to borrow from Joseph Heller again, the Crosbys eventually disappeared him.

According to Bing, and to Ted and Larry, who got their version of Bing's story from him, and to the several biographers who, having no reason to disbelieve him, perpetuated the story, the following sequence of events took place and resulted in Bing's rise to stardom: (1) The Rhythm Boys walked out on their contract with Abe Frank because Frank had refused to give them bonuses and raises as he had promised; (2) Frank retaliated by reporting The Rhythm Boys to the union, which resulted in their being blacklisted; (3) Everett sent a copy of Bing's "I Surrender, Dear" recording to both NBC and CBS radio and got favorable responses and invitations to New York for auditions; (4) Everett sold his car in order to raise the money needed to get himself and Bing (and their wives) back to New York for the auditions, for Bing had signed a personal-management contract with Everett because Ev had shown such initiative; (5) Everett negotiated with CBS in New York and emerged with the best-paying contract ever received to that date by an unsponsored radio soloist, a contract that launched Bing's singing career; (6) Bing missed his network debut on opening night and the following night because (there are two official Crosby versions) either his voice gave out from overuse, which resulted in nodes forming on his vocal chords, or his union blacklisting caught up with him; (7) Everett negotiated a contract with Paramount Publix for a twenty-week engagement at New York City's Paramount Theatre at up to $4,000 a week; and (8) Everett negotiated a contract for a starring role in the Paramount Pictures feature film *The Big Broadcast of 1932*, which resulted in

169

a three-picture deal with Paramount that launched his film career.

The above sequence of events represents revisionist biographical history fashioned by Bing and his organization and bears as little resemblance to the truth as did the official Crosby characterization of Dixie Lee Crosby. To be blunt, Bing's version of his rise to fame, which he told in his own book and retold to the authors of three authorized biographies of him, is a pack of lies. It's no wonder that he waxed evasive and self-effacing when pressed for specifics about his early career by interviewers like David Frost and Barbara Walters toward the end of his life.

What actually happened is that Bing double-crossed his way to the top, riding roughshod over people to do so. Then, having reached his goal, he covered his trail like a thief in the night by conjuring up a story of luck and of miraculous metamorphosis: Everett's overnight emergence from truck salesman to brilliant show-biz manager. Bing's machinations went deeply against the grain by his moral upbringing and religious training; it was a small wonder that he rarely passed a church thereafter without stopping in and bowing a pious head. It's unfortunate that he offered no atonement toward the people he stepped on.

That Everett Crosby could make the transition from truck salesman to ingenious personal artist's manager, guiding his brother through the complexities of the stage, movie, and radio business and the convolutions of legal contractual intricacies, is simply absurd. And people in the industry knew it. Such knowledgeable maneuvering requires contacts, training, and years of experience. Everett Crosby had neither the background nor the aptitude for it. The man who did everything that Everett was credited with was Roger Marchetti.

There were three Marchetti brothers in Los Angeles—Roger, Joseph, and Milo—and Bing eventually knew them all. Roger and Joseph were attorneys (Joseph, retired at this writing, was a municipal and superior court judge for thirty-five years). Milo, now retired also, was a business entrepreneur. All were extraordinarily successful, and all were well known in the highest of social, financial, and business circles. Milo, whom we mentioned earlier, not only owned Marchetti's restaurant but several others as well. He also owned a company that built bungalows and dressing rooms for movie studios on location shootings and that catered meals for the casts (he did many of DeMille's pictures, including *The Good Earth*, for which his company provided shelter for 5,000 extras and served them three meals a day). Among Milo's other business interests was his own talent agency. The Marchetti brothers also owned half of the Wilshire National Bank.

Roger Marchetti's interests weren't as diversified as brother Milo's. Roger was an attorney, not an agent, and while he represented clients like Mario and Amadeo Giannini, who founded in 1904 what is today the Bank of America, he also had dozens of entertainment-industry clients such as Irving Thalberg (one of the two men who built MGM), producer Myron Selznick, and the like. It was Roger Marchetti who brought Sir Alexander Korda from England to MGM. Such clients gave him a natural interest in and knowledge of all facets of show business, and there was hardly anyone in the entertainment industry, from coast to coast, whom Roger Marchetti didn't know personally.

It's not clear exactly when Marchetti began guiding Bing Crosby to stardom. If one considers that when Marchetti did enter the picture, Bing Crosby had a reputation as a drinker and an irresponsible performer, that he had been turned down by all the motion-picture companies that he approached, that he was well known only around Hollywood, that Everett couldn't even get him work on a local radio station, and that, when he married Dixie just a few months earlier, the marriage was reported only because Dixie was in the industry, one wonders about Mack Sennett's astonishing offer to star him in a film under his own name. We don't wish to detract from Sennett's genius for discovering and developing talent, but we question why he would have taken a chance and made such an offer to a reputedly drunken, irresponsible unknown. Maybe he did. But there are two other factors that make one wonder.

Roger Marchetti knew Mack Sennett well, and we'll document later that Marchetti spent a considerable amount of his own money to promote Bing. Sennett approached Bing in March of 1931, the same month that Bing—who couldn't get a $25-a-week radio job—was offered and signed a solo artist contract with Brunswick records. It's purely speculative on our part, but this sudden turn of good fortune seems ample evidence to justify raising the possibility that even as early as March of 1931, the influential Mr. Marchetti may have already been working on Bing's behalf.

What is not speculative is that Marchetti was making contracts and initiating meetings in the East on Bing's behalf by June of 1931. But from what we've learned of Marchetti, we doubt that he knew how Bing planned to get out of his Grove contract, for Bing's unconscionable action made Marchetti's job far more difficult. It's hard enough to "sell" a client who has a bad reputation—and the worst reputation one can have in the entertainment industry is uncontrollable drunkenness and a penchant for missing performances. And such reputations travel on the coast-to-coast show-business grapevine with the speed of light. It's harder still to get an institution like the then Columbia Broadcasting System to offer a contract to a performer who's available because he walked out of his previous contract and was blacklisted for doing so.

Bing may have told Marchetti (and perhaps he believed) that he could talk his way out of his contract with Abe Frank, just as he had talked his way out of the Whiteman contract. Bing's conduct at the Grove was certainly bad enough to make any club manager glad to be rid of him. But Bing hadn't been as buddy-buddy with Frank as he had been with Whiteman—far from it. And Abe Frank needed Bing and The Rhythm Boys far more than Whiteman had needed them. Consequently, Bing engineered an odious plan that tripped off the true sequence of events that led to his rise to stardom.

Bing wanted out of the Cocoanut Grove and out of the trio, but whether he ever approached Abe Frank on the subject or whether, knowing that Frank wouldn't let him out of his contract, Bing simply made demands of him that would justify—in Bing's mind—his walking out if Frank didn't meet them, we don't know. The evidence points to the latter.

Al Rinker recalled one confrontation between them shortly before the boys walked out of the Grove. "Bing and Abe had a big argument," Al told us. "I don't remember exactly what it was. Either Bing had borrowed money from Frank, or he wanted more money. I don't know. But there was a feud going on between them, and it seemed that they couldn't iron it out. All I know is that there was a big argument and that it was over money."

Ultimately Bing decided to break the contract by walking out, but he didn't want to walk alone, for to have done so would have meant assuming sole responsibility for his action, and that wasn't Bing's style. It's possible that he may have felt that if all three of them walked out together, perhaps the group would be blacklisted by the union and not necessarily the individual members of it. Or maybe he felt that at least all three of them would look bad, and not just himself. But for whatever reason, he wanted Al and Harry to join him, and he couldn't very well say to them, "I want to leave the trio and break the contract with the Grove, so I want you guys to walk with me and take some of the heat and get blacklisted." Instead, he took an insidious tack.

Bing met with Harry Barris and told him that the trio had no future, and that they could do better outside the Grove. There was movie work, for one thing—a Sennett series in the offing, and Bing had already used two Barris songs in his first Sennett film. Bing told him that he wanted to walk out of the Grove contract, and that he wanted Harry to join him. Harry agreed. It's not known whether Bing mentioned Al to Harry, but it is known that Harry assumed that the three of them would work together, but not as a trio.

Then Bing went to Al and implied that he and Harry had decided to walk out, thereby forcing Abe Frank to give all of them more money or at least give Bing more money for his solo work. Rinker agreed to go along with them; actually, Al had little choice in the matter.

So the stage was set. Harry knew that it was the end of The Rhythm Boys but assumed that they, as pals, were going on to better things. Al didn't know that the trio was breaking up and thought that the move was a part of Bing's plan to get himself—and them—a better deal with Abe Frank. Bing told them both that he would contact them, or at least that was implicit in his talks with them.

The following Sunday afternoon, at the Grove's Tea Dance, Loyce, who had been at the Grove only about eight weeks and didn't know exactly what was going on, overheard Bing say to Al and Harry, "Tomorrow we walk." The following day was a Monday, when the Grove was dark, so Bing's signal to the boys was that they wouldn't return to the Grove Tuesday.

"There had been a lot of tension," Loyce told us, "so I wasn't really surprised to hear Bing talking of their walking out. I didn't know whether they were walking for good or not. It wasn't until months later, after I'd married Harry, that I learned what Bing had done."

What Bing had done was double-cross both Al and Harry, for he never contacted either of them. He walked out of the Grove Sunday, and they didn't see him again. He couldn't even be found, for no one knew where he went. He wasn't home. He didn't go to Lakeside. He wasn't seen at any of his usual haunts.

We learned while interviewing Maybeth Carpenter why Bing couldn't be found. Maybeth was with Bing and Dixie at the time, fishing off the San Clemente Islands aboard Mack Sennett's boat, which Sennett had loaned Bing for the occasion. Naturally Bing had said nothing to Maybeth about leaving The Cocoanut Grove, but when he made no effort to get back to Los Angeles on Tuesday, she realized that something was happening.

Without contacting Al or Harry, Bing returned to Educational Studios and filmed *One More Chance*, directed by Mack Sennett, *Dream House*, directed by Del Lord, and *Billboard Girl*, also directed by Sennett. He finished them in time to leave for New York. Bing and Dixie and Everett and Naomie would all make the trip together.

In the family biography, Ted and Larry Crosby describe the train trip back East. In their last chapter, titled "Pennies from Heaven," they describe how Bing, apparently in a very thankful mood, went to the observation car before retiring on the first night and wrote a letter to Kate, telling her of his plans and asking for her prayers. Then he went out on the open platform, sat down on a folding chair, put his feet up on the railing, and, to the rhythm of the wheels on the track, sang "I Surrender, Dear."

How touching Harry Barris would have found the scene.

Roger Marchetti advanced the money for their trip back and for their three-week stay before the contracts he had negotiated were finally ready and signed. Everett and his wife had gone along because, in the interim, Bing had signed a ten-percent personal-management contract with Everett, and Ev's truck-selling days were over. The contract with his brother represented yet another trick Bing had up his sleeve.

The first result of their New York trip was announced in the trade papers. The following, in its entirety, is from the August 25, 1931, issue of *The Hollywood Reporter*:

BING CROSBY GOES COLUMBIA NETWORK

New York—Roger Marchetti has just closed a contract with Columbia Broadcasting Company for Bing Crosby. Contract calls for the largest pay check for any sustaining (unsponsored program) artist doing radio work. In order to accomplish this, the Crosby union difficulties have been satisfactorily adjusted.

Shortly thereafter, the publisher and founder of *The Hollywood Reporter*, W. R. "Billy" Wilkerson, printed the following item in his "Tradeviews" column:

> Bing Crosby grabbed himself a nice chunk in his new Paramount-Publix ticket. He gets 20 weeks in Publix theaters at $4,000 a week, plus lead in the Wild Waves picture [later retitled *The Big Broadcast of 1932*] for $35,000. Page Roger Marchetti.

So much for Bing's union problems—solved within eight weeks of his walkout. So much also for Everett Crosby's brilliant management and contract negotiations. But Bing wasn't finished. Less than a year later, he put the last double-cross in the triangle, clearing the way for himself, through brother Everett, to build a personal empire, and necessitating "disappearing" Roger Marchetti so that the Bing legend could be fashioned: the house that Crosby built. The sting was reported in another Wilkerson column, "The Low Down," (no pun intended; the column existed before this item was printed) in *The Hollywood Reporter*:

> Roger Marchetti dug Bing Crosby out of the Ambassador, fought his union battles through to victory, took him to New York and secured one of the best salaries a crooner ever received for broadcasting. Then his troubles began, with Marchetti finally selling out his interest to the crooner himself. Now the crooner is telling the world that he is sick of "paying 20 percent" to the man who made most of his success possible.

Marchetti sold all interest in Bing Crosby to Bing for about $40,000. People throughout the industry said that he shouldn't have done it. Bing, even then, was showing unlimited potential. Marchetti knew that. But Marchetti was wealthy and didn't need the money. And what was even more important to him, he didn't need the aggravation. Roger Marchetti had learned firsthand what other executives in various branches of the entertainment industry told us over and over again off the record: "Ask anyone who ever did business with them (Bing, Everett, and Larry). Everybody knew. They simply couldn't be trusted." But all knew, too, that Everett and Larry did only what Bing told them to do and were paid to take any heat generated by their actions. Bing was always blameless.

Everett's wasn't the only personal-management contract that Bing signed. In June of 1932, the late Edward Small, an agent who later turned film producer, filed suit in New York City against Bing for $20,000, claiming that amount was owed him under a personal-management contract that Bing had signed with him in June of 1930.

Roger Marchetti knew what he was doing when he shook Bing Crosby from his line.

One is reminded again of Bob Crosby's extraordinarily diplomatic statement about his jealous brother Bing's wanting him to stand on his own two feet and never letting him feel that he had a crutch. Bing managed to step on everybody's two feet but his own on the way to the top. And as for crutches, he surrounded himself with them, always. Most of them weren't as fortunate as Roger Marchetti; the two that Bing had literally abandoned in California were, for all Bing knew or cared, jobless and perhaps unable to get work because of their blacklisting.

Part Six:

Solo Artist

CHAPTER TWELVE

The ones who inflict such "little murders" are
the hollowest of all.

When more than a week passed with no word from Bing, Al Rinker knew what had happened. "I wasn't happy about the situation," Al told us, "but I wasn't shocked by it, either. I had come to know Bing Crosby pretty well in those last few months at the Grove. Pretty well. This wasn't the same guy I had come down from Spokane with nearly six years earlier. I saw the gradual change in him; a coldness emerged that wasn't evident before. I'm not saying that I understood him. I didn't. But I got to know him well enough in those last days to know that he had the *capacity* to do what he did. So I was neither shocked nor bewildered—puzzled, yes.

"I had seen what was happening at the Grove: Bing's rising popularity as a solo artist and Harry's flowering as a songwriter, and I knew that our days as a trio were numbered. When I look back on it now, I'm rather surprised at how philosophically I took it. But I was young (Al was 23), the times had been great, and the experience was invaluable for a guy as young as I was. Besides, I had things that I wanted to do, too. So it wasn't as rough on me as it was on Harry. I felt really sorry for Harry when I learned how he had taken the news. Harry was a nice fellow, and a very talented one. You don't write songs like he did—standards—without great talent."

As strange as it may seem under the circumstances, Al and Harry made no effort to get in touch with one another after the walkout. Like everyone else in town, both got news of Bing's activities through mutual friends long before it was reported in the trade papers. Gossip is by far the fastest news medium in Hollywood circles. "It would have been pointless for us to get together at the time," Rinker said. "It was over, and we both knew it. Years later, when we chanced to meet on an occasion or two, we discussed the walkout. Harry couldn't get over what Bing had done."

Apparently neither of them tried to get in touch with Bing at the time, either, and for the same reason. Loyce Whiteman Hubbard doesn't know positively whether Harry tried, but she doubts it. "I think Harry was too crushed and too proud to have done so," she told us. Al Rinker's reaction was similar: "As I said, I got to know Bing pretty well in those last days, and I had my pride, too. He knew how to find us both, had he wanted to."

Al Rinker took the opportunity to rest—his first vacation from performing in six years— during the first couple of weeks after the Grove episode. He spent most of his time playing golf and deciding what he was going to do next. It was from mutual friends of Bing and Al's at Lakeside that Al learned of Bing's activities, confirming what he already knew—that Bing wouldn't be back in touch with them. Bing, who usually haunted Lakeside, didn't go near the course until Al left town, which wasn't long afterward. Al went to New York, where he developed a vaudeville act with a young female singer;

their act was immediately signed for a forty-week tour of the East and Midwest.

In the meantime, Harry Barris hadn't fared so well. No one knows when Harry first learned of Bing's deceit, but the news so stunned him that he suffered a nervous breakdown. His mother had moved from Denver to Hollywood, and Harry was living with her at the time. She did what she could in an effort to pull him from his depression, but to no avail. Harry sank deeper into a state of withdrawal each day. At first he drank—as he always did—but eventually he stopped doing even that. He took to his bed, becoming more and more uncommunicative, and then, finally, physically ill. His mother attended to his needs around the clock and coaxed him to take nourishment occasionally. There was little more that she could do. Harry's spirit was completely broken.

Harry's reaction was so extreme, so ravaging to him both physically and mentally, that some exposition is called for here to preclude the possibility of interpreting the reaction as melodramatic or as a sign of weakness on Harry's part. Harry Barris wasn't a spiritually weak man. It's true that he was hounded—to his death—by whatever furies drive people to seek solace in the bottle; life may have presented more of a threat to him than it does to most of us. But anyone who knew him knew that he was intensely serious about his work and confident about his professional ability. His work was his life, and that's exactly where Bing's devastating blow fell. On a personal level, Bing's action represented to Harry, as it did to Al, a betrayal of their friendship and trust. But professionally, Harry had far more to lose than did Al Rinker by Bing's action.

With the advent of recorded sound, singers have quite literally rocketed from obscurity to stardom on the popularity of a single song, often within weeks, or even days. Mildred Bailey's hit with "Ol' Rockin' Chair's Got Me" is a good example. The song not only brought Mildred to the public's attention and made her famous, but, as Matty Malneck pointed out, it rekindled public interest once more in the entire Whiteman orchestra. Such is the power of the right song at the right time.

It naturally follows that writers of popular songs seek out singing stars to promote their songs and, in turn, are themselves much sought after by singers once they've been established as writers of hit songs. Such a symbiotic relationship developed between Bing and Harry Barris almost from the day Matty Malneck introduced them to one another in 1927.

The importance of Harry's songs to Bing Crosby's career is inestimable. Bing's marvelous voice, his public personality, and his development of a unique singing style almost discounts an argument such as: had it not been for Harry's songs (particularly "I Surrender, Dear") the right doors might never have opened to Crosby at the right time. Such a postulation would be trifling were it not for the fact that timing—being in the right place at the right time—is so vitally important in show business, and that, as we stated earlier, Crosby was a most unlikely candidate for stardom.

One can reject this view out of hand, but one can't reject the fact that, at the very least, Bing Crosby owed Harry Barris a debt of gratitude. Bing established himself as a solo artist and gained a degree of local fame by singing songs that the Grove patrons wanted to hear, and Harry Barris's numbers were very popular with them. Two out of the three songs sung by Bing in his hit Sennett comedy were Barris numbers. It was a *musical* comedy, and Harry's songs certainly contributed to its success. Finally, it was Harry's "I Surrender, Dear" that not only gave Bing his first recording as a solo artist that even remotely resembled a hit and that won him attention as a singer, but also won for him an audition with CBS Radio, which, indeed, launched him nationally as a solo artist.

Bing was no stranger to the symbiotic singer-songwriter relationship. Indeed, once he became famous, he counted songwriters among his closest friends.

And with due respect to all of them, none did more for Bing Crosby's career than Harry Barris. With the psychological edge of a symbiotic relationship with Bing—an edge that is extraordinarily beneficial to the creative process—Harry would have reached even greater heights; there's no doubt about it. But Harry had the misfortune of being a party to Bing's rise to stardom, and he was dispatched accordingly. Had Harry come into Bing's life *after* Bing was famous, so that, in effect, Bing would have been doing Harry a favor by singing one of his songs, Harry would have been accepted into the fold. But Harry helped Bing, and thus the symbiotic relationship was withdrawn with his friendship. The loss of this professional relationship when it was within his grasp reduced a proud and talented man to a groveling, fetuslike being. One rises and regains total dignity from such a position only in the world of fiction. Harry would get to his feet, of course, but, as Loyce Whiteman Hubbard told us, "He was never ever quite the same again." There would be a hollowness in him thereafter, and the ones who inflict such "little murders" are the hollowest of all.

Abe Frank came to Harry's rescue. Frank was furious at the walkout, but he wasn't stupid. If Bing thought that the union heat would be equally distributed among The Rhythm Boys, he was wrong. Frank surmised immediately who stood to profit most by breaking the Grove contract and filed a breach-of-contract complaint with the union against the profiteer: Bing Crosby. As nearly as we can determine, neither Al nor Harry was named in the complaint. And what Frank did for Barris makes it obvious that he held no rancor for the walkout victims.

Harry had lain in bed in a state of withdrawal for two weeks when word of his condition reached the Grove. Loyce remembers that the information was communicated somehow through philanthropist Cybil Brand, who was a friend of Harry's and who apparently learned of Harry's illness from his mother. Word eventually got to Loyce, who had been dating Harry occasionally but who hadn't seen him since the walkout. Loyce was alarmed when she heard the news about Harry, and she told Abe Frank about his condition. Abe was incensed by the news, and after muttering a few oaths and attaching numerous uncomplimentary adjectives to Bing's name, he said to Loyce, "Take a big bunch of flowers over to Harry, and tell him that I said he has a place here and that I want him to come back to work just as soon as he's able."

A week or so later, Harry was back at the Cocoanut Grove. But it was quite a different Harry from the one who had left. "He was never quite the same man after that," Loyce told us. "The cocky brashness that audiences found so entertaining eventually returned, but there was less confidence behind it, more show-acting. He used to say to me, 'If they [the patrons] ever find me out, I'm a goner,' and he was only half-joking. It was more an act, now, than a state of mind."

Loyce also said that for a long time, hearing a Crosby record or even the mention of his name affected Harry like a wound reopened. Naturally, people associated Bing with Harry and, not knowing the truth behind The Rhythm Boys' separation, they'd inevitably bring up Bing's name or relate some anecdote or bit of gossip about him, thinking that Harry would be interested or entertained by it. And Harry would become depressed. Eventually, of course, he became somewhat desensitized, but it took a long time.

Harry began working with Loyce, just as he had worked with Bing, when he returned to the Grove. Many theorized that he was trying to create with Loyce the relationship he had lost with Bing. And this is probably so. Loyce soloed on all the old songs, and Harry wrote new ones for her to introduce. They also worked up a duo, which was quite popular with the patrons.

Abe Frank, meanwhile, was juggling as best he could in an effort to fill the void left by Bing Crosby and The Rhythm Boys, particularly Bing. For all the aggravation Bing had wrought, he had packed them in at the Grove and had left the patrons with a taste for his singing style

that the patrons wanted to hear, Crosby or not. Jimmy
Grier, Gus Arnheim's arranger, had left Arnheim and
had formed his own band. And when Arnheim left the
Grove, Abe hired Grier's new band to replace him; at
least, the band sound would be the same. Abe also
added popular tenor Donald Novis to the show, as well
as a new trio, The Ambassadors (young Jack Smith,
who would eventually go out on his own as a soloist
and who later became the host of the popular television
program "You Asked for It," was a member of the
trio). And though Loyce Whiteman and Donald Novis
were very popular and kept the patrons happy, according to Kenny Allen in the interview conducted by Vern
Taylor, Abe Frank did everything imaginable to dupli-
cate the Crosby sound. "His [Crosby's] arrangements
were used by several of the singers," Allen said, "even
some of the girls." Allen also said that Abe brought in a
singer named Dick Webster, who tried, rather unsuccessfully, to imitate Bing and that Harry Barris, "who
was liked for his fast or cute stuff, even tried on some
of Bing's slower hits."

As persona non grata as Bing was at the Grove, and
as reviled as he was for his callous action, his incomparable talent prevailed. The thought of Harry Barris imi-
tating him at a time when the mere mention of Bing's
name made him recoil by reflex isn't at all incongruous.
Whatever Bing did—to himself and to others—was totally eclipsed by his talent.

Harry worked hard at the Grove, and the work was
therapeutic for him. He continued dating Loyce Whiteman, and after a few months, he proposed to her and
she accepted. Abe Frank was upset at this turn of
events. He took Loyce aside and offered her a bit of
fatherly advice. Frank liked Harry Barris, but he was
convinced that Harry wasn't good enough for Loyce.
Loyce had never been married and hadn't really been
around. Harry was the opposite. Frank told her that the
marriage could come to no good, that Harry drank too
much and that he was burning himself out by living the
fast life. Harry had already been married and divorced,

and he had a daughter, Zelle, by his first wife. Frank thought that Loyce deserved, and needed, someone more stable. Loyce was appreciative of Abe's concern, but, as usually happens in such matters, she didn't take his advice. The marriage was scheduled for November 22, 1931.

The news of Bing's first national radio show had been announced in the trade papers, and on the night that Bing finally broadcast his first show—September 2, 1931—Harry and Loyce got together to hear it. Harry could hardly contain himself; he knew that Bing would use "I Surrender, Dear" as his theme song; to Harry's way of thinking, it would compensate in part for what Bing had done and it would most certainly give Harry's career and deflated ego a boost. Bing was announced, and Harry gave the radio his undivided attention. Bing opened with his theme song: "Where the Blue of the Night Meets the Gold of the Day," and, according to Loyce, Harry cried like a baby; it was a clear signal that there'd be no help from Bing's quarter so far as Harry was concerned. Until then, he had still entertained hope. Bing's new theme song was written by Roy Turk and Fred Ahlert. It's claimed that Bing wrote the verse to it, which was tacked on after the song was written, but the writing credits on the sheet music read: Bing Crosby, Roy Turk, and Fred E. Ahlert. Ironically, as Laurence Zwisohn points out in his book *Bing Crosby, a Lifetime of Music* (containing the only complete discography of Bing's 1,600 recordings), Russ Columbo, Bing's chief rival at the time, recorded the song five days before Bing did.

Although Abe Frank was against Loyce and Harry's marriage, he pulled out all stops once Loyce had made her decision. The wedding and reception took place at the Cocoanut Grove, with the full Jimmy Grier orchestra playing and with all food and drink catered by the Ambassador Hotel. Abe provided and paid for everything. Then, as his wedding gift, Abe sent the couple on a honeymoon to San Francisco, where he not only

186

booked them into the Mark Hopkins Hotel but chartered a private plane to take them there.

Al Rinker's vaudeville act was booked into New York City at about the time Harry and Loyce were honeymooning in San Francisco. Al was staying at the Avon Hotel, a short distance from the Warwick, where Bing and Dixie were staying temporarily until Bing's radio show gained a sponsor and Bing was booked into the Paramount Theatre. Al, who at this writing still doesn't know the details of Bing's machinations, decided to let bygones be bygones, and telephoned Bing.

"I called him early one evening," Al said, "and suggested that we get together later on for dinner. Bing said it would be a good idea, and we talked briefly about what each of us had done since The Rhythm Boys broke up. He was casual and talkative to a point, and he told me that he'd get back to me a little bit later.

"About an hour later, I received a call from Tommy Dorsey, who informed me that Bing couldn't make it that night. I knew Dorsey. He was a very nice person, and I knew that Bing had delegated to him the chore of turning down my dinner invitation. It was typical of Bing. He never would face a problem squarely. He was an enigma if there ever was one. But from the tone of his voice when we first talked—a little guarded, hesitant—I can't say that I was very surprised when Tommy gave me the news. Bing just didn't have the decency and courage to call me back himself. That's the way he was."

In light of what Bing had done to his unsuspecting Spokane buddy, it's understandable that he didn't want to face him eye-to-eye across a dinner table. And while we agree with Al Rinker that Bing Crosby was as enigmatic a person as one is likely to encounter, there was nothing enigmatic about his actions that evening. Bing was guilt-ridden from intrigues that Rinker wasn't even aware had occurred. Al was in town for a while longer, but he didn't bother to call Bing back. Al would neither see nor talk to Bing again for twelve years.

187

Bing wasn't quite so evasive with Harry Barris. In May of 1932, toward the end of Bing's Paramount run and five months after he had rejected Al's dinner invitation, Harry and Loyce had finished their contract at the Grove and were successfully touring theaters across the country as a duo. When they arrived in New York City, they checked into a very plush suite at the Warwick, where most of the top musicians and singers stayed while they were in New York. The fraternity of musicians is a close one, so it wasn't long before Bing and Dixie, who had since moved to more permanent quarters at the Essex House, heard that Harry and Loyce were in town and dropped by the Warwick to see them.

One assumes that either Bing felt less guilty about dumping Harry than he had about dumping his hometown buddy, or that Dixie insisted that Bing take her to see them. The latter is probably the case, for Dixie had met Harry and liked him, and she had not yet met Loyce. She wasn't the kind of woman to let friends come to town without visiting them; then, too, she always acted as Bing's social conscience, often prodding him to do the proper thing, though Bing had little regard for such amenities.

Whatever the case, Bing and Dixie arrived at the Barrises' suite one day, unannounced. Loyce doesn't recall much about the visit except that it was her first meeting with Dixie, and that Dixie was friendly and sweet. What does stand out in her mind is Bing's presence. She hadn't seen him since the boys walked out of the Grove. Bing was quiet; he didn't say much, but he studied their suite closely and then finally said, "I can't see how you can afford to live like this." The remark impressed Loyce because she was a little miffed at Bing's condescending tone. The Depression had deepened by 1932, but everyone in the business knew from the trade papers that Bing was making more than five thousand dollars a week by then. It was a curious remark, as though Bing couldn't believe that Harry could do so well without him, as though he had expected to find Harry in the Warwick's cheapest room.

Considering the shape Bing had left Harry in, it *was* a marvelous recovery. Much of it was owing to Loyce, not only for the moral support and stability she gave him, but for her stage work. She was a fine and popular singer, and her soloing and duo teamwork with Harry made them a popular act. It wasn't until Harry's drinking got out of hand that they fell on much harder times. But that was years away, and when it happened, Bing didn't drop in to visit them.

CHAPTER THIRTEEN

. . . Crosby has begun to fade.

—*The Hollywood Reporter,* 1931

It took several weeks for Roger Marchetti to settle the legal problems that Bing had created for himself by walking out of the Grove. There was no problem with CBS. The network's president, William Paley, was very enthusiastic about Bing's singing, which accounted, in part, for Marchetti's getting for Bing an unheard-of $600 a week to do a fifteen-minute nightly radio show, for which the network had yet to find a sponsor. The snag was that Bing's network contract was contingent upon Marchetti's clearing up Bing's status with the American Federation of Musicians (AFM), and neither Bing nor Abe Frank was making the task an easy one.

When Abe Frank reported Bing's breach of contract, the AFM placed Bing on its "unfair" list, which meant that even though Bing wasn't a member of the union, until some restitution was made for the breach (usually by the offender paying a fine to the AFM and making a satisfactory settlement with the person to whom the offender was under contract), the offender could not perform with union musicians.

Bing is said to have gotten around his union problems on the Sennett films subsequent to leaving the

Grove by having the backgrounds to his songs recorded and then singing with the records rather than with a live orchestra. But he couldn't get away with that on network radio.

After the grievance had been arbitrated, Marchetti paid the union fine for Bing, but he ran into a tough negotiator in Abe Frank and a stubborn client in Bing Crosby. Bing alleges in his book that after leaving the Grove, he went to see Frank on at least two occasions in an attempt to settle their differences, but that they couldn't reach a settlement. Bing alludes to his own stubbornness as the primary cause of his failure to settle the dispute, but offers no specifics regarding his stubbornness. The official Crosby story was always that The Rhythm Boys walked out of their contract because Abe Frank had promised bonuses and raises and had never made good his promise. But, in fact, the boys had a clear-cut contract with the Grove that contained no such promises or provisions, and neither Al nor Harry was a party to such alleged discussions with Abe Frank or knew anything of the alleged promises. The boys were definitely underpaid at the Grove, but one gets the impression from talking to Al Rinker and Loyce Whiteman Hubbard that their attendance record hardly merited rewards from Abe Frank. Al Rinker's recollections are vague regarding such specifics, but when we asked Loyce about the boys' reputation for being, in the radio station manager's words, "just another drunken trio," she told us that she never knew Al Rinker to be a drinker. "He was always a quiet boy," she said, "and he just stayed in the background." Loyce also said that both Bing and Harry drank too much, but that drinking never interfered with Harry's work in those days. "Harry got peppier when he drank," she said, "but it seemed to work the opposite with Bing. They missed work a lot."

Although none was a party to the negotiations between Abe Frank and Bing, numerous interviewees told us that at first, Abe told Bing that the only way he could get off the unfair list was by returning to the

Grove and honoring his contract. But when Bing made it clear that he had no intention of returning, Abe is alleged to have demanded a considerable cash settlement and, as Bing held out, not wanting to pay anything, Abe is said to have raised his settlement demands. Perhaps it was Bing's refusal to make an early cash settlement that he was alluding to when he said later that he had been stubborn with Abe Frank. As it turned out, Marchetti is said to have paid a very substantial amount to Frank for "damages." Frank had gone to considerable trouble and expense to fill the void left by Bing at the Grove. Beyond this, Loyce Whiteman Hubbard says that Abe was furious with Bing for what he had done to Al and Harry. And many surmised that this, along with Bing's professed innocence and refusal to make a cash settlement, drove Abe Frank's settlement price into the high five-figure area.

It's ironic that just weeks after the settlement, Abe Frank gave one of the most lavish of West Coast weddings at the Cocoanut Grove for Harry Barris and Loyce. There's little doubt that Mr. Crosby unwittingly picked up the tab for his ex-partner's wedding and honeymoon. It's the kind of irony that Abe Frank would have relished.

Biographer Barry Ulanov says that when Frank finally caused Bing's name to be taken off the unfair list, he did so only outside the Los Angeles area and that for a period of time (undisclosed by Ulanov), Bing couldn't broadcast on the air from studios in the Los Angeles area. We couldn't verify Ulanov's statement, for AFM records don't go back to the thirties, but an AFM West Coast spokesman suggested that the restriction might well have been a personal action on Abe Frank's part, effected locally by his professional standing and influence in the community.

While Marchetti was negotiating with Abe Frank, Bing contacted his friend and former Whiteman sideman guitarist Eddie Lang. Bing wasn't familiar with the CBS studio orchestra, and vice versa, and as with any performing artist, he wanted someone at his side who was familiar with his style and who could fill in the kind of background that complemented it. Eddie Lang was just such a musician, and there was no better guitarist in his day. Eddie was the first guitarist to gain an international reputation as a soloist. His chord patterns were exquisite, and his single-string work was, quite literally, beyond compare. He was one of those persons gifted with an innate sense of music and a unique approach, and he was a master of his instrument. He was quite incapable of playing musical clichés, and he was also as close to Bing as anyone could be.

Bing wasn't the only person who knew of Eddie's consummate artistry. By the time Bing reached New York, Eddie had left the Whiteman orchestra and was booked solidly, playing regularly for several network radio shows and working for numerous recording studios. Most artists who came to town for recording sessions wanted Eddie Lang in the rhythm section and very often worked their recording dates around Eddie's schedule. But Bing was desperate to have Eddie at his side during his radio debut, and Bing was a friend; Eddie Lang would do anything for a friend.

Eddie's schedule conflicted with Bing's, but Eddie offered to quit one of his regular programs to accommodate Bing's need. Bing's program was a sustaining one, though, and could be canceled if a sponsor couldn't be found or if Bing didn't go over well. Bing didn't want Eddie to take the chance; then, too, Bing wasn't at all sure that he could make it as a solo artist on radio. The problem was that Eddie could make the broadcasts, but the rehearsal time conflicted with another show he was doing. It was finally decided that Eddie would do the broadcasts and would drop by the studio on his own time to look over the musical charts (the band's arrangements) to familiarize himself with the songs scheduled and their keys. Just the fact that Eddie would be backing him took enormous pressure off Bing, but not enough to keep him from nearly wrecking his radio career even before it began.

Bing was scheduled to make his network debut on

August 31, 1931, at 11:00 P.M. But when the time came, the announcer told the listening audience that the show had been postponed until the following evening because Bing was ill. The next night, September 1, the same announcement was made. The word on the show-business grapevine was that Bing was on a binge, and that Everett had tracked him down and was trying to get him straightened out to perform. Finally, on Wednesday, September 2, 1931, Bing performed as scheduled.

At the time, there was a good deal of talk about the controversy regarding his first network appearance and his self-destructive ways. Actually, he was behaving no differently from the way he had behaved at the Grove just a few months earlier. We wouldn't ordinarily devote much space to the controversy, except that four decades later, in Charles Thompson's book *Bing*, the matter was still being explored. The official story and its repercussions are exemplary of how zealous the Crosby organization was in revising Bing's biographical history and, through repetition, fooling even those who worked within the Crosby organization.

The family biography, written six years after the incident, attributes the broadcast delay to throat trouble. According to Ted and Larry Crosby, Bing was not only rehearsing for the show and making records but making the rounds of the Manhattan night spots and singing into the wee hours of the night, and playing golf in the rain. For these reasons, his vocal cords simply gave out. Allegedly, a throat specialist was consulted, and to everyone's alarm, it was discovered that nodes had developed on Bing's vocal cords that might alter his voice if they were operated upon.

Eleven years after the boys told their nodes story, author Barry Ulanov was led to believe and reported in *The Incredible Crosby* that Bing's show was delayed because of union problems. But since the union settlement had been announced in the trade papers a week before Bing was to broadcast, and since the network wouldn't have programmed Bing to go on without clearance in hand, Ulanov seems to have been led astray by someone in the Crosby organization.

Five years after Ulanov's biography, Bing published his own story and refuted the union story. In doing so, incidentally, he dispensed with a certain person (whom he had "disappeared") by saying that "a lawyer" had been unsuccessful in straightening out the union difficulty with Abe Frank, owing, Bing said, to his own stubbornness, until "We got ahold of that lawyer, and had him go to Abe Frank and make a settlement. Then I was free to go to work for Paley." Obviously "that lawyer," as Bing called him, was Roger Marchetti, and it's the only reference Bing made to Marchetti in his autobiography or in his conversations with interviewers and biographers. In fact, Bing places "that lawyer" in a context that leads the reader to infer that he's talking about John O'Melveny, the attorney who succeeded Marchetti and with whom Bing maintained a personal and professional relationship for the rest of his life. O'Melveny, by the way, did a brilli; t job in Marchetti's place, and although Bing acknowledges—and glowingly so—O'Melveny's role in his career, Everett was given credit, indirectly, for much of O'Melveny's work as well.

Bing assigned the reason for the broadcast delay to his habit of late-night saloon hopping—while "that lawyer" got his union problems straightened out—and to the air-conditioned CBS studio where he rehearsed—the first air-conditioned room he had ever been in. Bing said that he caught cold and called off the show twice because of his cold. He assigned Ted and Larry's nodes story to a few weeks later, when he was appearing at the Paramount Theatre. One presumes that he held onto the nodes story to preserve the veracity of the family biography. But there is absolutely no evidence that Bing ever missed a performance during his entire twenty-week engagement at the Paramount.

In the late forties or early fifties, just before Bing's autobiography was published, the nodes-on-the-vocal-cords tale was revived again. Teet Carl, who was head of publicity at Paramount when Bing was there, had the job of keeping the Paramount stars' names in print. He recalled to us that during one particularly slow news period, he and Ev Crosby were kicking around ideas to get Bing's name in the papers and magazines. Ev came up with the idea of attributing Bing's wonderfully husky tones to nodes on his vocal cords, which, if operated upon, might ruin his voice. As long as the nodes remained, the golden tones would remain, too.

Teet wrote up Ev's story, and it was picked up by the wire services, newspaper and magazine columnists and given a lot of attention and play. According to Teet, after the story was trumpeted in this country and abroad, Bing used to look at him and smile, then, shaking his head in "apparent" disbelief that such a rib could be pulled on the public, he'd say, "*Nodes* on the *vocal cords!*" Teet didn't know that the nodes story had been contrived twenty years earlier by the Crosby boys and that Bing was fully aware of the fact.

Ironically, the story got so much public play at the time that during our interviews, two people who were close to Bing and Dixie volunteered the information that they recalled something about Bing's having had a secret operation in the fifties to remove nodes from his vocal cords, but that the operation was reported to the press as something else. Bing did have an appendectomy and an operation to remove kidney stones (and continued to be plagued with stones), but many continue to believe the nodes story, and Bing inserted it in his autobiography shortly thereafter. Such is the stuff of which legends are made.

The tales of Bing's first network broadcast do something more than illustrate the adage about tangled webs that are woven from deception. Ev's role in Bing's life and career is revealed in them as well. Bing might have had a cold, too, at the time of his radio debut, but everyone in the business knew that the main reason he missed those first two nights was that he had gone off on one of his three-day binges and, in fact, was reported as being still in an alcoholic fog on the night of the broadcast. The family biography reported that on the evening of his broadcast, Bing left the following note for Everett:

Ev:
Cancel all contracts. I gave it all I had, and it's no go.
—Bing

Everett is said to have been alarmed and to have made a frantic search of the local speakeasies. He finally found Bing at a lunch counter, eating a dish of ice cream. Ev then bullied Bing into making the broadcast by calling him "yellow," showing him a cable from his mother, which reportedly referred to Bing's cold, and telling him that he would be the only Crosby who ever backed away from a challenge if he didn't make the broadcast. So Bing went on.

The story has the feel of an old, two-reeler melodrama. Young singing hero, losing his voice and feeling sorry for himself, tries to stuff himself into oblivion with ice cream but is saved in the nick of time by his brother, who, dashing from the wings, waves a tearful cable from mom and challenges his courage. The young singing hero, inspired by it all, shoves away the mound of ice cream before him, dashes to the radio studio, and becomes a star.

One wonders why the family biographers have Everett searching the speakeasies—that is, until one realizes that the story was fashioned at a time when everyone privy to the show-business grapevine knew the truth; thus, the searching of speakeasies saved the story—and Bing—from total hypocrisy and perhaps from being "exposed" by New York columnists. The story is also illustrative of Ev's role as a surrogate for Kate. For this reason, Everett was one of the few people who could handle Bing. That was his greatest contribution to Bing's early career, but one for which he couldn't be publicly recognized, so a whole new professional identity (with all of its skills) was fashioned for him.

In *Call Me Lucky*, Bing talks of Everett's influence

and, again, because of what everyone in the business knew, he had to come uncomfortably close to the truth. He said that he didn't think that he would have ended in the gutter with his head on a curb had it not been for Everett, but that Ev did contribute a great deal to his career. And indeed he did. Nearly all of the people with whom we spoke mentioned Bing's early-career binges and the fact that Ev (and occasionally Larry and/or Ted) sometimes had to sequester Bing to keep him away from the booze, dry him out, and put him back on the path to his commitments.

Bing's binge before broadcast time was probably one of the factors in Marchetti's decision to sell his interest in Bing back to Bing himself; it's no doubt also part of what *The Hollywood Reporter* publisher, Billy Wilkerson, was referring to when he alluded to Marchetti's assumption of the helm of Bing's career when he wrote, ". . . that's when his [Marchetti's] troubles began." After all of the work and money that Marchetti had put into the big push, he couldn't have been exactly pleased to see it nearly undone with a couple of bottles of Scotch.

The whole story seems inconsequential, but in fact it's significant when one considers that Bing was still trying to keep the lid on it more than four decades after the incident. Biographers continued to resurrect the story simply because the facts so obviously contradicted Bing's own account and because it was inconsistent with Bing's otherwise candid revelations. He had told of his alcoholic excesses with Whiteman and at the Grove. Why, then, wouldn't he be just as candid about that first broadcast? The facts notwithstanding, one is almost tempted to attribute the binge story to what songwriter Johnny Burke called the I Was There the Night He Fell Through the Drum Association, a group of detractors who Burke maintained attributed almost all of Bing's unusual actions to alcoholic excess.

In our opinion, Bing put a lid on the story and sat on it because it fell within that twilight zone in which he was re-creating himself in his own image, the image that the public identified with and accepted, the image that had "disappeared" what he had done to Rinker and Barris and Marchetti. He had to draw the line there. The post–Cocoanut Grove period was the era of the new image. There was no need to account for what went on before; it had been kid stuff, the unpredictable excesses of youth (even though Bing was 28 when he left the Grove).

Bing's talent prevailed on the night of the broadcast, and his radio debut met with favorable audience response. Bing's show was scheduled opposite that of a singer who would later rival him for a while, an acquaintance from the Cocoanut Grove days, Russ Columbo. So sure were people in the business that Columbo would eclipse Bing because of Bing's self-destructive bent that *The Hollywood Reporter* printed the following story on October 7, 1931, just five weeks after Bing's radio debut:

CROSBY UNDERSTUDY RADIO SENSATION

New York—Russ Columbo, former understudy of Bing Crosby, in California, is a radio sensation in the East. While Columbo is cutting his wide swath, Crosby has begun to fade.

It should be noted that Columbo was never Bing's understudy. He had been a violinist in Gus Arnheim's orchestra for a while when Bing was there, and he had done a little singing, but he left the Grove and opened his own club on Hollywood Boulevard months before The Rhythm Boys walked out and before Bing had established himself as a solo artist there. The understudy story stemmed, no doubt, from the fact that Columbo was at the Grove while Bing was there and from the fact that Columbo was a baritone who, reportedly, sounded like Crosby. Russ Columbo did emulate Bing's style, which was so haunting that no singer could escape its influence, and he had a beautiful, lyrical high-baritone voice, but he sounded no more like Bing Crosby than did Rudy Vallée.

The advertising agencies behind the networks tried to stir up radio-audience interest in the early thirties by creating a rivalry among Crosby, Columbo, and Vallée. Remarks alleged to have been uttered by one singer against one or both of the others were planted in the papers. Rumors about Rudy Vallée Fan Clubs deserting him en masse and joining the Bing Crosby Fan Club were circulated. A song and a cartoon film about Crosby, Columbo, and Vallée surfaced briefly. And it was said that neither Crosby nor Vallée would allow a picture of himself to appear on the sheet music to the song. None of this was true. All three singers had a high regard for one another's talent, and all three knew that there was room at the top for all of them.

Rudy Vallée was one of the first to predict that Bing would be a great star. He saw Bing at the Montmartre, when he was appearing with The Rhythm Boys. "Bing sang 'Montmartre Rose,'" Rudy told us. "There was no expression on his face whatsoever. Here he had knocked this audience for a loop—they were yelling and screaming—but no expression of exaltation or triumph or satisfaction—nothing. Just deadpan. He walked right by me, and I said, 'This guy's a hit and doesn't know it.'" When Vallée heard one of Bing's Brunswick recordings, he told whomever he was with, "This guy will dethrone me." And Bing did. Vallée maintained his position in radio, but his record sales were soon surpassed by Bing's. But then Bing's record sales surpassed everyone's until Elvis Presley came along.

There are those who still insist that had Russ Columbo lived, he'd have rivaled Bing and might have eclipsed him. Such talk is nonsense. Columbo had Valentino's good looks and a truly beautiful voice, but baritones with good looks and beautiful voices are not uncommon. Bing Crosby was uncommon. Only two singers in his lifetime who entered the field on Crosby's own turf, so to speak, have endured: Frank Sinatra, who was much influenced by Bing, and Tony Bennett who was influenced, in turn, by Sinatra. But they, too, endured because they are uniquely gifted, and they can no more be compared to Bing or to each other than Bing could be compared to Al Jolson (or Mildred Bailey), who influenced him. Elvis Presley, of course, was uniquely gifted as well, but he seldom touched Crosby's turf; his was a new game, for he revolutionized popular music.

Russ Columbo wasn't uniquely gifted, but he would have been a star. He had played the same theaters Bing played; he was under contract to Universal Pictures; he was recording and selling well; he was writing music and gathering a large radio following. Then his career ended, abruptly and tragically. Columbo was visiting a close friend, portrait photographer Lansing Brown, when it happened. Brown was living with his parents at 584 Lillian Way in Hollywood. Russ stopped in to see him, and they were lounging in Brown's den, talking. On his desk, Brown kept a pair of antique dueling pistols, which he had had for years. He was toying with one of them as he was talking, and when he lit a match to light his pipe, it ignited the fuse of the pistol, which Brown didn't even know was loaded. The pistol discharged a lead ball, which ricocheted off Brown's desk top and penetrated Columbo's left eye, lodging in his brain. Columbo was rushed to the hospital and died a few hours later, on September 2, 1934.

The writer for *The Hollywood Reporter* may have thought that Bing was fading in October 1931, but that opinion wasn't shared by the American Tobacco Company. Three weeks after the *Reporter* article was published, Cremo Cigars assumed sponsorship for Bing's radio show, complete with a new and better time slot: 7:15 each evening. A clause in Bing's American Tobacco Company contract made it evident that his reputation had drifted beyond show-business circles, though: it forbade him from drinking alcoholic spirits. The clause, incorporated in a contract that was written and signed during Prohibition, prompted Hollywood columnist Sidney Skolsky to comment wryly in his New York *Daily News* column: "There is also a *law* that forbids drinking."

At about the time that Bing signed with Cremo Cigars, he began a ten-week engagement at the Paramount Theatre, the scene of his 1927 bombing with Al Rinker. But this time Bing was a hit. His national radio show no doubt helped lure the patrons into the theater, but once in their seats, they discovered that Crosby had more going for him than his remarkable singing voice and style. He was showcased at the Paramount this time, with special-effects gimmicks including a crane that suspended him above the first few rows of his audience as he sang. And as the show's emcee, his relaxed manner, together with his natural wit and humor, was a pleasing "discovery" to the patrons. He was so popular that in mid-January (1932), Paramount Publix extended his engagement for another ten weeks.

Bing was into his second ten-week run when Paramount studios (it was known as Paramount Publix then and didn't become Paramount Pictures, Inc., until 1935) offered him a starring role in a film to be based on the Broadway musical comedy *Wild Waves* (tentatively titled *The Crooner,* but after a title dispute with another studio, it was changed to *The Big Broadcast of 1932*). Bing was making $4,000 a week at the Paramount Theatre and $600 a week on his nightly radio show, so he (and/or Marchetti) told Paramount that he wanted $5,000 a week to do the picture. Paramount thought the demand unreasonable, so they sounded out others, including Rudy Vallée, for the role. Eventually it was a toss-up between Bing and Rudy Vallée.

Rudy Vallée had established himself as *the* baritone of the airwaves fully two years before Bing made his network radio debut. He had also starred in *The Vagabond Lover* for RKO, so he was certainly qualified for the role. But according to Vallée, Paramount decided between him and Bing by conducting a poll among its executive-office personnel in New York and Hollywood to see who was the favored vocalist, and Vallée told us that Bing won by one vote—33 to 32. This seems a strange way to choose the lead for a motion picture, but Paramount often conducted such polls among its employees to name films and the like, and both men were qualified for the role.

Roger Marchetti set the deal with Paramount and got Bing $35,000 to do the part. Bing was the first member of the cast to be signed. And in May, the great husband-and-wife comedy team George Burns and Gracie Allen were signed for the picture. George and Gracie had been vaudeville headliners for six years and had done some two-reelers for Paramount in New York, but they came to the studio's attention as feature-film artists through their radio popularity. They had begun on radio with a guest appearance on "Rudy Vallée's Fleischmann Hour" and then on Guy Lombardo's half-hour musical program, on which they became regulars for several months. Thereafter, they got their own radio show (which ran for 19 years) and were summoned to Hollywood on a two-year feature-film contract. They brought with them a young radio writer named Carroll Carroll (his first assignment), who would eventually be very instrumental in Bing's biggest and longest-running radio success, "Kraft Music Hall."

When the 1931–32 radio season ended, Bing and Dixie returned to Hollywood, where they leased a house next door to their friend Sue Caroll, on Cromwell Avenue. Bing went to work on *The Big Broadcast*, which also starred Stuart Erwin, Leila Hyams, Sharon Lynne, and in addition to Burns and Allen, featured Kate Smith, Arthur Tracy, Donald Novis (one of the singers who had replaced Bing at the Grove), the Boswell Sisters, the Mills Brothers, and the orchestras of Cab Calloway and Vincent Lopez. Bing is said to have been offered top billing on this picture and to have turned it down, a practice that he continued throughout his movie career and which he admitted he did to keep from taking all the blame if the picture bombed.

Bing went on a tour of theaters throughout the Midwest and East after finishing *The Big Broadcast*, capitalizing on the movie publicity, his radio popularity, and the success of his Paramount Theatre run. During the summer, CBS Radio made him a number of attractive offers, mostly sustaining-show packages, to get him back on the network, but Bing was more sure-footed by then and wanted more money and artistic control over his shows, which CBS couldn't offer at the time. His theater tour wound up in New York City on December 2, 1932, at the Capitol Theater, where Bob Hope was appearing on the bill. Bing had actually met Hope a few weeks earlier, but he got acquainted with him at the Capitol.

Hope had toured vaudeville, had done some two-reelers for Educational in New York, and had created quite a stir in Broadway musicals such as *Roberta* and *Say When,* but it would be a few years before Paramount would put him under contract in Hollywood. (Al Rinker saw Hope in *Roberta* on Broadway, when Hope was relatively unknown. Rinker says that he was sensational, and that everyone wanted to know where he had come from; he was destined for stardom.) Hope, of course, was an extraordinary song-and-dance man, and Crosby could hold his own in wit and humor, so there was a natural good-natured rivalry between them from the start. Their friendly ribbing of one another didn't begin onstage at the Capitol, where they were in separate acts, but at the New York Friars' Club, to which both belonged.

While Bing was winding up his personal-appearance tour, CBS finally made him a proposal that met with his demands. The sponsor was Chesterfield cigarettes, and Bing began broadcasting a twice-weekly (Wednesday and Saturday nights) show for them with complete artistic control and a salary of several thousand dollars a week. Bing chose former Whiteman pianist and arranger Lennie Hayton to lead the studio orchestra, and, of course, Eddie Lang sat right behind him at the microphone; the guitar was always a key instrument in Crosby arrangements, and so Bing was always very choosy, utilizing only the best guitarists. It was on the

Chesterfield show that Bing began establishing a format that he would perfect later on the "Kraft Music Hall," employing writers and offering a combination of music and talk (pleasant banter, both written and ad-libbed—Bing was very sharp at ad-libbing) that would eventually make him one of the most popular radio personalities of all time. It was also on the Chesterfield show that he lost his closest and most influential musical companion, Eddie Lang.

Eddie had been having trouble with his tonsils for two years, and he was finally persuaded to have them removed. He informed Bing of his intention and made arrangements to play the Saturday-night radio show and to have the operation on Sunday, March 26, figuring to have recovered sufficiently to make the Wednesday-night show. But a postoperative blood clot caused a fatal heart attack the day of the operation.

Bing took Eddie's death very badly. He had known Eddie and his wife, Kitty (a former Ziegfeld Follies girl), since Eddie and Joe Venuti joined the Whiteman band in 1929. Kitty was accomplished at Italian cooking (though she wasn't of Italian descent—Eddie's real name was Salvatore Massaro), and Bing often dined at Kitty and Eddie's during his bachelor days and frequently went out on the town with them. When they were all reunited in New York, Dixie met Eddie and Kitty for the first time; they were Dixie's kind of people, gentle and unpretentious. They became very close friends and went out together almost every evening.

At Eddie's death, Bing was roundly criticized by his musician friends, who thought his public and private statements about Eddie should have had more emotion to them. They knew of Bing's cool side but didn't know that he was unable to express emotion without embarrassment, and they mistook his reserved reaction for the coldness that they had undoubtedly seen on other occasions. But this time his critics were wrong about him.

Eddie's widow, Kitty, recommended guitarist Perry Botkin to Bing, and Perry filled in for Eddie thereafter. After Eddie's funeral, Kitty joined Dixie on the West

Coast at the Crosby home on Cromwell and continued to live with the Crosbys for many years before she remarried. Kitty became Dixie's closest friend and confidante. She was with Dixie when each of the children was born and even worked as Dixie's stand-in when Dixie did *Manhattan Love Song* for Monogram Pictures after the birth of the Crosbys' first son, Gary Evan. Much later, Kitty married Bing's ranch manager and lived with him on the Elko, Nevada, ranch.

When the radio season ended, Bing returned to the Coast, where he was scheduled for another Paramount picture, *College Humor,* with Jack Oakie, Richard Arlen, and, again, Burns and Allen. During the filming, the Crosbys built their first home on a lot they had purchased in Toluca Lake, on Foreman Avenue, near the Lakeside Golf Course. Dixie's father, Evan Wyatt, supervised the building of the home and added a few innovations himself. One that he added, after conferring with Bing, was a stained-glass window with the first twelve notes of Bing's theme song, "Where the Blue of the Night Meets the Gold of the Day," leaded into it. Maybeth Carpenter told us that when Dixie saw the window for the first time, she said to Bing, "Why don't you just put a sign out on the front lawn that says Bing Crosby lives here?"

Dixie didn't go in much for ostentation.

CHAPTER FOURTEEN

He (Elvis Presley) never contributed a damn thing to
music!

—BING CROSBY TO JOHN SALISBURY

The Big Broadcast of 1932 had premiered in New
York while Bing was on tour, on October 14, 1932,
and the early box-office returns and good reviews were
enough to move Paramount to capitalize on its success
by bringing back Burns and Allen and Crosby for an
encore. But by the time they made their decision, Bing
had signed for the Chesterfield show, and the sponsors,
Liggett and Meyers, were reluctant to let Bing get involved in another entertainment medium during the
broadcast season. Paramount, however, had discovered
in Crosby what Mack Sennett and Bing's two-reeler
fans already knew: there was a charisma about him
quite different from that of any other screen star. So in
order to have Bing, Paramount announced its willing-
ness to hold up production on his next film, *College
Humor,* until March 15, when Bing would be free from
his radio commitment until the fall.

Bing definitely had his foot in the door of Paramount
after his performance in *The Big Braodcast,* but after
he did *College Humor,* and after it was released, Paramount opened its doors wide to him and rolled out the
red carpet. Columnist Helen Gwynne, writing from

New York for her *Hollywood Reporter* column on June 30, 1933, told how Bing was affecting Manhattan moviegoers:

> *College Humor,* by the way, is drawing the longest lines that have been seen in some time, and people are getting all excited over a new discovery—Bing Crosby. They've suddenly discovered what a grand personality the lad has, even when he isn't singing. The public is sometimes slow, but always proud of its discoveries.

With the success of *College Humor,* Paramount dusted off a previously shelved sequel to the Jack Oakie–Skeets Gallagher film *Close Harmony,* titled *Too Much Harmony,* and set their scriptwriters to work fashioning a large part for Bing Crosby. Bing and Jack Oakie scored high in the reviews, and Bing's motion-picture career was assured. The two-reelers he had made for Educational (*Dream House*) and Paramount (*Please*) were released to tie in with his new popularity. The two-reeler *Billboard Girl* was already in release, and *Blue of the Night* (both for Educational) would soon follow, and by June, MGM was trying to borrow Bing from Paramount. In July, it was announced that Marion Davies herself had asked for Bing to co-star with her in *Going Hollywood,* a Cosmopolitan–MGM release to be funded by William Randolph Hearst. Many in Hollywood viewed the move as a last-gasp attempt by Marion Davies to bolster her sagging film career, and she apparently figured that Bing's enormous growing popularity would assure a good box-office draw.

Going Hollywood didn't do much for Miss Davies, but her and MGM's interest in Bing couldn't have come at a better time for him. Bing had only a few months to go on his Paramount contract, and he used MGM's interest in him to advantage. Paramount immediately negotiated with him for a new three-picture deal; he was given $200,000 to do three films for 1934–35, and as a bonus for signing, Paramount allowed him to take $50,000 from MGM for his participation in the Davies picture. Bing and the family biographers reported that Everett pulled a coup in getting Bing a $5,000 weekly salary for the film, but the trades reported that it was a flat-fee deal.

By 1934, Bing was making a half-million dollars a year from his radio show, records, and motion pictures. And by September 1936, Bing was commanding $1 million for his three-picture deals with Paramount and was soon getting even more. Bing's association with Paramount Pictures would last twenty-five years; forty-five of his sixty-one feature films were Paramount releases, including his Academy Award—winning *Going My Way*. But the films that were destined to become classics were the seven *Road* pictures that he made with Leslie Townes Hope of Eltham, England.

Paramount finally brought Bob Hope to Hollywood for feature films in 1937, when he did *The Big Broadcast of 1938,* in which he sang Leo Robin and Ralph Rainger's "Thanks for the Memory" for the first time. After *Broadcast,* Paramount wasted him in half a dozen low-budget films until Bob hit it big on his Pepsodent radio show in the fall of 1938, bringing to Paramount's attention what a talent they had in him. Bob then starred in *The Cat and the Canary,* and after critical acclaim for that picture, together with the highly promotable and entertaining friendly rivalry he and Bing established on their radio shows, it became obvious even to the Paramount brass that they had a winning combination on the lot that cried out for exploitation.

Again, Paramount had a script on hand. Screenwriters Frank Butler and Don Hartman had refashioned a South Seas tale called *Beach of Dreams* as a vehicle for Burns and Allen and had renamed it *Road to Mandalay.* But Burns and Allen had turned it down, so it was offered to Jack Oakie and Fred MacMurray, who also turned it down. Bing and Bob signed to do it, but what premiered in New York City on April 13, 1940, under its new title, *Road to Singapore,* bore little resemblance to what Burns and Allen and Oakie and MacMurray had turned down. Bing and Bob, with the aid of sight gags and one-liners furnished by two fine gag writers named Barney Dean and Monty Brice (the brother of Fanny Brice), ribbed and ad-libbed their way through the picture in a manner that infuriated the scriptwriters, bewildered their feminine co-star Dorothy Lamour, and delighted audiences. The chemistry was exactly right, and the result was a series of seven pictures that became one of the most profitable film sequences in movie history. The series was so popular and profitable that by the time they made *Road to Rio*, Bing and Bob had struck a bargain with Paramount to split production costs and profits three ways, each taking a third—a deal about which Dorothy Lamour lamented in her autobiography, *My Side of the Road*, that she wasn't offered a share. Miss Lamour did profit from the pictures—they made her famous—but she was a little naive to think that she was deserving of a share in them. There were others, after all, who could have played her part equally as well, but no one could have replaced Bing and Bob. And in our opinion, Miss Lamour was even more naive to think that Bing and Bob, both of whom were obsessed with amassing fortunes, would even consider giving up any part of their share.

Miss Lamour did have a legitimate complaint with respect to the last *Road* picture, *Road to Hong Kong*, however, but she didn't take a full swing at Bing, who was more deserving of a haymaker than the jab she gave him. But her book was published in 1980, after his death, and this, one assumes, accounts for her treading so lightly.

Though Dorothy Lamour may not have deserved a full partnership in the *Road* pictures, she certainly deserved a full part in the last one (though at the time, of course, it wasn't considered the last; there was talk of doing *Road to the Moon* and *Road to the Fountain of Youth* right up to Crosby's death, but nothing ever came of the talk). Few could envision a *Road* picture without Dorothy Lamour, but Bing did. Miss Lamour was at her home in Baltimore, Maryland, when she first

1905—Bing and his mother, Kate. This photo was taken in Tacoma, Washington, a year before the Crosbys moved to Spokane. *Credit: Vernon Wesley Taylor.*

Bing and Mother Kate at his Holmby Hills home. *Credit: Peter Stackpole.*

1924—The Musicaladers *(l. to r.)*: Jimmy Heaton; Miles Rinker; Bing Crosby; Bob Pritchard; Clair Pritchard; and Alton "Al" Rinker. Posed at the Casino Theatre, Spokane, Washington. *Copyright © 1980: Al Rinker Collection.*

Bing Crosby and Paul "Pops" Whiteman. Exact time and place of photo is unknown—probably late 1930's or early 1940's in New York. *Credit: Vernon Wesley Taylor.*

1918—Jazz singer Mildred Bailey at age 17, Spokane, Washington. *Credit: Al Rinker Collection.*

1926—Al and Bing get a good notice in a San Diego, California paper for their appearance at the Spreckles Theatre. *Credit: Al Rinker Collection.*

1927—The Rhythm Boys *(l. to r.)*: Harry Barris, Bing Crosby, and Al Rinker. First photo ever taken of The Rhythm Boys; Paul White-man Club. *Credit: Al Rinker Collection.*

1930—A scene from Bing's first Sennett film, *I Surrender, Dear*.

1931—A formal portrait of Bing; he was still working the Cocoanut Grove with the Rhythm Boys when he posed for this photo.

1929—Dixie Lee, a Fox Studio publicity photo taken about the time she met Bing Crosby.

1929—Dixie Lee, a Fox Studio photo.

1930—Unpublished honeymoon snapshot of Bing and Dixie taken several days after they were married. *Credit: Sue Carol Ladd Collection.*

1933—Dixie Lee Crosby is shown here in the embrace of her closest friend, Kitty Lang.   *Credit: Kitty Lang Good.*

1935—Taken at Rancho Santa Fe: Bing; Dixie Lee; Gary Evans (standing); and twins Phil and Denny. *Credit: Paramount Pictures, Inc.*

1938—The Crosby family *(l. to r.)*: Dennis; Bing; Gary; Dixie, holding Lindsay; and Philip. *Credit: Sue Carol Ladd Collection.*

1943—The Rhythm Boys reunite for an NBC Radio program: Crosby, Barris, and Al Rinker. *Credit: Al Rinker Collection.*

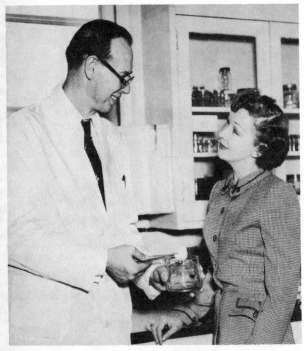

March, 1950—Dr. George Hummer and Dixie Lee Crosby, St. John's Hospital in Santa Monica. *Credit: Dr. George Hummer. Photo by Irving L. Antler.*

1952—Bing gives Jerry Lewis a lift on the Paramount lot. *Credit: Paramount Pictures, Inc.*

1976—Kathryn and Bing. *Credit: CBS.*

1977—Harry, Mary Frances, Nathaniel, Bing, Kathryn Crosby.
Credit: CBS.

read about another *Road* picture being prepared, but no one contacted her about it. Meanwhile, Bob was arguing in her favor and wanted her included, but Bing disagreed. Bing won, of course, and one assumes that if he hadn't, he might have given the picture his famous "walking brush-off." Since the film was to be made in England, Joan Collins was signed as the female lead; it was thought that her name would give the picture British-European draw. Dorothy was finally given a small part in the film, but one gathers that after co-starring in the first six *Road* pictures, the fact that she was reduced to a bit-part player in the seventh was a difficult experience for her.

If the *Hong Kong* experience wasn't humiliating enough for her, then Bing's second backhand was. After the film was complete, Bob Hope invited Dorothy to appear on one of his television specials to plug the picture. So she flew to Los Angeles and did the show. While she was in town, she heard that Bing was doing a special, too. She called Bing and asked if he wanted her for the show; she told him that she could stay over in Hollywood a few days if he did. Bing told her that it was too late to write her in. But when the special came to television, Dorothy watched it and was shocked to see that Bing had used large blow-up photographs of her and references were made to her throughout the show. Bing couldn't use her on the show, but he "used" her.

Bob Hope himself didn't get much better treatment from Bing. Though they had a forty-five-year acquaintanceship, they were never intimate friends, despite their occasional business ventures together. It's not that Hope wasn't willing, but he discovered the cool side of Mr. Crosby very early. Hope, of course, has never referred to Bing's cool side in public, but one doubts that he'd deny it if cornered. Actually, the ribbing rivalry between the two was several shades less than friendly; it had a cutting edge (particularly on Bing's part) that many on the Paramount lot and at the radio and TV studios had occasion to see. Most of the barbs were innocuous, and Bob's were always played for laughs, but occasionally Bing would take deadly aim below the belt. When referring once to Bob's investing in the Cleveland Indians baseball team, Bing said, "Hope doesn't come up with much money. He's a fast man with a squaw, but a slow man with a buck." Those who knew what Crosby thought of Hope knew that he wasn't kidding.

Bing would give co-billing or even top billing to anyone, but that's all he'd give. He was the top money-maker for Paramount when Hope was put under contract there, and Bob had to fight for a semblance of equality from the first day he arrived on the set of *Road to Singapore*—on screen and off. Crosby would have his own way. He didn't throw childish temper tantrums, as some Hollywood celebrities are notorious for doing; his was a more subtle approach. If he didn't get his way, he walked, and the powers that be didn't have to be told that he could be found at Lakeside *after* they scurried around to change whatever it was he wanted changed or effected whatever it was that he requested. He was also like a child who can hardly contain himself awaiting recess. If Bing was told that his call was from 10:00 A.M. until 1:30 P.M., when 1:30 came, he'd walk off the set even if they were in the middle of a scene.

Hope and Lamour were designated the unofficial greeters on the *Road* picture sets. Whenever studio brass ushered visiting dignitaries to the set—which was all too often in the opinion of the people who were trying to get their jobs done—Bing would rarely deign to meet such people. The Paramount brass were happy with the arrangement, for they never knew when Bing might give someone important the brush. And he often—and embarrassingly—did just that. Perry Botkin, the guitarist who replaced Eddie Lang, had an imaginary list that he called the PBOBBC List: People Brushed Off By Bing Crosby. Botkin didn't actually compile the list, of course, but it would have taken on the proportions of a good-size directory if he had.

The ultimate put-down of Bob Hope by Bing Crosby came after they had begun the *Road* pictures, in the early forties. The Friars' Club, to which both Bing and Bob belonged (in fact, Bing was an officer in the club, though he didn't attend meetings), gave Bob a testimonial dinner. Such functions are important to members of the entertainment industry, because one's presence is considered not just an act of friendship (very often that's not the case at all), but a tribute or acknowledgment of one's professional standing and a token of esteem. Bing was listed as a speaker, but the chair reserved for him at the speaker's table remained empty; Bing didn't show. When asked why later, Bing is reported to have quipped, "Because I wasn't hungry." Friars' Club members didn't think his remark funny. Later Bing told a reporter, "My friendship for Bob doesn't depend on appearing at testimonials." Bing's penchant for ignoring social amenities was notorious, but a professional put-down before one's peers was quite another matter. The Friars' Club members knew that had the testimonial been given for Bing, Bob Hope would have been among the first to arrive. Hope was genuinely hurt at Bing's slight. And the Friars' Club members were even more outraged when, awhile later, Bing showed up for a testimonial dinner given by the music industry for the "Dean" of song pluggers, Tubby Garron, whom Bing knew.

So Bing and Bob's relationship was almost purely business, and even then Bing was less than friendly. When Bob's production company did his film *My Favorite Brunette*, he wanted Bing for a cameo appearance that lasted only twenty seconds on the screen. Bing did it—for $25,000, which was donated to Gonzaga in Bing's name, a tax write-off for Crosby and a very expensive—and short—piece of film footage for Hope. Bing always contended that Hope was a slow man with the buck, but it was Hope who kept a small army of old vaudeville friends on salary when he worked and who sent his brother George out every Friday to deliver checks drawn on Bob's personal account

213

to old acquaintances, particularly to those who were ill. As with any star who hits it big, Bob had his share of people looking for a handout simply because he had money—stars are plagued by small armies of such people—but Bob never turned his back on a friend who was really in need or ill. He didn't "disappear" his friends and acquaintances. We might add that Bob didn't publicize his philanthropic acts; we know of them because we knew his brother George and on occasion accompanied him on his weekly check-delivering rounds. This is not to say that Bing wasn't charitable; he was—particularly to his alma mater, Gonzaga. But we're talking about philanthropy—humane acts—the kind involved with writing personal checks without benefit of tax advantages. And in this, Crosby was in no position to cast barbs. Philanthropic acts are usually not trumpeted in the trades, of course, but they often surface via the grateful recipients of them. One can hardly approach anyone in Hollywood or Palm Springs who doesn't have several stories involving Frank Sinatra's philanthropies, for example. But although Bing was one of the three or four wealthiest people in show business, one has to dig for stories. One story, which we'll go into later, involved a very humane act on the part of Sinatra and Jimmy Van Heusen, and when Bing entered the act, he attached strings to it.

Bing's last film for Paramount was *Anything Goes*, released in 1956, in which he played an aging matinee idol who teams up with a young television star (Donald O'Connor) to do a Broadway show. The timing of the picture coincided with the demise of Hollywood's star system. Paramount, like the other studios, was feeling the box-office pinch resulting from television's coming of age. The studios dropped their contract players and began hiring stars on a picture-by-picture basis. Both Crosby and Hope lost their places on dressing-room row and their multipicture contracts. Bing made nine pictures thereafter, and none was for Paramount. Even the last *Road* picture was a United Artists release. Bing did only two films after that one; his last was for Twentieth Century-Fox in 1966, a remake of the 1939 movie *Stagecoach*.

Bing's radio career lasted well into the television era. After the Chesterfield show, he was sponsored by Woodbury Soap, and his new program was produced by his old friend, Burt McMurtrie, who had produced Paul Whiteman's Old Gold show. It was on the Woodbury show that Bing first began using vocal backgrounds (like the Mills Brothers), and Burt had a hand in his doing so. Burt produced fifty-two Woodbury programs (two 26-week seasons) for Bing and was instrumental also in getting him to sing his first Christmas carol on the air. As with movies, later, Bing was set against performing anything remotely religious for fear that people would think that he was capitalizing on religion. But Burt proved his fears baseless.

A year before McMurtrie's death in 1979, he attended a luncheon in Tacoma, Washington, arranged by Ken Twiss, president of the Bing Crosby Historical Society. Other guests at the luncheon were Gordon Wall of Australia (which has a large Bing Crosby fan club), and Bill Osborn of Seattle and Vern Taylor of Portland, Oregon, both of whom are members of the society. Vern Taylor took notes at the luncheon, and the following quotes from McMurtrie are from a transcription reprinted here with Mr. Taylor's permission:

". . . I can remember the first time I asked Bing to sing a religious number," Burt told the group. "He absolutely refused. I told him, 'Bing, this is more than a religious number. I want you to do it on the Christmas show. You'll do a great job. It'll be wonderful.' But he backed off, claimed his audience wouldn't understand him singing that type of song. So I had to remind him of the promise he made to me in the beginning—that he would always do what I asked, at least to see how it might go. And he grumbled a little more, then agreed to do it.

"So, without telling him, I brought in four violinists

215

and planted them in the orchestra. Four extra violins! He hated it. Hated the whole idea. I can see him there, his back to the musicians; he's gazing out past his big, old box mike when the music comes up, then under. He closes his eyes and starts in. . . ."

(Burt's eyes suddenly fill with tears at the recollection. He shakes his head and smiles around the table.)

"Bing sang 'Silent Night' there for the first time. All by himself. He sang it like nobody—I mean, *nobody*—had ever sung it before. And all of us watching him stood stone still. It was unbelievable. So moving. Bing shouldn't have worried about it. Everything went off beautifully, and even before we went off the air, the telephones started ringing.

"But you see, it was like I have said. Bing could be a bad boy sometimes. He could screw things up when he didn't give a damn. Then he would do something like sing that first religious number, and all was forgiven."

When the 1934–35 radio season ended, Bing didn't renew his CBS contract, for there was an NBC show in the offing. It was the "Kraft Music Hall," an hour-long musical-variety program that aired every Thursday night and had been hosted by Paul Whiteman. Kraft decided mid-season that it wanted more variety than the orchestra leader was offering, and a deal was made with Bing.

The "Kraft Music Hall" had emanated from New York, and with Bing's signing, would transfer to the West Coast in January 1936. The first of four transitional programs took place on December 5, 1935, with Paul Whiteman and his orchestra broadcasting from New York, and Bing, backed by Jimmy Dorsey's orchestra, being piped in from the West Coast. When Bing assumed full control of the show on January 2, he inherited two people with the program who would contribute immeasurably to its success: writer Carroll Carroll and comedian Bob Burns.

Bob Burns was another Rudy Vallée discovery who had been holding down the comedy spot on the "Music Hall" in New York. He was a native of Van Buren,

Arkansas, was billed as "The Arkansas Hillbilly," and was "credited" with inventing the bazooka, a quasi-musical instrument that was named for the sound it made, which gives one a fairly good idea of the comedy esteem held for it by Bing and thousands of "Music Hall" fans. Burns and Bing hit it off immediately, for as we said earlier, Burns was the embodiment of the mythical Bingsville citizenry that entertained young Harry Crosby in Spokane and for whom he was nicknamed. Burns's country wit and wisdom and his tall tales of country relatives like Grandpa Snazzy broke Bing up—on the air and off—and served as a perfect counterpoise for Bing's longer-haired guests, which included classical musicians, dramatic actors, composers, and opera singers, among other types. Burns's slow Southern drawl was also a perfect foil for Bing's rapid-fire, intentionally hammy and pseudosophisticated oratorical style, a mixed bag of circumlocutory polysyllabical formal speech, incongruously peppered with jive talk. And some of the show's funniest moments were the dialogues between Burns and Crosby. Bob Burns gained a measure of fame on the "Kraft Music Hall," and Bing employed him in two of his films: *Rhythm on the Range* and *Waikiki Wedding*.

The man who wrote the entire Kraft show wasn't as readily accepted by Bing. Carroll Carroll had come west with Burns and Allen in 1931, when they did *The Big Broadcast* with Bing, but Carroll hadn't met Bing on that occasion. Carroll had been writing the "Music Hall" for Whiteman since its inception in 1934, when Al Jolson was Whiteman's first guest star. In the early spring of 1936, when it became evident that the West Coast writer assigned to the show wasn't going to stay with it, Carroll was again assigned to it. He arrived in Hollywood on broadcast day—the only day Bing ever went near the radio studio—and the show's producer, Cal Kuhl took him onto the stage to meet Bing.

"Bing was doping horses, with a scratch sheet in his hand," Carroll told us, "and Cal said, 'Bing, I want you to meet Carroll Carroll. He's going to write the show.'

217

And Bing said, 'Hi, Carroll,' and walked away. That was our entire contact for maybe six weeks."

Later, Carroll and Bing began having once-a-week script conferences over lunch at the Vine Street Brown Derby, but that was the only "socializing" they did in their entire nine-and-a-half-year association. Carroll visited Bing's house only twice in that time, and the visits were strictly business. "Nobody was close to Bing," Carroll told us. "He had little groups of friends—and *friends* is sort of a loose use of the term. He had fishing friends, golfing friends, racetrack friends. . . . He wasn't a loner, but he got together with people at his convenience—only those he wanted around, and at a time and place that he wanted them around. He didn't really have a social life."

Bing's tenure with Kraft spanned nearly ten years and came to an abrupt and rather stormy end. He walked out of his contract in June of 1945—fourteen years to the month from the time he walked out of his Cocoanut Grove contract. Kraft had Bing under contract until 1950, but Bing pointed to a California law under which personal contracts couldn't extend beyond seven years. The lines were drawn, and attorneys on each side quibbled for several months. Finally Kraft sued, and Bing settled with them by broadcasting another thirteen weeks in the spring of 1946. Then he was free to go elsewhere on radio, which is what he had been angling for.

The official Crosby line was that Bing broke with Kraft for financial reasons. They had offered him no tax shelter and, according to Bing's office, Bing was mad because he was keeping only one-ninth of his income—the rest was reportedly going to Uncle Sam. But the real reason he broke with Kraft couldn't be made public for fear of a backlash.

Bing was tired of having to be on hand every week for his radio broadcasts. He wanted to transcribe them with the newly developed audio-tape process (which his company, in affiliation with Ampex, brought back from Germany after the war and developed). The networks

218

were dead-set against transcriptions of any kind, figuring that without the immediacy of live programming, the broadcasts would suffer, people would turn off their radios, and sponsors would leave the shows. If the sponsors were paying for Bing Crosby, they argued, they wanted Bing Crosby, not a mechanical voice coming from an engineer's control booth. Their arguments had merit, but Bing was adamant.

Live programming and even live radio audiences didn't mean a thing to Bing—except more work. From the first Kraft show, he had insisted that there be no studio audience. He had also insisted that he didn't want to talk on the show—he had an announcer for that (Ken Carpenter); he just wanted to sing. His reluctance to talk may have stemmed from the Woodbury show days. The family biographers claim that Woodbury canceled the show because they didn't like the way Bing talked. Carroll Carroll and Cal Kuhl finally tricked Bing into talking on the "Music Hall" by giving guest stars wild lines that weren't in the script and to which Bing had to respond. Bing's natural wit pulled him through and gave him confidence, and Carroll began putting the wild lines into the script until the talking parts were as entertaining as Bing's singing.

Kuhl and Carroll also tricked Bing into using live studio audiences. Bing's main objection to doing so was his baldness; if an audience was present, he'd have to wear his toupee, which he hated, or his hat, which he finally accepted. Kuhl and Carroll convinced him that live studio-audience response was vital to the broadcasts. "We'll just invite family members of people affiliated with the show," they told him. Bing agreed, reluctantly, and as Carroll Carroll told us, on the first night, the line of "family members" extended clear around the building, waiting to get into the studio. It was obvious that the show had been opened to the public, but Bing took it well, and enjoyed playing before a live audience, and so the routine was established. But the advent of audio tape was something else. Bing figured that he could tape his shows in advance and be trout fishing in Canada while the show was being broadcast.

As was his habit by then, when neither NBC nor Kraft would give in to his demands, he walked. And as happened when he walked from the Grove, he left his victims. Carroll Carroll was one of them. He had written for Bing for almost ten years; he had written for the best of comedians, including Burns and Allen and Jack Benny (and dozens more). But as he describes in his book *My Life With,* Bing dropped him flat: no notice, no warning, no confrontation. Carroll was told that Bing would have a new radio program and therefore wanted all new personnel. It wasn't a very convincing reason, particularly when Bing took his engineer and John Scott Trotter with him. The writing assignment for Bing's new show went to Bing's fishing buddy and traveling companion, Bill Morrow.

In the summer of 1946, after Bing had fulfilled his settlement with Kraft, he announced that he was putting together a new radio show. Given his popularity and the quality of guest stars that he could draw, the sponsors lined up and began bidding for the show. Bing finally signed with Philco, the manufacturer of radios, who not only agreed to his transcribing the shows but gave him a handsome weekly program budget of $22,500 and a weekly salary of $7,500.

The network that broke broadcasting tradition by taking Bing's transcribed show was the American Broadcasting Company, which was newly franchised (in 1943) and composed of stations of the old NBC Blue network. ABC was so happy to get Bing that they not only broke the transcription barrier but allowed him to choose the programs that preceded and followed his. The Crosby organization explained that by doing so, they could keep the time surrounding Bing's program free of "offensive" programs that might lose listeners for Bing. One assumes that such "offensive programs" might have included radio shows like Frank Sinatra's. Bing had his own following, but why get into a ratings fight if one can manipulate a network?

Bing's association with ABC ended two years later when CBS president William Paley conducted an ingenious "raid" on NBC, from which he "stole" Amos 'n' Andy, Jack Benny, Edgar Bergen, and Red Skelton by making them multimillion-dollar capital-gains offers. And with the transcription barrier now broken, Bing left like a shot for CBS. And with Chesterfield as his sponsor, he remained with CBS until television replaced radio as the family entertainment medium.

At about the time that radio's golden age came to an end, another young man changed the sound of popular music just as Bing had done in the thirties. His name was Elvis Presley, and he hit the music world with such impact that it was never the same again. One is reminded of the Grove's singer Kenny Allen remarking that vocalists of his day hoped that Crosby's innovative style would just go away. The same can be said for other vocalists' attitude toward Presley. His new singing style was as revolutionary as Bing's had been during his era, but Presley introduced a new kind of popular music as well, and the latter "rocked" the industry, put popular music into the hands of youngsters, outraged most adults, and almost totally eclipsed the careers of male and female pop singers and traditional songwriters.

While it's true that Presley wreaked more havoc on the music industry as a whole than had the young Bing Crosby, Presley's effect on popular singers of the day was no more devastating than Bing's had been during his era. But as were most of the pre-Presley singers and songwriters, Bing was bitter and failed to see the parallel between his own emergence in the early thirties and Presley's in the mid-fifties.

Vern Taylor, who accompanied Portland, Oregon, radio celebrity and Crosby fan John Salisbury to Hillsborough for an interview with Bing, in the fall of 1975, describes how Salisbury tossed names at Bing for comment as he taped the interview for a broadcast. Bing spoke glowingly of Sinatra, Louis Armstrong, Connie Boswell, and the like, but when Salisbury mentioned

Elvis Presley, Taylor said that Bing's blue eyes suddenly went cold and he said, "He [Presley] never contributed a damn thing to music!"

Taylor says that Salisbury was startled by Bing's pronouncement and that he was momentarily nonplussed. "Elvis?" Salisbury said. "Elvis Presley?"

"No," Bing said. "He was successful—hard to account for. Oh, he sings well enough, I suppose."

And with that, Bing dimissed Elvis Presley. There wasn't much thought behind his remarks, but a lot of bitterness. They were gut-level, knee-jerk pronouncements, reflecting the view of dozens of singers whose careers ended abruptly or were unalterably changed after Elvis came to national attention. Presley had hurt Bing, too, but Bing had been more fortunate than most. He had become wealthy and had established himself in motion pictures. He wasn't dependent solely upon cabaret appearances and record revenues, as some were. But as with most popular singers of his day, Bing's record career was all but over, owing, ironically, to the self-taught young singer with a totally different style that other singers hoped would go away.

Bing became a wealthy man on his record sales alone. According to Laurence Zwisohn, in his book *Bing Crosby, a Lifetime of Music,* Bing recorded more than 1,600 songs (no one has topped that mark) and sold more than 500 million records—more than anyone before him. And what is truly astonishing, and a tribute to his talent, is that Bing launched his recording career from an unstable and sinking pad. For as Zwisohn points out, Bing's record career began during the depths of the Depression (1931–34) and despite the fact that record sales declined from $75 million in 1929 to $9 million in 1934. Bing attributes much of his success in records to a man named Jack Kapp, and rightly so.

It was during the Roger Marchetti–Cocoanut Grove transition that Bing began recording for Brunswick as a solo artist. Jack Kapp had become director of recording at Brunswick just the year before, and nobody knew the record business better than he. Kapp's father had been a record salesman, and Jack followed in his footsteps as a salesman until 1930, at age twenty-nine, when he became an executive with the company. Kapp and Crosby got along very well, and under Kapp's guidance, Bing's Brunswick showing was very impressive. But in 1933, Kapp was passed by for the presidency of Brunswick and, seeing no future with the company, he resigned.

Kapp had planned ahead, however. He and Ted (Sir Edward) Lewis made a deal with the Decca Company of England to market an American Decca label; then they offered Bing an opportunity to invest in the company, which he did, becoming a minority stockholder. Naturally Bing jumped from Brunswick and became the first artist to be signed by Decca (he was followed by Guy Lombardo and the Mills Brothers). Jack Kapp literally built Decca around Bing, even opening a recording studio on Melrose near Paramount for Bing's convenience. Decca's first release (D-100) was Bing's "I Love You Truly"/"Just A-Wearyin' For You," recorded on Wednesday, August 8, 1934, and Decca's blue label, with its 35¢ price (15¢ below that of the major competitive labels) was destined to become as popular as those of its chief competitors, Victor and Columbia.

Much of Decca's success is directly attributable to Jack Kapp's innovative approach and marketing knowhow. Bing was very impressed with him and, since it was his wont to do so anyway, he put his recording career in Jack's capable hands and credited Jack with the astounding breadth of his selections, which included semi-classics, jazz, Western, blues, Hawaiian, religious, Irish, novelty, Spanish, and other kinds of music that might never have occurred to Bing as being marketable. When Jack Kapp died in 1949, his brother Dave took over the reins and was a most capable replacement.

Part of Bing's record success can also be attributed to his movie tie-ins. When Bing became a money-maker for Paramount, thus gaining considerable influence and

223

power, he ensured the musical success of his films by employing some of the best songwriters in the business. He'd introduce the new songs in his films, record them before the films were released, and thereby get the jump on other recording artists. The films, of course, helped sell records. It was a business-wise and lucrative arrangement.

When Presley turned the record industry upside down, Bing, whose music was now passé in the industry, was more or less forced to leave Decca, for whom he had recorded exclusively for twenty-one years. After 1956, he continued to cut an occasional single or album for them, but he was really fighting against the tide. Soundtracks from his films were issued on the Columbia, Capitol, and Liberty labels, and he worked as a free-lancer, cutting albums for Sinatra's Reprise label and for Capitol, Daybreak, and Pickwick, among others. He also formed his own company, Project Records, in the late fifties and leased the tracks to major companies for distribution, including MGM, Decca, and Warner Brothers records.

Eventually Bing found that there wasn't a ready market for some of his recorded work and, like many another American recording artist, he turned to England, where there is still a pre-Presley popular market. Bing made his last recordings in England just days before his death. According to Laurence Zwisohn, twenty-two songs that Bing recorded for Project in 1962 have never been issued.

Bing turned reluctantly to television only after his career in radio, movies, and records was waning. It wasn't his favorite medium, to say the least. As in his movie work, he usually had to wear his toupee, but by the time he got into television rather heavily, it was the only game in town. Bob Hope was instrumental in dragging Bing before the unblinking eye for the first time. He talked Bing into appearing in a telethon to raise money for the Olympic fund on June 21, 1952. The following January Bing did his first half-hour special, which aired Saturday, January 3, 1953; Jack Benny was Bing's first guest. Then he did a few guest appearances, mostly for Bob Hope specials, before starring in "High Tor," a musical adapted for television from Maxwell Anderson's play, which received fair reviews.

In the fall of 1964, Bing made his only determined effort in the television medium with "The Bing Crosby Show," a half-hour situation comedy revolving around a family with teenagers in which Bing played the husband and father. After holding out for so long, Bing's debut as a television-series performer was eagerly anticipated. The show opened to good reviews, but the ratings soon slid, and Bing quit after doing twenty-two half-hour segments. Interest in the show seemed to slide with Bing's own interest. He hated the show and hated doing it. It took up more of his time than it was worth to him.

Bing continued making occasional guest appearances after his series failed. But he had no significant TV exposure until he was offered a spot on the popular Saturday-night variety hour called "The Hollywood Palace." Bing hosted the show every four weeks, alternating with Judy Garland, George Burns, and Martha Raye. He hosted sixteen of the shows between 1968 and 1970.

It was in 1966 that Bing did his first Christmas special, a one-hour show called "Bing Crosby's Christmas Eve Special," which became a holiday tradition and on which he always sang "White Christmas." The specials became a family tradition for millions of fans, as well. The last one was aired two months after his death and was presented in a format in which Bing's second family—Kathryn; Harry Lillis, Jr.; Mary; and Nathaniel—reminisced about the making of the taped show and about their life with Bing. It was very touching, but it would have been even more touching and meaningful had Bing's first four boys been invited to participate in the "live" portion of the presentation. Somehow it doesn't seem right that the family's farewell to Bing excluded his first four sons, even though they hadn't participated in the taped Christmas special segment. The four boys were, after all, Kathryn's stepsons and Bing's sons, too.

Part Seven:

Bing, Inc.

CHAPTER FIFTEEN

Hope? . . . he's got more money
on him than I *have.*

—BING CROSBY

Bing Crosby had one of the largest personal fortunes of anyone in show business. He made millions with his feature films and more millions with his records, which reached half a billion sales. He received a better than standard royalty for each record sold, and for twenty-one years, he owned an interest in the company that made and distributed his records. He would have been a multimillionaire even if he had let the Internal Revenue Service grab an unfair share of his earnings and if he had banked the remainder at simple interest. But he didn't.

By 1934, his career was on such solid footing that he was making more money than he could possibly spend, and when it became evident that there was no limit to his money-making potential—or to the federal government's greed—he took steps to protect his growing wealth. Up to that point, he had been operating out of an office at Paramount Pictures, where Ev and two full-time secretaries were kept busy with his growing enterprises. John O'Melveny had gotten Bing off to a good start by investing in tax-free municipal bonds for him. As Bing's earnings increased, O'Melveny and the money people with whom Bing was, in Dixie's words, hobnobbing at the time were offering him sound financial advice, and Bing was listening.

Bing decided to bring the Crosby clan together, except for brother Bob, who had already struck out on his own three years earlier. He brought his parents down from Spokane and bought them a fine house at 4366 Ponca Avenue, just a few blocks from his own home at Toluca Lake. Then he brought brother Larry down from Seattle, where he had been working in public relations after teaching at Gonzaga for a while. Larry is said to have had some newspaper background as well, and so he was appointed the official Crosby spokesman and the organization's public-relations director. Everett stayed on as Bing's personal manager and was, in effect, the top executive in the family business, next to Bing. And with attorney John O'Melveny to guide him, Everett eventually did a more than adequate job for the family business.

A number of people in the entertainment industry thought that Larry, rather than Everett, should have been Bing's chief executive. Larry had the college degree, and he was the more refined of the two. Everett wasn't a lout, but he was more abrasive, pugnacious, and forceful than Larry, qualities that Bing wanted in his front man, which is exactly what Ev was. Part of Ev's job was to be the bad guy of the Crosby organization, and that he was successful is attested to by the fact that in the industry he was known as "the wrong Crosby." It was the old Mutt-and-Jeff game that people in authority often play.

As we indicated earlier, there were numerous people

in the entertainment industry who wouldn't have any dealings with the Crosby organization, owing to a lack of trust. But, astonishingly, those who did didn't seem to recognize the Crosby technique. Bing Crosby, they thought, was too nice a guy, too easygoing to be behind Everett's maniacal, shouting demands, his desk pounding, his penchant for sending back contracts unread and demanding that better ones be offered. Such was the incredible effect of Bing's image. That "wrong Crosby," they thought, was drunk with power and was surely overstepping the bounds of his authority. If they could just get through to Bing, they reasoned, things would be different. But, of course, Ev acted as Bing's shield, taking the blame and the heat. That's what he was paid for.

Larry Crosby was intelligent enough, but he had a humane bent that wasn't conducive to operating in the tough business world—at least, not as practiced by the Crosby organization. He had a bad habit of questioning some of Bing's actions and orders. And the one thing Bing didn't need was another conscience, so he kept Larry in check by restricting his authority and by not letting Larry influence him, particularly with respect to helping those who had been hurt in one way or another by Bing's actions. Larry often tried to make amends for such actions but was frustrated in his attempts and often lamented that Bing simply wouldn't listen to him. Even so, Larry was intensely loyal and did a masterful job at public relations. Many people didn't think he did much; many thought that Bing's talent and superstardom and the high esteem in which people held him was all the public relations he needed. But, in fact, Bing's image had a tarnished side to it, and Larry was charged with keeping the shiny side up. In this, the mild-mannered brother excelled, for he was the most credible member of the organization.

Once Bing had gathered his family team, he purchased as his corporate headquarters a building at 9028 Sunset Boulevard, a modest, yellow-stucco, three-story building that still bears the Crosby name on its facade and which is still occupied by the Crosby organization, although at this writing, there are plans to close it down and vacate the premises. In its heyday, the basement of the building was occupied by the Finlandia Baths and the first- and second-floor offices were rented out. The Crosby business has always occupied the third floor.

A detailed study of Bing's corporation would be a book in itself. Bing incorporated in 1936 under the name Bing Crosby, Incorporated, and Bing Crosby, Limited. His subsequent dealings and holdings were locked in a maze of parent and subsidiary companies, which included Bing Crosby Enterprises; Bing Crosby Investment Corporation; Bing Crosby Research Foundation; Bing Crosby Productions; Bing's Things, Inc.; Decros (affiliated with Decca Records); Crosby-Jayson Corporation; and other companies, including limited partnerships, co-partnerships, and affiliations with companies like Ampex, Minute Maid, and several distribution companies.

A partial list of the activities and investments that his companies were involved in includes real estate, mines, oil wells, cattle, racehorses, a breeding farm for racehorses, music publishing, video and audio tape and machines, a racetrack, a percentage of the Pittsburgh Pirates and Detroit Tigers baseball teams, a percentage of the Los Angeles Rams football team, a professional hockey franchise, a resort complex, contracts of several prizefighters, ice-cream distribution, frozen-food distribution, a talent-booking agency, a record company, inventions and patents, toys, clothing, radio stations, television stations, business buildings, banks, savings and loan associations, motion-picture production, and television-series production.

The racetrack, of course, was Del Mar, on the Pacific, just north of San Diego, California. Bing had it built in 1936, and although several people like Edgar Bergen, Pat O'Brien, and Oliver Hardy went into the venture with him, Bing put up most of the money—his investment was reportedly half a million—to build it, and was its chairman of the board, chief stockholder, and biggest booster; he promoted it on his radio show until it became well known even among people who didn't follow the horses. When he sold his controlling interest in the track ten years later—a sale allegedly precipitated by a Supreme Court ruling that prohibited his owning a gambling facility (the track) while holding interest in a baseball team; he had purchased the Pittsburgh Pirates in August 1946—he was said to have had 35 percent of the stock, which was selling at $500 per share. It was reported that when he sold out, he kept one block of stock for Dixie and the four boys, which allowed him to remain on the track's board of diectors. Bing's interest in horses and racing was consuming. At one point, he owned a string of twenty-one racehorses in this country and abroad, and even after he sold his controlling interest in the track, he and Lindsay Howard continued operating the Bing-Lin Breeding Stables at Rancho Santa Fe, near San Diego.

Bing always denied owning a part of Minute Maid, the frozen orange juice company, but in fact he was in on it almost from its beginning. The process of freezing orange juice and then reconstituting it was developed during the war. In 1945, a man named John M. Fox refined the process and began marketing the drink under his company, Vacuum Foods Company. But he was underfinanced. The public needed to be educated about the product and, of course, the distribution problem was critical. In a time of small, independently owned neighborhood grocery stores that had little capital or incentive to buy the kind of equipment needed to keep the product frozen, the perishable commodity wasn't easy to push. Fox himself had sold it door-to-door. That's where the millionaire financier Jock Whitney came into the picture. Whitney raised the capital needed to get Vacuum Foods going, and he was a friend of Bing Crosby. In 1949, Bing began doing a fifteen-minute radio show for Vacuum Foods, and in lieu of money, he took twenty thousand shares in the parent company, which was soon renamed Minute Maid Corporation. In 1953, Minute Maid issued its first stock dividend, with a net exceeding $1 million. By 1954, its sales had reached $100 million, and it absorbed its chief rival, Snow Crop, and began marketing other frozen foods besides juice.

There is no indication that Bing ever sold his shares in the company; in fact, he had something that was perhaps even more profitable: distribution rights for five western states, including Arizona and California. Bing always denied being connected with Minute Maid, perhaps becuse he didn't want to be thought of as plugging his own product. Had he been cornered, he would have rationalized his denial on the technicality that he had a substantial chunk of Vacuum Foods, which only incidentally became Minute Maid.

Bing's corporation muddled along for nine years until the man behind his financial empire, Basil Grillo, came along. Grillo had been in credit management and tax auditing before Bing hired him to organize Bing Crosby Productions in 1945. Until Grillo's arrival, Bing had been putting much of his money into highly speculative ventures and non-income property. He had two business buildings, including his headquarters on Sunset, but he had also bought, traded, and sold a dozen ranches. And during one period alone, he had his mansion at Holmby Hills, a magnificent compound at Rancho Santa Fe near San Diego—which included huge stables, a tennis court and swimming pool, and several houses—a home in Palm Springs, a home at Pebble Beach in northern California, a vacation home on Hayden Lake in Coeur d' Alene, Idaho, and a three thousand-acre ranch in Elko, Nevada.

Grillo's behind-the-scenes financial maneuverings were brilliant. He organized and packaged Bing's talents, including his radio, television, movie, and record work. He helped manage Bing's other endeavors, including mining and oil, and steered him through the maze of negotiations in purchasing interests in numerous enterprises, including KMBY Radio in Monterey, California, which he bought with two other investors in 1951; Spokane's first television station, KLXY-TV, in

232

which he owned 47 percent interest in 1952; radio and television stations KFEQ and KFEQ-TV in St. Louis, Missouri, which he purchased with two other investors in 1955; KCOP-TV in Los Angeles, purchased in 1957 by Bing and a small group of investors for $4 million and for which Bing was named chairman of the board; KFOX AM and FM Radio in Long Beach, California, in 1957; and KPTV in Portland, Oregon, for which Bing was also named chairman of the board. He subsequently sold KCOP-TV in Los Angeles and KFOX Radio in Long Beach at enormous profits.

Another area that Grillo paid particular attention to was Bing Crosby Productions. The company had a dozen writers working full-time developing properties, including scores of films and such television series as "Ben Casey," "Slattery's People," "Breaking Point," "The Bing Crosby Show," "Hogan's Heroes," and "Wild, Wild West."

Less than five months before Bing's death, newswoman Barbara Walters interviewed him at his mansion in Hillsborough, a suburb of San Francisco. The taped interview aired during a "Barbara Walters Special" on the ABC network May 31, 1977. During the interview, Barbara asked Bing about an estimate that had been published of his wealth: $150 million. Bing said, "Oh, my God, Barbara!" then told her that he had just been working on his will (which was filed 27 days after the show was aired) and that, after taxes, he'd leave an estate of about $1,200,000. This "revelation" must have got a laugh from Barbara (off camera), for Bing made the statement from the spacious, well-manicured grounds of his mansion, which alone has an estimated worth of $1.5 million, and he had only moments before told her that he had kept his interest in an oil field that he and Bob Hope had invested in years before—not a well but a *field*, and a very productive one at that.

In Thompson's book *Bing*, which was published a year before the Walters interview, Bing was asked whether he or Hope was the wealthier, and Bing said,

"Hope? Oh! God, he's got more money *on* him than I *have*." And when asked about the estimated $150 million published figure, Bing called it completely preposterous and estimated his worth, after taxes, at $1.5 million.

Bing Crosby was no dummy, and he learned something from the financial wizard Basil Grillo in the more than thirty years they were associated (at Bing's death, Grillo was listed as his business manager). When Bing went into semi-retirement, for example, he sold Bing Crosby Productions to Cox Broadcasting Corporation of Atlanta, Georgia, for $2 million in stock. The following year, he purchased part interest in the First National Bank of Holbrook, Arizona, and was named chairman of the board. He enlarged the scope of his business interests during his semi-retirement from show business, and there is no indication that he sold his oil wells, his extensive real-estate holdings, his interests in banks, television stations, radio stations, savings and loan companies, and numerous other ventures that one would have to dig to find. Quite the contrary.

A person who was fairly close to the Crosby organization and who watched it grow over the years estimated Crosby's worth at about $80 million at his death. Then there's the published estimate of $150 million in 1975. If there's any truth to the estimate, and we think there is, Bing was worth more than $150 million at his death; those oil wells are still pumping.

CHAPTER SIXTEEN

If you're married to
a Crosby, you've *got* to drink!

—DIXIE LEE CROSBY

Bing and Dixie's marriage got off to a very rocky start with their separation and reconciliation in March of 1931; however, their next two years were not only their happiest together but the most trouble-free as well. Not once to our knowledge did Dixie talk of divorce or threaten to leave Bing during that period. And for good reason: she was happy. From March 1931 to March 1933, they were uprooted, unsettled, and inseparable—conditions that kept Bing off balance and that were not at all conducive to his establising the stereotypical *tableau vivant* he had in mind for Dixie.

They were an exciting two years, whirlwind years. Staying at New York City's Essex House; café society; Broadway plays; club-hopping with Everett and Naomie and Kitty and Eddie Lang and Sue Carol and others; Bing's successful radio debut, and a sponsor; Bing's smash at the Paramount Theatre, and a movie offer; back to the West Coast to do the movie, followed by a successful personal-appearance tour; and then back to New York and an even better radio offer. Bing's record sales soared with his radio and movie popularity. The big money began coming in. Dixie discovered that she was pregnant. Bing got an offer for a second Paramount film. It was, indeed, an exciting two years, and in that short period, Bing rose from the obscurity of a relatively unknown solo artist to the threshold of stardom. And Dixie was with him all the while, enjoying every minute of it.

At the end of the two-year period, in March 1933, Dixie went home to have their first child. She traveled by ship, via the Panama Canal, with a sightseeing stopover in Cuba, and was accompanied by Ev's wife Naomie, Sue Carol, and Sue's baby daughter, Carolee (who was named after Sue and Dixie and who is now the wife of Johnny Vietch, head of Columbia Pictures). Kitty Lang was scheduled to take the voyage with them, but Eddie decided to enter the hospital for a tonsillectomy. It was a minor operation, but Eddie was distrustful of doctors and hospitals, and Kitty stayed with him.

Dixie had just settled back into their leased house next to Sue Carol's and was awaiting Bing's return to Los Angeles when she learned of Eddie's death. She was six months pregnant and couldn't travel back to New York, but she insisted that Kitty join her in California after the funeral, which Kitty did. When the radio season ended shortly thereafter, Bing returned, and he and Dixie and Kitty went house hunting. The Crosbys would need larger quarters to accommodate the additions they'd be making to their family. It was on Forman Avenue, in fashionable Toluca Lake, that they bought their first home. For Dixie, it was the happiest time of her life; she had a husband she adored and whom she would soon make a father; she had a home of her own; and their financial worries and professional anxieties were behind them. She didn't know that she was now firmly snared in Bing's housetrap. Bing's stereotypical image was now complete. Dixie had everything a "mother" needed: a home, security, her own interests, and good friends. And while she did everything a mother was supposed to do, he ran and played again, just as he had done prior to their first separation.

The boys he played with this time were actors Richard Arlen, with whom he was making the film *College Humor*, and his old pal Gary Cooper. Like Dixie, Arlen's wife, Jobyna, was also expecting (the Crosbys and Arlens ultimately held a double christening of their offspring), and Bing and Richard were celebrating their impending fatherhood by doing a good deal of elbow bending at Hollywood's more fashionable watering holes. Bing reveled so much that it interfered with the picture he was supposed to be doing. It was Bing's big chance with Paramount, and one would have expected him to be on his good behavior. But Bing seldom did what one expected of him.

Mary Carlisle, who was also in *College Humor*, is quoted in Charles Thompson's book *Bing* about a big production number that was scheduled, and how the entire cast and crew were kept waiting for two hours by Bing before finally calling the shooting off for the day. Just as Miss Carlisle was leaving the set, Bing drove up, his eyes all bloodshot, and told her that he wasn't going to make it that day. Miss Carlisle said that he was so nice and apologetic that "nobody could get mad at him because he did it [apologized] so beautifully."

The boys had their days planned, too. The day before Bing's first son was born, the following blurb was printed in *The Hollywood Reporter:*

Gary Cooper, Bing Crosby, and Dick Arlen think they're leaving for a fishing trip in Mexican waters any minute.

Dixie, of course, was causing the delay, but on June 27, 1933, she finally cooperated by delivering the first of their four sons. He was named Gary Evan, after Gary Cooper and Dixie's father, Evan Wyatt. Bing is thought to have been on the golf course when Dixie was in labor, but wherever he was, Kitty Lang called him when Gary was born, and he went to the hospital to see Dixie and his son. Then he and Kitty celebrated the birth over ice-cream sodas at a nearby drugstore. Later, when speaking of his and Richard Arlen's newborns,

Bing said, "Not bad for a couple of old birds who are seldom on the nest."

The remark says a good deal about Bing's philosophy regarding marriage, and about Dixie's life with a man who was not only seldom on the nest, but who bragged about it in public—jokingly, of course—and who clearly believed that his attitude was a manly one: to Bing's way of thinking, flying free while the female tended the nest was the male prerogative and the right order of things. With such a male model, it's small wonder that Bing's first four sons have all had marriage problems; three of them had divorced before Bing died, and what is preposterous is that Bing was contemptuous of them because they couldn't make their marriages work. In the Barbara Walters interview in 1977, he was still lamenting the fact that "they married several times." He never forgave them for it.

Gary Cooper, the man for whom Bing's first boy was named, had much in common with Bing. Coop, as he was called, was also born in the northwest (Montana), within two years of Bing's birth; he, too, was a playboy; he, too, had an eye for younger, sophisticated women; he, too, loved fast horses, fishing, and the outdoor life; he, too, had extramarital affairs; and his marriage was also held together only by the devotion of his wife, who happened to be a Catholic (Cooper also converted to Roman Catholicism before his death from cancer). They made quite a pair.

In his biography of Gary Cooper, entitled *Coop,* author Stuart Kaminsky relates that in an interview with actress Patricia Neal (who had a three-year relationship with Cooper when she was 22 and he 47), she told Kaminsky that Cooper "adored people with money." Kaminsky also tells of Cooper's affair with a countess who took Coop on a grand tour of Europe, traveling in the highest social circles and acquainting him with the right people (Bing himself later developed a relationship with an aristocratic Frenchwoman). Cooper had married into an enormously wealthy family, so he was very much in a position to introduce Bing to the right people, and Bing was very much interested in being introduced to them.

During the mid-thirties, when Bing was establishing his corporation and beginning to make million-dollar picture deals and running with Coop, Bing went through a very snobbish phase. Sylvia Picker McGraw told us that for a while, Bing got out of touch with his old friends, and Dixie found herself entertaining millionaires rather than the musicians and show people with whom she was far more comfortable.

At the Burt McMurtrie luncheon, which was recorded by Vern Taylor and which we quoted from earlier, Burt gave the luncheon group an insight into this period. Burt was very close to both Bing and Dixie, and Dixie liked him very much because he was honest and outspoken.

"Bing's head began to swell about as soon as he began to make it big," Burt told the luncheon group. "His first movies; the great records; the radio show. All of a sudden, as far as Dixie was concerned, he had a whole new set of values. She didn't go for that. She had no pretensions herself, and it irked her when Bing began running around with the rich, important people who always seem to be around entertainers. He hung out more and more with them, instead of old friends.

"There was one time when the Whiteman guys were in town on one of their tours, and a lot of them were invited out to the Crosbys' for the evening. Well, old Bing didn't get home that night, so Dixie did all the hosting. They had their dinner, then sat around talking about the good old days. She made apologies all evening long, waiting for Bing to show up.

"She let him have it good after that. Really put him in his place—what did he mean by standing all his old pals up? Who did he think he was? She called him a hobnobber. Used some of her Deep South words on him, of which she knew a few, believe me. I can't remember now who told me about it. Probably Bing himself. 'You really have got yourself up in the air,' she told him. 'Do you *really* imagine those big shots give a

239

tinker's damn about you—*personally?* Why, all they want from you is what they expect from any other trained seal! They want you to stand up and burp for them!'

"Bing was a good learner. He got over it pretty fast. She was very good for him in those first years. He often admitted it. Your average . . . movie star would not have stood still for that one minute; he'd have closed the door behind him with a loud bang. . . . He [Bing] could dish it out, and when it came to taking it, he took it, and was glad for it later."

Bing's interest wasn't in the nouveau riche, whose ranks he was himself beginning to enter, but in those of inherited wealth and culture. The period in which he ran almost exclusively with them—particularly the Santa Barbara and Pasadena sets—lasted only eighteen months or so. But for the rest of his life, some of his closest friends were very wealthy people for whom he held great admiration. And even in the last few decades of his life, he was hobnobbing with wealth and royalty in Europe, where he went almost yearly.

As McMurtrie pointed out, Dixie, above all, noticed the change in Bing. His public image wasn't affected, but privately, Bing's values changed, and he was never quite the same person again. McMurtrie's views to the contrary, Bing did not get over the influence of his society period. Dixie could deal with the overt manifestations, but she was powerless to reach the psychic changes. Bing seemed so oblivious to them that Dixie worried that she herself might be unconsciously affected. In the late thirties, when she had begun to drink quite heavily, she sought Maybeth Carpenter's opinion. As was the case with all of Dixie's woman friends, Maybeth would tell the unvarnished truth if solicited to do so, and Dixie valued her opinion. Maybeth said that one day Dixie said to her, "Other than my drinking, Maybeth, do you think I've changed?" And when Maybeth told her sincerely that she didn't notice any difference in her, Dixie seemed satisfied.

It was during Bing's Gatsby period that he stopped drinking himself into unconsciousness. (He quit drinking entirely for a while, and when he resumed, he would drink occasionally, but never let the bottle get the best of him again.) This change occurred at about the time that superstar status was within his grasp (1936), when he incorporated himself, built a new mansion in Toluca Lake (which burned down January 2, 1943, when Christmas-tree lights shorted out), signed his million-dollar movie contract, and began revising his biographical history. The family biography was being written at this time; he was getting about ten thousand fan letters and requests for photographs each week; and a quarterly, twenty-four-page, digest-size magazine called *Bingang,* published by the Club Crosby of North Vassalboro, Maine, was about to be published for Bing's eighty-five fan clubs in this country and abroad. Bing was undergoing a lot of changes, and any one of them—or all of them—could have contributed to his new sobriety. Dixie had been after him constantly to stop his drinking to excess, for the way that liquor affected him would ruin his career, but one gathers from Dixie's friends that Dixie attributed his stopping not to her influence but to "high society" influences.

By the time Dixie had recovered from childbirth and Gary had grown from infant to toddler, she had taken a reckoning of married life à la Bing and had rebelled against his cozy-nest setup with its absentee lord. She signed with Monogram studios to go back to work. The film was *Manhattan Love Song* (1934). One of the provisions Dixie insisted upon at Monogram was that she be billed as Dixie Lee, not as Dixie Crosby. Friends say that she did so to keep producers from capitalizing on Bing's name. And this is certainly consistent with Dixie's character. But she was also a very intelligent and independent woman, and it no doubt crossed her mind that, under the circumstances, performing once again under the name she had used before marriage gave her a semblance of individuality (hopefully in

Bing's eyes) and perhaps even the self-respect that she was losing from assuming the hausfrau image Bing was imposing upon her.

The Crosby-organization line was that Dixie just wanted to get back in the swing of things after Gary's birth, but anyone who knew how excruciatingly painful it was for her to perform knew that she had to be either terribly angry or terribly desperate—or both—to be driven to such an extreme. Bing didn't want Dixie to work: the mother's place was in the home, minding *her* children. And by signing for the film, Dixie was not too subtly telling Bing what he could do with his stereotypical tableau. If Bing didn't feel obliged to stay home, then two could play the same game. Bing was very upset about her going back to work, and they fought about it, but nature interrupted the argument before it could be satisfactorily resolved. Dixie was pregnant again.

On July 13, 1934 (Friday the thirteenth), Dixie gave birth to twins: Philip Lang (named after guitarist Eddie Lang) and Dennis Michael (named after Bing's maternal grandfather Dennis Harrigan). Bing was on the golf course when the twins were born, and Dixie rubbed his nose in that fact for years afterward. She also resumed her rebellion six months later, when she went to Paramount to do the film *Love in Bloom* (1935), a musical in which she played the part of Violet Downey.

Dixie entered the enemy camp at Paramount, for at the time, Bing was having an affair with a well-known actress who was under contract there. Dixie's friends told us that they knew—or had heard—of the affair, but they don't know whether Dixie knew about it. Through all her martial problems, Dixie never talked with her friends about her personal relationship with Bing—his absences, yes; but nothing personal. She never hinted to anyone that she might have known about his extramarital activities. Bing was discreet in his affairs, but although, as columnist Florabel Muir pointed out in a 1950 Los Angeles *Mirror* column, "there had been the strangest conspiracy among even the gossip columnists to protect Bing and Dixie from any unfavorable stories," Bing's activities were well known to Hollywood insiders. Several of Dixie's friends told us, however, that by the early forties, she must have known that Bing was seeing other women.

Dixie finished *Love in Bloom* at Paramount, and on March 11, 1935 she recorded the first of two solo records that she did for Decca, "You Got Me Doin' Things"/"My Heart is an Open Book," then went to Fox, where she did *Redheads on Parade* (1935), in which she played opposite John Boles, the singer who had been given Bing's "Song of the Dawn" spot in *King of Jazz*. It's an irony that Dixie couldn't have overlooked. Bing, by the way, made an uncharacteristic appearance on the set of *Redheads on Parade* with Gary, Philip, and Dennis in tow. Whether this was a signal that he had capitulated, at least for the time being, isn't known, but *Redheads* was Dixie's last picture.

In July 1936, Dixie made her second solo recording for Decca, "When a Lady Meets a Gentleman Down South"/"Until the Real Thing Comes Along," and the following month she made her last recording—and the only one she ever made with Bing—a duet on the Decca label: "A Fine Romance"/"The Way You Look Tonight." It was also in 1936 that the Crosbys moved into their newly built home on Camarillo in Toluca Lake. It was a huge, two-story colonial structure with twenty-six rooms, ten baths, a tennis court, a swimming pool, and a U-shaped drive that cut across the six-acre estate. They lived there when the last of their four sons was born on January 5, 1938. He was named Lindsay Harry, after Bing's business partner, Lindsay Howard.

After Lindsay's birth, another major battle broke out at the Crosby household. Dixie didn't tell anyone what the battle was about, but it's known that she forced Bing to live in the servant's quarters above the garage—that is, when he was home. When the battle ended, Dixie seemed resigned to the kind of married life that Bing fashioned for her, though her friends say that it was at this point that Dixie began drinking very heavily as she rebelled periodically against his absences. She became known in film-colony circles as a recluse, for she seldom went out unless she could persuade Bing to take her somewhere, which wasn't very often.

There were times, though, when Bing would take Dixie out, and he could be extremely charming on such occasions. Maybeth Carpenter, who was a singer herself (her husband is trombonist Pete Carpenter, who also knew Bing and Dixie), was opening at the Beverly Wilshire Hotel in the mid-thirties. Dixie wanted to go, but Bing refused to take her, and since Dixie wouldn't go to clubs without Bing, she told Maybeth that she'd miss her opening. But on opening night, Bing came home and said to Dixie, "A fine friend you are. Here one of your best friends is opening at the Beverly Wilshire, and you're just sitting here." Maybeth was very surprised to see them walk in. Later in the evening, while Bing was dancing with Maybeth, he said, "I think I'll go up on the bandstand and sing two or three hundred songs." The band was Gus Arnheim's, and not only was Gus ecstatic about having Bing sing with him again, but so was the audience; Bing sang for nearly an hour.

Mostly, though, Dixie stayed home. But she entertained often, and it was always open house at Dixie's, a meeting place for all her friends. Dixie particularly loved babies and children, and whenever anyone got pregnant—friend, relative of a friend, or friend of a friend—Dixie threw a shower, and they were always lavish. She loved giving birthday and dinner parties, too. And as with most parties given for and by entertainers, all who attended usually performed. Once in a while Dixie could be prevailed upon to sing and to do her imitation of Bing, complete with mannerisms, which convulsed everyone, including Bing.

Christmas was Dixie's special time, and she always made a colossal production of it. Since she loved giving gifts, she'd start weeks in advance, setting up special tables in a room set aside for wrapping presents. She was an artist at gift-wrapping and spent a fortune on ribbons and bows and paper and ornaments to wrap with. She remembered everyone. All her friends said that she was incredibly generous and thoughtful, and that her presents were so beautifully wrapped that they hated to open them, feeling that they were destroying works of art. One of the reasons Dixie especially enjoyed Christmas is that it was a family occasion, and she loved having her entire family around her.

Despite Bing's knowledge of how meaningful Christmas was to Dixie, he didn't let the holiday interfere with whatever he had planned. He was home more often than not during the twenty-one Christmases they were married, and for a while, he established a tradition of Christmas caroling with his sons in their neighborhood, but not always. The late columnist Hedda Hopper, who never wrote a discouraging word about the Crosbys when Dixie was alive, filed a story with the wire services that was donated to the Academy of Motion Picture Arts and Sciences library a few months after Dixie's death. It's a sixteen-page typewritten tribute to her, and it may never have been published in its entirety. In the story, Miss Hopper tells of being at actress Merle Oberon's house for dinner one Christmas Eve, and for some reason, Merle Oberon wondered aloud what Dixie was doing. Hedda suggested that they call and find out. They learned from Dixie that the boys were asleep and that, except for the household help, she was alone and waiting for Bing.

"Why don't you come over and join us?" Merle asked.

Dixie reminded Merle that it was Christmas Eve and that she wanted to be home when Bing got there, although she didn't know when that would be.

Since Dixie was always giving parties for others, it was decided that the guests at Merle's would go over to Dixie's and bring her back to the party. When they got there, they found her alone. She was dressed up for Bing, wearing a black velvet gown, diamond earrings, clips, bracelet, and a diamond solitaire ring. Hedda said that she wasn't expecting anyone; she had dressed for Bing's arrival, and there had been no word from him.

Miss Hopper said that it took a lot of persuading, but they succeeded in taking Dixie back to Merle Oberon's, where she joined the others. "But I think I never saw a lonelier girl during the four hours she spent in our company," Miss Hopper reported. "She had only two drinks. Sitting on the floor, she reached out, touched Merle's hand, and said in a forlorn voice, 'Thank you. It means so much.' Miss Hopper added, "Her shyness, of which so few people knew, would not permit her to say more. But there was a world of gratitude in those few words."

Hedda Hopper also tells of being in New York on one of the few occasions that Dixie traveled there with Bing. Miss Hopper called Dixie to invite her for lunch. Dixie told her that if she had called the day before, she would have accepted the invitation "like a shot." But she added that she was packing to go home that evening.

"Home?" Miss Hopper said. "But Bing's staying another two weeks, isn't he?"

"Yes," Dixie said. "That's why I'm going. I'd rather be lonely at home than in New York. I'm staying at the Garden City Hotel in Long Island. Have you ever been there?"

The Garden City Hotel was a place where elderly people usually stayed. It had a long porch lined with rocking chairs, in which little old ladies usually sat and rocked and knitted and gossiped. But it was very near a fine tournament golf course. "Dixie had sat there three days, while Bing was out playing golf," Miss Hopper wrote. "She was not the rocking, knitting, gossiping type. So she went home. And who could blame her?"

Hedda Hopper also pointed out—"in fairness to Bing," she said—that she didn't think he neglected Dixie intentionally. "He had many friends for whom Dixie did not care," she wrote. Miss Hopper also said that Bing had become, in effect, "a citizen of the world, while Dixie had retired further and further into the small group that contained her family." Much of Bing's time, she wrote, was spent meeting people, doing benefits, and attending business affairs. "Dixie was proud of his success," she wrote, "but it did not detract from her loneliness."

As with other Hollywood columnists, Miss Hopper took indirect jabs at Bing but never threw a haymaker. Her point about Bing's not neglecting Dixie intentionally is probably, for the most part, true. But in this, Miss Hopper joined the ranks of others—even Dixie's friends—who dug up excuses and made apologies for Bing. In fact, whether his neglect of her was intentional is irrelevant. He neglected her. Constantly. She pleaded with him, and it didn't help. She left him once, and it didn't help. She went back to work in pictures, and it didn't help. She fought with him, and it didn't help. She drank, and it didn't help. She threatened him with divorce, and it didn't help. Dixie was a prisoner in her own home. Bing wouldn't let her go, and he wouldn't stay with her.

Bing's three thousand-acre ranch at Elko, Nevada, was another prison. The four boys were herded up there every summer, where they worked from sunrise to sunset for practically nothing, to teach them the value of money and of hard work. And it was tough, for it was a working cattle ranch, with several thousand head. Bing always said that the boys could choose their own professions, so long as they got their educations first. But he also let them know that it would please him if they became ranchers. None of the boys wanted to be a rancher, but Philip and Dennis enrolled in animal husbandry at Washington State College, mostly, no doubt, to please their father. And it no doubt displeased him when they didn't follow through after they were discharged from the service. Bing finally sold the ranch in the late fifties, when it became evident that Phil and Dennis preferred show business to herding cattle.

Nobody hated the ranch more than Dixie. She wasn't an outdoors woman at all, but Bing spent more time at the ranch than he did with her, so she began joining him just to be with him. But that didn't work, either.

Doodles Weaver, the musician who had known Dixie

back in the Grove days, was appearing at Elko with the Spike Jones band, and one evening Dixie drove from the ranch—at least an hour's drive—to see the band. She talked Doodles into coming back with her for dinner. Doddles said that the boys were there, but Bing wasn't. He told us that Dixie was angry at Bing because she had come up to spend a few weeks with him, and after they got there, he left to attend to a business matter. Dixie was particularly angry because Bing had done the same thing to her before. She told Doodles that on several occasions, they had come to the ranch, and after Bing was there a few days, he'd make some excuse to leave—usually business—saying that he'd be back soon, then never return.

Dixie began drinking so heavily that it worried her friends. Most thought that she drank partly because she was lonely and partly from pique. By this time, Bing seldom drank, and he hated Dixie to. She didn't drink every day; there were periods of weeks when she wouldn't drink at all. Then she'd drink for days or weeks. But she held the liquor well, and only once do any of her friends recall Dixie being really drunk. That was following the grand opening of Del Mar, when the Crosbys threw a party at their Rancho Santa Fe compound. And that was a few years before Dixie began drinking hard.

Dixie didn't drink much around her sons, as a general rule. And she held it well enough that even today, three of her sons don't believe, or don't want to believe, that she was an alcoholic. Gary knew otherwise. He became an alcoholic himself, and during a magazine interview and in an article, which caused ill feelings between his brothers and himself, he referred to his mother's alcoholism.

Bing knew that Dixie had a bad drinking problem, but rather than tracing it to its source—himself—he pointed to others, including Dixie's friends. The irony is that Dixie's friends weren't drinkers. Two of them, Kitty Lang and Sue Carol, didn't drink at all, and none of them drank to excess. But Bing had to blame some-

248

one. There was a rumor around Hollywood that Bing wouldn't let anyone bring a bottle in the house because of Dixie's drinking. The rumor was totally false. Every Crosby household had a complete, well-stocked bar.

Sylvia Picker McGraw told us that she was at Dixie's one day, and Dixie had been given a bottle of champagne and decided that they should have a glass of it. Sylvia doesn't like champagne, but Dixie was in a festive mood, and Sylvia didn't want to spoil it by refusing her invitation, so she agreed. Dixie had no sooner poured the first glass when Bing came home. He seemed in one of his cool moods, so Sylvia didn't pay much attention to his behavior, but when Sylvia was at NBC a day or so later to do the "Kraft Music Hall," on which she often played character roles or substituted for someone, Bing gave her his "walking brush." Sylvia is a small woman, but she's a tower of courage, and she confronted Bing about treating her so coldly. Bing told her that he was mad at her because she encouraged Dixie's drinking. That made Sylvia angry. He had known her since 1929, when she used to go out on dates with Bing and Dixie, and Bing knew she wasn't a drinker. But that didn't stop him from accusing her.

Dixie wasn't the only one in the family who was drinking. Everett's wife, Naomie, was having her problems, too. And when Everett divorced her, alleging that she was an alcoholic, Dixie was furious and, according to her friends, she didn't speak to him for nearly ten years afterward. In Naomie's defense, Dixie often told friends, "If you're married to a Crosby, you've *got* to drink!"

Dixie could tolerate Bing's inattention for certain lengths of time; then all hell would break loose. When the threat of divorce no longer worked in getting Bing's attention, she'd call her attorney. Then Bing would back off. But after this happened several times and she came to the realization that giving in to his charm resulted only in a temporary redress of her complaint, the charm no longer worked with her, and Bing would enlist other Crosby clan members to help him keep Dixie

249

from following through with her threat to divorce him. And they literally ganged up on her, appealing to her better judgment and persuading her to reconsider the consequences of such action in the light of Bing's religion and his career. It was always four to one—Bing, Larry, and Everett, and Kate's influence, if not her presence—against Dixie. And with Naomie gone, Dixie had no one on her side. June Crosby (Bob's wife) was Dixie's favorite sister-in-law, but when Bing and Bob had had a falling out in 1940 or '41, Bob refused to let June visit Bing's house.

On one occasion, when Dixie was really fed up with the family's arguments used in Bing's defense and didn't yield readily to their pressure, the family suggested that she needed a psychiatrist. "How do you like *that?*" Dixie said to her friends. "That whole damn bunch is nuts, and they want *me* to see a psychiatrist!"

After Dixie's death, it became widely believed that Bing and Dixie's last two years together were the happiest of their lives and that they had at last buried the hatchet. People we talked to who had worked with the Crosby organization believed this, and a couple of Dixie's friends volunteered the information, including Kitty Lang. But Kitty had been at Elko, Nevada, during that time, and none of the others was privy to what was really going on in the Crosby household. One can understand why people would like to believe the story; nothing could have made those who knew Dixie and knew something about her plight happier than to think that she had found happiness in her last years. And that's probably why so many people believed the story. Unfortunately, nothing could have been further from the truth.

CHAPTER SEVENTEEN

> If they (Bing and Dixie) take this
> to court, I hope it will be
> a legal separation, not a divorce.
> The family would want it that way.
>
> —LARRY CROSBY

Bing and Dixie's last two years were the strangest of their marriage, years marked by their longest separation from one another, by uncharacteristic behavior on both their parts, and by a surprising and mystifying candor on the part of the Crosby organization. This may have been prematurely precipitated by the promise of an impending financial settlement and legal separation and by a clandestine trip Bing made to Italy, evidence of which we stumbled upon during our research. There is no doubt that an irreparable breach had occurred between them at last, and that it was about to be resolved and made public.

In March of 1950, Bing had undergone an appendectomy, and it was announced that he planned to convalesce on his ranch at Elko. But instead, he taped a dozen or so radio shows in advance, put off discussions with Paramount regarding upcoming pictures until the end of June, and on April 14, he left for Europe. He was accompanied by his friend Bill Morrow, business associate John Mullin, and Morrow's secretary. Gossip

251

columnists reported that Dixie had wanted to go with him, and that Bing had refused to take her. When she was asked about Bing taking along Morrow and others instead of her, Dixie is said to have replied, "There'll always be a Morrow." Bing told reporters that his primary reason for going to Europe was to participate in the British Amateur Open Golf Tournament at St. Andrews, Scotland, which was scheduled from May twenty-second through the twenty-seventh, and he did play there.

Bing and his entourage checked into the Ritz in Paris, and, as usual, Bing played a lot of golf at St. Cloud and Chantilly. It looked as though his European trip would be a typical one, low profile and discreet. But back in California, the Crosby organization's "ice curtain" was suddenly and inexplicably raised. On May 8, Bing's attorney, John O'Melveny, confirmed a rumor that there were "strained relations" between Bing and Dixie. The confirmation alone was unprecedented, but Bing's representatives went even further, becoming almost voluble. The following day, the Los Angeles *Times* ran a story on the Crosbys' marital problems. The following are excerpts from the *Times* story:

> Bing Crosby's attorney intimated yesterday that the singer's 20-year-long marriage to actress Dixie Lee was headed for the rocks, but the film star in Paris denied it. Both attorney John O'Melveny and the singer's brother Larry said there had been a serious quarrel in the Crosby household, and the lawyer said there are "strained relations" there.
>
> . . . Mrs. Crosby could not be reached for comment. Her attorney, Brenton L. Metzler, said, "We have nothing to say at this time."
>
> . . . Larry Crosby said he had heard there had been a serious quarrel between his brother and his wife [sic] but knew nothing of a possible separation.
>
> "I know no settlement papers have been signed," he said. "If they take this to court, I hope it will be a legal separation, not a divorce. The family would want it that way.

He added, "They have these family battles about every six months—like every other husband and wife. . . ."

For fifteen years, it had been Larry's job to quell such rumors, and suddenly he was admitting that such problems recurred "about every six months" and that the "family" didn't want it to end in divorce, but rather in a legal separation. The fact that news of the rift had been broken by John O'Melveny, Bing's taciturn attorney, made it evident that his and Larry's revelations had been approved by Bing himself. Otherwise O'Melveny would have remained silent and Larry would have denied the rumors, as he had been doing for years.

The Crosby organization must have known, also, that their sudden candor with regard to Bing's marriage would seem an official signal to the press that restraint was no longer the order of the day. And columnist Florabel Muir was perhaps one of the most outspoken in discussing the overall implications of the Crosby organization's revelations. The following are excerpts from her May 9, 1950, syndicated column, which appeared the day after Bing's attorney publicly discussed the "strained relations":

Everybody in Hollywood has conspired to keep the public in the dark about the strained relations in the Bing Crosby menage that have been apparent for many years. But things got sort of out of hand yesterday. For the first time, Der Bingle's attorney admitted there is a rift, and his two brothers talked right out loud about a possible separate maintenance suit being filed.

Bing, of course, blithely denied it and, as usual, Dixie Crosby went into hiding and said nothing. But it was no secret around the film colony that when Bing took off for Europe early last month, his parting with Mrs. Crosby was definitely not on the amicable side.

This isn't the first time they have quarreled, and it may not be the last. Down in her heart, Dixie loves the golden-throated crooner better than her own life, and if he wants to exert that old charm he can put on and off like a coat, his little wife may not be able to resist him. At least, she never has up until now, but, of course, you never can tell. Perhaps, at long last, she's all fed up with the sort of life she leads, with so many days and nights alone, and this time she may stay mad.

. . . Bing has an amazing capacity for ignoring all criticism. He just doesn't hear it. He is so indifferent to the opinions, good and bad, of those with whom he comes in contact that it is surprising that he has so long kept such good public relations.

It is no doubt pressure from Hollywood that has kept this couple together all these years. This was one marriage that just couldn't fail. The world has so idealized Bing, and it just had to be kept believing he could do no wrong.

There has been the strangest conspiracy among even the gossip columnists to protect Bing and Dixie from any unfavorable stories. Any other film couple who made that sort of news found themselves plastered all over the front pages, but not the Crosbys. Bing has been much like Lindbergh after the flier crossed the ocean all alone that night back in 1927. The public made the blond eaglet a great hero and built him up with such enthusiasm none dared to spoil the illusion that had been created. . . .

Bing's actions in Paris are further indication that there had been a major development—or promise of a development—in the stalemate between himself and Dixie. On the day that he was quoted as denying any knowledge of trouble at home, he was photographed at Longchamps racetrack with an attractive young nightclub singer named Marilyn Gerson and with the countess and count of Segonzac. That evening, he was photographed at Maxim's in a black tie, all smiles, and sans toupee, dancing with Ghislain de Baysson, the Frenchwoman who was known as his frequent companion whenever he was in Paris. It was almost as though Bing himself was trying to shatter the illusion that columnist Florabel Muir had referred to the day before the photographs appeared in the papers. Bing was acting like a free man.

Then came the sudden reversal.

On May 9 (the day the photographs appeared), Bing denied the rumors of a possible break with Dixie. The following day, the Los Angeles *Examiner* quoted Dixie as saying, "If Bing says there's nothing to it, there's nothing to it. If anyone thinks differently, he can take it from there." Dixie explained that her attorney, Brenton L. Metzler, and Bing's attorney, John O'Melveny, were aiding them in working out financial matters, including trust funds for the boys. "Whenever you get money, there are problems," Dixie said. "A few months ago, we were doing some juggling, trying to separate money. I guess that's how it [the rumor] got started."

On May 10, the Los Angeles *Times* ran a story saying that Dixie's attorney continued his silence on the matter and told the *Times* reporter that he had not talked to Dixie and had no knowledge of her statements to the press. The article also pointed out that attorney John O'Melveny, who had confirmed a report of the quarrel two days earlier, had, in the meantime, talked to Bing in Paris. "I am pleased to hear that there is no trouble between them," O'Melveny said. "I wish to concur in the statements they make. Mr. Crosby will be home on June 25."

The ice curtain again dropped into place. There was no more talk of settlement papers that hadn't been signed. There were no more photographs of Bing living it up in Paris. It was as though Bing and Dixie had reunited while they were six thousand miles apart. It appeared that Bing's organization had sent up a trial balloon on Bing's own orders, and that Bing himself had shot it down the moment it was launched. It was an absurd turn of events.

During our interviews, one of Dixie's friends told us that in her opinion, Dixie stayed with Bing after the late forties partially out of economic necessity. Bing had their money so deeply buried in interconnecting corporations that Dixie could have been reduced to something tantamount to taking handouts from him if they separated, and she would definitely have been economically dependent upon Bing for the rest of her life (a condition that Bing's second wife, Kathryn, is presently subject to, which we'll discuss in Chapter 21). Dixie, the friend thought, undoubtedly felt that she had gone through enough hell with Bing to be deserving of total independence from him if they split up. But, in the friend's opinion, Bing's corporate structure precluded that. It should be emphasized that Dixie never told her friend this; it's an opinion she reached from comments Dixie had made once in a while relating to other matters.

From what we've learned of Dixie, she would never submit to being a kept woman, a ward of the Crosby organization, so to speak. It's most disconcerting to think of their relationship in monetary terms, but it seems to have come to that. Perhaps it explains why Larry had emphasized that "no settlement papers have been signed," when there had been no previous mention by anyone of settlement papers or their existence. Perhaps it explains, too, why Dixie had hired her own attorney in working out her and Bing's financial matters by, in Dixie's words, "trying to separate money." This was more than a year before Dixie made out her will. It appears that Bing and Dixie had come to an agreement about parting and that it would be effected when the financial terms had been arranged, but that when Dixie and her attorney ran into the corporate rat's nest, Dixie blew the whistle and Bing stopped dancing in Paris.

There is another factor in this curious episode. We learned from a most reliable person affiliated with the Crosby organization that Bing's primary reason for going to Europe was to have an audience with Pope Pius XII, whom Bing had met before and who was an admirer of Bing's work as Father O'Malley in his Academy Award–winning *Going My Way* (1944) and *The Bells of St. Mary's* (1945). According to our informant, Bing went to see Pope Pius XII in an effort to secure a special dispensation to annul his nineteen-year marriage on the grounds that Dixie was an incorrigible alcoholic.

We're acutely aware of the gravity of this information, and we should emphasize here that we've made a practice of excluding from this book matters that couldn't be verified or that came to us from questionable sources. In this matter, our source, who is unimpeachable, ultimately denied us an interview after this information was offered to us unsolicited. Not only did the person have no ax to grind with respect to Bing, but the information was offered in defense of Bing against criticism by others of his treatment of Dixie. The person who told us of Bing's visit to the Vatican in 1950 was apparently a believer in the Dixie Demon stories and told us out of a profound compassion for Bing's unfortunate "circumstances" in marriage.

As for other women in Bing's life, this person said, Bing would never have been unfaithful had his marriage been a good one. It was intimated that, under the circumstances, who could blame him for his little infidelities?

We have no idea what happened to Bing's petition to Pope Pius XII. We were going to follow up on the information during the interview. It appears from Bing's actions and from his representatives' actions that an agreement to separate had been reached before Bing left for Europe, but that for some reason, the announcement of an impending separation had to be withdrawn. Certainly, with the talk of settlement papers and the separation of monies, it's not at all unreasonable to assume that Dixie stopped the process as Larry seems to intimate, by refusing to sign the settlement papers that no one but Larry even mentioned. Whether Dixie stopped the process before or after Bing's intended trip to the Vatican isn't known. In any event, what followed proved conclusively that Bing and Dixie had not patched up their differences.

In an apparent effort to assure the press that there had been no truth to rumors that he and Dixie were separating, Bing boarded the *Queen Elizabeth* at Cherbourg, France, on June 9, telling newspeople that he would return to Europe soon with Dixie and "some, or all, of the kids." He arrived in New York on June 14, and when reporters confronted him with reports of a possible separation from Dixie, Bing said, "Really? I don't know anything about it." He added that Dixie was on her way from California to join him at the Waldorf-Astoria, where he would be staying. The following day Larry Crosby denied reports that Dixie would meet Bing in New York. And five days later, when Bing got off the train at Pasadena, California, to avoid reporters at Union Station in Los Angeles, he was met only by his chauffeur. It was the first time in anyone's recollection that Dixie had failed to meet him upon his return home.

That summer Bing and Dixie apparently formed an uneasy truce, and Bing devoted more time to his sons. On June 23, just four days before Gary's seventeenth birthday, Bing and Gary recorded their first record together, "Sam's Song" (which was named after Bing's friend and music-publishing associate, Sam Weiss) and "Play a Simple Melody." Then Bing and the boys went up to the ranch at Elko, and from there to Hayden Lake. It wasn't until Gary returned to school in September that he learned that the duet he had sung with his father was a hit.

In the late morning of October 4, Bing was returning to Los Angeles from the north when the California Highway Patrol stopped his car. They had been issued a bulletin to notify him that his father suffered a heart attack at his Toluca Lake home and was dying. Larry, Everett, and Bob were already at their father's side when Bing arrived. Harry Lowe Crosby died less than an hour later, at 2:30 P.M. He had been suffering from arterial schlerosis, and his health had been failing for a year. He was buried in Bing's newly purchased family plot at Holy Cross Cemetery on October 7.

Dad Crosby's death brought the family together again briefly. And then there were the Thanksgiving and Christmas holidays. But afterward, Bing and Dixie's relationship resumed its normal, strained routine. As happens with most people who consume large quantities of alcohol over a long period of time, Dixie's tolerance diminished as her need for it increased. She realized that she had a problem, and her close friends worried about her. There was talk that she might go on the Antibute treatment program; Antibute is a drug which, when it is present in the body, makes one very ill if the slightest amount of alcohol is consumed. But whether Dixie actually went on the program isn't known.

On March 21, 1951, Bing underwent surgery at St. John's Hospital in Santa Monica to remove a kidney stone, but this time, rather than Bing taking off for Europe after recuperating, Dixie did.

Dr. and Mrs. George Hummer, friends of both Bing and Dixie, mentioned to Dixie that they had planned a three-month trip to Europe, and Dixie told them, "You can't go without me." And so it was arranged. The Hummers planned to visit Spain, Italy, France, West Germany, Switzerland, Denmark, England, and Ireland. It was a coincidence (and a grim one) that Dr. Hummer, a pathologist, had been invited to speak at the University of Madrid and other medical centers on cancer control; Dixie's cancer wouldn't be detected for another fifteen months, and she may or may not have had it at the time of her trip.

The Hummers, Dixie, and her companion-aide Georgina Hardwicke boarded a plane for the transatlantic flight on March 12, 1951. Reporters at the airport asked Dixie if there was any truth to the new rumors that she and Bing were separating. Dixie replied, "No comment. You can make up your own story." When asked if she cared to deny the reports, Dixie said, "I do not wish to make any comment."

Through a friend at the Ford Motor Company, Bing had arranged to have a Mercury station wagon shipped to Paris for the Hummers and Dixie to use, and they drove throughout Europe. According to Dr. Hummer, Dixie was happy, cheerful, and healthy, and she enjoyed the trip very much. Dr. Hummer remembers that

Dixie treated them to a wonderful dinner party on Bing's birthday, and that Dixie called Bing that evening from France.

On June 1, Dixie returned to Los Angeles, where she was met at the airport by the family chauffeur and by her youngest son, Lindsay. Bing was on a fishing trip in Vancouver, British Columbia, with Bill Morrow.

Between June and November of 1951, Dixie became ill. On November 1, she gave herself a birthday party, and all her friends attended. She said nothing about her health to anyone, and no one suspected that she was quite ill. Sue Carol Ladd recalled seeing her quite a few times after Dixie had returned from Europe. "She was ill," Sue told us, "but I didn't know what was the matter with her. She knew I was going to Europe with Alan and the children for an extended stay, and she told me to come by once more before I left."

The day that Sue left for Europe, she stopped by Dixie's and was told by the maid that Dixie was upstairs in her bedroom. Sue found her in bed, resting. She was ambulatory, but Sue noticed that her lower abdomen was very swollen, though she said nothing about it to Dixie.

Dixie was very cheerful and didn't mention her health. As Sue was about to leave, she told Dixie that she had forgotten her white gloves and asked if she could borrow a pair. "Dixie was a most generous girl," Sue said, "and she dragged out about eighteen pair and said, 'Take them all.' I told her that I had no place to put them, and she said, 'Put them in a package. Maybe you can use them. I'll never use them.' Her remark bothered me terribly," Sue said, "because I had the feeling that she knew something that I didn't know. And, of course, it was later discovered that she had cancer. But I think she knew something was wrong even then. Why else would she give me eighteen pair of gloves and say, 'I'll never use them'?"

Sue's question remains a mystery. Dixie was partially bedridden, weak, losing weight, and had a distended abdomen. She also finished her will at the time; it was dated November 29, 1951. Yet she didn't see a doctor until the following June—more than seven months after she gave the gloves to Sue and made out her will. One can only guess at her reason for not seeking medical attention. And the only reason that seems logical is that she must have thought she had cirrhosis of the liver, which, in an advanced state, usually is manifested by an abnormal swelling of the abdomen. One of Dixie's closest friends was absolutely convinced that Dixie did have cirrhosis. We didn't pursue the fact because we were denied an interview. But it is reasonable to assume that Dixie's friend must have gotten that impression from Dixie herself. It's also reasonable to assume that Dixie must have been convinced that she was dying from the disease, and that she was either afraid that a doctor would confirm her suspicion, or she figured that it was too late to do anything about it anyway.

If our assumption is correct, then, tragically, Dixie's self-diagnosis may have cost her her life. Her old friend Dr. George Hummer is the pathologist who did the lab test during her exploratory operation, and Dr. Hummer told us that there was no cirrhosis—the organ is routinely checked when cancer is discovered to determine the extent of the cancer.

Despite her condition, Dixie got out of bed and threw a lavish surprise birthday party for Bing—it was a month before she underwent the exploratory surgery. The party planning must have taken her weeks. She sent out invitations to 175 guests, including family and Bing's closest friends. And Dixie's wit hadn't left her. The invitations read:

You are cordially invited to attend
A Surprise
Birthday Dinner
for
Bing Crosby
on Friday evening, May 2, 1952
BLACK TIE
(That'll surprise him!)

Dixie arranged for Gary, Philip, and Dennis to fly home from their schools on the day of the party, so that Bing wouldn't know they were in town. And after Bing left for Paramount that morning (he was filming *Road to Bali*), a crew came in and stretched a huge marquee over the entire backyard, set up tables with cloths and centerpieces to accommodate 175 dinner guests, temporarily planted live palms all around the patio, coverted the patio into a dance floor, and built a bandstand at the end of the garden. And when Bing walked to the back patio that evening, the entire Les Brown orchestra played "Happy Birthday." It was a typical Dixie Lee Crosby party production, and it was her last.

On Wednesday, June 18, Dixie entered St. John's Hospital for exploratory surgery, and on Wednesday, June 25, she was sent home to die. None of her friends knew, until the end, that she was dying. The newspapers were told only that she had had abdominal surgery and that she was going to Hayden Lake with Bing and the boys to convalesce. So friends didn't begin to call her until September, when they knew Lindsay had to be back at school.

When friends dropped around to see Dixie, Georgie (Georgina Hardwicke) put them off as best she could; Dixie refused to see any of them in her last days. To our knowledge, none of her women friends ever saw her again after she entered the hospital for the exploratory operation, with the possible exception of Kitty Lang Good. Dixie did take a few phone calls. Sue Carol Ladd called several times from England, but Dixie didn't even let on to Sue that she was sick, let alone dying. Dixie spoke lightly of her illness to Sylvia McGraw, telling her that she had had blood transfusions: "I'm so damn weak," she told Sylvia, "that they have to pump me up with blood." This alarmed Sylvia, but she didn't know that Dixie was mortally ill and, under the circumstances, Sylvia understood why Dixie didn't invite her to the house; she thought she would see Dixie when she had sufficiently recovered. Aside from Kitty Lang Good and the immediate family, Dixie saw only one other person: George Rosenberg, Bing's agent and old family friend. (Dixie's mother, Norma Wyatt, died in 1946 of cancer; she complained of illness for a year before her death, but doctors could find nothing wrong with her. The family was beginning to think that she was a hypochondriac, until the cancer was finally discovered—too late.)

Since Dixie's condition was terminal, and since she could die at any time within months or weeks or even days, grim plans had to be discussed and arrangements for the inevitable had to be made. As incredible as it seems, Bing was not too busy, however, to try to date a young Paramount actress while Dixie lay dying, an incident that will be discussed in the following chapter. Then he joined the boys at Elko and Hayden Lake, where they had all gone under the impression that their mother was recuperating from her "successful" operation. They returned in September. Gary, Philip, and Dennis went north to college, and Lindsay returned to Loyola High School. It's not known exactly how long Bing spent with Dixie—probably two weeks or less—before he boarded a train for New York and a ship for England. According to Kitty Lang Good, the moments that he did spend with her were tender, bittersweet ones, with Bing sitting in her bedroom for hours, Dixie on his lap, talking. They were perhaps the closest moments of their marriage, and they made Dixie very happy—despite the circumstances—and this makes Bing's going to Europe all the more mystifying. Kitty told us that Dixie insisted that Bing go. And we have no doubt at all that she did insist. That was Dixie's style. But Bing went. That was his style. (Kitty declined to grant us an interview because she's at work on her own memoirs, and since she was Dixie's best friend, lived in the Crosby household many years, and had known Bing from 1929 until his death, her book should be a fascinating one.)

After Dixie was buried, the older sons, who by then were young adults, resumed their lives, as adults must after losing a loved one. Lindsay, however, was only fourteen, and he couldn't be expected to go back to school as his more mature brothers had to do. So Bing kept Lindsay out of school for the rest of the term. Kate moved into the Mapleton house to take over the household, as only she could. With Dad Crosby gone, there was little reason for her to live alone in her own Toluca Lake house. While Kate was looking after things, Bing went back to Paramount and completed the interiors for *Little Boy Lost*. He also got acquainted with the woman who would eventually become the second Mrs. Crosby, nineteen-year-old Olive Kathryn Grandstaff, who would soon be under contract to Paramount as Kathryn Grandstaff (later Kathryn Grant). Though Kathryn wasn't put under contract at Paramount until August 22, 1952, she spent a good deal of time on the lot previous to signing and, in fact, we saw her on the *Road to Bali* set, which was before Bing left to do *Little Boy Lost*. This may account for the fact that Bing knew so much about her before, apparently, meeting her formally. One can't fail to deduce, even from Kathryn's own book, that Bing had eyes for her before the meeting she describes.

In *Bing and Other Things,* Kathryn tells of her meeting with Bing. She said that Bing had just returned from location shooting in Paris for *Little Boy Lost*. She doesn't establish the time, but since he was completing the interiors for the film (the 18-day completion schedule had been postponed because of Dixie's death), it was only a couple of weeks or so after Dixie died.

Bing and gag writer Barney Dean were standing outside the open door of Bing's dressing room when Kathryn passed by, and Bing called to her, "Howdy, Tex. What's your rush?" Kathryn wasn't in a rush when it came to Bing Crosby, so when Bing invited her to join Barney and him in the cool shade of his dressing room, she did, despite the fact that she had a pressing tennis date (which she missed). There was no need for introductions; she obviously knew who he was and he knew not only her name but something of her background as well. He talked to her with a Texas drawl, which she might ordinarily have taken exception to, but she intimates that the "full voltage" from his "robin's-egg-blue eyes" made it a matter of indifference to her.

Bing was very cordial. He showed her the floor-to-ceiling wall murals, all still photos from his motion pictures, and asked if she was a good tennis player (she was carrying a racket). She asked him if he played golf much, and he replied, "Just days," smiling, then told her that he played golf everywhere, every chance he got, in Europe, Canada, Mexico, Palm Springs. When Kathryn finally excused herself to leave, Bing, having learned that she was a tea drinker, invited her to come back for tea, telling her that they had tea every day at four in his dressing room. But it would be several months before she entered his life again.

After completing work on the film, Bing did the wise thing: he took Lindsay out of the Mapleton house, with its grim memories, and they stayed at the Palm Springs house until Bing took him to Europe in March. But Bing also did an unwise thing in Palm Springs. He invited twenty-six-year-old actress Mona Freeman to join Lindsay and him on their outings. The threesome played golf together and went to dinner together on several occasions. Columnists ignored the fact that Lindsay was present and immediately began drumming up a romance between Bing and Mona.

Somehow the rumor began to circulate that Bing and Mona would be married at St. Moritz, Switzerland, in December. The rumor caught up with Bing in London, while he was on the European tour with Lindsay, and he denied it. But he had so often denied what was later found to be the truth that the rumors persisted. Mona Freeman was terribly embarrassed by the reports. After all, Dixie had been dead only a couple of months when the columns began appearing. She issued her own denials, assuming that the rumors would stop, but they didn't. In September of 1953, she finally sent a letter to all of the columnists, explaining that she had been a guest of both Bing and Lindsay's earlier that year, enjoyed herself, and would be their guest again if asked, but that she hadn't seen Bing since that time and hadn't heard from him in weeks. Her letter was also published in the Hollywood *Citizen News,* and in it she explained why she was writing to the columnists: ". . . the courtesy I'm hoping for is that you will discredit whatever you hear on the subject [of their alleged romance]."

Mona Freeman must have been even more embarrassed when, just four weeks later, Bing got into an auto accident that eventually linked her name with his in newspapers for nearly a year. The accident occurred on October 11, 1953, at the intersection of Wilshire and Sepulveda boulevards in West Los Angeles. At 5:30 A.M., Bing's new Mercedes struck another vehicle. Bing escaped without serious injury, even though the whole front of his car was demolished, but the three occupants of the other vehicle were hurt, two of them seriously but not fatally.

According to the first newspaper reports, Bing had been returning from a dinner party at a producer's home in West Los Angeles when the accident occurred. Bing said that he had given his version of the accident to the police and then had been taken home by a passing motorist. But when the accident victims filed a $1 million suit against him and depositions were taken, it was learned that while the crash victims were taken away in an ambulance, Bing was taken home not by a passing motorist but by the police. The suit charged him with driving under the influence of alcohol (although this wasn't noted on the police report). Bing immediately accused the other driver of being at fault and of driving under the influence of alcohol. His story sounded like his version of the 1929 accident that had gotten him thrown in jail.

As it turned out, Bing had been drinking but was not drunk, and the other driver apparently had not been drinking at all. Bing settled out of court thirteen months later for $100,000. During the court battle, it was established that Bing's date that night had been Mona Freeman, whom he had taken home minutes before the accident. Mona's name and photograph appeared in the newspapers numerous times during the thirteen-month time span between the accident and the settlement, firing the rumors that she and Bing were definitely an item. The rumors, however, finally died of natural causes, as Bing turned his attention to other women, including Olive Kathryn Grandstaff.

CHAPTER EIGHTEEN

I don't want to get into specifics
about . . . "the dark side of Mr. Crosby,"
but yes, there were women:
many, many, many of them.

—A FORMER CROSBY ASSOCIATE

Except for Howard Hughes, who once said that he could pay for all the publicity he wanted or pay all he wanted for no publicity, Bing Crosby got away with more improprieties than any celebrity in Hollywood. There are those with cleaner slates than his, of course, but those were the ones who lived cleaner lives—and contrary to popular belief, most people in the entertainment industry live more decent lives than people in almost any other profession. But owing to the industry's high profile, it only takes one Errol Flynn to give the entire industry a reputation it can't live down.

In Bing's heyday, when studios had millions invested in their contract players and millions more in their stars, the industry was terrified of scandal magazines. It had good reason to be; an untimely exposé of a star who was at work on a million-dollar film, for example, could ruin the star in the eyes of Middle America and, worse—so far as the studio was concerned—destroy the million-dollar product at the box office. And since the making of films is primarily a business, trade-offs were not altogether uncommon. If a production company learned, for example, that a scandal magazine was about to break a story on one of its top stars, it might trade the magazine two stories on two of its other stars to "kill" the one they didn't want published. The hapless victims of the trade-offs were usually "problem" actors or actresses whom the production company considered expendable, or stars on their way down, or stars whose contracts were running out and who no longer showed box-office clout, or the like.

Another way of getting in or out of the news was through the use of gifts or cash. The lesser scribes who covered the Hollywood scene were notoriously underpaid and overprivileged. And there was hardly a public-relations man who didn't curry the favor of such scribes with bottles or cases of Scotch—depending upon what they wanted planted in the paper—or cash or cars or all-expense-paid vacations to cover almost any plug or to kill or discount almost any story. And it's still being done today. We know a prominent columnist who works for peanuts because the fringe benefits in prestige and gifts more than make up for the individual's absurdly low salary. On the day before the Christmas holidays, the columnist spends most of the day loading and hauling home the automobile trunkfuls of gifts that are brought to the office the week before Christmas. Some of the gifts are delivered in Rolls-Royces by chauffeurs; others are delivered by the exclusive shops from which they were purchased; still others are hand-delivered by young and not-so-young aspirants and down-on-their-luck actors who can ill afford to give such gifts.

We talked to a number of publicists about what columnist Florabel Muir called the strange conspiracy to protect Bing Crosby from bad publicity. The publicists felt that Bing himself and the organizations to whom he was under contract bought a lot of "washed-out ink," as they put it. One of them, who was on the Hollywood beat in those days and who is now retired, said that this was probably true in the mid- and late-thirties, but not afterward. "Bing was built up as being such a devoted father and family man," the publicist said, "and enjoying the ideal marriage to Dixie Lee, that even if one of those stories leaked out, Bing would deny it, the public wouldn't believe it, and whoever revealed it would be discredited more than Bing."

Bing's improprieties weren't of an alcoholic nature. He had quit drinking before it affected his career, and he had been such a spectacular drunk that there was no way his drinking could have been kept from the public, anyway. His improprieties were his many women. And he was as discreet with women as he had been indiscreet with booze.

Aside from the possibility—and some say the probability—that gifts and influence kept Bing's early infidelities out of the press, there were four other reasons that he escaped being exposed in print. To begin with, Bing compartmentalized his friendships, so that each of his friends knew a little about him and about his feminine companions, but very few knew much, and none knew all. Another reason is that Bing was very cautious. Of all the people we talked to, only three women's names were mentioned by all; one was his leading lady in the mid-thirties, an affair that took place before people began being so protective of his image; another was a mid-forties affair, and the leading lady was not only very aggressive, but also talkative and indiscreet—the one exception to the kind of woman Bing was usually attracted to; the third was an affair of such long duration—though it was intermittent—that it finally became known to almost everyone in town.

The third reason that Bing's affairs weren't known to all was because of the kind of woman he was attracted to. Bing wasn't a "skirt chaser"; for the most part, the women he sought had the kind of class that was rare among women with careers in show business. All were quiet, intelligent women who weren't egomaniacal and who wouldn't do just anything to further their careers; in fact, most of them weren't at all stagestruck or career oriented.

270

The final and most significant reason that Bing seemed immune to bad press was, in our opinion, Dixie's undeserved reputation, which not only contributed to the desire of others to protect Bing, but no doubt helped the objects of his affection return his interest with fairly clear consciences: he was married in name only, they thought, a trapped, lonely man in need of the female companionship that he deserved and that he didn't have at home. If the latter weren't truly believed, it's unlikely that some of his relationships would have developed at all, for several of the women who found him attractive were the kind who probably wouldn't have gotten involved with a married man under any other circumstance.

Because of the fact that most people with whom we spoke regarding Bing's affairs didn't know any more about him than Bing himself or his biographers revealed, they were still protective of his image. They didn't deny his affairs, but to one degree or another, they thought them justified and were hesitant to discuss them. As one person who had worked closely with Bing for a dozen years in the thirties and forties told us, "I don't want to get into specifics about what my wife calls the dark side of Mr. Crosby, but yes, there were women: many, many, many of them."

One person who lived in Beverly Hills, fairly close to the Crosbys' Holmby Hills home, told us off the record that in the late forties and early fifties, Bing used to bring his dates to that person's home to visit and to go swimming. "It was very embarrassing," the person told us, "for we knew the entire Crosby family so well. We didn't like the idea of his doing so, but there was nothing we could do about it without insulting him. And, of course, he knew that we'd never say anything to Dixie about his visits."

Dixie was a homebody and rarely went anywhere without Bing, so it wasn't hard for him to avoid the possibility of running into her while he was escorting someone else. Her shyness and penchant for staying home also made it easier for people to believe almost

271

anything that was said about her, for they never had an opportunity to meet her. She never talked to reporters, and only gave three or four interviews in her entire life—and two of these were by phone. She didn't even like shopping. Her friends or servants would shop for her. She bought her clothes from fine stores but shopped by phone, having the clothes sent out on approval, and she had Sylvia McGraw's aunt alter them for her.

One publicist told us that one has only to examine the casts of Bing's films from the mid-thirties through the mid-fifties to determine whom he was involved with. Those who appeared in two successive Crosby films were likely to have been on the receiving end of Bing's attention. There were exceptions to this, of course, but very few. Bing wasn't the most aggressively romantic of men, and symbiosis was an important factor in his romantic relationships. He generally dated only women with whom he worked or with whom he came into contact while he was working. His approach was usually low key and friendly, so that the woman in question was never quite sure whether he was just being friendly or was genuinely interested. If he asked her out to dinner, which is the way all of his relationships began, and they accepted, then he knew they were interested. Most of his affairs involved actresses, except for an affair with a well-known singer who never appeared in a film with him.

In the previous chapter, we mentioned that Bing had approached an actress at Paramount less than two weeks after Dixie had been sent home from the hospital, terminally ill. The actress was Ann Robinson, a member of what was called the Golden Circle at Paramount—a group of about a dozen contract players at Paramount who were young and promising—and it should be emphasized that at the time Bing approached her, no one knew that Dixie was dying of cancer and not everyone knew that she had had an operation. Also, when we talked to Miss Robinson, it was twenty-eight

272

years after the fact, and she still doesn't know how ill-timed Bing's approach to her was.

Ann Robinson starred in George Pal's science-fiction classic *War of the Worlds*, which was made on the Paramount lot in 1952. She was called back to do some pickup shots and publicity stills for the film shortly after July 4. She had seen Bing on the lot before, of course, and had chatted with him; they had a sort of nodding acquaintance. But he had never asked her for a date.

"One evening after work," Miss Robinson told us, "I saw Bing near his dressing room, and he smiled and said hello, then asked how the picture was coming along, and I told him that it was fine. After some small talk, he asked me if I'd like to have dinner with him that night. I was flattered, but also a little embarrassed. I told him that I couldn't make it, but thanked him for the invitation. He asked if it could be possible for the next night, and again I said that I couldn't, and thanked him.

"It must have been a terrible put-down for a man of his importance in the business to be turned down by an actress, but I had my reasons. I knew that he was married to Dixie, and I wasn't about to go out with a married man. The cardinal rule for all the girls in the Golden Circle was not to date any male on the lot. One girl violated that part of her contract by dating a top male star, and she was immediately fired."

Miss Robinson told us, however, that Bing was so influential at Paramount that he could probably have gotten away with violating the Golden Circle's rule. And at the time, this was probably true; however, when he finally got around to dating Kathryn Grant (they went to dinner at Chasen's on January 24, 1954), Kathryn says in her book that her option was dropped by Paramount the following day. Kathryn may have been a victim of the Golden Circle rule without realizing it, or it may have been purely coincidental. It happened at about the time that the star system was being abandoned and contract players let go, and Kathryn's contract was due to expire on February 22, anyway. By 1954, Bing wasn't very influential at Paramount, and he made only one more film for them two years later.

After Dixie's death, Bing dated openly. Within weeks, he was linked with two actresses, who reportedly visited his Palm Springs home. Then he began seeing Mona Freeman, Grace Kelly, Kathryn, and others. Dixie's friends knew that Bing would remarry, and most of them were rooting for Mona Freeman, including Sylvia McGraw. "Mona would have been perfect for Bing," Sylvia told us. "She was a darling girl and a lot like Dixie: intelligent, down-to-earth, good sense of humor, very unpretentious and, like Dixie, acting wasn't very important to her. She would have made Bing a good wife. He needed someone like her."

A number of people we talked with felt the same way about Mona, but it wasn't to be. What they didn't take into consideration was the fact that Mona had been divorced; she had married very young, and the marriage hadn't worked out. And with Bing, being a divorcée was tantamount to wearing a scarlet letter. For this reason, Mona never had a chance, even though Bing was enormously attracted to her.

Two other actresses that Bing fell very hard for were Grace Kelly and Rhonda Fleming. Bing was intimidated by Grace Kelly's noble bearing and beauty at first, but after working with her in *The Country Girl* (released in 1954), for which she won an Academy Award and for which Bing was nominated (but lost to Marlon Brando), Bing dated her on several occasions. But as one columnist commented, Grace didn't go much for American men. (In Bing's favorite film, *High Society* [1956], he sang "True Love" to Grace aboard ship, which Bing said was his favorite scene. Later, Bing named his 55-foot fishing cruiser *True Love*.) Rhonda Fleming was involved with someone else when Bing made it known that he was interested in her; by the time her involvement ended, it was too late; Bing was involved with Kathryn Grant. Years later, Rhonda

Fleming expressed regret that Bing's interest was so ill-timed, for she thought him quite a fascinating man.

The woman who finally snared Bing Crosby wasn't even considered a contender by the movie colony. She was thirty years younger than Bing and five months younger than his eldest son, Gary. But those who dismissed her as one of Bing's passing fancies totally underestimated her. Kathryn Grant was not only a Southern belle like Dixie and the image of Bing's first love, Peggy Bernier, but also a woman after Kate Crosby's heart, and that alone gave Kathryn the inside track. The fact that she was a smart distance runner and had the instincts of a world-class poker player gave her the win.

Part Eight:

The Final Round

***

CHAPTER NINETEEN

***

Is this a wedding date, or not?

—KATHRYN CROSBY, FROM *Bing and Other Things*

Landing Bing Crosby was neither the easiest task in the world nor the most pleasant. It's generally believed by those who knew him that he was so supersensitive to public opinion with respect to the possibility of his remarrying that he dove for cover at the pop of a flashbulb or the hint of a rumor. For this reason, it was thought, although he hooked himself firmly on actress Kathryn Grant, he wiggled off the hook five times, only to hook himself again each time. By the fifth time, however, Kathryn had learned a good deal about angling. She stopped fighting to land him and simply played the line out, letting him run. And when he grew tired of running and realized that he was still hooked, he gave up the struggle. But it was a very long run.

In her book, *Bing and Other Things* (1967), Kathryn

says about the struggle, "It was simple. Love without responsibility is not love, and Bing and I were both being more responsible to the public, to the press, to the mysterious 'they' out there, than we were to each other."

There is more profundity to Kathryn's statement than is apparent at first reading. She may have thrust straight to the heart of the problem, whether consciously, or not: love without responsibility is not love. It would have been a fitting epitaph for Bing and Dixie's marriage, a marriage that had died of terminal irresponsibility on Bing's part long before Dixie's untimely and tragic death. It's very possible that Bing's inordinate fear of publicity was simply a rationalization, a cover-up for his real fear. Certainly he worried about what people would think of his marrying someone thirty years younger than himself. But Bing always did exactly what he wanted to whenever he wanted to. Public opinion would not dictate the terms of his personal life.

In backing out of the fourth planned wedding date with Kathryn at Hayden Lake in the fall of 1956, Bing told her that he had had a long talk with his old Gonzaga chum, Father Francis Corkery, who was supposed to have performed the ceremony. Then, in reference to the publicity surrounding his impending marriage, Bing suggested to Kathryn that perhaps "the world is trying to tell us something." But in context of the historic reality of the Church, how momentous could the objection of a few fans to the marriage of two actors in Idaho be? Would it have shaken the earth? Would it have collapsed the Catholic Church? How absurd to think that Father Corkery "discussed at length" with Harry Lillis Crosby the implications of the publicity attendant on his proposed marriage. "Corky" would have kicked Bing in the hind end for such frivolity. No, one must assume that Bing had grave misgivings that had nothing at all to do with publicity and very little to do with his image.

In an interview with Barbara Walters, which was

aired on an ABC Barbara Walters special just five months before his death, Bing said of breaking his wedding dates with Kathryn, "I lost my guts." He was afraid to marry. He gave no explanation for his fear, but he must (and should) have been haunted by the specter of his failed marriage with Dixie. He loved Kathryn and obviously wanted to assume the responsibilities of marriage. The question was whether he was indeed capable of making the commitment and of assuming the responsibility that the commitment entailed; whether, in fact, he was capable of sustaining love for another person. If he hadn't met a woman like Kathryn Grant, a woman of almost incredible tenacity, he might never have overcome his fears and might not have remarried.

The nineteen-year-old that Bing had stopped in front of his dressing room at Paramount shortly after Dixie's death had all the qualities he admired in women: she was beautiful, petite, intelligent, and very independent. At Paramount, she was under contract as Kathryn Grandstaff, which she changed to Kathryn Grant when she went to Columbia Pictures. She had been born Olive Kathryn Grandstaff in West Columbia, Texas, on November 25, 1933. And she was from a family of achievers. Her mother and father married in 1920 and shortly thereafter decided that they each should have a college education. So they went to school during the summers and taught during the winters. Kathryn's father, Delbert E. Grandstaff, earned his bachelor's degree nine years later; her mother, Olive, whose education was interrupted by the births of a son, Emery, a daughter, Frances Ruth, and then by Kathryn, persisted and finally took her B.A. thirty years later, in 1950, and her M.A. in 1961. Tenacity was a family trait, and Kathryn inherited a strong streak of it. She won her first beauty contest at age three, when she became Splash Day Princess, then went on to win several others over the next fifteen years before she was spotted during her reign as a rodeo queen and was eventually signed to a contract with Paramount. She had been at Paramount only a short time when she met Bing Crosby.

After their initial meeting, Bing took Lindsay to Europe and didn't return until June of 1953. The shooting of his next film, *White Christmas*, had been postponed from January to mid-August because of Dixie's death. Bing had been working on the film for several weeks when he again saw Kathryn, who was escorting a sorority friend from the University of Texas around the lot. Bing was riding his bicycle toward Stage 9, where *White Christmas* was being shot, and he stopped to chat with Kathryn and her girl friend, finally inviting them to visit the set. They did, and Bing had arranged for Kathryn to have a chair next to his on the set; Kathryn's girl friend was left standing—and ignored—as Bing and Kathryn got better acquainted.

Kathryn had arranged to do a column, "Texas Girl in Hollywood," for a chain of newspapers in her home state owned by Glen McCarthy, and she naturally arranged an interview with Bing a few weeks after their visit on the *White Christmas* set. By this time (mid-January, 1954), Bing was filming *The Country Girl*, and the first thing Kathryn learned during the interview was that Bing had tried to call her at Christmastime, but she had gone home to Texas for the holidays. Bing compounded his obvious interest by suggesting that they resume their interview in more depth at dinner on the following Sunday, January 24, at the film colony's most fashionable and expensive restaurant, Chasen's.

The day following their dinner date, Kathryn says she was dropped by Paramount, the UCLA drama department, and the chain of Texas newspapers. She continued her academic work at UCLA toward a degree at the University of Texas, and by September, she was signed as a contract player by Columbia Pictures. It may have been coincidental, but Bing's production company wasn't without influence at Columbia; the studio's irascible mogul, Harry Cohn, was uncommonly civil to Kathryn, considering that she was just a contract player, and, later, a phone call from Bing got Kathryn out of a commitment with the studio when Bing wanted to set a wedding date that conflicted with her schedule. Bing took Kathryn to a Los Angeles Rams football game to celebrate her signing with the studio.

Kathryn had meanwhile moved to the San Fernando Valley, where she shared a place with her aunt Mary Banks' daughter, Marilyn. Bing was treated to a home-cooked meal at their Valley place, and after dinner, as he was talking with her and smoking, she realized that he was putting his ashes in his pants cuff (Bing occasionally smoked cigarettes) because there were no ash-trays in evidence. Kathryn got Bing a saucer to use, telling him that she was trying to break her cousin of the smoking habit and had disposed of all the ashtrays in her effort to do so. The incident is an example of the kind of take-charge woman Kathryn was at twenty; she would impose her will on others—for their own good—whether they liked it or not.

In October, Bing invited Kathryn and her cousin, Marilyn, to his Palm Springs home for the weekend, and on Saturday evening, October 30, 1954, Bing proposed to her—in his fashion. He told her that he had a question that he wanted to ask her as soon as he knew what the answer would be. Then he talked on, intimating that she might fit into his plans for the future. When she seemed obviously interested, Bing said, "You mean you might want to marry me?" And Kathryn replied, rather casually, she thought, "Yes, I believe so."

The wedding date was set for February 7, 1955. They were to be married at an old Spanish mission in Carmel, California, near Bing's Pebble Beach home. It would not be their only wedding date. As Kathryn commented in her book, so many wedding dates were set and missed that she used to wake up in the mornings wondering, "Is this a wedding date, or not?"

After the date was set, Kathryn joined a USO tour of Europe for the 1954 Christmas season. Then on January 9, Bing was operated on for the removal of another kidney stone (the same kind of operation he had had three years earlier). He went to his Pebble Beach home to recuperate and refused to let Kathryn see him until he was well again. The operation and convalescence forced the cancellation of their first wedding date.

The second date was set for May 2, Bing's birthday, and although Kathryn intimates that a picture assignment interfered with the date, two big occurrences in her life took place at about that time: she took her final examinations for her B.A. degree at the University of Texas at Austin, and she took instruction there to convert to the Catholic faith (she had been a Baptist). Kathryn says that Bing never urged her to become a Catholic. She says that attending Catholic services at a cathedral in Paris during her USO tour inspired her to convert. But the consideration that Bing was Catholic and that he had been through one rocky marriage with a Protestant must have influenced her decision.

September 10, 1955, was the third wedding date. Kathryn went up to Hayden Lake, Idaho, which is just east of Spokane, across the Washington state line. At the lake were Bill Morrow and his girl friend, Mary Henderson—who would later marry and who were to be best man and maid of honor—and Bing's youngest son, Lindsay, and his girl friend. Before the ceremony was to take place, Bing took Kathryn to Spokane, showing her his boyhood home on Sharp Street, and they stopped by St. Aloysius Church, where Father Corkery, who was to perform the wedding ceremony, gave Kathryn instructions in the ceremony before they headed back to Hayden Lake.

Kathryn had arrived at the lake on September 3, but by September 6, she was still single and on her way back to Los Angeles, alone. She attributes "cold feet" to her fleeing before the wedding could take place, but she wrote her autobiography when Bing was still living, and there was obviously more to her leaving Hayden Lake than that. Everything was supposed to have been arranged for the wedding, yet Kathryn says in her book that Bing was waiting for his baptismal certificate to arrive from Tacoma and for a letter from Kate, whom he is said to have written, asking for her blessing, which, obviously, he could have gotten by phone, if need be. But in fact Bing had had eleven months (since he first proposed to Kathryn) and two canceled wedding dates to secure Kate's blessing and his baptismal certificate. If Kathryn had cold feet, Bing certainly didn't; they must have been burning up from the friction of his dragging them. Kathryn got the message, and it must have been an increasingly embarrassing one, with Bing stalling while Bill Morrow and Lindsay and their girl friends looked on, no doubt as nonplussed as Kathryn must have been.

Many in Hollywood attribute their third false start to the news that leaked two months earlier that Kathryn had ordered a wedding gown from designer Danny Lanson in Hollywood. Bing, who was just leaving for a fishing trip when the wedding-gown news was broken, at first refused to comment, but later, when a reporter asked about the gown, Bing denied that he was marrying Kathryn or anyone else. As to the wedding gown, Bing said, "I hope she gets a chance to use it." She didn't.

Kathryn went back to work at Columbia, then did *Mister Corey* with Tony Curtis at Universal before flying to Seattle, where she joined her mother and father and Aunt Frances for a brief vacation, and where Bing joined them, meeting Kathryn's parents for the first time. A fourth wedding date was set, again for September 10 (a year later) and again for Hayden Lake. This time it looked as though the wedding might actually occur.

The apparent fact that it wasn't only Kathryn's cold feet that sent her scurrying from Hayden Lake the year before was evident when Kathryn's aunt Mary warned against her going up there again. But Bing seemed determined to be married at St. Aloysius by Father Corkery. Bill and Mary Morrow (they had since married) were there again, and again it was planned that they would be best man and maid of honor. In Spokane,

Bing broke ground for the new Crosby Library at Gonzaga University, while Kathryn "sneaked" in for more instruction from Father Corkery at St. Aloysius. But it was at this time that Bing told Kathryn about his lengthy talk with Father Corkery and gave her the "maybe the world is trying to tell us something" line. He suggested that he'd take Kathryn to the airport the following morning, but Kathryn was furious, telling him that if she stayed one more night at Hayden Lake, she'd "stay on to the bitter end" and that he'd have to work something out. She stayed, and the next days Bing worked out a plan, à la Crosby: they'd drive to Fall River Mills where Bing had scheduled a hospital-benefit performance, then they'd slip into Las Vegas and be married.

Following the hospital benefit, Bing is alleged to have called Las Vegas and to have learned that there were newspeople lurking about. And as though Las Vegas were the only town in Nevada where they could be married, Bing decided that it would be best to go instead to Pebble Beach, where, coincidentally, he was scheduled to do a television show. So the caravan of two cars—Bing and Kathryn and Bill and Mary Morrow and Leo Lynn had driven two cars down from Idaho—headed for Pebble Beach. Bing told Kathryn that after the television show, they'd "fly somewhere and get married."

The morning after the television show, Bing went golfing. Kathryn walked the beach and came to the decision that she'd be better off in Los Angeles again. She seems to have worried whether Columbia would take her back, since she had turned down a "Ford Theatre" television show to get married. But whether she knew it or not, Bing had arranged with Columbia personally to get her out of the show. Kathryn went back to the Pebble Beach house and packed her bags, and when Bing returned from playing golf, she told him that she had to go back to Los Angeles. All Bing said in reply was, "Fine, dear."

Kathryn returned to Columbia again and joined a

USO tour going to Korea for the Christmas holidays (1956). When she returned from the tour in January, she settled into her own apartment in Hollywood and got a call from Bing at the studio. He wanted to know if he could call on her for tea. She agreed, but when at tea he asked her to go out to dinner, she refused, and from January to July 1957, she didn't hear from him again. In July, she got a letter from Bing telling her that he was the defendant in a lawsuit and asking her to call his Sunset Boulevard office and talk to an attorney. It was all a ruse on Bing's part; there was no such suit and no such attorney, but Kathryn didn't know that. Bing told her in his letter that although it was just a nuisance suit, the attorney would probably need a deposition from her regarding places Bing had been at times that Kathryn would have knowledge of.

It was a nuisance suit for Kathryn, too. She had entered the nursing program at Queen of Angels Hospital, where she planned to become a registered nurse, and she was leaving for Spain in two days to film *The Seventh Voyage of Sinbad* for Columbia. She called Bing's office and discovered that they had never heard of the attorney that Bing had asked her to call. But, they said, she could call Mr. Crosby, if she wished. Kathryn told them that she had no intention of calling Mr. Crosby and that if it was important, he could call *her*; she'd be home for two hours. Then, according to Kathryn, she sat by the phone, fully intending never to leave it until he called even if it took forever. But a couple of minutes later, he called. She was all business on the phone; he seemed more interested in how she was than in the lawsuit. When he learned that she was going to Spain, he told her that the deposition could wait. That was the last week of July.

Kathryn returned from Spain about eight weeks later and found a note from Bing waiting when she arrived. He said that the lawsuit had been settled, but that he'd be coming down to Los Angeles from Pebble Beach in a few days; he asked her to drop a line to him at his Mapleton Drive address in Holmby Hills, informing him whether he could call on her. He apparently also asked if she was still interested in him. She wrote to him, saying that she loved him but that she wouldn't see him. On October 8, she received another letter from him, special delivery. She didn't answer it. On October 15, another letter arrived, asking if he could see her for a "brief chat." She didn't answer that one, either. Five days later, while attending a studio function—a hairdresser's show in Los Angeles at which she was to appear—she stopped in at an Edsel exhibition with a publicity woman from Columbia; it was in the same building as the hairdresser's show. Bing apparently made a guest appearance on the Edsel show.

They didn't meet there, but columnist Army Archerd noted in *Daily Variety* the following day: "Watching the Edsel Spec last Sunday, Kathy Grant's beautiful eyes filled with tears when Bing bounced in." Kathryn said in her book that she suspected that the publicity girl told Archerd. It worked. The next day Bing wrote another note, referring to the Archerd column. Kathryn didn't answer this note, either, but she sought the advice of Father Elwood Keiser, the priest at St. Paul's Church in Westwood, whose services Bing occasionally attended. Father Keiser advised Kathryn to continue doing what she was doing regarding Bing: nothing. She followed his advice, and on Tuesday, October 22, Bing wrote the following note to her (which she later kept in a frame in the master bedroom at Hillsborough):

Dearest Kathryn:
I guess this will be my last letter to you, since you won't see me. I do feel I should tell you what I want to say. I want to marry you—anytime, any place you wish. I really feel this proposal deserves a personal response.
Love, Bing

Kathryn says in her book that she had a restless night pondering his proposal and that toward dawn, she had the answer, "The only answer I could ever have given him, from the first 'Hi, Tex' on the Paramount lot." But not only had she learned a good deal about angling, she had also apparently decided not to let herself in for another fall. As she said in her book, ". . . promises had been made, broken, made again." Kathryn would be a tougher negotiator this time.

The following morning she called her aunt Mary and learned that Bing was on her aunt's other line, talking to her. Aunt Mary, Kathryn said in her book, was crying because Bing sounded so lonely and sad. Kathryn had apparently gotten an unlisted phone in the interim and had made her aunt promise not to give the number to Bing, so she told her aunt that she would go over to her house. When she got there, she didn't talk to Bing. She decided that she couldn't; she decided also to let her aunt do the negotiating for her. Half an hour later, Aunt Mary and Bing were on the phone again. The wedding plans were mapped out like a military assault: logistics, rendezvous, plans to evade the enemy (news media). After they were worked out, Kathryn made two demands, through her aunt. They were non-negotiable: she could continue her nursing studies and her acting. Bing agreed. Kathryn, having still not talked to him directly, left her aunt's' for the studio, while Bing, presumably, worked out the details and made reservations. At about three that afternoon, Kathryn called her aunt to learn the results: they were booked for a five P.M. flight for Las Vegas.

Kathryn and her aunt, Mary Banks, were booked into the Desert Inn. Bing had checked into The Sands with Leo Lynn, and he called her that evening and told her to meet him at seven-thirty the following morning in The Sands parking lot. Leo Lynn, Bing's old school buddy and aide, hustled around Las Vegas that night to buy a plain gold wedding band and a corsage for Kathryn. In the morning, he was waiting in the lobby of the Desert Inn when she and her aunt came down. He drove them to The Sands parking lot, where Bing was waiting. Bing got into the front of the car with Leo, and they drove to the marriage license bureau, then on to St. Anne's Church, where Monsignor John J. Ryan was waiting for them. The monsignor bolted the church doors to afford complete privacy, and performed the Nuptial Mass. Leo Lynn and Mary Banks were best man and maid of honor; the only others present were two altar boys. At the end of the ceremony, Bing didn't kiss the bride; he patted her on the cheek.

A wedding breakfast was held at The Sands, with toasting all around. Kathryn called her parents, and Bing called Kate. After breakfast, Mary Banks took a plane back to Los Angeles, and the newlyweds boarded a Western Airlines plane at noon for Palm Springs. Bing had just completed a new home there, at Palm Desert, just outside Palm Springs (the home in which President John Kennedy later stayed on two occasions). It was a beautiful, ranch-style house that Bing is said to have had a hand in designing. Its spacious grounds, with Y-shaped swimming pool, were bordered with an adobe brick wall. Set into the entrance near the gate was a Madonna and Child, and the Crosby family crest was set in tile at the entrance to the house, at the base of its Spanish door, which had come from the Hearst Castle.

Bing and Kathryn spent their first evening dining on quail at the home of Phil and Alice (Faye) Harris. The following day Lindsay and his girl friend, Sally, came to visit and to go swimming. After swimming, Kathryn, who hadn't known where they would spend their honeymoon and who had packed clothes too hot for the desert, slipped on a pair of tennis shorts to lounge at the pool. When Bing came out and saw the shorts, he said to her, "I think those shorts are just fine for writing letters in your room. They look more like Sunset Strip than Abercrombie and Fitch." So Kathryn went in and put on a wool dress.

They were married on Thursday, October 24, and they both had to be back to work on Monday, the twenty-eighth. (They did spend three days the following weekend with Kathryn's parents in Texas.) When they arrived at their Holmby Hills home that Sunday night, Kate met them at the door, saying, "Congratulations, and I'm leaving." Her bags were all packed, and her chauffeur, Louis Serpe, was waiting. (Kate needed a chauffeur because she went to the racetrack daily during the racing season; she also never missed a Kentucky Derby.) Bing and Kathryn both talked Kate out of leaving, saying that she was needed. So she stayed.

Kate was of great help to Kathryn the following day. It was apparent to Kathryn that Bing hadn't given much thought to his bride's arrival at the Mapleton Drive home, nor had Kate. When Kathryn went to retire that evening, the bed was covered with a spread upon which Dixie's initials, DLC, were monogrammed. Then, in the master bedroom, she found a large framed photo of Dixie inscribed, "To my angel, Bing." Kathryn says that although she had never met Dixie, who, she says in her book, ". . . had died several years before I met Bing" (it had actually been several weeks, not years), she felt a little jealous and out of place. So rather than broach the subject with Bing, she spoke to Kate over coffee the following morning, and when Kathryn returned from the studio that evening, the bed cover and framed photo were gone. Kate had taken care of it, and probably with little remorse. Dixie and Kate's relationship was, at best, a chilly truce; they were both very strongwilled women. Kathryn was, too, but she was far more flexible than Dixie had been, and though she was as honest, she was less outspoken than Dixie, too—unless she got mad.

As had happened to her mother, Kathryn's plans to study nursing and to continue her career were occasionally interrupted. Ten months after she married Bing, she gave birth to their first child. He was named Harry Lillis Crosby, Jr. and he was born August 8, 1958, at 11:32 A.M. at Queen of Angels Hospital, across the freeway from Hollywood. (It should be noted that although the press still insists on placing Roman numerals after Harry Junior's name—he's often referred to as Harry Lillis Crosby III—as did whoever captioned the photograph of him on the back of the dust jacket to his mother's book, Bing's father's name was Harry Lowe, not Lillis; therefore, Jr., not III, is correct.)

Thirteen months later, their second child—and Bing's only daughter—was born at the same hospital on September 14, 1959, and was named Mary Frances. Lindsay, who had just been discharged from the service and was pursuing a singing career at the time, was named Mary's godfather. Bing had, indeed, changed; he drove Kathryn to the hospital for both Harry, Jr., and Mary Frances. Kitty Lang had done the driving, or at least the escorting, for Dixie when her four sons were born.

After Mary's birth, Kathryn got a breather. It would be two years before their third and last child was born. Bing and Kathryn took a vacation in Europe and had an audience with Pope John XXIII. Afterward, the last *Road* picture, *Road to Hong Kong,* was scheduled for production in England. Kathryn saw Bing, Bob and Dolores Hope, and the Hopes' children, Tony and Linda, off to London, where they would look for a suitable place to stay before Kathryn and Harry, Jr., joined them. Bing and Bob leased a huge country home just outside London called Cranbourne Court, and the Hopes and Crosbys shared it. Two-year-old Mary Frances stayed in the United States with Kathryn's sister, Frances.

While Bing and Bob made the picture and played golf, Kathryn and Dolores combed the area for antiques and went with Tony and Linda Hope to the Continent; they visited Paris, then heard mass with Pope John XXIII (Dolores was also Catholic). Meanwhile, Bing and Bob worked out a routine whereby they appeared on the set of *Road to Hong Kong* early, left at five, and rushed to Wentworth or Sunningdale to get in nearly a full round of golf before dinner.

It was at Cranbourne Court that Kathryn met Alan and Norma Fisher, the English butler and maid who would eventually work for the Crosbys for nearly twenty years. Kathryn interviewed Alan Fisher in London, when she was looking for servants to work for them in the United States. Fisher had come highly recommended in England, but he had sent a letter to Kathryn, apologizing for not accepting their offer to be in their employ. He was not at all the stereotypical English butler. He is a big, rugged man who had been born in the slums and worked his way up from footman to butler in service to the rich and noble. And he is most outspoken. In an interview with Jody Jacobs for the Los Angeles *Times,* printed on December 10, 1978, Jacobs says that Fisher is a self-confessed supersnob who was not at all thrilled with the prospect of working for a singer. "Money was not important," he told Jacobs. "I had worked for a Scottish duke who had his own private Leonardo da Vinci. So what did an entertainer have to offer me?"

Even though Bing Crosby was perhaps more popular in England than he was in the United States at the time—if that's possible—Fisher was still unimpressed. "I was working for a German-Jewish banker who I liked and who had more charm than eight Bing Crosbys," Fisher told Jacobs. "When you've worked for the duke of Windsor [which he had], you're not going to impress me if you're Rock Hudson or Carol Burnett."

After screening all the applicants, Kathryn called Fisher again, then sent their leased Rolls-Royce to pick him up for an interview. Fisher said of Kathryn, "She was seven months pregnant (with Nathaniel) and looking fabulous in black. She paused at the door, making an entrance, and I thought she was the prettiest woman I'd seen, but so theatrical—off the wallpaper." (We said Fisher was outspoken; he was still working for Kathryn at the time of the interview.)

At the end of their meeting, Fisher told Kathryn that he wasn't interested; but, undaunted, Kathryn replied, "You're the man I want. It may take five years, but rest assured you will come with us." Fisher said that Bing felt a little differently toward him, considering him "an unnecessary evil. He could not envisage a butler in his life." But Kathryn kept calling Fisher after that, raising her offer for his services each time. "Everybody said I'd be stupid not to go," Fisher told Jacobs. "Mrs. Crosby said if you come to us and you don't like it, we'll send you home. The offer was really so adorable." Eventually, true to Kathryn's prediction, Alan and Norma Fisher did go to work for the Crosbys.

Carl Johnston, a Los Angeles–based writer and promoter who was, at Bing's death, working on a film script about whales in which Bing was very interested, had occasion to meet Alan Fisher. Johnston says that while Fisher may claim to be a supersnob, he's really a very nice man. Johnston said that Fisher didn't like Bing's singing, either, and used to tell Bing so. And while Fisher may have felt that Bing never really accepted him, Johnston got quite the opposite impression from Bing, and he thinks that Fisher's loyalty in the Crosby household went to the children first, Bing second, and then Kathryn.

In October 1961, as Bing and Bob completed *Road to Hong Kong,* Kathryn returned to California to have her third child. They expected to have another girl and had planned on naming her Catherine Harrigan, after Kate, but at 11:20 P.M. on October 29, 1961, Kathryn delivered another son at Queen of Angels Hospital. He was named Nathaniel Patrick, after Bing's paternal grandfather.

Between the births of Mary Frances and Nathaniel Patrick, Kathryn had enrolled in the registered nursing course at Queen of Angels, and despite the fact that she took two vacations in Europe, played summer stock, and had Nathaniel, she completed the course in three years, graduating on December 19, 1963, just in time to join Bing for some marlin fishing at their home in Las Cruces, at the tip of Baja, California. The children were in the capable hands of Alan and Norma Fisher, who had finally been coaxed from England and were now in the service of the Crosby family in their Holmby Hills home. In the meantime, Bing had been looking for a quiet place to raise his new family, and he found it about twenty miles south of San Francisco, in an exclusive area called Hillsborough. Bing had placed his Palm Desert home on the market for $175,000, but pulled it back off when he sold the Holmby Hills place for a quarter-million dollars. The Crosbys would make the move to northern California the following month, January 1964, and were looking forward to it, but the New Year started off on a sad note for them.

Kate Crosby had been ailing for two years. In the fall of 1963, she suffered a disabling stroke and was placed in the Santa Monica Convalarium, where she suffered several more strokes. She had gone into coma about mid-December, from which she never recovered. She died on January 7, 1964, exactly one month before her ninety-first birthday. All of her children except Everett attended her funeral. Everett was in New York City's Mt. Sinai Hospital. In June of 1963, one of his legs had been amputated below the knee because of poor circulation complicated by diabetes. The other leg was amputated the day before Kate's death.

Requiem Mass was held for Kate on January 9, following a eulogy delivered by Father Francis Corkery. Kate was buried in the Grotto of Our Lady of Lourdes at Holy Cross Cemetery, next to Dad Crosby and Dixie.

Later in the month, the Crosbys moved to Hillsborough. And in March, Kathryn took her two-day state board examination for her license as a registered nurse. Bing and the children were at La Paz (near Las Cruces) on his fishing cruiser. After the exam, Kathryn joined them. It would be six weeks before she knew the outcome of her examination, but as it turned out, she scored in the upper five percent of those taking the exam. She was now Kathryn Crosby, B.A., R.N., and she announced that she intended to donate her free time to hospitals near San Francisco; she also set up a little clinic in Mexico, near their Las Cruces home.

CHAPTER TWENTY

> Bing had never been that demonstrative
> to an audience in his life.
>
> —ROSEMARY CLOONEY

By Bing's sixty-first birthday, in May 1964, the Crosbys were settled in at their Hillsborough home with their staff of four servants, including Alan and Norma Fisher, an Irish cook, and a nurse for the children. The move to Hillsborough was Bing's idea entirely, and there is little doubt that Kathryn wasn't terribly thrilled with relocating to such splendid isolation. But Bing wanted out of the smog and away from the movie colony, an environmental influence that he thought had contributed adversely to the upbringing of his first four boys and which he didn't want affecting his second crop.

Hillsborough is on the San Francisco peninsula, with the Pacific Ocean to its west and the San Francisco Bay to the east. Bing purchased the house from the estate of the late Phoebe Alexander. It's a marvelous, rambling, twenty-five-room, Tudor-style mansion. A winding drive spans the fifty meters or so between the road and the mansion, leading to a red flagstone terrace and the front entrance, which is flanked by two giant urns. For the first ten years that the Crosbys occupied the house, its multiacre grounds edged imperceptively into the surrounding countryside, giving the place an open, expansive feel that both Bing and Kathryn loved. But the Crosbys were neighbors of the William Randolph Hearsts, and when the so-called Symbionese Liberation Army "kidnapped" Patricia Hearst in February 1974, their action frightened Bing, and he hemmed in his estate with an eight-foot ornamental iron fence complete with sensors, an electronically controlled gate, and a bell-horn two-way speaker. Ever since the Lindbergh kidnap-murder of the thirties, when Bing and Dixie had received kidnap threats, Bing had been fearful of such a possibility, and the close proximity of the Hearst home to his own focused more media attention on the area than was comfortable. Still, Bing wasn't the kind of man to be fenced in; he hated it and lamented the need for such protective measures.

It was generally believed by the Hollywood crowd that Kathryn had herself a bed of roses up north, and that Bing had changed completely, becoming a more attentive husband and father. But in truth, had Kathryn been as reclusive and shy as Dixie Lee, she would have suffered much the same life that Dixie had. Bing had stopped seeing other women when he married Kathryn, but he didn't stop being the absentee house lord, and his primitive view of home and hearth and obedient wife and adult children didn't change. He was as dogmatic and set in his ways as ever. Aside from the isolation, there were only two differences between the first and second Crosby households. The first was with respect to the treatment of the children. Bing was a stern taskmaster with all of them. He laid down the law, complete with written lists of chores, and he expected his laws to be followed to the letter. He had often disciplined his first four boys himself, using a hairbrush or a leather belt. Sometimes he would punish them again for an infringement that Dixie had already punished them for. And this double punishment often caused arguments between Dixie and Bing. He laid down the law for his last three children, too, but this time he left the punishing to Kathryn—and complained that she was too strict with the children.

In Jody Jacobs's interview with Alan Fisher, he is quoted as saying, "Most of the discipline was meted out by Mrs. Crosby with a well-worn tortoise hairbrush, which was very much battered. I felt sorry for that brush, never for the children. She's very strict, but they can talk to her." He added that as a disciplinarian, Bing was the joke of the year. His discipline consisted of his ". . . running around with a rolled-up newspaper and shouting, 'This has got to stop!' " Obviously, most of the discipline was meted out by Kathryn because Bing wasn't there most of the time when it was called for.

Another difference in the households was, of course, that between Kathryn and Dixie. Kathryn was the more malleable of the two, and although their marriages weren't comparable, Kathryn was more subservient than Dixie and, in this respect, she was a better wife for Bing and was certainly more attuned to how he had changed than Dixie was. Kathryn's malleability, however, has caused her to have a good many detractors among some of Bing's old acquaintances and friends. Kathryn went along with Bing's "Gatsby" complex, for example, which Dixie had fought against. For this reason, there are some who consider Kathryn a social climber and a snob. The late Burt McMurtrie, Bing's old Tacoma and radio-producer friend, was one of them.

In the luncheon interview recorded by Vern Taylor, McMurtrie said of Kathryn, "Mrs. Crosby has no time for me, and she knows how I feel about her. She [Dixie] was a different story. Nobody would ever have accused little Dixie of being a snob or a social climber. She was a warm, down-to-earth kind of woman, but she was shy and timid around strangers. I often think she must have detested all the falderal of show business, and was just glad to be able to settle down and raise her family."

There are many others who knew both Bing and Dixie who share McMurtrie's opinion of Kathryn. She has been described to us often enough as prissy and snobbish to warrant our not totally discounting that view of her, but in all fairness and in light of revelations about Bing's actions that we have set down here and that people like Burt McMurtrie didn't know about—particularly Bing's mental trick of "disappearing" people—it should be considered that in some instances, Bing might have played the game, while Kathryn was stuck with the blame. We know, for example, that Kathryn made a lot of enemies with Bing's funeral arrangements (which we'll go into later). In carrying out his wishes, she took personal blame from every quarter for deterring many of his old friends from paying their last respects to Bing. She could have said, "I'm simply carrying out Bing's last wishes," but she refused to blame her dead husband for all of the hard feelings that the funeral caused. She took a bum rap and kept her mouth shut. Thus, on one side of the Hollywood fence, we have the Dixie Demon stories, and on both sides of the fence, we have the Kathryn Demon stories. Bing was, of course, blameless.

The fact is that Kathryn had an incredibly tough act to follow, in the opinion of those who had had the privilege of knowing Dixie Lee Crosby. And the fact is that Kathryn, by her own admission, was more than a little jealous of Dixie; anyone in her place would have been. All of the people we interviewed who really knew Dixie loved her without reservation and were fanatically devoted to her. And rightly so. Her loyalty to friends and her generosity and unpretentiousness is legendary among them. It's not easy to follow a legend, particularly on the legend's own turf, and one can hardly blame Kathryn for shying away from those who would compare her with Dixie. It was difficult enough to live up to Dixie's better qualities in her husband's own eyes, let alone stride gracefully—at the age of twenty-four—through the mobs in the "enemy" camp. Kathryn got enough flack from strangers who wrote asking how she dared marry sweet Dixie's widower; she was even accosted in church on her honeymoon by a woman who was apparently crazed by the idea that anyone dared take Dixie's place.

Perhaps Kathryn was influential in severing ties with some who had been friends of both Bing and Dixie, but it should be remembered that Bing was king of the castle; there were no old friendships and acquaintanceships severed that he didn't want severed. No doubt Kathryn became the scapegoat for many who were "disappeared" after Dixie's death.

While at first Kathryn and the children were isolated at Hillsborough, Bing was not. The year they moved there, he began taping his television series, "The Bing Crosby Show," taking an apartment in West Los Angeles to do so and commuting between Hollywood and Hillsborough by chartered jet. Then he did his last film, *Stagecoach*, for Twentieth Century-Fox. And after his TV series failed, he began hosting "The Hollywood Palace." Aside from his guest appearances on television—primarily "The Dean Martin Show" and Bob Hope specials—and his annual golf classic and Christmas specials, he was through with films and television, but he continued to make record albums here and in England and did a few single records, as well. Then, for about ten years, Bing devoted most of his time to the activities that gave him the most pleasure: golf, his ever-growing business interests, traveling, sports events, partridge shooting in Spain, pheasant shooting in Scotland, grouse hunting in Canada, a safari to Africa (with Phil Harris and then-Governor John Connally, which was filmed by ABC's "American Sportsman" television series), and, of course, countless fishing trips to Canada and Mexico. It would be a long time before Bing would again get the urge to perform.

On July 13, 1966, Everett died at age seventy of throat cancer at Sharon Hospital in Connecticut. He had lived on his farm in Salisbury, Connecticut, since he had left the Crosby organization in 1962, at which time he had tried unsuccessfully to establish an independent film company in the East. He was confined to a wheelchair for the last two years of his life. He was survived by his second wife, Florence George Gutherie Crosby, a former singer; his daughter by his first marriage, Mrs. Mary Sue Shannon, of Seattle; three grandchildren; and, of course, brothers Bing, Larry, Ted, and Bob, and sisters Mary Rose and Catherine, all of whom attended the funeral in Connecticut, where he was buried.

It is still rumored in Hollywood that Bing and Ev had a parting of the ways in 1962 (about the time that Kate suffered her disabling stroke) and that there was ill feeling between them. Those who might have known whether there was any truth to the rumor were instructed by the Crosby office not to give us interviews, on the grounds that Kathryn was writing another book. Leo Lynn told us by phone, however, that Everett simply got tired of the business and retired.

During the early years of their marriage, Bing and Kathryn strove for the togetherness that Bing's first marriage had lacked. In her surprisingly candid book, *Bing and Other Things,* Kathryn says that she knew even before she married Bing that he was a man's man and that he "only wanted a 'buddy,' not a sweetheart." Instead of an engagement ring, Bing gave her a saddle. And soon after they were married, he gave her a twenty-gauge Berretta and took her to a ranch where, with the aid of a hunting guide, he gave her some basic training in game shooting. Then there were the golf lessons she took (a failure: the pro was afraid to unleash her on the course), and fishing—freshwater and ocean. She never became a convert to the great outdoors, but she at least learned the rudiments and gained enough insight and interest so that she wasn't bored by the golf and other sports talk at the dinner table.

When they began having children, Kathryn was quite occupied with home life, and there were times when she could have been reading from Dixie's script in her complaints about Bing's frequent absences. But later, when she began to get out more and Bing complained that he wanted her to stay home with the children, she pointed out to him that even when he announced that he would be home for a couple of weeks, this meant four hours of golf every morning, then into San Francisco for lunch with his business associates, and not returning until dinnertime. Then, of course, it was early to bed, and up for golf bright and early. In this sense, he hadn't changed at all. A couple of times after Bing had been hospitalized and was recuperating at home, Kathryn said that she enjoyed him when he was convalescing because he was confined to the house and she had him all to herself.

Kathryn also gave Bing a taste of his own wanderlust. She didn't let him renege on his before-marriage promise that she could continue her acting. She joined the American Conservatory Theater, a repertory group in San Francisco. She also did summer stock and winter stock, appearing in plays all over the country, often for as long as thirty-nine weeks at a stretch. Very often when they were on their separate ventures, Kathryn would take one or two of the children with her, while Bing took the other one; then they'd trade off. And much to Bing's chagrin, Kathryn took modeling and substitute-teaching jobs in addition to her theater work (Kathryn had gotten her teaching credentials while she was at home with the children in their formative years).

Bing didn't care much for her being away from home so much with her acting. "I want you to stay home and raise your family," he'd tell her. But Kathryn wasn't buying the hausfrau image. When all of the children reached school age, they were often left in the capable hands of Alan Fisher. In fact, it wouldn't be too much of an exaggeration to say that he practically raised them from school age to young adulthood. The children were the main reason the Fishers stayed with the Crosbys for so long. It's quite evident that Fisher loved the children very much, and they returned his love. And while Bing spent a good deal more time with his second family than he had with his first, once the children reached school age, the Fishers had as much to do with raising them as Bing and Kathryn did.

In the early seventies, Bing spent more time at home,

and very often it was Kathryn who was on the road. Bing would arise at 6:45 every morning and have breakfast at 7:30. When the children were in school, they all had breakfast together, and after they left, he'd usually go up the winding staircase to his den and attend to his correspondence. Throughout his career, Bing was scrupulous about answering his fan mail, often with personally handwritten notes. At Hillsborough, he continued to use the services and personnel of his Hollywood office. He dictated his letters and sent the dictaphone belts to his secretary, Lillian Murphy, and she'd type the letters and send them back to him for his approval and signature.

If the weather was fair, he'd go golfing. And, as Kathryn complained, he spent a good deal of time in San Francisco on business. As his career activity tapered off, he focused much more of his time and energy on business matters, and he had a number of new business partners in San Francisco. In the late sixties and early seventies, he got involved more heavily in real estate. And as late as 1974, he was in partnership with two San Francisco entrepreneurs in purchasing Warner Hot Springs, a resort north of San Diego that occupies some two hundred acres of land that has since skyrocketed in value.

There is evidence, though, that Bing's semi-retirement didn't wear well on him. By the mid-seventies his interest in business pursuits weren't as fulfilling to him as they had been. There was the problem of the winter months, too, when he couldn't lose himself on the golf course or in other outdoor activities that he pursued all his life. He had sold the ranch, too, when it became evident that Phil and Dennis wouldn't become ranchers and look after it for him. He got restless, particularly when Kathryn was on the road; he had led too active a life for such quietude. When John Salisbury and Vern Taylor visited Bing to tape a radio show in the fall of 1975, he was alone in the house, except for the servants, and puttering around his cluttered den. One gets the impression from the mood piece written by

Taylor about the visit that Bing was frustrated, coiled like a spring (our words, not Taylor's). He had something to attend to following the taping, but he wasn't really pressed for time, and one senses that he would have liked to be.

The pencils in Bing's wastebasket belied the myth of his imperturbable calm. When he was a child, it's said that he chewed pencils; he'd chew a new one down to a nub before his first-period class was over. As an adult, he broke them, snapped them in two—new pencils, often unsharpened. He broke them in the den of his North Hollywood home in the thirties and forties; he broke them in his den at Holmby Hills in the fifties and sixties; and he broke a lot of them in his den at Hillsborough. Such actions are, quite obviously, indicative of anger and frustration. He was quite a troubled man, and his semi-retirement made him more troubled.

On Christmas Day 1973, Dixie's father, Evan E. Wyatt, died in Camarillo, California, near Santa Barbara. Bing couldn't attend his funeral, for he was ill himself. He had become sick over the holidays, and on New Year's Day, Kathryn drove him to Burlingame Hospital, where he was admitted. It was discovered that he had an abscess on his left lung and that it was caused by a tumor that was growing at an alarming rate. The decision was made to operate on the thirteenth. Kathryn stayed through the night with him at the hospital, then at 6:00 A.M. she went to mass and prayed that Bing didn't have cancer. The fact that Everett had died of cancer seven years earlier is something the family didn't want to think about.

Bing's illness made headlines around the world, and millions were relieved when it was discovered that the tumor wasn't malignant. Half of Bing's left lung was removed during the operation. Astonishingly for a man his age, he was recuperating at home thirteen days later. And even more astonishingly, six weeks later he was on his cruiser *Dorado*, fishing off the coast of Mexico. He stayed at his Mexican vacation home another six weeks and celebrated his seventieth birthday there.

The Crosbys' delight at Bing's narrow escape and incredible recovery was somewhat blunted later that year by the death of Bing's sister Catherine. The following year (1974), brother Ted died in Spokane. And on February 12, 1975, brother Larry died of a heart attack in Hollywood. He was buried at Holy Cross on February 15. Of the seven Crosby children, only Bing, Bob, and Mary Rose remained.

After half of Bing's lung was removed, there was speculation about whether his voice would be affected. But when he began performing again, the speculation ended. His voice was as good as ever. Naturally, as with the "nodes" story, there were those who claimed that his voice was even better and his range higher, which wasn't true.

In 1975, Bing ended his semi-retirement and began making personal appearances with a show he put together called *Bing Crosby and Friends;* the friends were Kathryn, Rosemary Clooney, and the Joe Bushkin combo. It was a fine show, and what was truly remarkable is that Bing's voice was truly as good as ever—and he was seventy-two years old. The troupe gave concerts in Los Angeles; northern California; Las Vegas; Miami Beach; New York; London; and Oslo, Norway, over the next two and a half years before Bing's death.

Bing again made world headlines in 1977, when on March 3, while taping a CBS special commemorating his fiftieth anniversary in show business at the Ambassador Auditorium in Pasadena, California, he fell into a twenty-foot-deep orchestra pit as the audience of 1,200 was giving him a standing ovation. The pit had been the focus of a couple of jokes during the three-hour taping session. It housed the band platform, which could be raised from the basement to stage level. The third time that the Bushkin combo was lowered during the taping, Bushkin quipped, "We're going down for the third time—like the *Titanic*." And once Bing peered into the gloom of the pit, saying, "I hope they don't get lost down there." But at the end of the taping that evening, Bing apparently thought that the band platform had been raised again, and as he was taking bows, he backed into the pit.

Fortunately, he instinctively grabbed for a piece of the scenery as he toppled, and it helped break his fall. He seemed to be shaken up and bruised, but in good shape. Kathryn rushed to his side after the fall, as did Bob Hope and Paul Anka, who were on the show. Three doctors from the audience attended him until the ambulance arrived; one of them was Dr. J. DeWitt Fox, who had seen Bing's embarrassing performance at the Beverly Wilshire back in the thirties. Bing joked about the fall, and it was reported that he sang to the paramedics in the ambulance on his way to Pasadena's Huntington Memorial Hospital.

There were no fractures, but he had ruptured a disc at the base of his spine, between the fifth lumbar and the sacrum. After three weeks at Huntington Memorial, Bing was flown by special air ambulance to Peninsula Hospital in Millbrae, California, near Hillsborough, where he spent another two weeks before he was released.

It pained him very much to stand. He could have had an operation to correct the problem, but he and his doctor decided to wait. At his age, no one knew exactly how he would be affected. He was soon getting around with the aid of a cane, and his chief worry was whether he'd be able to play golf well again. Eleven weeks from the day he fell into the pit, he was seen on the May 1977 "Barbara Walters Special," walking arm-in-arm with Barbara beneath an umbrella (it was drizzling) and doing a little dance step with her as they walked, singing a few bars of "Singin' in the Rain." He was seventy-three and seemingly indestructible.

Soon he was playing golf again, and in mid-August, he was back in harness when his *Bing Crosby and Friends* did a one-night concert at Concord, California, across the bay from his Hillsborough home; it was a warm-up for the show they'd take to London the following month, and a crowd of five thousand enthusiastic fans greeted Bing's first return to the boards since the accident five months earlier. Bing was in fine voice and spirits.

On September 26, 1977, the show opened at London's Palladium, and in addition to its regulars, Harry Lillis Crosby, Jr., and comedian Ted Rogers were featured. They played to a sell-out crowd for the two-week engagement, and *Variety* reviewed the show. It was to be Bing's last review:

Undoubtedly, highlight of this two and a half hour show, in for two weeks at this vaud flagship, is a stint when Bing Crosby and the Joe Bushkin Quartet glide smoothly through a medley of chestnuts including "White Christmas" and an up-beat arrangement of "Old Man River."

Crooner always looked relaxed and confident, whether gagging with the capacity audience, duetting with wife, Kathryn, or son, Harry, or singing along with Rosemary Clooney. Latter was also in fine form during a solo spot when she warbled past pops such as "Come On-a My House" and "Tea for Two."

Audience was predominantly middle-aged to elderly, and much of Crosby's show is designed to take advantage of the singer's tremendous nostalgia appeal.

Harry Crosby showed a certain instrumental accomplishment on both an acoustic guitar and piano, and comedian Ted Rogers provided his own brand of amusing if sometimes scathing practical jokes.

In the paperback edition of Rosemary Clooney's autobiography, *This For Remembrance* (written with Raymond Strait), Miss Clooney noted that although Bing seemed to have no serious physical problem with his back at the Palladium, rather than standing in the wings, as he usually did when someone else was on, he sat in a chair provided for him. She also noticed a phenomenal occurrence on the next-to-closing night. When he was taking his final bows to thundering applause, he stepped away from the mike, and said, "I love you," to the audience. Then he closed his arms, hugging himself, to demonstrate how much he loved them. Miss Clooney said she couldn't believe her eyes or her ears, and that "Bing had never been that demonstrative to an audience in his life."

Just prior to opening at the Palladium, Bing had taped his annual Christmas show in London for CBS. Titled "Bing Crosby's Merrie Olde Christmas" (his forty-second Christmas show, counting his radio programs), it was scheduled for airing on November 30 and was shown after Bing's death.

The Palladium engagement ended on October 10, and Bing left Kathryn, Harry, Jr., and Alan Fisher in London while he went to Spain, where he planned to play golf at several of Spain's fine courses and perhaps do a little game shooting. It's said that Kathryn didn't want him to make the trip; perhaps as a trained nurse, she sensed that he needed more sedentary relaxation after his busy recording and performing schedule in London and Norway. But he went. Kathryn left for Hillsborough, and Alan Fisher stayed behind to help get Harry, Jr., settled, for Harry was entering the London Academy of Music and Dramatic Arts, where he would study for the next three years.

Four days later, on Friday, October 14, 1977, Bing had just finished the seventeenth hole at the La Moralejo Golf Club when he was felled by a massive heart attack. His golf partners thought he had slipped and fallen, but he didn't move, and he never regained consciousness. He died en route to the Red Cross Hospital in Madrid.

The American ambassador to Spain called Kathryn immediately, and the news was flashed around the world. It happened so quickly that although Kathryn was on the phone notifying people all night, most of those who were close to Bing, including his four oldest sons, learned of his death through the news media. Bob Hope, who was in New York at the time and was scheduled to do a benefit, is said to have canceled a show for the first time in his life. President Carter issued a statement praising Bing. Rosemary Clooney flew from Beverly Hills to Hillsborough as soon as she heard the news. Kathryn, her aunt, Mrs. Leonard Meyer, Nathaniel, Mary, and Bing's business manager, Basil Grillo, attended mass at Our Lady of Angels Church in Hillsborough, and a special prayer was said for Bing by Reverend Gerald Barron. It was the local church that Bing had often attended, usually wearing his crumpled golf hat.

It fell to nineteen-year-old Harry, Jr., and Alan Fisher to claim Bing's body. An autopsy was performed on Saturday by Spanish authorities, who confirmed the cause of death. It took another day to process the death certificate and to secure the proper clearances to ship the body from Spain. And on Monday, October 17, Harry and Alan Fisher accompanied the casket bearing Bing's body and brought his golf clubs with them. They arrived in Los Angeles that same night, on TWA Flight 11 from New York. Kathryn, Mary, and Nathaniel met the plane, and after the casket was loaded into a waiting hearse, they went to an upstairs room at the airport terminal for a brief press conference.

Many funeral masses were held around the world for Bing. More than three thousand worshipers jammed into New York City's St. Patrick's Cathedral alone, which was exactly what Bing didn't want for his own funeral and which he left explicit instructions to avoid. Kathryn carried out the instructions almost to the letter, but not quite. According to one member of the family, who doesn't wish to be quoted, Bing's instructions were that only Kathryn and his seven children were to attend his funeral.

Kathryn was very distressed at these orders. How could she not invite Bing's only living brother and sister, Bob and Mary Rose? And she couldn't bring herself not to invite Bob and Dolores Hope, and Phil Harris and Rosemary Clooney. And where does one draw the line? That's about where Kathryn drew it, although the press reported that there were a few others in attendance, as well, including Bing's attorney, John O'Melveny, and his business manager, Basil Grillo.

The night before the funeral, an old-fashioned wake

was held for Bing at a West Los Angeles hotel where Kathryn had taken an entire floor as her Los Angeles headquarters for handling all the details that she had to attend to and accommodate friends and relatives. In her autobiography, Rosemary Clooney says that all of Bing's old drinking, golf, hunting, and fishing buddies attended the wake. Bob Hope didn't, for Dolores's mother had just died.

The services were held, unannounced, on Tuesday, October 19, 1977, at St. Paul's Church, near the UCLA campus in Westwood, a church that Bing had often attended when he lived in Holmby Hills. Bing had requested a simple service. Father Elwood Keiser, who had known him and who had counseled Kathryn during their stormy courtship, recited the Mass of the Resurrection. The service took less than an hour. The only flowers in the chapel were a blanket of red roses that draped the casket. Members of the press, including television newsmen, had shown up for the service and were most respectful, attempting no interviews, asking no questions. There was not one fan in evidence, which is the way Bing wanted it.

It was still almost dark when the pre-dawn mourners traveled the five miles or so from St. Paul's Church to Holy Cross Cemetery. And there, too, there were no fans. Folding chairs were set up at the grave. Bing's six sons were the pallbearers. The graveside rites were simple, as Bing had requested, and after the mourners left, Bing's oak casket was lowered into plot number 119, beside the grave of his first wife, Dixie. To the right of Dixie's grave is that of Dad Crosby, and to the right of that is Kate's. The grave markers at Holy Cross are flush with the ground and of granite, embedded in a concrete border. As we noted earlier, Bing's marker bears the wrong birthdate. It says: Bing Crosby 1904-1977.

There was much speculation about whether Bing would be buried next to Dixie. And if so, what about Kathryn? Bing had purchased only four plots when his father died in 1950; they were for himself, Dixie, his mother, and his father. By 1957, when he married Kathryn, the adjacent plots were taken—in fact, occupied. But Bing's funeral instructions had allowed for this problem, too.

Instead of the customary six-foot depth, Bing had himself buried at a depth of eight to nine feet, so that if Kathryn wishes, she can be buried in his plot, above him, and the marker can be removed and replaced with one bearing both their names.

Part Nine:

Epilogue

CHAPTER TWENTY-ONE

Where there's a will, there's a way.

There's an adage about money: you can't take it with you. It used to be a comforting little proverb, sort of a cracker-barrel philosophical reminder that it's more rewarding to focus one's attention on the business of living than on the business of the marketplace. It was especially true in the days when a man was nothing more or less than a man, when all he had in the end to shuffle off was his mortal coil. That, of course, was before man learned to recreate himself in another image: the Corporate Entity, whose immortality and impenetrability could be guarded by legal armies of the night forever and ever. This miracle of creation brought a degree of obsolescence to the cracker-barrel adage and new significance to another adage: where there's a will, there's a way.

When the details of Bing's will were made known to his heirs following his death, it was evident that in his

311

will, he had, in effect, found a way to take his money with him that is totally in keeping with the true nature of the man.

A person's last will and testament speaks volumes about him. It's his last act, the instrument by which, in sober moments of reflection upon the reality of his own mortality, he reveals his true feelings, his values, and much about his philosophy. Bing's reflected a man who was secretive, ungrateful, domineering, dogmatic, and unforgiving.

The will was filed on June 27, 1977, about four months before his death. Bing worked on it during his convalescence from the fall he had taken at the Ambassador Auditorium, a fall that apparently spurred him to think in terms of his last will and which gave him the time to do so. Bing had always been secretive about personal matters, and he was doubly secretive about money matters—even his wife, Kathryn, was kept totally in the dark about them. So when the will became a matter of public record in San Mateo County, newspeople rushed for particulars. And they were stopped cold. They discovered that the will was as enigmatic as the man had been. Only $400,000 was bequeathed under its terms. The rest, described legally as "the residue after charges, taxes, and bequests," was to be deposited in the Harry L. Crosby Trust, a confidential trust established in Bing's name the day that the will was filed. Technically, it's sometimes called an intervivos trust, or, in lay terms, "a living trust." Under California law, such a trust offers a blanket or tax shelter, for it precludes the levying of probate fees and taxes. There was no indication in the will of the value of the estate left in trust, and particulars regarding the trust are to be made known only to parties named therein and, of course, to concerned government agencies.

In the will itself, Bing bequeathed money in the following manner: $150,000 to his wife, Kathryn; $50,000 each to Gonzaga High School and Gonzaga University; $25,000 to Basil Grillo (Bing's tax man and business manager); $20,000 to Leo Lynn (Bing's boyhood pal who, at this writing, is still employed by the Crosby organization); $20,000 to Mary Rose Pool (Bing's only surviving sister); $15,000 to Lillian Murphy (Bing's secretary); $15,000 to Carolyn Miller (Mary Rose's daughter); $15,000 to Marilyn McLachlin (the daughter of Bing's late sister, Catherine); $10,000 to Louis Serpe (who was Kate's chauffeur); $10,000 to Catherine Crosby (his late brother Ted's daughter); $10,000 to Mary Sue Shannon (Everett's daughter); $5,000 to Marian Harrigan (a cousin); and $5,000 to St. Aloysius Church.

Those who were not named in the will or the trust and who were bequeathed nothing were: all male cousins and nephews; all divorced female cousins and nieces; Bing's only living brother, Bob, and his daughters, Cathleen and Junie. We were told by a member of the family that Bing's sister, Mary Rose, was led to believe that she would be well provided for in Bing's will; it was believed that the bequest would be several hundred thousand dollars. She was left only $20,000, which was less than Bing left his tax man, whom he had known only since the mid-forties. Allegedly, Mary Rose was left a token bequest because she had twice divorced.

In addition to the above bequests, Bing said in his will: "I give all of my automobiles, jewelry, silverware, books, paintings, works of art, household furniture and furnishings, clothing and other personal effects, and any insurance policies covering the foregoing, to my wife, Kathryn, if she survives me."

Bing also noted in the nine-page will that Kathryn was to receive her half-interest in all community property. Then he added Catch-22: "most of my property is my separate property and the rest is community property of my wife and me." This is probably the weakest link in the trust, particularly if Kathryn didn't sign a contract with Bing concerning separate and community property. And there is no evidence, to our knowledge, that she did.

Kathryn was furious when the contents of the will

313

and the trust were made known to her. She had good reason to be. Bing left her the household furniture and furnishings, for example, but he left their Hillsborough home to the trust. But through the magnanimity of the trust arrangement, Kathryn *can* live in her home if she wants to. That absurdity alone is enough to make a widow mad.

The will also says: "Except as otherwise provided in this will, and in the Trust referred to . . . I have intentionally and with full knowledge omitted to provide for my heirs, and I have specifically failed to provide for any child of mine, whether mentioned in this will or in said Trust or otherwise." The clause keeps anyone from challenging the will with claims that they were inadvertently overlooked or forgotten. A number of persons and publications mistakenly inferred from this bit of legalese that Bing wasn't leaving his children anything, but in fact, they were all provided for in the trust. It was rumored that of his first four sons, only Gary had been provided for because he had sufficiently rehabilitated himself in Bing's eyes to have been deserving of a bequest—as though the other three sons were lying somewhere with their heads on a curb, as Bing used to do—which is not at all true.

As nearly as we can determine from our sources, Gary was indeed provided immediately with an inheritance, but it's our understanding that he receives only the interest on the sum of money provided for him in trust. When, or if, he receives the full amount set aside in trust is anyone's guess. Philip, Dennis, and Lindsay are also provided for—in time. They won't come into their inheritance until they reach specific ages. At this writing, the fall of 1980, they have not yet reached those ages, and one wonders if they'll be too old to spend it when they finally get it. Philip and Dennis are forty-six. Lindsay is forty-two. When Bing filed the will and established the trust, Gary was a month from his forty-fourth birthday; Philip and Dennis were two months from their forty-third birthdays; and Lindsay was thirty-nine. Apparently none was old enough, in Bing's opinion, to handle money.

The one who was most hurt by Bing's "living trust" and his apparent distrust is Kathryn. She holds no control over the trust whatever, only the interest generated by it. Now that she's alone, her husband dead, her children having gone their separate ways, the prospect of living by herself in a twenty-five-room mansion whose upkeep alone would take a fairly good percentage of her income from the trust is an absurd one to contemplate. One can only wonder in bewilderment at a man's motivation for placing his wife in such a position. She was married to him for twenty years, suffered his dominance, his inattention, his absences, and bore him three children, and posthumously he tells her, in effect, what was ours isn't yours now that I'm gone.

One is reminded of the 1951 battle between Bing and Dixie, when Bing went off to Europe acting very much like a soon-to-be eligible bachelor, while Dixie's attorney was apparently battling the Crosby organization for something more than a monthly handout. With Dixie, it wasn't the money, but the principle: freedom from domination—economic and otherwise. Kathryn may now know the feeling well.

People have speculated, privately and in the press, that Bing considered Kathryn too generous with money, that he was so distressed when she allegedly pledged $1 million to the now-defunct Immaculate Heart College in Hollywood that he didn't trust her with large sums of money. There may be some truth to the speculation, but it's probable that he would have made the same trust-fund arrangement regardless of Kathryn's generosity. Bing obviously didn't trust anyone with his money, not even his forty-year-old sons.

The hypocrisy of his attitude is mind boggling. Here was a man who was described from childhood as indolent and who never worked a hard day in his life unless the work was fun to do. Here was a man who, owing to his superb, God-given talent, never had to struggle (connive, yes, but not struggle) to reach the top of his profession. Here was a man who, from 1925 to 1930, made what is today equivalent to $1,500 a week and who blew every penny of it. Here was a man who was flat broke when he married at age twenty-seven. Here was a man who spent more money in his life gambling at the dice tables, the racetracks, and the golf courses than the average man makes in a lifetime of hard labor. And he judged, at age seventy-four, that those who survived him couldn't manage his "hard-earned" money.

According to the terms of the trust, all seven of Bing's children will come into their inheritances when they reach specified ages. Kathryn wasn't so lucky. Apparently she is doomed to be a ward of the trust for the rest of her life, getting only the interest earned by it. It's still a lot of money, of course—reportedly $200,000 to $300,000 yearly. But with Kathryn, as with Dixie, it's a matter of principle, and she's allegedly challenging the trust in order to break it. And with her tenacity, she just might do it.

CHAPTER TWENTY-TWO

Bing says he wants perfect children. . . .

—KATHRYN CROSBY

The task set before the wives of Bing Crosby was to raise children who would be unaffected by the celebrity of their famous father. Bing and Dixie and Kathryn didn't want show-business brats who, from mingling with the stars, would be ill prepared for a down-to-earth life. In this, both Dixie and Kathryn were successful parents. Bing was not—at least, not in his estimation.

What Bing Crosby didn't realize, or wouldn't accept, is that we all muddle through parenthood. We raise our children by imitation, learning from what we judge to be the good or bad example set by our own parents and adjusting accordingly. Usually we overcompensate, becoming too strict or too permissive or, worse yet, both. It has always been so. Parenting is an awesome task and an art—when the results are judged to be good—never a science; there are too many variables for that. Moral and social standards change from one generation to the next; each family unit is different from the ones the parents were raised in; each newborn is unique. For all of our studies in sociology and behavioral and child psychology, parenting remains a matter of trial and error, and to err is human.

Bing would accept none of this. As a parent, he strove for and demanded perfection and agonized that he didn't get it. To some of his seven children, his expectations were bewildering. It was as though their father envisioned a Platonic master pattern for the perfect child that was known only to him, but to which they had to conform. Worse yet, at least for his first four sons, the master pattern wasn't even made known to them until after they had apparently not measured up to it. Then it was too late. Bing's first four sons were publicly "disappeared," and his only daughter, Mary, was dangerously close to the same fate at the time of Bing's death.

Mary Crosby did what so many young people began doing quite openly in the seventies: she lived out of wedlock with the man who was later to become her husband. And in an interview with Barbara Walters just five months before his death, Bing made it clear what he would do if one of his children cohabited out of wedlock. ". . . if one of them did that," Bing told Walters, "I wouldn't speak to them ever again." Many people we interviewed who had seen the program felt that Bing was issuing a public ultimatum to his daughter. And when Mary got married after her father's death, it became apparent that Kathryn had been very much attuned to Bing's way of thinking. She didn't approve of her daughter's relationship with the young man, and she went to extremes to show her disapproval: she didn't attend her only daughter's wedding. The family butler, Alan Fisher, represented the family at the reception and later made excuses for Kathryn's action. He said that Mary had set the wedding date astrologically, and the date she chose conflicted with a performance Kathryn had committed herself to with the American Conservatory Theater, the San Francisco repertory group. Kathryn's action further strained her relationship with Mary, who, among other things, had dropped out of college, as Bing's first-family boys had done, and at this writing, it's alleged that their differences have yet to be resolved.

We mentioned earlier the dichotomous relationship between the first and second Crosby families with respect to public appearances, particularly concerning the annual Christmas shows. It would be absurd to speculate that the absence of the first four Crosby boys from the annual Crosby "family" specials was unintentional. Gary, Philip, Dennis, and Lindsay all visited the second-family home in Hillsborough many times, but still they were never invited to participate in the televised Christmas specials. They were, in fact, so cut off from the second family in the public's mind that it's almost necessary to remind the public that the boys were not only Bing's sons but Kathryn's stepsons and Harry, Mary, and Nathaniel's half-brothers. Obviously, Bing disappeared them. And just as obviously, Kathryn has carried on the tradition. She had an opportunity to make amends. She had done so by bending Bing's funeral directions to include brother Bob and Bob Hope and Rosemary Clooney, but didn't let her stepsons back into the fold by inviting them to participate in a farewell tribute to their father's last televised performance. It wasn't always so.

Before Bing married Kathryn, the boys performed professionally with him and had participated in several of his Christmas radio shows. Gary had cut two single records with him, and one of them, "Sam's Song," had gone gold, with more than a million sales. Gary had begun appearing with Bing during World War II, when he was only eight; he toured military camps in California, Arizona, and Texas, singing "Rose O' Day," among other songs, to the men in uniform.

In 1942, Gary appeared with Bing in the film *Star Spangled Rhythm,* in which he had two lines. And in 1945, all four boys appeared in the film *Duffy's Tavern.* The only son who performed with Bing after he married Kathryn was Philip, who had a part with Bing in the 1964 film *Robin and the Seven Hoods.*

Gary was sixteen when he made his radio debut on Bing's show, and he was so popular that he became a weekly guest star and eventually had his own show,

"The Gary Crosby Show," which replaced Bing's during the summer season. On March 15, 1950, the twins, Phil and Dennis, made their radio debut on Bing's show, too. Phil sang "Thanks" and Dennis sang "Flight of the Wild Goose." Lindsay, then only fourteen, stayed in the wings, but he was ushered out with the rest of the boys on September 5, 1950, when Bing and his sons recorded the two-record album "A Crosby Christmas" for Decca.

The boys then acceded to Bing's wishes that they get their educations before pursuing careers. But by the time they were ready to enter show business, their relationship with Bing and his new family wasn't conducive to their appearing together. Gary went off to Stanford, and Phil and Dennis were just starting Washington State College when Dixie died. After Dixie's death, Gary, then Dennis, then Phil eventually dropped out of college and went into the army. Lindsay eventually joined the army, too. It was during the time that the three older boys were just entering the service that Bing decided to marry Kathryn. And by the time the boys had served their two-year tours of duty and were back home again, Bing was still setting wedding dates and breaking them.

Several things happened in the middle and late fifties that caused hard feelings between Bing and the boys. In 1954, Gary came of age and took over the holding of his trust, which had been established in 1941 with $50,000 and which had grown with his earnings from records, radio, and movies and from the money left to him by Dixie to nearly $220,000. The following year Phil and Dennis took over their trusts of $204,000 and $205,000 respectively (Lindsay took over his trust in 1959, which totaled $227,000).

When Gary, Phil, and Dennis got out of the army, they decided to form a quartet called The Crosby Boys and waited for Lindsay to finish his tour of duty in the army and join them. Meanwhile, there was no thought of going back to college or of running the Elko ranch, which displeased Bing no end. Worse yet, it was party time for the boys, and that displeased Bing even more. But the temptation was just too much for them: they were single, had almost a million dollars among them, and after two years in the army, there was a lot of lost living to catch up on. It was wine, women, and song until Lindsay was discharged. And that was cause to celebrate with more wine, women, and song. Bing was more than a little miffed with them for their youthful abandon, and they were more than a little miffed with him when it became evident that he finally intended to go through with his marriage to Kathryn.

No one could replace their mother, of course. Even so, the boys understood Bing's wish to remarry and respected it. But with the possible exception of Lindsay, they were all against Kathryn. It would be tough enough for them to relate to a stepmother, but to have one that was younger than Gary and only eight months older than Phil and Dennis was just too incredible for them to imagine. They spoke bitterly and reproachfully about the impending marriage among themselves, hoping that it would fall through again and for good, but whether they approached Bing about the subject isn't known.

After Bing and Kathryn were married, there were attempts at a truce between Bing and the boys. Lindsay broke the ice by visiting the newlyweds at the Palm Desert house during their short honeymoon. Then all four boys went to the Holmby Hills house for dinner frequently, and over the next few years, the boys and their wives attended family lawn-party get-togethers. But incidents kept interrupting the truce. It started with the boys' visit to the Holmby Hills house on Christmas 1957, two months after Bing and Kathryn were married. Christmas had been Dixie's favorite holiday, and her presence was bound to be felt in the house. Bing and Kathryn would have been wise to have had the family Christmas get-together in Palm Desert, which was neutral territory—a house that had been built after Dixie died. But they didn't.

The boys were shocked to find that all traces of their

321

mother's existence had been removed from the house, which probably wouldn't have bothered them so had it not been such a sentimental time of year. What bothered the boys most was that Dixie's belongings had been boxed and stored in the garage like so much junk and had not been offered to them. One could hardly blame Kathryn for not wanting reminders of her predecessor everywhere she turned. Apparently, Kate swept the house clean of Dixie's belongings, but it was up to Bing to offer the boys their mother's things. He hadn't, and the incident caused hard feelings.

The second occurrence that rubbed the boys the wrong way was the firing of Georgina Hardwicke, known to the family as Georgie. Georgie had been fanatically devoted to Dixie and the boys, and was practically their second mother. After Kathryn took over the household, Georgie came to work one morning and found a dismissal note in the kitchen, signed by Kathryn. It was really Bing's obligation to notify her, but he let Kathryn do it, and she took the heat from the boys for her action. It's understandable that they would be hurt by Georgie's dismissal, even though Bing is alleged to have given her a good pension when she left. It's equally understandable why Kathryn would feel uncomfortable having the boys' "second mother" and Dixie's devoted confidante in the house. Ironically, Gary hired Georgie on a part-time basis to keep his bachelor apartment on Sunset Plaza Drive in order and eventually fired her himself, according to the other brothers. But Gary was drinking very heavily at the time and bringing women to his apartment, and there's little doubt that Georgie let him know that she didn't approve of such goings-on. There's little doubt, too, that Georgie kept Bing posted about Gary's activities, for Bing stopped by to have long talks with Gary. Gary probably felt that Georgie was spying on him, even though she had his best interests at heart, so he let her go.

Another incident took place during Christmas of 1958. Bing and Kathryn had invited Lindsay to spend Christmas with them at the Holmby Hills house. But

Lindsay decided to spend Christmas with Gary instead, perhaps to console Gary, for Harry Lillis Crosby, Jr., had been born two months earlier. Before leaving for Las Vegas, Lindsay had his Christmas presents for Bing, Kathryn, and Harry, Jr., sent to the Holmby Hills house. Bing and Kathryn returned the presents to him unopened because they felt that Lindsay had slighted them. Gary was furious that they would do such a thing to his kid brother, and, naturally, Lindsay was deeply hurt by Bing and Kathryn's callousness. The wound healed, of course, but thirteen months later, Kathryn reopened it; on February 6, 1960, Lindsay married Barbara Frederickson, a Las Vegas showgirl whom Kathryn thoroughly approved of. It was the first wedding of any of his sons that Bing attended. The reception was held at the Holmby Hills house, and all went well until Kathryn learned that Lindsay had invited Georgie to the reception.

We were told by several people that Kathryn apparently vowed that she'd stay upstairs if Georgie set foot in the house. Georgie came, and Kathryn disappeared. The slight wasn't overlooked, for in those days, if you slighted one of the boys, you slighted them all—particularly if Lindsay was the one who was slighted; the other three boys were very protective of their kid brother. All of them were offended when Kathryn snubbed Georgie.

The on-again, off-again feuds between Bing and his sons only reinforced the public's low opinion of Bing and Dixie's boys. Like Dixie, the boys were publicly maligned. We approached the writing of this book with the same preconception of them that most outsiders have: that they were hell-raisers who got into all kinds of serious trouble and who caused Bing a great deal of disappointment and embarrassment. But what we found during our research is that the facts don't suport what is generally believed about them.

Owing to Bing's fame and particularly to his all-American father and nice-guy image, the boys got away in the press with much less than most young people do.

The news media focused on and amplified their every transgression. And it turns out that their transgressions were few. In fact, except for an embarrassing paternity suit filed against Dennis, the boys represented the Crosby name better than their elders. It's interesting to consider what the other Crosbys were doing while the boys were supposedly getting into "serious trouble."

Just before entering the army in January 1954, Dennis was arrested, not for drunk driving but for being drunk while he was a passenger in an automobile that was stopped by the police. His record was so clean that the charge was dropped. Four months earlier, the boys' Uncle Larry was jailed, convicted of drunk driving, and fined $500.

In May of 1954, Gary was involved in a two-car accident near Santa Clara, California; the driver of the other vehicle was at fault. Seven months before that, Bing was involved in the automobile accident that he finally settled out of court for $100,000; he had been drinking, and he lied about the details of the accident to the press.

Philip is alleged to have been arrested for drunk driving in Tacoma, Washington, but tests showed that he wasn't drunk. In November of 1958, Kathryn plowed her Thunderbird into the rear of another vehicle that was stopped at a red light, knocking the vehicle clear across the intersection and leaving its sixty-year-old driver dazed (later hospitalized) and wondering what had hit him. It was an unavoidable accident; Kathryn's high heel got caught and she couldn't brake in time, but she left the scene of the accident before police arrived (which is against the law) in order to have a minor cut on her chin attended to by her personal physician.

Dennis was arrested for drunk driving in 1962; there was no accident involved, but Dennis apologized to the police and to the public, through the press, saying that he was glad that no one was injured by his foolish action. The only other "serious problem" the boys got into that made the newspapers occurred when Gary got

324

into a scuffle in a cocktail lounge with a man who reportedly insulted his mother (a similar incident occurred in Germany, when a sergeant made the mistake of calling the late Dixie Lee an alcoholic). And, finally, Lindsay is reported to have taken a dip in a ski-resort swimming pool sans his trunks.

Except for the news they made with their various marriages and divorces, that's about it for the Crosby boys' serious troubles. Compared with their father's behavior when he was their age, they were saints. Compared with the records of most young men, in fact, the boys were quite well behaved. So where did we and others get the impression that they had been such bad kids? It became obvious from our research that the general and false impression of them came from the same quarter as the general and false impression people had of their mother: from Crosby associates and from Bing himself. It came as fall-out, so to speak, from Bing's obsession with having perfect children.

On March 31, 1959, Bing gave an interview to the Associated Press writer Joe Hyams, saying that he failed the boys "by giving them too much work and discipline, too much money, and too little time and attention." And he added, "I just wanted them to be nice guys. I don't care how big they are or how important. I'd just like them to be the kind that other people would like to have around. And I want them to be thoughtful of other people. I hate thoughtlessness, rudeness, and arrogance."

What could people think of such remarks coming from Bing? The implication is that by failing them, they were failures. Worse—they were not, one assumes, nice guys; they were not the kind that people like to have around; they were thoughtless, rude, and arrogant. To this, Hyams added, "Crosby said he kept the boys on a tight string until they were 17; home at 10:00 P.M., whipped with a leather belt when necessary, earning their own spending money. But, he said, it didn't produce the boys he hoped for." Bing repeated this last refrain over and over during interviews, saying, in effect—and often specifically—that he did his best, but that as soon as they left the house, they'd fall under the influence of someone else, and all his advice to them was wasted. What can one infer from such remarks? The boys must have been a really bad lot. Bing should know. He was their father. But the facts simply don't support his allusions.

It was neither the first nor the last time that Bing referred to the boys' failure in his eyes and to their troubles. Eighteen years later, in the 1977 interview with Barbara Walters, he said that the boys had finally quieted down, but said they had had "a lot of trouble," citing their many marriages and the problems they had on the road with their quartet—quarreling with their agents, their wives, the club managers, and among themselves. It seemed that Bing would always find something to criticize them about.

Since Bing's relationship with the boys in the latter 1950s was restricted largely to their visits to the Holmby Hills home, one must assume that what he called their thoughtlessness, their rudeness, and their arrogance was based on his perception of their behavior toward Kathryn and himself, not toward people in general. Perhaps he was really saying, "I'd like them to be the kind that Kathryn and I would like to have around." Bing certainly wasn't traveling in the boys' circles, and it's difficult to think of any other means by which he could make such judgments of them. The people we talked to who knew the boys during that stage of their lives certainly didn't consider them rude or arrogant or thoughtless. Quite the opposite. But what appear to be sweeping generalizations on Bing's part were accepted as gospel by outsiders, and so it was generally accepted that Dixie had produced a bad crop.

The son who in 1959 might have occasionally exhibited some of the negative qualities that Bing attributed to all of his sons was Gary. By this time, Gary was an alcoholic and didn't know it. But it's not at all surprising that he was.

Of all the Crosby children, including those of the second family, the first born, Gary, was the most like Bing. Gary looked like him and acted like him and walked like him and talked like him. By the time he reached school age, Gary already had a deep, husky voice, which was startling coming from such a small boy. Gary also inherited Bing's build and blue eyes. One recalls Al Rinker's description of the then-thirteen-year-old Bing Crosby as a "towheaded, pudgy little fellow." Gary, too, was towheaded and pudgy. But rather than giving Gary an affectionate nickname, as was his practice with the children of his second family (he called Harry, Jr., Tex and Mary, Sis), Bing called Gary fat and stupid throughout most of his childhood. He rode Gary unmercifully about his weight, criticizing him in front of his friends and even in the press. In the mid-forties, when one interviewer asked about his sons, Bing said that Lindsay was beginning to exhibit some musical ability, but that Gary was just getting fat. He added that even at the ranch, they couldn't keep Gary from the refrigerator. Gary saw the interview and was very hurt by it. It's little wonder that he grew up with a whopping inferiority complex.

Gary overcame his weight problem—as his dad had—and by 1954, when he was twenty-one, he was generally recognized as the heir apparent and was beginning to be called the young Bing Crosby by some. But he had an impossible act to follow, and eventually it took its toll on him, though at that time, there seemed no limit to his potential.

After doing his own radio show for CBS in the 8 P.M. Sunday-night time slot during the summer of 1954, Gary quit Stanford, and in March of 1955, he signed an exclusive CBS radio and television contract. He did radio and TV work until he went on the road with Louis Armstrong; he was with Armstrong in Australia when he received his draft notice in the late spring of 1956.

There's a distinct possibility that even at this writing, Gary doesn't know the extent of his dad's bouts with the bottle early in his career, for Bing covered his trail well. But unknowingly, perhaps, Gary followed in his father's footsteps. And since there would be no equivalent of Bing's Dixie Lee in Gary's life until 1962, Gary staggered beyond the trail left by his father.

By the time his draft notice caught up with him in Australia, Gary, by his own admission, was downing nearly two quarts of liquor a night. It's alleged that, unlike his father, he didn't miss any performances while drinking, but after each performance, he'd drink himself into oblivion. On one occasion, when it came time for the troupe to make a charter flight to their next stop, Gary didn't show, and two members of the group went looking for him. They didn't have far to look; he was still in his hotel room, in bed and drunk. When they revived him, he clutched the mattress and refused to budge, so he was carried, mattress and all, to a waiting car and was driven to the airport, where he was poured into the plane.

Induction into the army didn't stop Gary's drinking. While he was stationed in Frankfurt, Germany, Gary says that he was drinking three or four bottles of cognac a day. In an interview with Muriel Davidson for an article published in *Good Housekeeping* magazine in September 1967, Gary said that he was drunk nearly every second of the time he was in the army. In the article, he told Davidson:

> If for some reason I couldn't get any [liquor] for 24 hours, I'd go right on my head, as if I were having an epileptic seizure. Then I'd end up in the Section Eight psychiatric ward, where they'd take away my belt and matches and things . . . but the medics never could find anything wrong with me. The minute they let me out of the hospital, I'd go right back to drinking.

When Gary was discharged in May 1958, the Presley revolution had changed the music industry. Presley's "Hound Dog" and "Don't be Cruel" were recorded the year Gary went into the army, and when he returned from Germany two years later, the music industry was upside down. Even Bing was free-lancing his records, having severed his relationship with Decca, and was having trouble pushing the kind of music that Gary had been brought up on. Radio was also a medium of the past; three years earlier, Gary had been under exclusive contract to CBS radio, and now there was no place for him. The young balladeer decided to hit the road with his brothers just as soon as Lindsay got out of the service. Meanwhile, Gary turned to acting.

Three months after Gary got out of the service, Bing and Kathryn had the first of their three children, and they named him Harry Lillis Crosby, Jr. It had to be a crushing blow to whatever was left of Gary's ego. Characteristically, Bing "credited" Kathryn with naming their firstborn, thus absolving himself from the deed. Gary has never said anything on the subject, to our knowledge, but he must have been devastated, and it's our guess that it may have been the underlying factor in Gary's bitterness and often bellicose behavior over the next few years toward his father. It should have been.

Gary would have had to be totally insensitive not to have been crushed by Bing and Kathryn's action. The honor of being named after the father should have gone to the firstborn son, who, ironically, is the only one who looked like a Bing Crosby, Jr., and still looks like a Bing Crosby, Jr. It was bad enough that Gary truly believed that his father didn't love him. It was bad enough that Bing began putting down his first son as soon as he learned to walk and talk. It was bad enough that he gave his fifth son his name. But then he rubbed it in. Publicly.

After casting more aspersions at his first four boys, Bing told reporters that, with the birth of Harry, Jr., he felt he had a second chance at being a good father, as though he had given up being a father to his first brood and had written them off. He added that he was going to keep a close eye on "Tex" (Harry, Jr.) and that he had forgotten how much fun it was to have a baby around the house—as though he had ever noticed. If Gary hadn't been drinking hard at the time, he might well have begun at that point.

Gary had hardly settled into his Sunset Plaza apartment—three months before Harry was born—when the Crosby family friend and Bing's agent George Rosenberg got him a two-year contract with Twentieth Century-Fox at $50,000 a picture. Gary did *Holiday for Lovers, Mardi Gras,* and *Private Affair* for his mother's old film company, but his drinking was now beginning to interfere with his work, putting him in dark moods and giving him a bad reputation on the lot. In her *Good Housekeeping* article, Muriel Davidson quotes George Rosenberg as saying,

> . . . he [Gary] was headed for a great career on his own. But then he began to need liquor to get himself on the set [one is reminded of Gary's mother, who also drank at Fox to bolster her nerve]. Not only did he *look* exactly like his father, he was trying too hard to *be* his father. He didn't realize that he was much too good himself to have to try to be somebody he couldn't be.

Author Nancy Bacon was going with Gary at the time and told us that looking back now, she realizes that Gary did have a drinking problem, but that she was simply too young and naive in those days to realize it or to understand the hell that Gary was going through. She says that Gary had Bing's records at his Sunset Plaza apartment, and that they played them often. They also watched Bing whenever he was on television. Nancy told us that whenever Gary got drunk, which was very, very often, he would break down, crying about the death of his mother, whom he loved and who he said had killed herself, and how he loved his father, but that his father didn't love him. From what Gary said during his drunken crying jags, Nancy got the distinct impression that Gary felt guilty for being rejected by his father, as though he felt that *he* had done something wrong, something deserving of rejection, but he didn't know what.

While he was still at Fox, Gary worked on an act with his brothers to be called The Crosby Boys, and on June 9, 1959, they opened at the Sky Room in Tucson,

Arizona. From Tucson, they played Chicago; Washington, D.C.; and other cities in preparation for opening at the Hotel Sahara in Las Vegas. The prospect of seeing the sons of the famous entertainer appealed to the public, and the boys were booked far in advance all over the country and Canada. Gary, who was the oldest and most experienced of them, was chosen as their leader, and he had tentative plans for taking the act to England, too. They would have been a smash in England, where their father was enormously popular, but the act had a spectacular breakup less than a year from its inception.

When they opened in Las Vegas and Bing was nowhere in evidence, Gary gave a United Press International reporter an interview about what the reporter called his "bitter estrangement" from his father. "Dad did something last Christmas that I felt was far from right," Gary said. He also criticized "all that propaganda Pop spread about us wanting to be ranchers." Gary said he had no intention of inviting his father to see the act, which he had yet to see. "The other boys can invite him if they want," he said.

The UPI release led many to believe that Bing never saw the boys at the Sahara, but he and Kathryn did go to see the act before its run ended there. Nancy Bacon was there; she was supposed to have made the trip to Las Vegas with Bing and Kathryn, but Gary wouldn't let her travel with Bing. "He'd have you in tears before you got to Vegas," he told her. Nancy doesn't know whether Bing went backstage to see the boys after the show, but it's doubtful that Gary talked with him if he did. It wasn't until the boys played the Moulin Rouge in Hollywood (now the Aquarius Theater) on Saturday, October 16, that they patched up their differences—for a while.

Bing didn't sit with the theater audience at the Moulin Rouge but watched the show from a glassed-in control booth above and behind the audience. He went backstage after the show and reportedly told the boys that they were great and that the act was great. He spent twenty minutes with them in the privacy of their dressing room before posing for pictures. Reporters speculated that Bing's asking Lindsay to be newborn Mary's godfather apparently made up for the Christmas slight in Gary's eyes and resulted in what UPI correspondent Rick Dubrow described as "an emotional dressing room scene," in which Gary "threw his arms around the crooner's shoulder and posed for a picture that also included three of Bing's other sons, Dennis, Philip, and Lindsay."

Gary was the only one of the boys who didn't attend Mary's baptism. He is said to have overslept. And it wasn't until after the baptism and five days before the boys' Moulin Rouge engagement was to end that Bing went to the theater with agent George Rosenberg. In the meantime, the other three boys had been seen at football games with Bing, but not Gary.

It wasn't long after Bing and Gary patched up their differences that the Crosby boys broke up their act. There were a number of factors that contributed to the dissolution, but chief among them was Gary's drinking, with its resultant actions and attitude. The other boys had chosen Gary as leader, but they had obviously expected a more sober one. The situation finally came to an impasse in Montreal and ended with a dressing-room brawl. During the scuffle, while Phil and Dennis were holding Gary, Lindsay threw a wild punch that caught Gary square in the face. To this day, Gary apparently doesn't know which of his brothers socked him, but he didn't suspect his kid brother.

There's rarely a specific reason for such fights, particularly among brothers. It was no doubt the culmination of many grievances, but it was apparently touched off by an interview that Gary had given in which he had made references to his mother's alcoholism. Dixie's drinking, in fact, still seems a touchy issue with Phil, Dennis, and Lindsay, who are apparently troubled by the stigma of alcoholism, looking upon it as a weakness rather than the sickness it is. As a recovered alcoholic, Gary is more inclined to speak freely about the disease and about its influence on his mother and himself, and his frankness has caused a breach between his brothers and himself that is as bitter today as it was when the fight ended their professional relationship twenty-one years ago.

After the fight, Gary struck out on his own as a solo artist, which was something that he had wanted to do even before he and his brothers formed the quartet. But as the older brother and the more experienced in show business, he had apparently felt an obligation to his brothers and a genuine desire to establish and maintain a close family group. Unfortunately, his drinking destroyed the relationship and inflicted wounds that wouldn't heal even after Gary overcame his drinking problem in 1962.

In July 1960, Gary opened to good reviews at the Flamingo Hotel in Las Vegas. Like Bing, Gary had a tendency to put on weight when he was drinking (Bing had to wear a girdle when he was making *Mississippi* in 1935 and still drinking too much). But rather than giving up booze, Gary took diet pills to reduce, and he continued drinking. He began to suffer blackouts from the combination of pills and liquor, but he admitted that he was so far gone as an alcoholic that he tolerated the blackouts rather than give up the liquor.

Gary did cut down on his drinking when he was getting his solo act together before his Las Vegas opening. It was at the Flamingo that he met dancer Barbara Consentino, who two years later would become his wife. Gary did all right as a solo artist, but like his mother, he was terrified of performing. Unlike his mother, though, alcohol did to him almost exactly what it did to his father before he straightened out. Exactly a year after he began his solo career, it ended on a stage at the Tradewinds nightclub in Chicago. Just before he was announced to go onstage, Gary downed half a bottle of vodka. He was already dead drunk, as usual, but he was usually able to perform, doing so on instinct, as a prizefighter who's out on his feet. The orchestra repeated the four-bar intro to his song, but Gary just stood there, his blue eyes staring blankly at the audience, not responding to the music at all, not responding to anything. Finally the emcee pulled him offstage. His singing career was at an end. Like the "nodes on the tonsils" story that had been concocted for his father, the trade papers and newspapers announced that Gary had "ruptured his throat."

Gary's bouts with the bottle ended in 1962, the year that he married his wife, Barbara. He says that he hasn't touched a drop of alcohol since then, and he attributes much of his success in recovering from his illness to Barbara. Since 1962, he has concentrated on acting, particularly on television, and he's appeared in the "Chase," "Emergency," and "Adam 12" series among others. He's a much better actor than he probably realizes.

The only one of the boys who hasn't yet divorced is Gary—he was like his father in that respect, too. The others have nine marriages among them. At this writing, however, Gary and his wife of eighteen years have separated, and there is talk of divorce. Gary is living in Las Vegas and finishing his autobiography, which he's writing with author Ross Firestone and which is scheduled for 1981 publication.

Typically, several columnists have jumped on Gary with both feet about his book, even though none of them has seen a page of it. The panning started in January 1980, when columnist Marilyn Beck wrote an item headlined: *Insiders are calling Gary Crosby's book on father a "Daddy Dearest."* The reference was to the exposé that Christina Crawford wrote about her mother, Joan Crawford, entitled *Mommie Dearest*. The columnist intimated that Gary's book, which she hadn't seen and which wasn't half-written, would be in the same genre. Her source, Beck said, was "industry insiders." After Beck's column appeared, other columnists jumped on the "Daddy Dearest" theme with no more evidence than Beck had until Beck's second column on the subject appeared three months later, with the banner: *No "Daddy Dearest" from Bing's son Gary.* Apparently Gary's representative, or Gary himself, had contacted her and told her that he was writing an autobiography, not an exposé of his father, and that he could hardly write the story of his life without mentioning Bing and Bing's influence on his own life. Even so, Gary is quoted as telling Beck that the book will "probably end up making half the world hate me."

Unfortunately, the columns contained misinformation that succeeded only in widening the breach between the Crosby brothers. Philip was particularly upset about the first Beck column, and he called columnist James Bacon, telling him that he couldn't track Gary down because "He's up in Las Vegas getting a divorce." But Phil added that, speaking for himself and brothers Dennis and Lindsay, he wanted it known that they considered Bing a good father, strict and old-fashioned, but not cruel. "He just reared us the way Grandma Kate Harrigan brought him up," Phil told Bacon.

Bacon checked with Gary's wife, who confirmed their separation, and he reported the news in his syndicated column. Marilyn Beck reported that Gary planned to remarry when his divorce was final.

Gary is the only son of the first family who doesn't have children of his own, although he did adopt a son, Steven, Barbara Consentino's child by a previous marriage. The other three boys gave Bing fourteen grandchildren, including one named Dixie Lee (by Philip and his former wife, Sandra Drummond), who at this writing is working in a Beverly Hills gift shop. Phil's other child by Sandra, Brian Patrick, was killed in a motorcycle accident in Beverly Hills a year to the month after Bing died. Brian Patrick was eighteen at the time of his death.

Of Bing's seven children, only two have chosen careers outside show business. Dennis is married and lives in Palm Springs, where he's involved in a business or two, including an electronics firm. Nathaniel, nineteen at this writing, is a student at the University of Miami, at Coral Gables, Florida, where he's on the golf team.

He has plans of continuing the Crosby golf tournament at Pebble Beach, the oldest of the celebrity tournaments, and of becoming a professional golfer; it's said that he's exceptionally talented at the game.

Phil is the only Crosby offspring who's still singing professionally at this writing. He sings in clubs and has several records on the market under his own label, Dixie Lee Records. Phil's also a restaurateur on the side; he had an interest in a chain of Mexican food stands in the Los Angeles area for several years and is currently half-owner of a plush restaurant on the outskirts of Atlanta, Georgia—appropriately called Crosby's—where he often joins in the entertainment. He commutes between Atlanta and his home in the San Fernando Valley. We called Phil several times during the writing of this book, and he returned our calls. He was most cordial, but said that in light of Gary's forthcoming book, he, Dennis, and Lindsay preferred not to be interviewed. We did spend several hours talking to him about everything from sports to show business, however, and found him very friendly and pleasant.

Lindsay continued his show-business career by acting in numerous independent films, which he was doing when we first met him in the sixties. He still takes an occasional acting job, but spends most of his time on his San Fernando Valley ranch, where he raises horses.

Harry Junior has completed his three years at the London Academy of Music and Dramatic Arts and is concentrating at this time on acting. He did a movie in England, *Friday the 13th,* and recently completed a one-hour American television pilot, "Riding for the Pony Express." The pilot, which aired on CBS in September of 1980, got bad reviews, but Harry and his co-star, John Hammond, rose above the material and received favorable notices.

The most active Crosby in show business, and certainly the most visible at this writing, is Bing's daughter, Mary. In the paperback edition of Carroll Carroll's book, entitled *My Life With* (it was originally published in hardcover under the title *None of Your Busi-*

ness), he tells a delightful story about Mary Crosby, one that leaves no doubt that she was a precocious child of firm convictions even in grammar school.

Carroll had occasion in 1968 to supervise the filming of a short film clip of Bing apologizing for not personally attending an industry function. Carroll arrived in Hillsborough early on the morning of the filming, and while Bing got in a round of golf, he directed the crew in setting up the camera, blocking out the movements, and readying the cue cards.

While the crew was setting up, Carroll noticed that Mary was sitting on the grass nearby, watching. He had seen her in a teleplay with her father and thought she was quite good, so he sat down beside her and told her so. She thanked him, and after Carroll learned from her that she was nine years old, he told her that he had a granddaughter just her age in New York.

"In New York?" Mary said. "She's lucky."

"What's lucky about being in New York?"

"That's where the *action* is," Mary said.

Carroll was amused by her reply. He looked around the quiet, spacious Hillsborough grounds for a moment, taking note of the clear, sunny, northern California sky, and he said to Mary, "You know, New York isn't quiet like this. New York is busy and crowded and noisy and dirty."

Mary nodded in agreement with all the adjectives that Carroll applied to New York but interrupted the description with, "Yes, but if you want action, you've got to have busy and crowded and noisy and dirty."

At fifteen, Mary was enrolled as a drama major in her mother's alma mater, the University of Texas, but she soon grew impatient with having to wade through all the academic subjects in order to get just a few hours of drama training a week, so she quit and returned to San Francisco, where she spent two years with the American Conservatory Theater. In 1976, she moved to Malibu, a beach community north of Hollywood, to pursue her acting career.

Thus far, Mary has had a major role in the television

film *Pearl*, the lead in another film for television, *With This Ring*, a starring role in the TV series "Brothers and Sisters," and, at this writing, she has just finished another film, *Dick Turpin*, and another television series pilot, "Golden Gates," after leaving the internationally syndicated television series "Dallas," from which she quit for fear of being typecast. Mary gained more fame by leaving the series than she had by acting in it. She portrayed Kristin Shepherd, the mistress of the series' antagonist, J. R. Ewing, portrayed by actor Larry Hagman. And when Mary decided that she wanted to leave the show, the producers decided to write her out of it by having her shoot J. R., the antagonist, in a cliffhanging last episode of the season. J. R.'s assailant would remain a mystery until the 1980-1981 season began, and it was the most successful publicity gimmick in television history. When the episode revealing that Kristin had shot J. R. was broadcast, the story and Mary Crosby's photograph made the newspapers in all of the 57 countries in which the program was syndicated.

In September 1980, Mary appeared on Dinah Shore's television talk show, and when Dinah mentioned Bing's having moved his second family out of the show business community, Mary, who by then had long been where the action is, said that she was glad her dad had taken them to Hillsborough. Mary felt better adjusted, she said, for having been raised in an "upper-middle-class" environment rather than in the film colony. A $1.5 million mansion for a home, with a nurse, a cook, two maids, and an English butler who had once worked for the duke of Windsor was what Mary considered upper-middle-class. One wonders how the upper class lives.

CHAPTER TWENTY-THREE

I wouldn't waste a dime calling him.

—HARRY BARRIS, REFERRING TO BING

On the Fourth of July, 1943, Bing Crosby, Al Rinker, and Harry Barris got together once more at the CBS Radio studios on Sunset Boulevard in Hollywood. The occasion was the reunion of The Rhythm Boys on Paul Whiteman's summer radio show. As one can imagine, Bing wasn't too thrilled with the idea, but he did it as a favor to Whiteman. Afterward, speaking of the show and of Whiteman, he remarked to one of his associates, "Now we're even." It seemed a curious remark, considering all that Whiteman had done for Bing, but then the associate didn't realize what a costly favor the half-hour reunion was to Bing Crosby: it took a lot of nerve for him even to face Al and Harry again, let alone perform with them.

Al Rinker hadn't seen Bing since the trio split in 1931. Harry had seen him only once, when Bing and Dixie visited at the Warwick Hotel in May of 1932. Rinker says of the reunion that there was little need of rehearsing their songs; though a dozen years had passed since they had sung together, they picked up right where they had left off, performing the numbers flawlessly on the first run-through. Part of the broadcast was reproduced in a multi-record album commemorating Whiteman's fiftieth year in show business, which was narrated by Whiteman. Dinah Shore took part and played Whiteman's secretary in a comedy skit with The Rhythm Boys, but her voice had to be taken from the soundtrack and her lines dubbed by a radio actress, because her record company wouldn't allow her to be heard on another record label.

After the rehearsal and before the evening show, Bing said to Rinker, "I'm going out for a round of golf. You wanna come along?"

Al accepted the invitation, and Bing drove. He decided to stop by the house for some reason, and Al went in with him (the Holmby Hills place). Al didn't see Dixie or any of the boys, but Bing's parents were in the living room when they walked in. Bing headed directly for the stairway and said to his parents as he passed them, "You remember Al, don't you?"

"I thought I had Bing figured pretty well," Rinker told us. "I grew to expect the unexpected from him, but he surprised even me with that one. Here I had known his parents since 1923 or '24, had hung around with Bing at his house as a kid, had even lived with them at his home when we were on our way to join Whiteman, and he asked them if they remembered me. It was as though I were a hitchhiker that he had picked up by chance once before.

"What a thing to say. It certainly lacked warmth of any kind. I mean, you or I would have said, 'Hey! Guess who's *here?*' or 'Look who's with me!' But not Bing."

Rinker said that Bing's parents greeted him warmly. "The old man threw his arms around me, and we talked until Bing came back. Then we went out to Bel-Air and played a round of golf before going back and doing the Whiteman show."

After the show, Al and Harry had a couple of drinks together at a nearby cocktail lounge and talked about old times. They hadn't seen one another for several years. Bing had been invited to join them. He didn't accompany them but dropped in later for about five minutes, then left. It was the last time Harry Barris ever saw him.

When Harry married Loyce Whiteman, they bought a house in Glendale, where they lived when they weren't on the road. Both Bob and Larry Crosby were guests at their house, at different times. Bob Crosby stayed with them after singing with Anson Weeks and while casting around for work; he finally landed a job as a vocalist with the Tommy Dorsey orchestra. Larry lived there for a while when he first came to Hollywood to join the Crosby organization. He knew nothing about show business and often conferred with Harry about different facets of the business and what he should do as Bing's public-relations director. He had been given an office and a title, and he was totally bewildered; he kept saying to Harry, "I don't know what to do. What can I do to help him [Bing]?"

Because of his drinking, Harry Barris fell on bad times. He and Loyce had a very good act and headlined in the best theaters and clubs, but his drinking began interfering. During one engagement in San Francisco, he had to be put in a sanitarium for alcoholics while Loyce finished their engagement at the club where they were booked. It wasn't long before word got around to the club and theater owners, and he could no longer get bookings.

Harry was very proud and would starve before asking anyone for help. Loyce Whiteman Hubbard doesn't recall his ever trying to contact Bing after the trio split, but Al Rinker has vague recollections about Harry mentioning that he had. Al thinks that Harry may have called twice—getting through to him once, and Bing's not returning his calls after that. Both Al and Loyce recall that whenever anyone mentioned the idea of calling Bing or contacting him for some reason, Harry would always say, "I wouldn't waste a dime calling him."

From 1937 to 1944, Barris appeared in six Bing Crosby pictures. He was never offered work as a composer but was given walk-ons or bit parts as an actor. Usually he was cast as a jive-talking musician or orchestra leader. His agent tried to get him larger parts in the Crosby films but wasn't successful, and it frustrated both Harry and his agent. Harry was happy to get work, of course, but his work on Bing's films was a source of embarrassment to him eventually. Hollywood can be a cruel place for a proud man. Many people in the business thought that Bing was throwing him bones and that he was accepting them. And rather than being critical of Bing for not giving Harry a better chance, they were derisive of Harry for taking the small roles. But the fact is that Harry was working at other studios and on other pictures, and with the exception of perhaps one or two of the Crosby films, Harry got the parts through his agent and Paramount casting, never directly from Bing. In addition to the Crosby pictures, he did *Two Plus Four* and *Spirit of Notre Dame* for Universal, and *Every Night At Eight, After the Dance,* and *Love Me Forever* at Paramount, in addition to a few shorts for the small independent companies. His parts in the Crosby pictures were so small that they weren't even mentioned in his trade-paper obituaries.

In January 1962, Harry was admitted to St. Joseph's Hospital in Burbank, California, for an operation. It was reported that he received more than two hundred letters when his impending operation was announced. No word from Bing. St. Joseph's Hospital is next door to the NBC television complex in Burbank, where Bing did a lot of work. It's also less than a mile from the Lakeside Golf Course, which Bing frequented. Yet when Barris was again hospitalized there in September of 1962 and remained there until his death on December 13, Bing didn't go to see him. He didn't even send flowers to Harry's funeral.

Al Rinker became a radio producer after he left vaudeville. A year or so after the reunion on Paul Whiteman's show, Al was working for J. Walter Thompson, the advertising agency that handled Bing's "Kraft Music Hall" show, and Al was sent from New York to Hollywood to produce the show for one season. Bing had nothing to do with the assignment; he inherited Al just as he had inherited the previous producer and Bob Burns and writer Carroll Carroll.

Rinker doesn't know whether Bing knew that he was coming West to do the show or not. We asked him what Bing's reaction was when he walked into the studio for the first time. Rinker says that Bing simply said, "Hi, Al," and that was that. They worked together for a season, and Rinker saw Bing only once a week, on broadcast day. There were no invitations to lunch. No invitations to the house. Nothing. Bing wasn't unfriendly, just all business. "After I left the show, I only saw Bing a couple of times," Rinker told us. "Once at Lakeside [golf course], we talked for a minute or two about Spokane, and then a few years later, I saw him at the Bel-Air Country Club. I had just finished a round of golf and was crossing a bridge toward the clubhouse when I saw Bing coming out of the building. When he saw me, he ducked back inside—I mean he really ducked. My guess is that he was embarrassed, that he didn't know what to say to me if we came face to face. I remember once, too, when I chanced to meet him on the street in New York City. He seemed ill at ease, embarrassed then. I was producing radio shows at the time, and he said, 'I'll have to have you over [to his radio show] to do a couple of numbers.' But, of course, he never called me. He was just making conversation."

It wasn't easy for Bing to avoid Barrises or Rinkers; he kept running into them when he least expected it. Al's wife, Elizabeth, was a singer, too, and when the Rinkers settled on the West Coast, Elizabeth did a lot of free-lance singing, mostly backup for record, radio, and movie studios. She was in a number of Bing's Paramount pictures and on some of his Decca records before he knew who she was. Finally someone introduced them, and Elizabeth says that Bing was very cordial, asking about Al and wanting to see any family pictures she might have. After that one occasion, though, Bing didn't talk to her again, except maybe to say hello, even though Elizabeth continued running into him while doing free-lance work as a "utility" singer.

The same is true for Al and Elizabeth's daughter, Julia Rinker Miller. Julia, who's still active as a backup singer and composer of special material for musical shows, used to work with the Earl Brown Singers, who backed Danny Kaye's television shows in 1966 and 1967 and his Las Vegas nightclub act. Julia did numerous record dates singing backup for Bing and worked on a couple of his television specials, too. She was once introduced to Bing as Al Rinker's daughter, and she told us that Bing was pleasant, saying something like, "Hello. How are you?" and that he didn't make any reference to his past with her dad. "I got the impression that he [Bing] was freer than maybe most people give him credit for," she told us. "He had outgrown the past and was very much in the present, without need of dwelling on the past, as some people do."

Harry and Loyce had a daughter who sang, too. She's Frances Maurine Barris, known today as Marti Barris Porter. Like her mother, Marti became a band singer and for a while was the featured vocalist with Freddy Martin's orchestra. After Harry's death, Larry Crosby invited Marti to sing at Pebble Beach in the variety show that Bing always put on for the participants in his golf tournament on the night before the tournament was to begin. Larry suggested that Loyce travel with Marti, and they flew to Pebble Beach along with Harry James and Ben Hogan.

Kathryn was at the festivities that night, too. Bing didn't speak to Loyce or Marti, and he didn't bother introducing them to Kathryn. Larry Crosby tried to get Bing to do a few Harry Barris numbers with Marti, who played piano like her dad, but Bing ignored Larry's suggestions. Marti performed for the gathering that night, and when she did her father's arrangement of "Mississippi Mud," Bing joined her on the last chorus. But according to Loyce, he didn't speak to either of them afterward.

The Crosby boys knew Marti, and Loyce told us that Gary often mentioned to Marti that he couldn't understand why his father didn't offer to help her with her career, which he could easily have done. Larry tried to get Bing interested in doing so, even taking Marti's records to Bing. And Loyce contacted Bing once on her daughter's behalf. "It's the only thing I ever asked of Bing," Loyce told us, "but he never did anything for her."

Then there was the great jazz singer Mildred Bailey. We mentioned in an earlier chapter that composer Jimmy Van Heusen and Frank Sinatra had been involved in a deed to which Bing had apparently attached strings. We learned about it while reading Laurence Zwisohn's book, *Bing Crosby, a Lifetime of Music,* to which Van Heusen wrote the foreward. In his foreword, Van Heusen pointed out that although he had worked with Bing for thirty-eight years, there was a modest and secretive side to him that few knew much about— including Van Heusen. As an example, Van Heusen cited something that Bing had done for Al Rinker's sister, Mildred Bailey, that he didn't think Al knew about.

Van Heusen said that while taking part in the filming of an ABC television special, "Bing Crosby: His Life and Legend," which was filmed and aired after Bing's death, the show's producer mentioned that he had filmed Al Rinker, and that Al was upset that Bing had totally neglected Mildred Bailey after he had gained fame (Al didn't say this on the show but mentioned it to the producer in a private, off-camera conversation). To set the record straight, Van Heusen told the producer the story about Bing regarding Mildred, which he also related in the forward to Zwisohn's book.

Van Heusen got a call one evening from composer-conductor Alec Wilder, who informed him that Mildred

Bailey was in a hospital in the East, on an open ward, deathly ill and unable to pay the hospital or the doctor. Wilder wanted to know if Van Heusen would be willing to pay to get her into a private room. Van Heusen said that he would, and that he'd be willing also to pay for a doctor and for anything else Mildred needed.

The call to Van Heusen had been relayed to Frank Sinatra's house, where he had gone for the evening. When Van Heusen got off the phone, Sinatra offered to go fifty-fifty with him to help Mildred. So it was settled; Van Heusen and Sinatra would pay Mildred's medical bills. Van Heusen was working on a film at Paramount with Bing at the time, so he told Bing of the call and asked if Bing wanted to go thirds on Mildred's bill, along with Sinatra and him. Bing said he would, and nothing more was said about the incident.

Eventually only one or two bills were sent to Van Heusen, and when they stopped coming, he suspected that Bing had taken over the entire problem and confronted him about his suspicion. He learned that Bing had sent an accountant and an attorney back East to look over Mildred's situation, and that he had not only taken over the expenses but had paid off the mortgage on Mildred's farm, had brought her out to St. John's hospital in Santa Monica, California, and had arranged for her to stay in a Toluca Lake house when she got out of the hospital. The point of Van Heusen's telling the story was that Bing was secretive about such things. "The sadness of the story," Van Heusen wrote, "is that Mildred Bailey never told her brother, Al Rinker, what Bing had done for her . . . and, of course, secretive Bing never told the guy he started out with, Al Rinker, that he saved his sister's life."

When we read Mr. Van Heusen's foreword, we were puzzled. Al had contributed an interview to Mr. Zwisohn's book, and he had loaned us his copy because the book was available only by mail order. We wondered why Rinker hadn't mentioned the incident about Mildred to us and why Bing would send an attorney

346

and an accountant back East rather than simply taking care of the bills, as Van Heusen and Sinatra had planned on doing. So we went back to see Rinker about the matter.

Al Rinker had suffered a very bad heart attack at about the time of the book's publication, and he was still recovering from it when he finally granted us an interview (he had refused to grant an interview in August 1979, when we first called him, and it wasn't until February 1980, after several calls, that he finally agreed to talk to us). Since he was convalescing from his heart attack, he hadn't read Van Heusen's foreword to the book. When we brought it to his attention, he was pleased to hear that Van Heusen and Sinatra, both of whom he admires very much, had helped his sister. And he was very grateful to them. He told us that at the time of his sister's illness, he was in no financial position to help her. He knew of Bing's involvement, though, and he added a postscript to the story that the secretive Mr. Crosby neglected to tell Mr. Van Heusen.

Bing had indeed sent an accountant and an attorney back East to see Mildred. Mildred was taken ill suddenly and was apparently strapped for ready cash at the time, but she was an art collector and, as a show person, she had a lot of furs and jewelry. She gave twenty to thirty thousand dollars' worth of jewelry to whomever Bing had sent East to see her, which more than covered her doctor and hospital bills and the mortgage on her farm, which, as Al recalls, was about seven thousand dollars. Rinker says that the medical expenses were taken care of but that Mildred never saw any of her jewelry again. In those days—the forties—medical care was reasonably priced, and it appears that the Crosby organization didn't lose any money in helping Mildred. Rinker also said that he didn't know anything about the house in Toluca Lake, where she may well have stayed for a while, but that she lived with a friend of the family until she returned East again.

What had begun as a purely philanthropic act on the

parts of Jimmy Van Heusen and Frank Sinatra was apparently turned into a cool business deal by the man whom Mildred Bailey had helped get established in show business.

And that is the sadness of the story.

CHAPTER TWENTY-FOUR

Not easy thinking these things about Bing.

—A FAN

At the outset of our look at the man beneath the image, we noted the almost incredible disparity between what he was and what he appeared to be. The man, in fact, was the antithesis not only of his screen image but also of his public image. We said also at the outset that one can't peruse the details of his personal life and of his associations with others without running headlong into a quagmire of psychological and philosophical considerations. And having examined the record with us, the reader should now understand, if not appreciate, our dilemma. Bing Crosby's behavior toward others is almost incomprehensible. We set out to write the story of a wonderfully witty, bright, talented, and charismatic man, and found also the stuff that Shakespeare's plays are made of. And that was the last thing in the world we expected. This man Bing Crosby was many things to many people, but he did some monstrously callous things to those who were nearest and who should have been dearest to him.

We have neither the inclination nor the training to conduct a psychological autopsy on the man, but such a study would be fascinating. Still, one can't stumble across such incongruities without wondering about them

349

and examining them with whatever light one has at hand. It doesn't take a trained eye to see that Bing was no better off than was Dixie. The difference was that Bing was one of the *walking* wounded to whom the emotionally dependent Dixie fell prey. Bing seemed emotionally impotent, a hollow man.

Enigmatic was the adjective most often applied to Bing by those who were as close to him as one could get. And he was that. One of his most paradoxical characteristics was that he wasn't a loner, but that he couldn't relate to others. He had, perhaps, the emotional makeup of a loner, but he couldn't bring himself to attempt anything alone. He needed people. He couldn't relate to them in a meaningful way, and more often than not, he didn't even want them around—but he needed them. The result was that he used people. He was a user, and an insidious one, for he didn't seem to bear the distinctive marks of a user. When he no longer had a use for people or a need for them, he discarded then, apparently without emotions like remorse. Intellectually, he knew better. Intellectually, he would reach inside himself for the proper emotional response, which was always suppressed beyond his grasp, and he always came up empty-handed. His treatment of Dixie is but one obvious example.

Bing's autobiography, *Call Me Lucky*, was finished and at the publisher's when Dixie died. Since the book was to be published after Dixie's death, Bing couldn't let it be released without a reference to her passing, so he added a four-page chapter titled "What a Lady!" in which he very obliquely discussed facets of his marriage for which he had obviously been criticized. "When I've had to be abroad or on tour, working," he wrote, "I've got letters, most of them anonymous, from people taking me to task because I didn't spend more time with Dixie. They pictured her as lonely and forgotten. That was not true. Dixie had a host of friends. . . ."

Did he truly believe that *friends* could take his place? That with friends around, Dixie wouldn't be lonely? Apparently so. Perhaps Bing was projecting his own feelings; he wasn't lonely for Dixie when he was with *his* friends; why should Dixie be lonely for him when she was surrounded by her friends? For twenty years, Dixie battled with him on that very point. Again, intellectually, he knew better, but he didn't feel it. And if Bing didn't feel like doing something, that was that. He was a great one for lecturing and for expecting others to do the right thing, but he did only what he felt like doing. And the nature of his feelings seemed to be, like tactile pleasures, self-limiting.

Dixie had been a good friend to him. He "eulogized" her by saying in his autobiography, "Any mawkish sentimentality [written] about her would have made her wince." And he went on to praise her "steadfast and constructive support" of him, her honesty toward him, and her obvious devotion to him. In a quintessential display of antimawkishness, he didn't even tell his readers that he loved her. No. What he told them was, "I'm going to sorely miss *her* love. . . ." (Emphasis ours.)

Kathryn pointed out in her book that Bing said he felt awkward and graceless saying *I love you.* Songwriters were driven to distraction to keep from using the phrase when they were writing songs for Bing; he rejected such "mushy stuff." One can, of course, feel love for someone without being able to tell them so face-to-face. But it seems incredible that he couldn't write *I loved her* in a eulogy to a wife of twenty-two years who had just died of cancer. He didn't say it and he didn't write it. Also, he didn't show it. In fact, he made a spectacularly long display of indifference. One can't help but wonder whether Bing was capable of loving anyone. Certainly he wanted to; certainly he knew that he should; but maybe it just wasn't in him. The fact that he raised the possibility of saying something that might smack of "mawkish sentimentality" indicates that he knew his eulogy was the place for it.

Kathryn knew what she was talking about when she said that Bing only wanted a buddy, not a sweetheart. He needed female companionship, but he didn't want strings attached. Kathryn was an achiever, but being the wife of Bing Crosby had to be the most challenging endeavor she ever undertook. Bing expected his wife to make a vocation of marriage, while he made an avocation of it.

Bing's friendships were avocational ones, too. He seemed to categorize his friends: business friends, golf friends, hunting and fishing and music and racetrack friends. One of the prerequisites to friendship with Bing was to stay on the surface—keep it light and, preferably, zany. Bing had a great sense of humor; if one is always looking on the light side of things, there's little danger of profundity, of having to probe within. One seldom got personally serious with Bing. He didn't like having to reach down inside himself for something that wasn't there and coming up empty-handed. It was an embarrassment to him. One shouldn't embarrass him by saying something heartfelt. He couldn't respond. Criticism was fine. He could absorb it or ignore it. But compliments were fraught with obligation. One can't absorb or ignore a compliment; one is expected to respond. Compliments are warm, and warmth made Bing uncomfortable.

Bing's embarrassment at any display of emotion on his part or on the part of others toward him seems symptomatic not just of feelings of inferiority but of self-hatred—and here one is reminded that up to a certain point in his life, Bing tried to drink a part of himself into oblivion. You don't do that if you like yourself. He was almost unbelievably self-effacing with respect to his abilities and accomplishments as an actor and a singer; these were things that came from within, products of the self, and he constantly downplayed their worth and, in effect, his own worth. His self-effacement doesn't appear to have been false humility on his part. He seemed the embodiment of the satiric line: I wouldn't belong to any organization that would have the likes of me as a member.

One wonders if there was substance to his apparent self-hatred. If there was, it could account for much that seemed enigmatic about him: I wouldn't have a wife who would marry the likes of me; I wouldn't have a child fathered by the likes of me; I wouldn't have a friend who would help the likes of me. Considering his treatment of wives and children and people who helped him rise above himself, one wonders.

Anyone who genuinely contributed to Bing's rise to fame—not to his fame once it was established, for that was a fair trade-off, but to his *rise*—was summarily "disappeared" by Bing, no matter how infinitesimal or great the contribution or claim. Like a little dictator establishing a personal empire and jealously guarding it, he systematically eliminated all who could lay claim to having helped establish him on the throne. They ceased to exist in Bing's mind, and, where possible, they were ruthlessly purged from his life (like Roger Marchetti) or, in the case of those whose total "disappearance" would leave inexplicable gaps in his life (Rinker and Barris), they were portrayed as having disassociated themselves from him of their own volition and of having participated only tangentially in his life. His self-made-man image thus established by revision and implication (he needn't claim publicly to being a self-made man, for his "edited" life story made that evident), he would wear his rumpled, loud-shirted humility in public and privately counsel others to make it on their own—just as he had done. To his family, he was the demanding apostle of self-reliance, the prince of virtue, the preacher of all he was taught by the Jesuit fathers, but which he failed to practice himself.

A proud side of him finally emerged and caused him to get a little puffed up and big-headed. Looking at what he pointed to with pride tells us something about the new, self-made man. Was he the proud husband, the proud father, the proud friend, the proud entertainer? No. Those were all manifestations of the hollow man. He was the proud millionaire. He pointed to his financial status—not publicly—and he guarded it jealously. Can one imagine the humble Bing Crosby on national television sporting the family crest on his blazer? Bing Crosby having the family crest set in tiles at the

Hearst-Castle-door entrance to his Palm Desert home? His den at Hillsborough lined with wood paneling from the Hearst Castle? Bing Crosby with an English butler? The latter was attributed to Kathryn's influence, but Bing was the master of the castle, and an English butler wouldn't darken his door if he didn't personally want him. And Bing was up to his ears in Hearst-Castle trappings long before he married Kathryn.

Bing's pride began surfacing when he was hobnobbing, during his early and more overt Gatsby years. His first million was at hand; the family crest was dug up; the family was brought down from Spokane; the Crosby building appeared on the Sunset Strip; he became a corporate entity. The pride in the family crest was in its heritage, not necessarily in the immediate members. Those who showed their allegiance by becoming vassals were accepted; those who didn't were banished. And God had to help the ones who dared trade on the family name he established; Bing certainly wouldn't.

Inside, though, it was still hollow. It was a curse to him and to those who tried to touch him. He was a victim of himself, as well. He was a very tortured man, a very unhappy man who played the clown. On the stairs leading to his den at Hillsborough he kept a portrait of himself as a clown. And one senses that the laughter, too, was hollow.

Author Gene Fowler once wrote that a book is never finished; it's abandoned. It's an epigram that has particular significance when the book is about as complex a man as Bing Crosby. We can think of no more fitting way to abandon this one than with the words of Bing's old Washington State pal, the late Burt McMurtrie, who had been moved to tears with his recollection of Bing singing that first Christmas carol.

At the luncheon we spoke of earlier, Burt had told a few of Bing's fans about a side of him that they weren't accustomed to hearing—nothing terribly revealing, just a drinking incident and a reference to Bing's "snobbish" phase. One of the fans seated at the luncheon table sighed, then shook his head, saying, "Not easy thinking these things about Bing."

Burt was rather startled by the fan's reaction. "Why?" he asked, looking around the table at each of them. "Well . . . Don't misunderstand me," he added. "I loved the man deeply, and I mean this truly, yet he was capable of doing stupid things. He was always the first to admit it. It doesn't do Bing or Dixie any credit to believe either one of them wasn't very human, or that they were not pretty much like everybody else. If you want my personal opinion, I wouldn't want Bing any other way. Even his music seems to be better for his being just an ordinary kind of person. Mind you, I don't think he was just plain old Harry L. Crosby who was born here in Tacoma and grew up over east of the mountains in Spokane. Hell's bells! Why, no one in this wide world ever did nor ever will sing so beautifully. In that, he was superhuman."

FILMOGRAPHY

The following is a chronological listing of *all* Bing Crosby films, including shorts, features, cameo appearances, and documentaries.

1. *King of Jazz* (Universal Pictures, 1930). Dir., John Murray Anderson. This lavish all-talking, all-color (Technicolor) production was one of the most expensive musicals ever made. It was especially written as a screenplay for Paul Whiteman and his Orchestra, capitalizing upon his immense popularity. Bing's featured number, "Song of the Dawn," was given to John Boles as a result of Bing's auto accident and stint in jail. He did sing "Music Has Charms" over the opening title and sang four songs as a member of The Rhythm Boys (Crosby, Al Rinker, Harry Barris). George Gershwin made a rare film appearance and played "Rhapsody in Blue" (which was Whiteman's theme song). *Cast:* John Boles, The Brox Sisters, Janette Loff, Laura La-Plante, Merna Kennedy, Glenn Tryon. (100 minutes.)

2. *Ripstitch the Tailor* (Pathé Films, 1930). Dir., Raymond McCarey. This two-reel short was never released.

3. *Two Plus Fours* (Pathé Films, 1930). Dir., Raymond McCarey; story by Raymond McCarey and Charles Callahan (2-reel short).

4. *Check and Double Check* (RKO Radio Pictures, 1930). Dir., Melville Brown; original story, lyrics and music by Bert Kalmar and Harry Ruby. Starring radio's all-time favorites, Amos 'n' Andy (Charles Correll and Freeman Gosden). Bing appeared with Al Rinker and Harry Barris (The Rhythm Boys), who sang "Three Little Words" in a brief appearance with Duke Ellington's Orchestra. *Cast:* Sue Carol, Irene Rich, Charles Morton, Ralf Harolde, Rita LaRoy, Edward Martindel. (85 minutes.)

5. *Reaching for the Moon* (United Artists Studios, 1931). Dir., Edmund Goulding; original story by Irving Berlin. Bing sang "When the Folks Up High Do the Mean Low Down" in an unbilled bit part. *Cast:* Douglas Fairbanks, Sr., Bebe Daniels, Edward Everett Horton, June MacCloy, Helen Jerome Eddy, Claude Allister, Jack Mulhall, Walter Walker. (90 minutes.)

6. *I Surrender, Dear* (Educational Films, 1931). Dir., Mack Sennett. Bing introduced Harry Barris's new song in this musical comedy, which also provided the title (2-reel short).

7. *Confessions of a Coed* (Paramount Publix, 1931). Dirs., Dudley Murphy and David Burton. Bing sang "Just One More Chance" in an unbilled bit, off-camera. *Cast:* Norman Foster, Sylvia Sidney, Phillips Holmes, Claudia Dell, George Irving, Martha Sleeper, Florence Britton. College drama in which four students become involved in campus problems and scandals. (75 minutes.)

8. *One More Chance* (Educational Films, 1931). Dir., Mack Sennett. Bing scores again in another situation-comedy musical (2-reel short).

9. *Dream House* (Educational Films, 1931). Dir., Del Lord. Another musical-comedy capitalizing upon Bing's voice and comedy ability (2-reel short).

10. *Billboard Girl* (Educational Films, 1931). Dir., Mack Sennett. Bing combines singing and comedy. *Cast:* Franklin Pangborn, Babe Kane (2-reel short).

11. *Blue of the Night* (Educational Films, 1931). Dir., Leslie Pierce; prod., Mack Sennett. Bing vocalizes in this comedy-musical, singing his famous theme song (2-reel short).

12. *Sing, Bing, Sing* (Educational Films, 1932). Dir., Babe Stafford; prod., Mack Sennett. Bing at his best in two-reelers. *Cast:* Franklin Pangborn, Lloyd Bacon, Florence McKinney.

13. *The Big Broadcast* (Paramount Publix, 1932). Dir., Frank Tuttle. Based on the play *Wild Waves* by William F. Manley; screenplay, George Marion, Jr.; dir. of photography, George Folsey; songs by Leo Robin and Ralph Rainger. *Cast:* Stu Erwin, George Burns, Gracie Allen, Sharon Lynne, Ralph Robertson, Anna Chandler, Spec O'Donnell, George Barbier, Leila Hyams, Alex Melish, Tom Carrigan, Mills Brothers, Arthur Tracy (The Street Singer), Cab Calloway, Boswell Sisters, Vincent Lopez, Donald Novis. Bing gets his big movie break in this excellent comedy in which he portrays a happy-go-lucky crooner singing at a failing radio station operated by George Burns. Stu Erwin, an eccentric millionaire, comes to the rescue, saves the station with a lineup of "big broadcast" names. (85 minutes.)

14. *College Humor* (Paramount, 1933). Dir., Wesley Ruggles; based on a story by Dean Fales; adapted for the screen by Frank Butler and Claude Binyon; dir. of photography, Leo Tover; songs by Arthur Johnston and Sam Coslow. *Cast:* Richard Arlen, Jack Oakie, Mary Carlisle, George Burns and Gracie Allen, Mary Kornman, Eddie Nugent, Joseph Sawyer, Lona Andre. Singing professor Bing Crosby is sought after by pretty coed, Mary Carlisle, making her boyfriend Richard Arlen mad in this zany comedy-musical in which Jack Oakie and Arlen face each other on the football field. (80 minutes.)

15. *Star Night at the Cocoanut Grove* (Metro-Goldwyn-Mayer, 1933). Bing sang "I Saw Stars" with a full orchestra in this two-reel short.

16. *Too Much Harmony* (Paramount, 1933). Dir., Edward A. Sutherland; original story and screenplay by Joseph L. Mankiewicz and Harry Ruskin; songs by Sam Coslow and Arthur Johnston. *Cast:* Jack Oakie, Judith Allen, Harry Green, Skeets Gallagher, Ned Sparks, Lilyan Tishman, Kitty Kelly, Evelyn Oakie, Grace Bradley, Shirley Grey, and Billy Bevan. Bing portrays an easy-going singer torn between two girls, one bad and one good, but he succeeds in a vaudeville act that lands him back on Broadway. (75 minutes.)

17. *Going Hollywood* (Cosmopolitan Pictures Production of an MGM Release, 1933). Dir., Raoul Walsh; original story, Frances Marion; screenplay, Donald Ogden Stewart; songs by Arthur Freed and Nacio H. Brown; musical dir., Lennie Hayton; dir. of photography, George Folsey. *Cast:* Marion Davies, Fifi D'Orsay, Ned Sparks, Patsy Kelly, Stu Erwin, and Bobby Watson. Bing again plays a radio crooner; Marion Davies portrays a French instructor at a girls' school. She falls in love with him, follows him to Hollywood, and becomes a star with his help. (77 minutes.)

18. *Please* (Paramount, 1933). Dir., Arvid E. Gillstrom. A musical short capitalizing upon Bing's singing and popularity (two-reel musical short).

19. *Bring on Bing* (Educational Films, 1933). Dir., Mack Sennett. Capitalizing on Bing's rise to stardom, this comedy-musical combines footage from some of Bing's earlier films for Sennett, which were shot in 1931 (three-reel musical-comedy short).

20. *Hollywood on Parade* (Paramount, 1933). A short-subject film promoting the top Paramount stars at work, play, sports. Bing is one of more than a dozen, including Jack Oakie, Gary Cooper, and others (two-reel short).

21. *We're Not Dressing* (Paramount, 1934). Dir., Norman Taurog. Adapted from J. M. Barrie's *The Admirable Crichton;* screenplay, Benjamin Glazer: songs by Mack Gordon and Harry Revel; dir. of photography, Charles Lang. *Cast:* Carole Lombard, George Burns, Gracie Allen, Leon Errol, Charles Morris, Raymond Milland, Ethel Merman, Jay Henry, John Irwin, Ted Oliver, and Ben Hendricks. Bing plays a singing deckhand on Leon Errol's yacht which beaches itself on a small island. Lombard is a millionairess whom Bing wins from two other rivals. (80 minutes.)

22. *Just an Echo* (Paramount, 1934). Dir., Arvid E. Gillstrom. Another Crosby musical short capitalizing on Bing's crooning style (two-reel musical short).

23. *She Loves Me Not* (Paramount, 1934). Dir., Elliot Nugent; based upon a play by Howard Lindsay and from the novel by Edward Hope; screenplay and producer, Benjamin Glazer; dir. of photography, Charles Lang; songs by Mack Gordon and Harry Revel, Edward Hey-

man, Arthur Schwartz plus Ralph Rainger and Leo Robin. *Cast:* Miriam Hopkins, Henry Stephenson, Edward Nugent, Kitty Carlisle, Warren Hymer, Lynne Overman, Judith Allen, George Barbier, Margaret Armstrong, Henry Kolker, Ralf Harolde, Maude Gordon, and Matt McHugh. Bing and Ed Nugent portray Princeton prep students who take it upon themselves to hide showgirl Miriam Hopkins—after she has witnessed a murder—by disguising her as a man. (83 minutes.)

24. *Here Is My Heart* (Paramount, 1934). Dir., Frank Tuttle; based upon the play, *The Grand Duchess and the Waiter*, by Alfred Savoir; secreenplay, Harlan Thompson and Edwin Justus Mayer; produced by Louis D. Lighton; dir. of photography, Karl Struss; songs by Lewis Gensler, Ralph Rainger and Leo Robin. *Cast:* Kitty Carlisle, Reginald Owen, Akim Tamiroff, William Frawley, Roland Young, Cecelia Parker, Charles Wilson, Marian Mansfield, Charles Arnt, Arthur Houseman, and Cromwell McKechnie. Bing portrays an American millionaire abroad who falls in love with Kitty Carlisle, a European princess; he poses as a waiter, learns of her problems, and marries her before the end. (75 minutes.)

25. *Mississippi* (Paramount, 1935). Dir., Edward A. Sutherland; produced by Arthur Hornblow, Jr.; adapted from Booth Tarkington's "Magnolia"; screenplay, Claude Binyon, Francis Martin, Herbert Fields, and Jack Cunningham; dir. of photography, Charles Lang; songs by Richard Rodgers and Lorenz Hart. *Cast:* W. C. Fields, Joan Bennett, Queenie Smith, Gail Patrick, Fred Kohler, Sr., John Miljan, Jack Mulhall, Libby Taylor, Paul Hurst, John Larkin, Harry Meyers, Theresa Conover, Bruce Covington, Jules Cowles, Ed Pawley, King Baggott, Mahlon Hamilton, and Clarence Geldert. Bing flees to a riverboat after being disgraced by fiancée Gail Patrick and her family, becomes known as The Singing Killer in Field's showboat troupe, winning the hand of Joan Bennett after he redeems himself. (74 minutes.)

26. *Two for Tonight* (Paramount, 1935). Dir., Frank Tuttle; based upon the play by Max Lief and J. O. Lief; screenplay, Jane Storm and George Marion, Jr.; additional dialogue by Harry Ruskin; dir. of photography, Karl Struss; songs by Harry Revel and Mack Gordon.

Cast: Joan Bennett, Lynne Overman, Douglas Fowley, Thelma Todd, Mary Boland, James Blakeley, Charles Lane, John Gough, Charles Arnt, Maurice Cass, and Ernest Cossart. Bing plays one of the three songwriting sons of Mary Boland, falls in love with Joan Bennett, and poses as a playwright who turns out a musical show in a matter of a few days. (62 minutes.)

27. *The Big Broadcast of 1936* (Paramount, 1935). Dir., Norman Taurog; screenplay, Ralph Spense, Walter De-Leon, Francis Martin; songs by Leo Robin and Ralph Rainger, Mack Gordon and Harry Revel, Dorothy Parker and Richard Whiting. *Cast*: Jack Oakie, Wendy Barrie, Lyda Roberti, Samuel S. Hinds, Gail Patrick, George Burns, Gracie Allen, Akim Tamiroff, Benny Baker, Henry Wadsworth, Ethel Merman, Virginia Weidler, Amos 'n' Andy, Ina Ray Hutton, Bill Robinson, Ray Noble, Charles Ruggles, and Mary Boland. Bing did only a guest appearance in this film, singing "I Wished on the Moon" and "Why Dream?" (97 minutes.)

28. *Anything Goes* (Paramount, 1936). Dir., Lewis Milestone; prod., Benjamin Glazer; adapted from the musical comedy by Howard Lindsay and Russel Crouse; songs by Cole Porter, Richard Whiting, Leo Robin, Frederick Hollander, Hoagy Carmichael, Edward Heyman; dir. of photography, Karl Struss. *Cast*: Ida Lupino, Ethel Merman, Charles Ruggles, Grace Bradley, Arthur Treacher, Margaret Dumont, Matt Moore, Edward Gargan, Robert McWade, Richard Carle. Bing follows pretty Ida Lupino after he sees her forced to board an ocean liner. Believing she is being kidnapped, he poses as an accomplice of gangster Ruggles, only to discover that Lupino is an English heiress being brought back to London. After some hectic moments and a shipboard romance, Bing wins her hand. (92 minutes.)

29. *Rhythm on the Range* (Paramount, 1936). Dir., Norman Taurog; prod., Benjamin Glazer; from a story by Mervin J. Houser; screenplay, Francis Martin, Walter DeLeon, John C. Moffitt, Sidney Salkow; dir. of photography, Karl Struss; songs by Richard Whiting, Frederick Hollander, Johnny Mercer, Leo Robin, Sam Coslow, Bager Clark, Billy Hill, Ralph Rainger, J. K. Brennan, Gertrude Ross, Waller Bullock; musical dir., Boris Morros. *Cast*: Frances Farmer, Bob Burns, Samuel S. Hinds, Martha Raye, George E. Stone, Martha Sleeper, Clem Bevans, Lucille Webster Gleason, James

Burke, James Thompson, Herbert Ashley, Emmett Vogan, Leonid Kinskey, Duke York, James Blaine. Bing is cast as the owner of a fancy dude ranch in California. In New York, he and Bob Burns win a rodeo prize—a champion bull—and head West with it. In the railroad stockcar, he discovers Frances Farmer, in jewels and furs, as a stowaway; she tells him she is running away from her fiancé. Bing suggests she stay at his ranch. By the time they get to California, they have fallen in love; she likes ranch life, and they are married. (87 minutes.)

30. *Pennies from Heaven* (Columbia, 1936). Dir., Norman Z. McLeod; prod., Emmanuel Cohen; based upon "The Peacock Feather" by Katherine Leslie Moore; screenplay, Jo Swerling; dir. of photography, Robert Pittack; musical arrangements by John Scott Trotter; songs by Arthur Johnston and Johnny Burke; *Cast:* Madge Evans, Donald Meek, Louis Armstrong, Edith Fellows, Tom Dugan, William Stack, Tom Ricketts, Nana Bryant, Noble Chissell, John Gallaudet. Bing plays the part of a convict who, in prison, meets a man who is on his way to the death chamber. The man gives him a note with the names of the only living relatives of the man he killed and who need help. Bing looks them up when he gets out, meets social worker Madge Evans. He finds them an old house in which he opens a roadside restaurant and becomes a singing troubador, in an effort that rewards him by adopting the child and marrying the pretty social worker. (81 minutes.)

31. *Waikiki Wedding* (Paramount, 1937). Dir., Frank Tuttle; based on a story by Don Hartman and Frank Butler; screenplay, Frank Butler, Don Hartman, Walter DeLeon, Francis Martin; prod., Arthur Hornblow, Jr.; dir. of photography, Karl Struss; musical director, Boris Morros; orchestrations by Victor Young; arrangements by Arthur Franklin and Al Siegel; Hawaiian lyrics by Jimmy Lovell; songs by Harry Owens, Ralph Rainger, and Leo Robin. *Cast:* Shirley Ross, Bob Burns, Leif Erickson, Martha Raye, Anthony Quinn, Grady Sutton, George Barbier, Maurice Liu, Raquel Echeverria, Miri Rei, Alexander Leftwich, Spencer Charters, Nick Lukats, Prince Leilani, Granville Bates, Michell Lewis. Bing is a hotshot publicist who persuades Shirley Ross, a winner in the Pineapple Princess contest, of the beauty of Hawaii, subsequently falling in love with each other and fighting off natives who are bent on kidnapping. (89 minutes.)

32. *Double or Nothing* (Paramount, 1937). Dir., Theodore Reed; prod., Benjamin Glazer; story by M. Coates Webster; screenplay, Charles Lederer, Edwin Gelsey, John C. Moffitt, Duke Atterberry; dir. of photography, Karl Struss; musical director, Boris Morros; vocal arrangements, Victor Young and Max Terr; vocal supervision, Al Siegel; musical advisor, Arthur Franklin; songs by Sam Coslow, Johnny Burke, Arthur Johnston, Burton Lane, Ralph Freed, Al Siegel. *Cast:* Andy Devine, Martha Raye, Mary Carlisle, Samuel S. Hinds, Benny Baker, Fay Holden, Harry Barris, William Frawley, William Henry, Walter Kingsford, John Gallaudet, Gilbert Emery, and Frances Faye. An unusual will poses a problem for Bing, Raye, Frawley, and Devine, as they are four down-and-out individuals about to inherit the money if they can double it in thirty days. Bing guides them to victory, winning the love of Mary Carlisle. This marked the first appearance in a Crosby film of Bing's old partner, Harry Barris.

33. *Swing with Bing* (Universal, 1937). Dir., Herbert Polesie. This was a short subject covering the first Bing Crosby Golf Tournament. Bing sang "The Little White Pill on the Little Green Hill" (30-minute sports short subject, 3 reels).

34. *Doctor Rhythm* (Paramount, 1938). Dir., Frank Tuttle; prod., Emmanuel Cohen; based on O. Henry's famous short story, "The Badge of Policeman O'Roon"; screenplay, Jo Swerling and Richard Connell; dir. of photography, Charles Lang; musical director, George Stoll; orchestrations by John Scott Trotter; songs by Johnny Burke and James V. Monaco. *Cast:* Mary Carlisle, Beatrice Lillie, Rufe Davis, Fred Keating, Louis Armstrong, Andy Devine, Laura Hope Crews, Sterling Holloway, Franklin Pangborn, John Hamilton, William Austin, Emory Parnell, Dolores Casey, Allen Matthews, Harry Stubbs, Frank Elliot, and Henry Wadsworth. Bing becomes a policeman to substitute for ailing Andy Devine, watching over heiress Mary Carlisle in her aunt's home. The latter is trying to prevent her elopement with an entertainer. Bing's closeness with the pretty heiress ends with their romance in full bloom, and she falls for Bing. (80 minutes.)

35. *Don't Hook Now* (Paramount, 1938). Documents the second annual Bing Crosby Golf Tournament; Bob Hope appears with Bing (32-minute sports short subject, 3 reels).

36. *Sing You Sinners* (Paramount, 1938). Dir. and prod., Wesley Ruggles; original story, screenplay, Claude Binyon; dir. of photography, Karl Struss; musical director, Boris Morros; vocal arrangements, Max Terr; songs by James Monaco and Johnny Burke, Frank Loesser and Hoagy Carmichael. *Cast:* Ellen Drew, Fred MacMurray, Elizabeth Patterson, Donald O'Connor, William Haade, Irving Bacon, Herbert Corthell, Tom Dugan, Paul White, John Gallaudet. Bing plays a down-and-out character who leaves his two brothers and mother, goes to Los Angeles, opens a small shop, sends for his family. They arrive only to discover Bing has sold the business and bought a racehorse. The brothers reunite, establish a singing act, while the horse is put through the paces for an important race. Much to everyone's surprise, the horse wins, and Fred MacMurray ends up with the girl, Ellen Drew. (90 minutes.)

37. *Paris Honeymoon* (Paramount, 1939). Dir., Frank Tuttle; prod., Harlan Thompson; dir. of photography, Karl Struss; based upon a story by Angela Sherwood; screenplay, Don Hartman and Frank Butler; songs by Leo Robin and Ralph Rainger, Gordon Graham and Spencer Williams. *Cast:* Shirley Ross, Franciska Gaal, Edward Everett Horton, Victor Killian, Akim Tamiroff, Ben Blue, Gregory Gaye, Raymond Hatton, Rafaela Ottiano, Alex Melish, Keith Kenneth, Michael Visaroff. Bing portrays a Texas millionaire who goes abroad to be near his equally wealthy love, Shirley Ross. On the way, in a fictitious country, Bing meets a beautiful peasant girl, Franciska Gaal, falls in love with her, and soon forgets his first love. (92 minutes.)

38. *East Side of Heaven* (Universal, 1939). Dir., David Butler; original story by David Butler and Herbert Polesie; screenplay, William Conselman; dir. of photography, George Robinson; songs by Johnny Burke and James Monaco. *Cast:* Irene Hervey, Mischa Auer, Joan Blondell, C. Aubrey Smith, Baby Sandy Henville, Helen Warner, Jerome Cowan, Robert Kent, Mary Carr, Dorothy Christie, J. Farrell MacDonald, Jackie Gerlich, Russell Hicks, Douglas Wood, Edward Earle, Jane Jones, Arthur Hoyt, Matty Malneck and his Orchestra. Bing plays an easygoing taxi driver who sings while he drives, but suddenly is thrown into a position of taking care of a small infant. Bing and girl friend Blondell successfully turn the child over to its millionaire grandfather, who decides to sponsor a radio show with Bing as a successful crooner. (89 minutes.)

39. *The Star Maker* (Paramount, 1939). Dir., Roy Del
Ruth; prod., Charles R. Rogers; original story by Ar-
thur Caesar and William Pierce; screenplay, Frank
Butler, Don Hartman, Arthur Caesar; dir. of photography, Karl Struss; musical direction, Alfred Newman;
songs by Johnny Burke and James Monaco. *Cast:*
Linda Ware, Louise Campbell, Ned Sparks, Janet
Waldo, Laura Hope Crews, Walter Damrosch, Billy
Gilbert, and Thurston Hall. Bing plays an unsuccessful
singer and songwriter who settles with wife, Louise
Campbell, taking a job in a department store, but still
has the urge to return to show business. He forms a
vaudeville troupe with all young boys and showcases
his new musical at a local theater where it wins acclaim, then takes to the road-circuit vaudeville houses.
Just as things are going fine, he is hit by the child-
welfare rep, who tells him that children can't work
after eight P.M.; said to be the life of Gus Edwards, it
bears only a meager resemblance to Edwards's flamboyant career. (93 minutes.)

40. *Road to Singapore* (Paramount, 1940). Dir., Victor
Schertzinger; prod., Harlan Thompson; story by Harry
Hervey; screenplay, Frank Butler and Don Hartman;
dir. of photography, William Mellor; musical director,
Victor Young; dances staged by LeRoy Prinz. *Cast:*
Bob Hope, Dorothy Lamour, Anthony Quinn, Edward
Gargan, Jerry Colonna, Charles Coburn, Judith Barrett,
Pierre Watkin, Johnny Arthur, Miles Mander, Great
Granstedt, Kitty Kelly, John Kelly, Pedro Regas,
Gloria Franklin, Harry Bradley, and Carmen D'Anto-
nio. Bing comes from a wealthy ship-building family
but is unhappy with his life and fiancée; he and old
pal Hope take off on a freighter just to get away from
it all. They meet up with Lamour, whom they rescue
from abductors, and she lives with them as their maid.
Bing finally decides his place is back home, since he
believes that Lamour is really in love with Hope, for
whom she shows inordinate interest. Back home, he
discovers that she only did so to not interfere between
him and his fiancée. Bing boards the next boat out for
Singapore to seek his new love and throw a few quips
at old buddy Hope, who loses Lamour to Bing. This
was the first *Road* picture and said to be the weakest of
them all, although it was a big box-office hit. (93 minutes.)

41. *If I Had My Way* (Universal, 1940). Dir. and prod.,
David Butler; story by David Butler, William Consel-

man, James V. Kern; screenplay, William Conselman and James V. Kern; dir. of photography. George Robinson; songs by Johnny Burke and James Monaco. *Cast*: Gloria Jean, Charles Winninger, Donald Woods, Allyn Joslyn, Trixie Friganza, El Brendel, Claire Dodd, Moroni Olsen, Blanche Ring, Grace LaRue, Eddie Leonard, Nana Bryant, Kathryn Adams, and Joe King. Bing is a singing factory worker who agrees to take charge of a friend's daughter after her father dies in an accident; Bing takes her to New York to locate her grand-uncle, a former vaudevillian. Bing's sidekick loses their bankroll when he buys a failing restaurant. Bing comes to the rescue by restoring it to a fancy nightclub, and all ends well. (92 minutes.)

42. *Rhythm on the River* (Paramount, 1940). Dir., Victor Schertzinger; prod., William Le Baron; original story by Billy Wilder and Jacques Thery; screenplay, Dwight Taylor; dir. of photography, Ted Tetzlaff; musical director, Victor Young; orchestration by John Scott Trotter; songs by Johnny Burke and James Monaco. *Cast:* Mary Martin, Oscar Levant, Basil Rathbone, William Frawley, Jeanne Cagney, Phyllis Kennedy, Harry Barris, John Scott Trotter, Charles Grapewin, Wingy Manone, Oscar Shaw, Lillian Cornell, Charles Lane, Billy Benedict, Pierre Watkin, and Brandon Hurst. Bing plays an unambitious singer and songwriter who ghost-writes songs for Rathbone rather than trying to do it for himself; this work is shared with him by Mary Martin, and they decide to write songs under their own names. Music publishers believe they are peddling Rathbone's tunes, since his style is now identifiable, and Bing goes back to the farm and Martin pursues a career as a singer in nightclubs. Meanwhile, Rathbone panics when he runs dry of material and announces he is going to introduce a new song, one that Bing told him never to use; Rathbone finally comes clean, announcing that his new partners are Bing and Martin, who will write the songs for his musical, and all ends well. (This was the second Crosby film in which former Rhythm Boys member Harry Barris appeared.) (92 minutes.)

43. *Road to Zanzibar* (Paramount, 1941). Dir., Victor Schertzinger; prod., Paul Jones; story by Don Hartman and Sy Bartlett; screenplay, Don Hartman and Frank Butler; dir. of photography, Ted Tetzlaff; musical director, Victor Young; dance director, LeRoy Prinz; songs by Johnny Burke and Jimmy Van Heusen. *Cast:*

Bob Hope, Dorothy Lamour, Eric Blore, Una Merkel, Iris Adrian, Ethel Greer, Lionel Royce, Joan Marsh, Douglas Dumbrille, Leo Gorcey, Georges Renavent, Luis Alberi, Noble Johnson, Charles Gemora, Buck Woods, and Leigh Whipper. Bing and Bob are two con men on the run who flee to Zanzibar. They meet Lamour and Merkel, who talk them into making a safari with them to locate Lamour's lost brother. The boys discover that Lamour has tricked them, actually trying to seek out the wealthy plantation owner she plans to marry. The girls take off, leaving the boys stranded in the jungle. They decide to return to Zanzibar and are captured by a cannibal tribe who believe them to be mysterious gods from a strange place. After a series of belly laughs, Bob and Bing meet up with the two girls and walk into the sunset. (This has been said to be the best of the *Road* pictures, and its success prompted Paramount to make the series of *Road* films.) (92 minutes.)

44. *Birth of the Blues* (Paramount, 1941). Dir., Victor Schertzinger; prod., B. G. DeSylva; story by Harry Tugend; screenplay, Harry Tugend and Walter De-Leon; dir. of photography, William Mellor; musical director, Robert Emmett Dolan; songs by Robert Emmett Dolan, Johnny Mercer, W. C. Handy, Edward Madden and Gus Edwards, Harry Tugend, B. G. De-Sylva, Ray Henderson, Lew Brown. *Cast:* Mary Martin, Brian Donlevy, J. Carrol Naish, Horace MacMahon, Eddie "Rochester" Anderson, Minor Watson, Carolyn Lee, Harry Barris, Wingy Manone, Ruby Elzy, Perry Botkin, Barbara Pepper, Dan Beck, Cecil Kellaway, Jack Teagarden and his Orchestra, Harry Rosenthal, Donald Kerr, and Ronnie Cosbey. Bing is portrayed as a boy by Ronnie Cosbey in this musical offering about a clarinet player (Cosbey-Crosby) who organized a jazz band; staged in a typical New Orleans Bourbon Street background; the title of the picture is the theme of the story. (85 minutes.)

45. *Holiday Inn* (Paramount, 1942). Dir. and prod., Mark Sandrich; original story by Irving Berlin; adapted by Elmer Rice; screenplay, Claude Binyon; dir. of photography, David Abel; musical dir., Robert Emmett Dolan; songs, Irving Berlin. *Cast:* Fred Astaire, Marjorie Reynolds, Walter Abel, Virginia Dale, Louise Beavers, James Bell, John Gallaudet, Irving Bacon, Leon Belasco, Judith Gibson, Shelby Bacon, Harry Barris, and Katharine Booth. Bing plays the role of a happy-go-

lucky singer who owns an exclusive night club in New England that is open only on holidays. A love triangle develops among Crosby, Astaire and Reynolds. A movie company rents the place for a location, and Astaire and Reynolds go on to bigger things, including an engagement to be married. Bing finds her unhappy in Hollywood, and she cancels her contract and returns East with him. In the end, Astaire winds up with his old fiancée, Virginia Dale, and everybody is happy again. (102 minutes.)

46. *Angels of Mercy* (Metrotone News, 1942). This is a war effort short, filmed for the American Red Cross. Bing sang the title song, which was written by Irving Berlin, and the film was distributed in three different versions by MGM, Paramount, and Twentieth Century-Fox, each of them using their own stock-library footage of the Red Cross in action, but all of them using Bing's song over the stock footage.

47. *Road to Morocco* (Paramount, 1942). Dir., David Butler; assoc. prod., Paul Jones (no producer credited); orig. screenplay, Don Hartman and Paul Jones; dir. of photography, William Mellor; musical director, Victor Young; songs by Jimmy Van Heusen and Johnny Burke. *Cast:* Bob Hope, Dorothy Lamour, Dona Drake, Anthony Quinn, Vladimar Sokoloff, Yvonne de Carlo, Laura La Plante, Mikhail Rasumny, Monte Blue, George Lloyd, Andrew Tombes, George Givot, Brandon Hurst, Richard Loo, Sammy Stein, Ralph Penney, Dan Seymour, Pete Katchenaro, and Leo Mostovoy. Survivors of a sunken freighter, Bing and Bob head for Morocco, where they meet the princess, none other than Lamour. Bing falls for her and Bob ends up with Dona Drake, and the foursome set sail for home. An explosion takes place, and the four of them end up on a life raft heading for Manhattan. (83 minutes.)

48. *Star Spangled Rhythm* (Paramount, 1942). Dir., George Marshall; assoc. prod., Joe Sistrom (no producer credited); orig. screenplay, Harry Tugend; dir. of photography, Leo Tover; musical score and director, Robert Emmett Dolan; vocal arrangements, Joseph J. Lilley; dance dir., Danny Dare; sketches by Norman Panama and Mel Frank, George Kaufman, Arthur Ross; songs by Johnny Mercer and Harold Arlen. *Cast:* Eddie Bracken, Betty Hutton, Anne Revere, Gil Lamb, Cass Daley, Victor Moore, Fred MacMurray, Ray Milland, Veronica Lake, Franchot Tone, Alan

369

Ladd, Mary Martin, Vera Zorina, Susan Hayward, Paulette Goddard, Eddie "Rochester" Anderson, Jerry Colonna, Lynne Overman, Albert Dekker, Walter Abel, Preston Sturges, William Bendix, and Cecil B. DeMille. This was Paramount's patriotic effort during the war, enlisting cameo performances from many of the top contract players on the lot for a series of sketches and blackouts, thinly disguised with a story line of a studio story. Bob Hope is master of ceremonies for the film, while Bing sings "Old Glory" in the finale against a studio background of Mt. Rushmore. It should be noted that this was Gary Crosby's first screen appearance, although his name does not appear in any of the credits. (99 minutes.)

49. *My Favorite Blonde* (Paramount, 1942). Dir., Sidney Lanfield. Bing made a cameo appearance; his first in a Hope film. (78 minutes.)

50. *Dixie* (Paramount, 1943). Dir., Edward Sutherland; assoc. prod., Paul Jones (no producer credited); story by William Rankin; adapted to the screen by Claude Binyon; screenplay, Karl Tunberg and Darrell Ware; dir. of photography, William Mellor; musical director, Robert Emmett Dolan; vocal arrangements, Joseph J. Lilley; songs by Johnny Burke and Jimmy Van Heusen. *Cast:* Marjorie Reynolds, Dorothy Lamour, Lynne Overman, Billy DeWolfe, Raymond Walburn, Grant Mitchell, Eddie Foy, Jr., Stanley Andrews, James Burke, Sam Flint, Clara Blandick, Tom Herbert, Olin Howlin, Hope Landin, Robert Warrick, Norma Varden, Harry Barris, and Sam Flint. This was Bing's first picture in Technicolor as a star (*King of Jazz*, 1930, was his first appearance on the screen in Technicolor). Bing plays the role of songwriter Daniel Decater Emmett, who marries Marjorie Reynolds, then with pal Billy DeWolfe goes through some hard times, forming a minstrel troupe, doing a blackface act, and eventually writing the title song, "Dixie," which became the war cry of the Confederacy. Unfortunately, Emmett's life was not portrayed properly in this fictional account, as the real story would have been more interesting and logical; this was merely a fictional piece based upon history to provide a musical hit for Bing. It also marked another time old pal Harry Barris appeared with Bing, playing a drum. (90 minutes.)

51. *Going My Way* (Paramount, 1944). Dir. and prod., Leo McCarey; orig. story, Leo McCarey; screenplay by

Frank Butler and Frank Cavatt; dir. of photography, Lionel Linden; musical director, Robert Emmett Dolan; songs by Johnny Burke and Jimmy Van Heusen, J. R. Shannon. *Cast:* Barry Fitzgerald, Barry Stevens, Frank McHugh, Stanley Clements, Porter Hall, Jean Heather, Gene Lockhart, William Frawley, Fortunio Bonavova, Carl Switzer, George McKay, Eily Malyon, George Nokes, Hugh Maguire, Adeline Reynolds, Gibson Gowland, Jack Norton, Jimmy Dundee, Anita Bolster, Sybil Lewis, Tom Dillon, and the Robert Mitchell Boys Choir. Bing won an Academy Award for his performance as Father O'Malley in this story about a young priest sent to aid an elderly one, and their mutual efforts to save the church in a lower middle-class neighborhood. (129 minutes.)

52. *The Road to Victory* (Warner Bros., 1944). Charles Ruggles and Cary Grant appeared in this one-reeler for the War Activities Commission, in which Bing sang the title song. (12 minutes.)

53. *The Princess and the Pirate* (Samuel Goldwyn Studios, 1944). Dir., David Butler. More than halfway through this Bob Hope film with Virginia Mayo, taking place mostly aboard a pirate ship, Bing makes a brief appearance and Hope looks into the camera and comments on Bing's interrupting the story. (94 minutes.)

54. *Here Come the Waves* (Paramount, 1944). Dir. and prod., Mark Sandrich; orig. screenplay, Ken Englund and Zion Myers, Allan Scott; dir. of photography, Charles Lang, Jr.; musical director, Robert Emmett Dolan; songs by Harold Arlen and Johnny Mercer. *Cast:* Betty Hutton, Ann Doran, Sonny Tufts, Noel Neill, Catherine Craig, Harry Barris, Mae Clarke, Oscar O'Shea, Marjorie Henshaw, Mona Freeman, Jimmy Dundee, James Flavin, Yvonne DeCarlo, Lillian Bronson, Kit Guard, Guy Zanett, Carlotta Jelm, Roberta Jonay, and James Flavin. Bing and buddy Sonny Tufts are sailors who meet so-called twins, both played by Betty Hutton, in this wartime comedy. (99 minutes.)

55. *Out of This World* (Paramount, 1945). Dir., Hal Walker; screenplay, Arthur Phillips and Walter DeLeon; songs by Johnny Mercer and Harold Arlen. *Cast:* Eddie Bracken, Diana Lynn, Parkyakarkus, Veronica Lake, Olga San Juan, Ted Fiorioto, Joe Richman, Ray Noble, Donald McBride, Florence Bates, Cass Daley, Henry King, Carmen Cavallaro, Gary

Crosby, Phillip Crosby, Lindsay Crosby, and Dennis Crosby. A satire on a famous singing personality played by Eddie Bracken and featuring Bing's four sons. Bing never appeared in this film, but his voice was dubbed for the crooning done by Bracken. (97 minutes.)

56. *All-Star Bond Rally* (Twentieth Century-Fox, 1945). Dir., Michael Audley. Another film for the War Activities Committee, and the United States Treasury Dept., with a star-studded cast including Frank Sinatra, Bob Hope, Harpo Marx, Linda Darnell, Betty Grable, Jeanne Craig, Harry James and Orchestra, Fibber McGee and Molly. Bing sang one song, "Buy Bonds." (11 minutes.)

57. *Hollywood Victory Caravan* (Paramount, 1945). Dir., William Russell. Another production of the War Activities Committee and the United States Treasury Dept., in a brief screenplay by Mel Shavelson, featuring stars Alan Ladd, Humphrey Bogart, Bob Hope, William Demarest, Betty Hutton, Olga San Juan, Barbara Stanwyck, Dona Drake, Franklin Pangborn, Robert Benchley, Carmen Cavallaro, Diana Lynn. In this film, Bing sang "We've Got Another Bond to Buy." (21 minutes.)

58. *Duffy's Tavern* (Paramount, 1945). Dir., Hal Walker; screenplay, Norman Panama and Mel Frank; songs by Johnny Burke and Jimmy Van Heusen, Bernie Wayne and Ben Raleigh. *Cast:* Marjorie Reynolds, Barry Sullivan, Victor Moore, Ed Gardner, Charles Cantor, Ann Thomas, Betty Hutton, Robert Benchley, Cass Daley, Diana Lynn, Sonny Tufts, Howard DeSilva, Billy DeWolfe, Gary and Dennis, Lindsay and Phillip Crosby. Based upon the popular radio show of the era, everybody on the Paramount lot was in this film except Bob Hope. Benchley tells the four young Crosby children about their father. (97 minutes.)

59. *The Bells of St. Mary's* (A Rainbow—RKO Film, 1945). Dir. and prod., Leo McCarey; orig. story, Leo McCarey; screenplay, Dudley Nichols; dir. of photography, George Barnes; musical score, Robert Emmett Dolan; songs by Jimmy Van Heusen, Grant Clarke, Johnny Burke, George Meyer, A. Emmett Adams, and Douglas Furber. *Cast:* Ingrid Bergman, William Gargan, Ruth Donnelly, Henry Travers, Martha Sleeper, Una O'Connor, Bobby Frasco, Edna Wonacott, Dickie

Tyler, Cora Shannon, Rhys Williams, Joan Carroll, Matt McHugh, Minerva Urecal, Eva Novak, Gwen Crawford, and Aina Constant. Bing again plays the Father O'Malley role (*Going My Way*), this time coming to the rescue of a destitute parochial school, finally inducing a wealthy man to contribute a building for their purposes. Meanwhile, Ingrid Bergman as Sister Benedict is discovered suffering from tuberculosis and it is suggested that she be transferred to a more adaptable climate without telling her of her ailment; Bing steps in and explains that transferring her without telling her the real reason would break her heart, so he levels with her and informs her of her plight. (126 minutes.)

60. *Road to Utopia* (Paramount, 1946). Dir., Hal Walker; prod., Paul Jones; screenplay, Norman Panama and Mel Frank; dir. of photography, Lionel Linden; music director, Robert Emmett Dolan; score by Leigh Harline; dance director, Danny Dare; songs by Johnny Burke and Jimmy Van Heusen. *Cast:* Bob Hope, Dorothy Lamour, Hillary Brooke, Robert Benchley, Jimmy Dundee, Jack LaRue, Douglas Dumbrille, Alan Bridge, Nestor Paiva, Robert Barrat, Will Wright, Billy Benedict, Edward Emerson, George McKay, Charles Gemora, Larry Daniels, Paul Newlan, Romaine Callender, and Ronnie Rondell. Bing and Bob play vaudevillians who end up in the Klondike's gold rush, meet Lamour, who is a singer in a dance saloon and on the trail of gold and fortune. (90 minutes.)

61. *Road to Hollywood* (Astor Pictures Release, 1946). An enterprising producer, hoping to capitalize upon the popularity of the famous Paramount *Road* pictures, bought the rights to Mack Sennett's old Crosby two-reelers—"I Surrender Dear," "Billboard Girl," "One More Chance," and "Dream House"—to edit together some of Bing's old footage (minus the appearance of Hope and Lamour). (56 minutes.)

62. *Blue Skies* (Paramount, 1946). Dir., Stuart Heisler; prod., Sol Siegel; dir. of photography, Charles Lang, Jr.; from an idea by Irving Berlin; adapted by Allan Scott; screenplay, Arthur Sheekman; musical director, Robert Emmett Dolan; dance director, Hermes Pan; vocal arrangements, Joseph L. Lilley; songs by Irving Berlin. *Cast:* Joan Caulfield, Fred Astaire, Billy DeWolfe, Karolyn Grimes, Frank Faylen, Olga San Juan, Victoria Horne, Roy Gordon, Jack Norton, Neal Dodd,

Joan Woodbury, Roberta Jonay, Cliff Nazarro, Clarence Brooks, Michael Brandon, John Gallaudet, and John Kelly. Fred Astaire narrates this love triangle comprised of himself, Bing, and Joan Caulfield over a period of years. (104 minutes.)

63. *Variety Girl* (Paramount, 1947). Dir., George Marshall; screenplay, Edmund Hartmann, Frank Tashlin, Monte Brice, Robert Welch; songs by Jimmy Van Heusen, Frank Loesser, Johnny Burke. *Cast:* Olga San Juan, Mary Hatcher, Frank Faylen, William Demarest, Gary Cooper, Paulette Goddard, Bob Hope, Ray Milland, Burt Lancaster, Dorothy Lamour, Robert Preston, William Bendix, Patrick Knowles, Veronica Lake, Billy DeWolfe, Joan Caulfield, William Holden, and Barbara Stanwyck. A tribute to the Variety Clubs of America, utilizing all of Paramount's top stars. Bing and Bob appeared in a golfing sketch. (94 minutes.)

64. *My Favorite Brunette* (Paramount, 1947). Dir., Elliott Nugent; screenplay, Edmund Beloin, Jack Rose; prod., Daniel Dare; musical score, Robert Emmett Dolan; dir. of photography, Lionel Linden. *Cast:* Bob Hope, Peter Lorre, Dorothy Lamour, Lon Chaney, Charles Dingle, Frank Puglia, Ann Doran, Jack LaRue, John Hoyt, Reginald Denney, and Willard Robinson. Bing makes another cameo appearance as Hope's executioner at the end of the film. (87 minutes.)

65. *Welcome Stranger* (Paramount, 1947). Dir., Elliott Nugent; prod., Sol Siegel; orig. story, Frank Butler; screenplay, Arthur Sheekman; dir. of photography, Lionel Linden; musical director, Robert Emmett Dolan; songs by Jimmy Van Heusen and Johnny Burke. *Cast:* Barry Fitzgerald, Joan Caulfield, Wanda Hendrix, Elizabeth Patterson, Frank Faylen, Percy Kilbride, Charles Dingle, Don Beddoe, Paul Stanton, Larry Young, Robert Shayne, Milton Kibbee, Thurston Hall, Charles Middleton, John Westley, Ethel Wales, Edward Clark, and Clarence Muse. Bing plays the part of a young singing physician taking over the practice of an ailing doctor, Barry Fitzgerald. Bing romances Joan Caulfield, and finally saves the life of the old doctor. (106 minutes.)

66. *Road to Rio* (Paramount, 1947). Dir., Norman Z. McLeod; prod., Daniel Dare; dir. of photography, Ernest Lazlo; screenplay, Jack Rose and Edmund Beloin; music director, Robert Emmett Dolan; dance directors,

Billy Daniel and Bernard Pearce; songs by Jimmy Van Heusen and Johnny Burke. *Cast:* Bob Hope, Dorothy Lamour, Jerry Colonna, Frank Faylen, Gale Sondergaard, The Andrews Sisters, Nestor Paiva, Frank Puglia, The Wiere Brothers, Charles Middleton, Tor Johnson, Gino Corrado, Ray Teal, Donald Kerr, George Chandler, Stanley Andrews, and Joseph Vitale. Bing and Bob play musicians who accidentally set fire to a carnival, then escape by boat to South America. They meet Lamour, and the intrigue begins there and ends in Rio. (100 minutes.)

67. *The Emperor Waltz* (Paramount, 1948). Dir., Billy Wilder; prod., Charles Brackett; dir. of photography, George Barnes; musical score, Victor Young; songs by Richard Heuberger and Johnny Burke, James Van Heusen and Johnny Burke, Ralph Erwin and Fritz Rotter, and Johnny Burke basing his songs upon Johann Strauss. *Cast:* Joan Fontaine, Richard Hayden, Lucille Waston, Roberta Jonay, Julia Dean, James Vincent, Harold Vermilyea, Roland Culver, William Haade, Doris Dowling, Harry Allen, Frank Elliott, John Gargan, Frank Corsaro, Cyril Delevanti, John Goldsworthy and Sig Ruman. Bing plays the role of a supersalesman in Austria, who introduces the phonograph to royalty; his encounters with Emperor Franz Josef result in his love affair with Austrian countess Joan Fontaine. (106 minutes.)

68. *A Connecticut Yankee in King Arthur's Court* (Paramount, 1948). Dir., Tay Garnett; prod., Robert Fellows; based upon an original story by Mark Twain; screenplay, Edmund Beloin; dir. of photography, Ray Rennahan; music by Victor Young; songs by Johnny Burke and Jimmy Van Heusen. *Cast:* Rhonda Fleming, Richard Webb, William Bendix, Virginia Field, Henry Wilcoxon, Sir Cedric Hardwicke, Murvyn Vye, Alan Napier, Julia Faye. Bing plays the blacksmith who, after his horse runs into a tree during a violent rainstorm, awakens to find himself as a member of King Arthur's Round Table in the days of Camelot. (107 minutes.)

69. *Top o' the Morning* (Paramount, 1949). Dir., David Miller; prod., Robert Welch; screenplay, Richard Breen and Edmund Beloin; dir. of photography, Lionel Linden; music director, Robert Emmett Dolan; vocal arrangements, Joseph J. Lilley; dance director, Eddie Prinz; songs by Jimmy Van Heusen and Johnny Burke.

Cast: Ann Blyth, Barry Fitzgerald, John McIntire, Tudor Owen, Eileen Crowe, Hume Cronyn, John Eldridge, Mary Fields, John Costello, Dick Ryan, and Jimmy Hunt. Bing plays an insurance investigator dispatched to Ireland to find the missing Blarney Stone. The result is finding love with Fitzgerald's daughter, Ann Blyth, and a smooth romance. (99 minutes.)

70. *The Adventures of Ichabod and Mr. Toad* (Walt Disney–RKO Radio Pictures, 1949). Dirs., James Algar, John Kinney, Clyde Geronimi. This feature-length cartoon featured Bing's and Basil Rathbone's voices; Bing sings three songs written by Gene DePaul and Don Raye. (69 minutes.)

71. *Down Memory Lane* (Eagle-Lion Pictures, 1949). This is a compilation of some Mack Sennett footage, including *Sing, Bing, Sing* and *Blue of the Night,* which Bing starred in about 1931. Also included is W. C. Fields's hilarious short, *The Dentist.* (67 minutes.)

72. *Riding High* (Paramount, 1950). Dir. and prod., Frank Capra; based on Mark Hellinger's short story "Broadway Bill"; screenplay, Robert Riskin; add'l dialogue, Jack Rose and Mel Shavelson; dirs. of photography, George Barnes and Ernest Lazlo; musical director, Victor Young; musical assoc., Troy Sanders; vocal arrangements, Joseph J. Lilley; songs by Johnny Burke and Jimmy Van Heusen. *Cast:* Colleen Gray, Charles Bickford, Frances Gifford, Ward Bond, William Demarest, Oliver Hardy, Margaret Hamilton, Max Baer, Frankie Darro, James Gleason, Harry Davenport, Joe Frisco, Irving Bacon, Douglas Dumbrille, Clarence Muse, Raymond Walburn, Marjorie Lord, Percy Kilbride, Gene Lockhart, and Charles Lane. Bing plays a carefree racehorse buff in this exciting and tender story of the turf, a remake of Capra's original *Broadway Bill* (1934). Bing trains his horse for a big race; it wins and then dies. (111 minutes.)

73. *Mr. Music* (Paramount, 1950). Dir., Richard Haydn; prod., Robert Welch; from Samson Raphaelson's play, *Accent on Youth;* screenplay, Arthur Sheekman; dir. of photography, George Barnes; musical director, Van Cleave; vocal arrangements, Joseph J. Lilley; dance dir., Gower Champion; songs by Johnny Burke and Jimmy Van Heusen. *Cast:* Nancy Olson, Ruth Hussey, Charles Coburn, Tom Ewell, Robert Stack, Charles Kemper, Groucho Marx, Peggy Lee, Ida Moore, Don-

ald Woods, Gower and Marge Champion, Clause Curdle, Dorothy Kirsten, and The Merry Macs. Bing plays a song-writing golfer who hits the skids but is put back on the track again by Charles Coburn, a producer, who hires pretty Nancy Olson to get him serious about his music again. (113 minutes.)

74. *Angels in the Outfield* (Metro-Goldwyn-Mayer, 1951). Bing makes a cameo appearance in this zany baseball farce starring Paul Douglas and Janet Leigh. (102 minutes.)

75. *Here Comes the Groom* (Paramount, 1951). Dir. and prod., Frank Capra; orig. story, Robert Riskin and Liam O'Brien; screenplay, Virginia Van Upp, Myles Connolly, Liam O'Brien; dir. of photography, George Barnes; musical director, Joseph J. Lilley; songs by Jay Livingston and Ray Evans, Hoagy Carmichael and Johnny Mercer. *Cast:* Jane Wyman, Alexis Smith, Franchot Tone, James Barton, Anna Maria Alberghetti, Connie Gilchrist, Robert Keith, Walter Catlett, H. B. Warner, Alan Reed, Nicholas Joy, Beverly Washburn, Minna Gombell, Maidel Turner, Howard Freeman, Ellen Corby, Irving Bacon, James Burke, and Ian Wolfe, with cameo appearances by Phil Harris, Cass Daley, Louis Armstrong, and Dorothy Lamour. Bing is the third corner of a love triangle involving Franchot Tone and Jane Wyman as he portrays a reporter who has just five days to marry so that he can retain custody of two French orphans. (113 minutes.)

76. *The Greatest Show on Earth* (Paramount, 1952). Dir., Cecil B. DeMille. Bing makes a cameo appearance with Bob Hope in this star-studded film depicting life under the big top, utilizing the Ringling Bros. Circus. (153 minutes.)

77. *Son of Paleface* (Paramount, 1952). Dir., Frank Tashlin; prod., Robert Welch; dir. of photography, Harry Wild; musical score, Lyn Murray. *Cast:* Bob Hope, Jane Russell, Roy Rogers, Harry von Zell, Wee Willie Davis, Iron Eyes Cody, Charles Cooley, Paul E. Burns, Douglas Dumbrille, Bill Williams, and Lloyd Corrigan. Bob goes West to claim his fortune and finds a lot of problems, including a cameo appearance by old friend, Bing Crosby. (104 minutes.)

78. *Just for You* (Paramount, 1952). Dir., Elliott Nugent; prod., Pat Duggan; based on "Famous" story by Ste-

phen Vincent Benet; screenplay, Robert Carson; dir. of photography, George Barnes; musical director, Emil Newman; songs by Leo Robin and Harry Warren. *Cast:* Jane Wyman, Natalie Wood, Ethel Barrymore, Robert Arthur, Regis Toomey, Willia Bouchey, Cora Witherspoon, Ben Lessy, Herbert Vigram, and Art Smith. Bing is a producer-songwriter who feels guilty for neglecting his two children in favor of a Broadway actress but redeems himself by writing a hit song, the title of the film. (95 minutes.)

79. *Road to Bali* (Paramount, 1952). Dir., Hal Walker; prod., Harry Tugend; screenplay, Hal Kanter, Frank
— Butler, William Morrow; dir. of photography, George Barnes; musical dir., Joseph J. Lilley; musical numbers staged by Charles O'Curran; orchestral arrangements, Van Cleave; songs by Johnny Burke and Jimmy Van Heusen. *Cast:* Bob Hope, Dorothy Lamour, Peter Coe, Ralph Moody, Murvyn Vye, Leon Askin, Bunny Lewbel, Donald Lawton, Jack Claus, Jan Kayne, Bernie Gozier, Herman Cantor, Carolyn Jones, Michael Ansara, Larry Chance; cameo appearances by Humphrey Bogart, Jane Russell, Bob Crosby, Dean Martin, and Jerry Lewis. Bing and Bob in their first *Road* picture in color, again as a pair of vaudevillians who get conned into diving for sunken treasure, ending up on the island of Bali, with lots of pretty girls and funny gags. This marked the first and only film that Bob Crosby ever appeared in with Bing. (90 minutes.)

80. *Scared Stiff* (Paramount, 1952). Dir., George Marshall. Bing and Bob (Hope) make a cameo appearance in this Dean Martin–Jerry Lewis film, with Elizabeth Scott and Carmen Miranda. (108 minutes.)

81. *Little Boy Lost* (Paramount, 1953). Dir., George Seaton; prod., William Perlberg; dir. of photography, George Barnes; based on a story by Margharita Laski; screenplay, George Seaton; musical dir., Victor Young; songs by Johnny Burke and Jimmy Van Heusen. *Cast:* Nichole Maurey, Claude Dauphin, Gabrielle Dorziat, Christian Forcade, Georgette Anys, Peter Baldwin, Adele St. Maur, Jacques Gillo, Arthur Dulac, Ninon Stratly, Karen Vengay, Tina Blagoi, Gladys de Segonzac, Colette Dereal, and Jean Del Val. Bing is an American journalist who returns to France after the war to find his lost son, in this sentimental story of a man caught up in doubt, accepting the child he found in an orphanage as his own. (It was during the filming

of this picture, right after Bing returned to Hollywood from French locations, that his wife Dixie died in November, 1952.) (97 minutes.)

82. *White Christmas* (Paramount, 1954). Dir., Michael Curtiz; prod., Robert Emmett Dolan; screenplay, Norman Panama, Mel Frank, Norman Krasna; dir. of photography, Loyal Griggs; musical dir., Joseph J. Lilley; songs by Irving Berlin. *Cast*: Rosemary Clooney, Danny Kaye, Vera-Ellen, Mary Wickes, Dean Jagger, Sig Ruman, Barrie Chase, Ann Whitefield, Robert Crosson, Gavin Gordon, Johnny Grant, Richard Shannon, Grady Sutton, and John Brascia. Bing and Kaye are song-and-dance men who got together in the service and pursue their act after the war; they discover their old commanding officer has a failing New England resort, and they come to his rescue through their combined talents. (This was the first motion picture by Paramount to be filmed in the new process of VistaVision.) (120 minutes.)

83. *The Country Girl* (Paramount, 1954). Dir., George Seaton; A Perlberg-Seaton Picture; from the play by Clifford Odets; screenplay, George Seaton; dir. of photography, George Warren; musical score, Victor Young; musical numbers staged by Robert Alton; songs by Harold Arlen and Ira Gershwin. *Cast:* Grace Kelly, William Holden, Gene Reynolds, Jacqueline Fontaine, Ida Moore, Anthony Ross, Eddie Ryder, Robert Kent, Frank Scanell, Howard Joslin, John W. Reynolds, Charles Tannen, Chester Jones, Ruth Rickaby, Jon Provost, and Hal Dawson. Bing plays a has-been Broadway actor, an alcoholic, who is given a second chance by William Holden, a young and dedicated stage director, who succeeds in his endeavors to arrange a comeback for the once-famous actor through the actor's determined wife, Grace Kelly. (104 minutes.)

84. *Anything Goes* (Paramount, 1956). Dir., Robert Lewis; prod., Robert Emmett Dolan; from the play by Guy Bolton and P. G. Wodehouse; screenplay, Sidney Sheldon; dir. of photography, John Warren; musical direction, Joseph J. Lilley; orchestral arrangements, Van Cleave; choreography, Nick Castle; songs by Sammy Cahn and Jimmy Van Heusen. *Cast:* Mitzi Gaynor, Donald O'Connor, Jeanmaire, Phil Harris, Archer MacDonald, Kurt Kasznar, Richard Erdman, James Griffith, Argentina Brunetti, Walter Sande, and Alma

Macrorie. Bing is an aging actor who meets young television star Donald O'Connor, and they team up to find two female leads for their proposed quartet, doing song-and-dance routines. Their search takes them to Europe, where they discover Mitzi Gaynor and Jeanmaire. This was the last film that Bing was to make under his Paramount contract. (106 minutes.)

85. *Bing Presents Oreste* (Paramount, 1956). This was made while Bing was still on the lot in 1956, introducing on the screen a new Paramount find, opera singer Oreste. Bing made the introduction, but Oreste did the singing. (A one-reel short, 11 minutes.)

86. *High Society* (Metro-Goldwyn-Mayer, 1956). Dir., Charles Walters; prod., Sol Siegel; dir. of photography, Paul Vogel; from Philip Barry's *The Philadelphia Story*; screenplay, John Patrick; songs by Cole Porter. *Cast:* Grace Kelly, Frank Sinatra, Celeste Holm, Sidney Blackmer, John Lund, Louis Armstrong, Louis Calhern, Richard Keene, Margalo Gillmore, and Lydia Reed. Bing is a country gentleman–songwriter who takes offense at his ex-wife Kelly marrying John Lund; Frank Sinatra plays a reporter who helps Bing break up the wedding. (107 minutes.)

87. *Man on Fire* (Metro-Goldwyn-Mayer, 1957). Dir., Ranald MacDougall; prod., Sol Siegel; from an original story by Jack Jacobs and Malvin Wald; screenplay, Ranald MacDougall; dir. of photography, Joseph Ruttenburg; musical score, David Raksin; songs by Sammy Fain and Paul Francis Webster. *Cast:* Inger Stevens, Mary Fickett, E. G. Marshall, Richard Eastham, Anne Seymour, Malcolm Brodrick, and Dan Riss. Bing plays a successful businessman who fights for custody of his child after his marriage breakup, but finally realizes that he has been fighting a lost battle. Bing also sings the title song. (96 minutes.)

88. *Showdown at Ulcer Gulch* (1958). This was an institutional film for *The Saturday Evening Post,* which was billed as an adult Eastern and, in addition to Bing, also boasted such stars as Ernie Kovacs, Groucho Marx, Edie Adams, Orson Bean, Bob Hope, Salome Jens, and Chico Marx.

89. *Say One for Me* (Twentieth Century-Fox, 1959). Dir. and prod., Frank Tashlin; dir. of photography, Leo

Tover; screenplay, Robert O'Brien; musical director, Lionel Newman; dance director, Alex Romero; vocal supervision, Charles Henderson; songs by Sammy Cahn and Jimmy Van Heusen. *Cast:* Debbie Reynolds, Robert Wagner, Les Tremayne, Frank McHugh, Connie Gilchrist, Ray Walston, Sebastian Cabot, Joe Besser, Stella Stevens, Judy Harriet, Richard Collier, Thomas Henry, Murray Alper, and David Leonard. Bing dons the white collar as a priest for his third movie role playing this character, best remembered from *Going My Way*. His church is near Broadway, and he tries to solve showgirl Debbie Reynolds' problems, over the protests of club owner Wagner. (119 minutes.)

90. *Alias Jesse James* (United Artists–Hope Enterprises, 1959). Dir., Norman Z. McLeod; prod., Jack Hope; story by Robert St. Aubrey and Bert Lawrence; screenplay, William Bowers and Daniel Beacham; music arranged and conducted by Joseph J. Lilley; dir. of photography, Lionel Linden. Bing made a guest appearance in this film starring Bob Hope. Other guest stars were Gary Cooper, Gene Autry, Roy Rogers, James Arness, Hugh O'Brien, Ward Bond, Gail Davis, James Garner, and Jay Silverheels. A Western comedy; one of Hope's better film efforts. (92 minutes.)

91. *Let's Make Love* (Twentieth Century-Fox, 1960). Dir., George Cukor. Marilyn Monroe and Yves Montand star; Bing makes a cameo appearance, also supplemented by Milton Berle and Gene Kelly. (118 minutes.)

92. *Pepe* (Columbia Pictures, 1960). Dir., George Sidney. Starring Cantinflas and Dan Dailey, Maurice Chevalier and Frank Sinatra, in which Bing makes a cameo appearance. (195 minutes.)

93. *High Time* (Twentieth Century-Fox, 1960). Dir., Blake Edwards; prod., Charles Brackett (A Bing Crosby Production); based on a story by Garson Kanin; screenplay, Frank and Tom Waldman; dir. of photography, Ellsworth Fredericks; musical score, Henry Mancini; songs by Sammy Cahn and Jimmy Van Heusen. *Cast:* Tuesday Weld, Nichole Maurey. Fabian, Jimmy Boyd, Richard Beymer, Yvonne Craig, Kenneth MacKenna, Agnes Duncan, Dick Crockett, Paul Schreiber, Gavin McLeod, and Nina Shipman. Bing is a middle-aged widower who decides to get the college

education he never had; he is in love with a 'French professor, Nichole Maurey; the rest is farce and comedy. (102 minutes.)

94. *Road to Hong Kong* (United Artists, 1962). Dir., Norman Panama; prod., Mel Frank; screenplay, Mel Frank and Norman Panama; dir. of photography, Jack Hilyard; music by Robert Farnom; songs by Jimmy Van Heusen and Sammy Kahn (A Melnor Pictures Production). *Cast:* Bob Hope, Joan Collins, Dorothy Lamour, Robert Morley, Walter Gotell, Jacqueline Jones, Robert Ayres, Robin Hughes, Bill Nagy, Alan Gifford, Julian Sherrier, Roger Delgado, Simon Levy, Harry Baird, Mei Ling, Edwina Carroll, Sein Short, Zoe Zephyr, Irving Allen, Diane Valentine, Lier Hwang, Camilla Brockman, Guy Standeven, Victor Brooks, Felix Ahymer, Roy Patrick, David Randall, Katya Douglas, April Ashley, Michelle Molk, Yvonne Sihma, Lena Margot, Sherry Winton, Michael Wynne, John McCarthy, John Dearth; guest stars: Frank Sinatra, Dean Martin, Jerry Colonna, Peter Sellers, David Niven, Bing and Bob are hoofers again, but Bob is suffering from amnesia, so Bing takes him to Tibet for treatment by a High Lama. He regains his memory and also picks up total recall plus a photographic memory, which helps out when he discovers a formula for secret rocket fuel, which eventually involves them with secret agents and going off into space. (91 minutes.)

95. *The Sound of Laughter* (Union Pictures, 1963). This feature-length film is composed of various comics doing sketches from their routines of the late twenties and thirties. Narrated by Ed Wynn, there are interesting shots of Bing in some segments. (75 minutes.)

96. *Robin and the Seven Hoods* (Warner Bros., 1964). Dir., Gordon Douglas; prod., Frank Sinatra; dir. of photography, William Daniels; screenplay, David R. Schwartz; executive producer, Howard W. Koch; assoc. prod., William Daniels; musical score and direction, Nelson Riddle; songs by Jimmy Van Heusen and Sammy Cahn. *Cast:* Frank Sinatra, Dean Martin, Peter Falk, Sammy Davis, Jr., Edward G. Robinson, Victor Buono, Phil Crosby, Sig Ruman, Hank Henry, Jack LaRue, Robert Morley, Barbara Rush, Allen Jenkins, Harry Swoger, Milton Rudin, Maurice Manson, Phil Arnold, Robert Carricart, Barry Kelley, Robert Foulk, Joseph Ruskin, Bernard Fein, Richard Bakalyan, and Sonny King. Bing's role is supporting, not starring, in

this 1920s gangster story in which he plays a revivalist and sings a fitting song, "Mr. Booze." (123 minutes.)

97. *Stagecoach* (Twentieth Century-Fox, 1966). Dir., Gordon Douglas; based upon the Ernest Haycox story, "Stage to Lordsburg"; screenplay by Joseph Landon, adapted from the original screenplay by Dudley Nichols; prod., Martin Rackin; dir. of photography, William Clothier; music by Jerry Goldsmith. *Cast:* Ann-Margret, Alex Cord, Red Buttons, Van Heflin, Robert Cummings, Slim Pickens, Stefanie Powers, Michael Connors, Brett Pearson, Keenan Wynn, John Gabriel, Joseph Hoover, Brad Weston, Bruce Mars, and Oliver McGowan. Bing plays the drunken doctor role in this remake of John Ford's classic, in the original of which Thomas Mitchell, as the doctor, won an Academy Award, and John Wayne became a full-fledged star. Bing's attempt at character acting was short-lived. (114 minutes.)

98. *Cinerama's Russian Adventure* (United Roadshow Presentations, 1966). Bing narrated this Cinerama travelogue of Russia. (121 minutes.)

99. *Bing Crosby's Washington State* (Cinecrest Pictures, 1968). Bing narrated this travelogue showing his home state at its best. (30 minutes.)

100. *Cancel My Reservation* (Warner Bros., 1972). Dir., Paul Bogart; prod., Gordon Oliver; exec. prod., Bob Hope; screenplay, Arthur Marx and Robert Fisher. Dir. of Photography, Russell Metty; music, Dominic Frontiere. *Cast:* Bob Hope, Eva Marie Saint, Forrest Tucker, Keenan Wynn, Doodles Weaver, Betty Ann Carr, Anne Archer, Pat Morita, Herb Vigran, Chief Dan George, and Suzanne Beaumont. Bob and Eva Marie Saint are hosts of a daytime television show in New York when they get into an argument over women's rights. Bob's doctor advises him to take a rest. In Arizona, he finds the body of a dead Indian girl in his car and the plot unfolds, with Bing Crosby making a brief cameo appearance. (95 minutes.)

1. *Fox Movietone Follies of 1929* (Fox Film Corporation, 1929)
2. *Happy Days* (Fox Film Corporation, 1929)
3. *Cheer Up and Smile* (Fox Film Corporation, 1929)
4. *The Big Party* (Fox Film Corporation, 1929)
5. *Let's Go Places* (Fox Film Corporation, 1929)
6. *Why Leave Home* (Fox Film Corporation, 1929)
7. *Harmony at Home* (Fox Film Corporation, 1930)
8. *Manhattan Love Song* (Monogram, 1934)
9. *Love in Bloom* (Paramount, 1935)
10. *Redheads on Parade* (Twentieth Century-Fox, 1935)

The Films of Kathryn Grant

1. *Arrowhead* (Paramount, 1953)
2. *Casanova's Big Night* (Paramount, 1954)
3. *Forever Female* (Paramount, 1954)
4. *Living It Up* (Paramount, 1954)
5. *Rear Window* (Paramount, 1954)
6. *Five Against the House* (Columbia, 1955)
7. *Cell 2455, Death Row* (Columbia, 1955)
8. *Phenix City Story* (Allied Artists, 1955)
9. *Tight Spot* (Columbia, 1955)
10. *Unchained* (Warner Bros., 1955)
11. *Reprisal* (Columbia, 1956)
12. *The Wild Party* (United Artists, 1956)
13. *The Brothers Rico* (Columbia, 1957)
14. *Guns of Fort Petticoat* (Columbia, 1957)
15. *Mister Corey* (Universal, 1957)
16. *The Night the World Exploded* (Columbia, 1957)
17. *Operation Mad Ball* (Columbia, 1957)
18. *The Seventh Voyage of Sinbad* (Columbia, 1957)
19. *The Big Circus* (United Artists, 1959)
20. *Anatomy of a Murder* (Columbia, 1959)

DISCOGRAPHY

Bing Crosby recorded more than sixteen hundred songs during his fifty-one-year recording career, and a complete listing of them would probably be of interest only to record buffs. For this reason, we are including here only those few of Bing's records that we find of special biographical interest. For those interested in a book containing the complete recordings of Bing Crosby, including record labels, recording dates, and other relevant matter, we recommend Lawrence J. Zwisohn's *Bing Crosby, A Lifetime of Music* (Palm Tree Library; Los Angeles, California; 148 pages).

Recordings of special biographical interest:

I've Got the Girl (Columbia); recorded October 18, 1926. This is the first record ever made by either Bing Crosby or Al Rinker; a duet, it was recorded with Don Clark's orchestra in Los Angeles and is significant because it's the only extant record of what "Crosby and Rinker" sounded like before joining Paul Whiteman. For more details on the recording, see the index. "I've Got the Girl" is available on a limited-edition LP issued by The Bing Crosby Historical Society, Tacoma, Washington. At this writing, there is a plan in the works at Columbia Records to reissue this and other early Crosby recordings in a special album.

Wistful and Blue (Victor #20418); recorded December 22, 1926. This is the second record made by Crosby and Rinker and their first with Paul Whiteman; recorded at the Concert

Hall on Michigan Avenue in Chicago, it featured the fine violin of Matty Malneck.

Muddy Water (Victor #20508); recorded March 7, 1927. This is the first solo Bing ever recorded; it was made with Paul Whiteman's orchestra at Liederkranz Hall in Manhattan; Bing was a member of The Rhythm Boys at the time.

Side by Side (Victor #20627); recorded April 29, 1927. This is the first record made by The Rhythm Boys, and was recorded also at Liederkranz Hall in Manhattan with Paul Whiteman's orchestra. Whiteman and The Rhythm Boys were appearing in the Broadway show *Lucky* when this song was recorded. Two months later, The Rhythm Boys signed their own recording contract—independent of Whiteman—with Victor.

I Surrender, Dear (Victor #22618); recorded January 19, 1931. This record, made with Gus Arnheim's orchestra while The Rhythm Boys were at the Cocoanut Grove, is generally credited with being the recording instrumental in getting the attention of CBS president William Paley, which subsequently led to Bing's first radio contract.

Ho Hum (Victor #22691); recorded May 1, 1931. This is the only duet Bing recorded with Loyce Whiteman; they were backed by Gus Arnheim's orchestra; Loyce had recently signed with the Cocoanut Grove, and within weeks of this recording, Bing walked out on his contract, which broke up The Rhythm Boys.

Out Of Nowhere (Brunswick #6090); recorded March 30, 1931. This was Bing's first record under an independent-solo-artist contract.

I Love You Truly (Decca #100); recorded August 8, 1934. This was not only the first record Bing made for Decca, but also the first record made and released by the newly-formed company, which was built around Bing and in which he owned stock. The flip side of the record was Bing's recording of "Just A-Wearyin' For You."

A Fine Romance (Decca #907); recorded August 19, 1936. This is the only record Bing and Dixie made. Bing said that it took some fast talking just to get Dixie to consider the idea, but she had made a solo record at Decca the previous month. The flip side is their duet of "The Way You Look Tonight."

Suspense (Decca); recorded June 12, 1947. This is the only one of Al Rinker's compositions that Bing ever recorded. ·

Sam's Song (Decca); recorded June 23, 1950. This is the first duet recorded by Bing and his first son, Gary, when Gary was only 17. The flip side is "Play a Simple Melody"; more than a million copies of the record sold. Later, Bing and Gary also recorded "Moonlight Bay"/"When You and I Were Young Maggie Blues."

A Crosby Christmas (Decca); recorded September 5, 1950. This is a two-record album recorded by Bing and all of his first four sons, and the only time they ever recorded together.

A Tribute To Duke (Concord Jazz); recorded April 15, 1977. Bing sang one tune, "Don't Get Around Much Anymore," for this tribute to Duke Ellington. It was recorded in San Francisco, and was the last recording Bing made in the United States.

Seasons (Polydor, London, England); recorded September 12, 13, and 14, 1977, just four weeks before his death. This was Bing's last record, an album that featured, among other songs, "Yesterday When I Was Young" and "Spring Will Be a Little Late This Year." At this writing, the album has not been released in the United States.

390

399

400

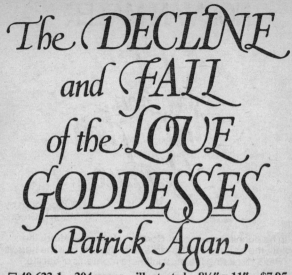

The DECLINE and FALL of the LOVE GODDESSES

Patrick Agan

☐ **40-623-1**   **304 pages**   **illustrated**   **8½" x 11"**   **$7.95**

Between the covers of this book are the dazzling, behind-the-klieg lights stories of ten internationally famous film stars who made it to the top, held the world in the palm of their hands, then let it all slip through their fingers...victims of their own weaknesses, of changing times, of men who used them. With photographs as poignant as his words, Patrick Agan delves behind the headlines to present the *real* story—what made them tick, and what made the ticking stop.

The Love Goddesses: Rita Hayworth, Jayne Mansfield, Betty Hutton, Linda Darnell, Veronica Lake, Betty Grable, Susan Hayward, Dorothy Dandridge, Frances Farmer, and of course, Marilyn Monroe.